THIS IS MY PHILOSOPHY

THIS IS MY PHILOSOPHY

Twenty of the World's Outstanding Thinkers
reveal the Deepest Meanings
they have found in Life

EDITED BY WHIT BURNETT

Ruskin House
GEORGE ALLEN & UNWIN LTD
MUSEUM STREET LONDON

First Published in Great Britain in 1958
Second Impression 1958

This book is copyright under the Berne Convention. Apart from
any fair dealing for the purposes of private study, research,
criticism or review, as permitted under the Copyright Act, 1956,
no portion may be reproduced by any process without written
permission. Enquiry should be made to the publisher.

© *George Allen & Unwin Ltd.*, 1958

Printed in Great Britain
by Bradford & Dickens
*London W.C.*1

Grateful acknowledgment is made to the following for permission to reprint selections included in this book:

J. B. S. Haldane, Princeton University Press, Princeton, New Jersey and Oxford University Press, London, for "Human Evolution: Past and Future" from *Genetics, Paleontology and Evolution*. Edited by Glenn L. Jepsen, George Gaylord Simpson and Ernst Mayr. Copyright, 1949, by Princeton University Press.

Werner Heisenberg, Pantheon Books, Inc., New York and Faber & Faber, Ltd., London, for "Science as a Means of International Understanding" from *The Philosophical Problems of Nuclear Science*. Copyright, 1952, by Pantheon Books, Inc. and Faber & Faber, Ltd.

William Ernest Hocking and Harper & Brothers, New York, for "Tentative Outlook for State and Church" from *The Coming World Civilization*. Copyright © 1956 by William Ernest Hocking.

Aldous Huxley, Harper & Brothers, New York and Chatto & Windus, Ltd., London for "The Double Crisis" from *Themes and Variations*. Copyright, 1950, by Aldous Huxley.

Karl Jaspers for "The Task of Philosophy in Our Day."

Carl Gustav Jung and The Bollingen Foundation, Inc., New York for "The Spirit of Psychology" from Volume I, *Spirit and Nature, Papers from the Eranos Yearbooks,* published for The Bollingen Foundation by Pantheon Books, Inc. Copyright, 1954, by Bollingen Foundation, Inc.

Salvador de Madariaga and Calmann-Levy, Paris, for "Introduction," "Universal Federation: The Co-World" and "Conclusion" from *De l'angoisse à la liberté*. Copyright, 1954, by Calmann-Levy.

Gabriel Marcel, Henry Regnery Company, Chicago and The Harvill Press, Ltd., London, for "The Universal Against the Masses (I and II)," Preface and Conclusion from *Man Against Mass Society*. First published by The Harvill Press, London, under the title of *Man Against Humanity*, 1952.

Jacques Maritain, Charles Scribner's Sons, New York, and Geoffrey Bles, Ltd., London, for "Confession of Faith" from *The Social and Political Philosophy of Jacques Maritain*. Edited by Joseph W. Evans and Leo R. Ward. Copyright, 1955, by Charles Scribner's Sons.

Lewis Mumford, Harcourt, Brace and Company, Inc., New York, and Martin Secker & Warburg, Ltd., London, for selections from *The Conduct of Life,* Copyright, 1951, by Lewis Mumford, and *The Condition of Man*, Copyright, 1944, by Lewis Mumford.

Reinhold Niebuhr, Charles Scribner's Sons, New York and James Nisbet & Co., Ltd., London, for "On Freedom, Virtue, Faith" from *Faith and History*. Copyright, 1949, by Charles Scribner's Sons.

J. Robert Oppenheimer and Simon and Schuster, Inc., New York, for "Prospects in the Arts and Sciences" from *The Open Mind*. Copyright © 1955 by J. Robert Oppenheimer.

Sarvepalli Radhakrishnan and The Library of Living Philosophers, Inc., Evanston, Illinois, for "The Religion of the Spirit and the World's Needs" from *The Philosophy of Sarvepalli Radhakrishnan*. Copyright, 1952, by The Library of Living Philosophers, Inc.

Bertrand Russell, Simon and Schuster, Inc., New York, and George Allen & Unwin, Ltd., London, for "Prologue or Epilogue?" from *Human Society in Ethics and Politics*. Copyright © 1952, 1954, 1955, by Bertrand Russell; copyright under the Berne Convention by George Allen & Unwin, Ltd.

Jean-Paul Sartre and Philosophical Library, New York for selections from *Being and Nothingness*. Copyright, 1956, by Philosophical Library, Inc.

Albert Schweitzer, Henry Holt and Company, Inc., New York and George Allen & Unwin, Ltd., London, for "From Elemental Thinking: Reverence for Life" from *Out of My Life and Thought*. Copyright, 1933, 1949, by Henry Holt and Company, Inc.

Ignazio Silone, *Dissent* Magazine, New York, and *Encounter* Magazine, London, for "The Choice of Comrades," published in the December, 1954, issue of *Encounter* and in the Winter, 1955, issue of *Dissent*. Copyright, 1955, by Dissent Publishing Company.

Pitirim A. Sorokin for "Integralism Is My Philosophy."

G. M. Trevelyan and Longmans, Green & Company, Ltd., London, for "Stray Thoughts on History" from *Autobiography and Other Essays*.

Frank Lloyd Wright and Horizon Press, Inc., New York, for "The Language of Organic Architecture" from *The Future of Architecture*, Copyright, 1953, by Horizon Press, Inc.; "Integrity: In a House as in an Individual" and "Grammar: The House as a Work of Art" from *The Natural House*, Copyright, 1954, by Horizon Press, Inc.

CONTENTS

CONTENTS

ACKNOWLEDGMENTS

THE EDITOR WISHES TO THANK THE DISTINGUISHED CONTRIBUTORS TO THIS
volume for their many acts of co-operation, and the publishers in the
United States, England, France and Switzerland who have permitted
the use of their authors' material, in some cases even before they have
used it themselves.

The editor is also indebted for much help to the American Library in
Paris, the Bibliothèque Nationale, and the Library of the University of
London; and also, for special consideration, to Mrs. A. Jaffé of the
Institute for Analytical Psychology at Zurich, Miss Vaun Gillmor of
the Bollingen Foundation, and Kyrill Schabert of the Pantheon Press,
New York.

He must also express a particular gratefulness for the time and advice
of Professor George P. Conger, head of the department of philosophy
at the University of Minnesota, whom he encountered in Paris, midway
between his home in America, and India, whence he was returning
from making the Ghosh Lectures on the unification of the faiths at
Calcutta.

THIS IS A WORLD in which each of us, knowing his limitations, knowing the evils of superficiality and the terrors of fatigue, will have to cling to what is close to him, to what he knows, to what he can do, to his friends and his tradition and his love, lest he be dissolved in a universal confusion and know nothing and love nothing. . . . This balance, this perpetual, precarious, impossible balance between the infinitely open and the intimate, this time— our twentieth century—has been long in coming; but it has come. It is, I think, for us and our children, our only way . . . to make partial order in total chaos.

J. Robert Oppenheimer, New York,
nuclear physicist

PHILOSOPHY TODAY is the responsibility of man as Man. In opposition to supposedly total knowledge, philosophy is charged with the duty of keeping awake the faculty of independent thought and therewith the independence of the individual which totalitarian powers seek to extinguish. Philosophy must remind every individual that he *can* be *himself*, and that he ceases to be a man if he relinquishes this privilege.

Karl Jaspers, Basel,
philosopher

MISGUIDED DEVELOPMENT of the soul must lead to psychic mass destruction. The present situation is so sinister that one cannot suppress the suspicion that the Creator is planning another deluge that will finally exterminate the existing race of man. . . .

Carl Gustav Jung, Zurich,
analytic psychologist

LIBERTY IS THE practical recognition of human polymorphism. . . . Liberty demands not only equality of opportunity but a variety of opportunities, and a tolerance of those who fail to conform to standards which may be desirable but are not essential for the function of society.

J. B. S. Haldane, London,
biologist

MEN STRAIN AT the skies for miracles, when the sky itself is an illusion and marvels of atoms and cells and nervous systems, which make miracles seem trivial, lie all around them. To look for miracles is like looking for the end of the rainbow. The rainbow is not painted; it is pervasive.

George P. Conger, Minnesota,
philosopher

FOREWORD: AS A DEDICATION
TO TWENTY MEN

IN PLATO'S DAY THE INSPIRED MEN WERE MOSTLY IN ONE PLACE, IN ATHENS. Today they may be in Paris, London, Princeton, Rome, New York, in the heart of Africa, or in Delhi. Our only way to meet them is through books.

This book brings together twenty of the world's outstanding thinkers with substantial selections of their works, which show the deepest meanings they have found in life.

Not an analysis of systems of thought, nor the hairsplitting of differing philosophical theories, *This Is My Philosophy* is the varied thinking of men in different spheres of activity. Independent of each other, not knowing in advance what the other had to say, each has expressed his thought in the terms and climate of his work, his life, and his beliefs.

Some, like the venerable Trevelyan, may view things lyrically, and even history, the subject nearest him, as something fading as it recedes, as poetry. Some expressions have writhed through doubt and disillusion and, as in the Italian Silone's case, the words seem penned in pain. None is an offhand, glib confection. Intimate as some are, each has sought the universal in all men. This is the world we live in—its conflicts and its problems—a shrinking and expanding world, a world of as many possibilities for evil, it seems, as for good. And if all men, when they think, philosophize, this might be called a book about ourselves, in those rare, deep moments when the human spirit meets the test of thought.

What is man and where is he going?

To these twenty men, who have taken thought, he is going to heaven or to hell, and maybe faster than he thinks. The pace, thinks Bertrand Russell, is being set in our day. "It is impossible to guess which we shall choose. . . ."

Not all these men are professional philosophers. One is an architect; two are nuclear physicists; one is a biologist; another a missionary and a doctor. Two or three are authors. One is a theologian. Another a psychoanalyst.

And not all have led a wholly bookish life. One was the maker of a weapon that has altered the relationship of nations and might conceivably wipe out mankind. Another was six times imprisoned and once, confined in Russia's Fortress of Peter and Paul, condemned to death for fighting Communists. Another was hunted by Fascists in the hills of Italy. One is the vice-president of India, that vast and fecund land teetering in the neutral air between the East and West.

To them all, philosophy is less as Russell sees it, "something intermediate between theology and science," than it is a discipline of the whole mind and being. "Philosophy exists wherever man becomes conscious of his being through thought. Philosophy with a capital letter," says Gabriel Marcel, "is an idol; what is real is a kind of life of reflective thought that can and ought to be pursued at every level of human activity.

"The philosopher," adds this French contributor, "can help to save man from himself (and the destructive tendencies inherent in him) only by a pitiless and unwearying denunciation of the spirit of abstraction. . . . The philosopher knows that the mass itself is a lie and it is against the mass and for the universal in man that he must bear witness. . . ."

This is a book in which twenty exceptional men bear witness.

Not forty. Nor a hundred. Statistics of quantity always try in these days to sway our judgments. We live in an era when attempts are made to prove almost anything by numbers. This book has fewer men, but, we believe, deeper ones. "Inward men," as Dr. Schweitzer would advocate, and "men with an active, outward ethic."

Few of the contributions are set pieces, written for the occasion or the moment. They represent each man in longer thought, often at the very core of his lifetime's work, and what is here is here for a total and all-encompassing meaning and of enough length and substance to give a reader not a journalistic response to a question but the flavor and the style of thinking of an integrated personality.

If a writer like Lewis Mumford has concentrated for twenty years on one series of books designed to plead the necessary wholeness of man in a divisive and a loveless world, surely a reader who might turn to a book like this will reasonably consent to spend time on the four long fragments the philosopher has selected from such labors. Those who have an interest in the "psyche," as Carl Gustav Jung calls the old mysterious soul, may here read *all* that Dr. Jung wishes to say about it, albeit the thoughts of the soul are long, long thoughts, and here run to some twenty-five thousand words, some in Greek and Latin.

After length and substance, it might be pertinent to say something of nationality.

Five of the authors are American: Lewis Mumford, J. Robert Oppenheimer, Frank Lloyd Wright, Reinhold Niebuhr, William Ernest Hocking, and Pitirim A. Sorokin, who is the Russian-born, naturalized sociologist at Harvard.

Four are British: Lord Bertrand Russell, J. B. S. Haldane, Aldous Huxley and George Macaulay Trevelyan.

Three are French: Jean-Paul Sartre, Jacques Maritain, Gabriel Marcel.

Albert Schweitzer is Alsatian.

Two are German: Werner Heisenberg, of Göttingen, and Karl Jaspers, now a resident of Switzerland.

Carl Gustav Jung is Swiss.

Ignazio Silone is Italian.

Salvador de Madariaga is a Spaniard who lives at Oxford.

Sir Sarvepalli Radhakrishnan is of India.

From such a list it will be plain that these are not young men and new to the world of thought, experience and the gift of expression. None is a bright young genius—even Sartre is past fifty—none is a specialist in some technical field who has come up like a rocket and sputtered out as briefly in his illumination of our times. Many are in their seasoned seventies. They have lived their philosophy as well as thought it. Lord Russell and Professor Hocking, at the poles in their approaches to philosophy, are practically twins in years, both, as this is written, eighty-four years old. Frank Lloyd Wright, who bounces about the country, tossing his vital white hair and quipping at banquet audiences when he is not out in Wisconsin or in Arizona, building "natural" houses, or "organic" skyscrapers, or light and soaring, circular museums, is eighty-eight, but his philosophy is invigorated by the same integrity today as forcefully as it was at any earlier age. Indeed, the combined ages of these twenty men represent a total of 1,422 years, a length of time one philosopher's life less than the time covered from the birth of Christianity to the discovery of America, or if concentrated in the intellectually active periods of the world would be represented through two or three centuries of Chinese and Indian philosophy, the three or four hundred years of the Athenian ascendancy, the eleventh to thirteenth centuries of the late Middle Ages, the two hundred years of the Renaissance, the eighteenth century of the Enlightenment, and practically the whole 350 years of modern times since Descartes—all periods our thinkers here have delved in and profited from. These men are elders who have seen Susanna, they have heard Cassandra wail, and, in the patience of their wisdom, some at least have caught fleeting glimpses of Esperanza—the other sister—Hope.

Started as private reading a dozen years ago, this volume represents an editor's sense of the need of many for some representative assertion of ethical standards for today, and an anthologist's sense of gathering the men and their writings to that end. Some years ago he had editorially plucked the sleeves of other thinkers.[1] Santayana. Ortega y Gasset. Croce. Dewey. Einstein. Whitehead. Thomas Mann. Men now dead, no longer to be sought and asked to share the generosity of their wisdom with the rest of us. But others are still writing, and the world has changed, even in a decade. But has it changed, essentially? What are the best men thinking today, and what of their conclusions in the past do they still hold to now?

How do these men characterize our present age, in the light of their knowledge of history? What are the important trends of thought, seriously considered and judiciously accepted by men who have dedicated 1,422 years to the end of knowing? What do they consider man's greatest social need? What does the future hold for each of them, I asked, and how has your personal philosophy been affected by the work to which you have devoted the mature years of your life?

These were some of the queries.

Others were: What sort of creatures are we, biologically, historically, spiritually, as we race through our days? Is improvement possible? Can we alter man and add a cubit to our stature by taking thought, by love, genetics, or by force of law?

It seems fitting that a big question comes first, from Lord Russell. Will we survive our own technically increasing knowledge which makes it possible now to exterminate us all? And it seems just as inevitable—for, Lord Russell, musing on the proper men turning up, is hopeful—that the book should end with another question, from philosopher-statesman Radhakrishnan, functioning as prophet as well: Can the world, having found a single body, find its soul? He thinks it can.

[1] *The World's Best* (Dial, 1950).

A preoccupation with Christianity flows, not surprisingly, through these pages. Science, the god of the age, is not all. With its weapons and its automation, Science has ridden roughshod, and taken rebuffs with its progress, and philosophy has often been publicly scored as a useless waste, in these days, of our energy. Yet each has its defenders in this symposium. The two men of nuclear physics speak with measure and responsibility. The philosophers have gone beyond the boundaries of their books. Many sought their horizon in religion.

"Philosophy," says Professor Hocking, "is but a remote indicator of the secret struggles of countless human souls carrying on the query-laden enterprise of living under existing conditions.

"Religion meets these struggles directly.

"But the philosophy that lives, lives only because those who struggle find it helpfully interpreting that struggle. It is not something apart from religion—it is an organ of the human thought without which religion is but a blind survival impulse, sometimes usurping the name of 'faith'—which is never blind. Christianity, holding itself duly independent of philosophy (and on occasion unduly despising it), has no choice but to come to terms with the concepts which the time spirit finds expressive of its own groping for light."

If this is approaching religion with a bias toward philosophy, then this it is. Some thinkers approach philosophy with a bias toward religion—Maritain and Niebuhr and Marcel. In Dr. Schweitzer's case, philosophy was only a first step. Reverence for Life, the basis of his fundamental thinking, he says, is the ethic of love widened into universality. "It is the ethic of Jesus, now recognized as a necessity of thought." For Dr. Schweitzer the basic need of man in the world is the power and the courage to think, deeply and honestly; not impossible, he holds, within a Christian framework. For the Russian-born sociologist, Sorokin, the greatest need of mankind at the moment is creative love.

Not all the thinkers here are Christian. Sartre is an atheist. And yet, *de profundis,* in nausea and despair, what denial of negativeness lies behind the hope that his existentialism will, in the end, furnish its own psychoanalysis as a therapy of his age? *Désespoir,* says Hocking, sympathetically, contains in itself *espoir.*

Isaiah's voice is raised on many sides. Woe. Man is not redeemed by the simple fact of his historical development. The human self in its integrity and unity, says Dr. Niebuhr, has been lost. We live on our planet like a swarm of destructive parasites, Aldous Huxley warns;

nature will exact her penalty. We do not think, says Schweitzer. Progress is no longer glowingly inevitable, raising man generation by generation to new heights of virtue and prosperity; man is as capable of evil, as he has shown in this generation, as he is capable of good. The comrades, workers, are not *ipso facto* angels who by right of inherent superior qualities will inherit as the onward-marching proletariat. So thinks Silone. Men as mobs, says Marcel, are less than men; only passion and violence rule them. Numbers are not magical, it is only man conscious of himself as man, thinking and responsible, who is capable of the good, the true or the beautiful.

"In all philosophical interpretation," writes Sir Sarvepalli Radhakrishnan, shuttler between Oxford and Benares, an intimate of Gandhi, Tagore and Nehru, "the right method is to interpret thinkers at their best in the light of what they say in the moments of their clearest insights. There is no reason why philosophical writers should not be judged as other creative writers are, at least in the main, on the basis of their finest inspirations."

So let it be.

But, in judging these men, many readers will be judging, too, themselves. These men are not alone in their thoughts. There are twenty more who think like them and twenty many times over. So, many may find expressed here their own unvoiced feelings. *These* men have thought their feelings through, if even they have not found all the ready answers. They have not shut their eyes to the squalors in the world or their hearts to its beauties shimmering through, nor have they shut their minds, ungenerously, to the contradictions and dilemmas of society.

Thus, peculiarly, as personal and professional evidence of thought, *This Is My Philosophy* is an almost wholly selfless book. What these men do and say is more than self. And they do not fear to think, or speak, or feel compassion for the lot of man and a "love of things good and a hatred of things evil."

If the temper of the age is scientific, the specialist who does not look beyond his field upon a larger frame of life is not to go unwarned.

Werner Heisenberg, speaking before the youth of a one-time warring country, says: "You are gathered here to contribute in your circle to an understanding between the peoples. There can be no better way of doing this than by getting to know, with the freedom and spontaneity of youth, people of other nations, their ways of thought and their feelings. Take from your scientific work a serious and incorruptible method of thought, help to spread it, because no understanding is possible without it.

"Revere those things beyond science which really matter and about which it is so difficult to speak."

When thoughtful men speak about such things, let us listen.

What follows is the testament of twenty such men.

—THE EDITOR

THIS IS MY PHILOSOPHY

1 / A PHILOSOPHER WITH A QUESTION

WINNER OF THE NOBEL PRIZE, IN 1950, FOR LITERATURE, BERTRAND Russell, English philosopher, mathematician and author, is a contemporary world thinker whose multiple aspects were specifically cited in the award: "In recognition of his many-sided and significant authorship, in which he has constantly figured as a defender of humanity and freedom of thought."

Bertrand Russell was born in 1872, and thus near eighty-five, is one of the deans in this book. He is known not only to book readers in most parts of the English-reading world, but to lecture audiences in the United States, China and Europe. He taught at two different periods of his life at his alma mater, Trinity College, Cambridge; his fellowship there was withdrawn during the First World War for his activities in behalf of peace; he was prosecuted, fined and sentenced to six months in jail for an article printed in leaflet form. In 1944 he returned to Trinity College with a fellowship and there he completed one of his most representative works, his "philosophical testament," *Human Knowledge: Its Scope and Its Limits*. He is the author of a *History of Western Philosophy,* which grew out of a series of lectures for which he was dismissed from a five-year teaching contract at the Barnes Foundation in Marion, Pennsylvania, in 1942, an act for which he sued and recovered damages. His generally considered greatest work, on which he collaborated with the late Alfred North Whitehead, is the *Principia Mathematica* (1910-13), in which he attempts to find a mutual meeting place for mathematics and philosophy in "symbolic" or mathematical logic.

Of late years Lord Russell has concentrated on political writing, essays, and has even written a book of short stories.

"My intelligence," he wrote in 1951, "such as it is, has been steadily decaying since the age of twenty. When I was young I liked mathematics. When this became too difficult for me, I took to philosophy, and when philosophy became too difficult, I took to politics. Since then I have concentrated on detective stories."

On the air, at eighty-one, he said: "I think one of the troubles of

I

the world has been the habit of dogmatically believing something or other, and I think all these matters are full of doubt and the rational man will not be too sure that he is right. I think that we ought always to entertain our opinions with some measure of doubt."

The philosopher has been four times married. He lives, as he says, "in serene old age" in the English countryside at an ancestral home in Wales. He succeeded to his title in 1931. His last divorce was in 1952, at the age of eighty. In the same year he married Edith Finch of New York.

His response to this symposium was as immediate as his response to most calls upon his time and energy. He was asked if his personal philosophy had been affected by his professional work and answered: "Less than most people think. My professional work has led me to reject the dogmas of all known religions and to be suspicious of philosophies which make a liberal use of the concept of organism."

Was there any period or place in history which he finds more satisfactory than the present?

"The answer," he wrote back, "must depend on income. The Athens of Pericles was pleasant for rich men but not for slaves or women. France in the last decades before the Revolution was pleasant for philosophers and liberal aristocrats.

"I suppose Elizabethan England was pleasant for Sir Philip Sidney. But I doubt whether at any earlier period there has been a wider diffusion of well-being than there is at present in Western Europe and America."

How, he was asked, *would you characterize our present age if you were viewing it from the perspective of history?*

"This is quite impossible to answer until we see how the present age turns out. Before the year 1000 people thought the end of the world imminent. This made their judgment of their own times erroneous. Two gateways stand before us, one leading to heaven and one to hell. It is impossible to guess which we shall choose."

Although students of Lord Russell will find his views as a philosopher, embodied in many of his books, notably in the *Introduction to Mathematical Philosophy, 1919,* and in *Human Knowledge, 1948,* the *Outline of Philosophy, 1927,* and *History of Western Philosophy, 1945* (all published by George Allen & Unwin, Ltd.), he has chosen to represent himself in *This is My Philosophy* with the following pages, "Prologue or Epilogue?" the last chapter of his *Human Society in Ethics and Politics,* Published in England by George Allen & Unwin Ltd. and in the United States by Simon & Schuster.

Prologue or Epilogue?

BY BERTRAND RUSSELL

Man, as time counts in geology and in the history of evolution, is a very recent arrival on his planet. For countless millions of years only very simple animals existed. During other countless millions, new type gradually evolved—fishes, reptiles, birds and, at last, mammals. Man, the species to which we happen to belong, has existed for, at most, a million years, and has possessed his present brain capacity for only about half that time. But recent as is the emergence of man in the history of the universe, and even in the history of life, the emergence of his titanic powers, at once terrifying and splendid, is very much more recent. It is only about six thousand years since man discovered his capacity for distinctively human activities. These began, we may say, with the invention of writing and the organization of government. Since the beginning of recorded history progress has not been steady, but has been a matter of fits and starts. After the Age of the Pyramids, the first really noteworthy advance was in the time of the Greeks, and after them there was no further advance of comparable importance until about five hundred years ago. During the last five hundred years changes have occurred with continually increasing frequency, and have at last become so swift that an old man can scarcely hope to understand the world in which he finds himself. It seems hardly possible that a state of affairs differing so profoundly from everything that has existed since first there were living organisms, can continue without bringing some kind of dizziness, some calamitous vertigo, that will end the maddening acceleration in which heart and brain become increasingly exhausted. Such fears are not irrational: the state of the world encourages them, and the contrast between the hustling present and the leisurely past brings them to the imagination of the contemplative historian.

But when, forgetting our present perplexities, we view the world as astronomers view it, we find ourselves thinking of the future as extending through many more ages than even those contemplated in geology. There appears to be no reason in physical nature to prevent our planet from remaining habitable for another million million years, and if man can survive, in spite of the dangers produced by his own frenzies, there is no reason why he should not continue the career of triumph upon which he has so recently embarked. Man's destiny for many millions of years to come is, so far as our present knowledge shows, in his own hands. It rests with him to decide whether he will plunge into disaster or climb to undreamt-of heights. Shakespeare speaks of

> The prophetic soul
> Of the wide world dreaming on things to come.

Are we to think that the dream is not prophetic? Is it no more than a deceiving vision ending in death? Or may we think that the drama is only just begun, that we have heard the first syllables of the prologue, and as yet no more?

Man, as the Orphics said, is a child of earth and of the starry heaven; or, in more recent language, a combination of god and beast. There are those who shut their eyes to the beast, and there are those who shut their eyes to the god. It is all too easy to make a picture of man as unmixed beast. Swift did it in his Yahoos, and did it in a manner so convincing that to many of us the impress is ineffaceable. But Swift's Yahoos, repulsive as they are, lack the worst qualities of modern man, since they lack his intelligence. To describe man as a mixture of god and beast is hardly fair to the beasts. He must rather be conceived as a mixture of god and devil. No beast and no Yahoo could commit the crimes committed by Hitler and Stalin. There seems no limit to the horrors that can be inflicted by a combination of scientific intelligence with the malevolence of Satan. When we contemplate the tortures of Hitler and Stalin, and when we reflect that the species which they disgraced is our own, it is easy to feel that the Yahoos, for all their degradation, are far less dreadful than some of the human beings who actually wield power in great modern States. Human imagination long ago pictured Hell, but it is only through recent skill that men have been able to give reality to what they had imagined. The human mind is strangely poised between the bright vault of Heaven and the dark pit of Hell. It can find satisfaction in the contemplation of either, and it cannot be said that either is more natural to it than the other.

Sometimes, in moments of horror, I have been tempted to doubt whether there is any reason to wish that such a creature as man should continue to exist. It is easy to see man as dark and cruel, as an embodiment of diabolic power, and as a blot upon the fair face of the universe. But this is not the whole truth, and is not the last word of wisdom.

Man, as the Orphics said, is also the child of the starry Heaven. Man, though his body is insignificant and powerless in comparison with the great bodies of the astronomer's world, is yet able to mirror that world, is able to travel in imagination and scientific knowledge through enormous abysses of space and time. What he knows already of the world in which he lives would be unbelievable to his ancestors of a thousand years ago; and in view of the speed with which he is acquiring knowledge there is every reason to think that, if he continues on his present course, what he will know a thousand years from now will be equally beyond what *we* can imagine. But it is not only, or even principally, in knowledge that man at his best deserves admiration. Men have created beauty; they have had strange visions that seemed like the first glimpse of a land of wonder; they have been capable of love, of sympathy for the whole human race, of vast hopes for mankind as a whole. These achievements, it is true, have been those of exceptional men, and have very frequently met with hostility from the herd. But there is no reason why, in the ages to come, the sort of man who is now exceptional should not become usual, and if that were to happen, the exceptional man in the new world would rise as far above Shakespeare as Shakespeare now rises above the common man. So much evil use has been made of knowledge that our imagination does not readily rise to the thought of the good uses that are possible in the raising of the level of excellence in the population at large to that which is now only achieved by men of genius. When I allow myself to hope that the world will emerge from its present troubles, and that it will some day learn to give the direction of its affairs, not to cruel mountebanks, but to men possessed of wisdom and courage, I see before me a shining vision: a world where none are hungry, where few are ill, where work is pleasant and not excessive, where kindly feeling is common, and where minds released from fear create delight for eye and ear and heart. Do not say this is impossible. It is not impossible. I do not say it can be done tomorrow, but I do say that it could be done within a thousand years, if men would bend their minds to the achievement of the kind of happiness that should be distinctive of man. I say the kind of happiness distinctive of man, because the happiness of pigs, which the enemies of Epicurus accused him of seeking, is not possible for men. If you try to make yourself content with the happiness of a pig, your suppressed potentialities will make you miserable. True happiness for human beings is possible only to those who develop their godlike potentialities to the utmost. For such men, in the world of the present day, happiness must be mixed with much pain, since they cannot escape

5

sympathetic suffering in the spectacle of the sufferings of others. But in a society where this source of pain no longer existed, there could be a human happiness more complete, more infused with imagination and knowledge and sympathy, than anything that is possible to those condemned to live in our present gloomy epoch.

Is all this hope to count for nothing? Are we to continue entrusting our affairs to men without sympathy, without knowledge, without imagination, and having nothing to recommend them except methodical hatred and skill in vituperation? (I do not mean this as an indictment of all statesmen; but it applies to those who guide the destinies of Russia and to some who have influence in other countries.) When Othello is about to kill Desdemona, he says, "But yet the pity of it, Iago! O Iago, the pity of it!" I doubt whether the ruler of Russia and his opposite number, as they prepare the extermination of mankind, have enough pity in their character to be capable of this exclamation, or even to realize the nature of what they are preparing. I suppose that never for a moment have they thought of man as a single species with possibilities that may be realized or thwarted. Never have their minds risen beyond the daily considerations of momentary expediency in the narrow contest for brief power. And yet there must, in every country, be many who can rise to a wider point of view. It is to men with such capabilities, in whatever country, that the friends of man must appeal. The future of man is at stake, and if enough men become aware of this his future is assured. Those who are to lead the world out of its troubles will need courage, hope and love. Whether they will prevail, I do not know; but, beyond all reason, I am unconquerably persuaded that they will.

II / A PHILOSOPHER OF RENEWAL

For twenty-one of the mature years of his life, Lewis Mumford has been engaged in a task of presenting his interpretation, in book form, of a philosophy of human development. In 1951, in his own mid-fifties, the final volume in his four-volume *Renewal of Life Series* made its appearance. It was *The Conduct of Life.* The series began with *Technics and Civilization,* 1934; followed by *The Culture of Cities,* 1938, and *The Condition of Man,* 1944.

On publication of the final volume, Mr. Mumford wrote: "In these volumes I have sought to deal in a unified way with man's nature, his work, and his life-dramas, as revealed in the development of contemporary Western civilization. By intention, these books outline a philosophy, demonstrate a method of synthesis, and project further a new pattern of life that has, for at least a century, been in process of emergence. . . .

"During the period covered by the writing of these books grave changes for the worse have taken place throughout the world. But if the evils that now threaten mankind are more appalling than ever before, the reward for facing them and overcoming them promises also to be greater. . . . Despite the shocks and sorrows of the last two decades, Hope abides and 'maketh not ashamed.' Even if the present crisis continues for another generation, even if it brings forth a succession of catastrophes, it is already time to prepare for the renewal of life. To that end these four books have, from the beginning, been dedicated. . . ."

Mr. Mumford, who lives with his wife in the quiet of the Berkshire foothills at Amenia, New York, was born in Flushing, Long Island, beyond the shadow of the New York skyscrapers, October 19, 1895. He was educated at City College, Columbia University and the New School for Social Research. He contributed to the *Freeman,* the *New Republic, American Mercury,* the *Journal of the American Institute of Architects,* and other periodicals. His pioneer studies in American culture (the arts, literature, architecture, etc.), *The Golden Day, The*

Brown Decades, Sticks and Stones and *Herman Melville,* prepared him for his larger work. His constant preoccupation has been to interpret, in a rounded fashion, man's life, his work and the society in which he lives. In his nonliterary activities, he has pursued the same end in interesting himself actively in education, first as a member of the Board of Higher Education in New York, then as a member of the Commission on Teacher Education of the American Council on Education, as professor of humanities at Stanford University and professor of city planning at the University of Pennsylvania from 1951 onward. He has been widely esteemed as a critic of architecture, although he says, "My main work during the past fifteen years has been within the fields of education, politics, religion and philosophy."

Van Wyck Brooks has said of him, "He carries on, like no one else living in America today, the tradition of Emerson, Whitman, and William James."

Mr. Mumford's selections are from *The Conduct of Life* and *The Condition of Man* in which, as the exponent of what he has called the "open synthesis," he directs attention to the whole personality of man, disposes of "systems" of philosophy as too partial and lopsided, asks for balance, a reformation of individual man and concludes with citing the life and philosophy of Albert Schweitzer as evidence of the possibility of man's capacity for renewal at a time of catastrophe.

"My philosophy," Mr. Mumford wrote the editor, "has doubtless matured, as my own life has matured, with sundry additions and a certain generosity toward contradictions and residual mysteries: but the outlines of it are already visible in my earliest books, *The Story of Utopias* (1922) and *The Golden Day* (1926).

"I have lived this philosophy as well as thought it: indeed without the living the thought would be immature, if not meaningless: so for many readers the core of it would be found in the little biography I wrote of my son Geddes (who was killed in the Second World War), *Green Memories.*"

The Fulfillment of Man

BY LEWIS MUMFORD

I. TRIUMPH OVER SYSTEMS

Most ethical philosophies have sought to isolate and standardize the goods of life, and to make one or another set of purposes supreme. They have looked upon pleasure or social efficiency or duty, upon imperturbability or rationality or self-annihilation as the chief crown of a disciplined and cultivated spirit. This effort to whittle down valuable conduct to a single set of consistent principles and ideal ends does not do justice to the nature of life, with its paradoxes, its complicated processes, its internal conflicts, its sometimes unresolvable dilemmas.

In order to reduce life to a single clear intellectually consistent pattern, a system tends to neglect the varied factors that belong to life by reason of its complex organic needs and its ever-developing purposes: indeed, each historic ethical system, whether rational or utilitarian or transcendental, blandly overlooks the aspects of life that are covered by rival systems; and in practice each will accuse the other of inconsistency precisely at those imperative moments when common sense happily intervenes to save the system from defeat. This accounts for a general failure in every rigorously formulated system to meet all of life's diverse and contradictory occasions. Hedonism is of no use in a shipwreck. There is a time to laugh and a time to weep, as The Preacher reminds us; but the pessimists forget the first clause and the optimists the second.

The fallacy of systems is a very general one; and we can follow its ethical consequences best, perhaps, in education. The moral becomes equally plain, whether we consider a fictional or an autobiographic account. One thinks, for example, of Sir Austin Feverel's system in Meredith's *The Ordeal of Richard Feverel*. Full of reasoned contempt for the ordinary educational procedures of his culture, Sir Austin contrives a watchful private system, designed to avoid current errors and to produce a spirited, intellectually sound, thoroughly awakened, finely disciplined young man. But the system-maker had not reckoned upon the fact that a young man, so trained, might, as the very proof of the

9

education, fall in love with a young girl not duly accounted for in the system and elope with her in marriage; and that when the system intervenes in this marriage in order to carry out its own purposes, it would bring on a far more harrowing tragedy than any purely conventional mode of education, less confident of its high intentions, less set on its special ends, would have produced.

Or take an even better case, none the worse for being real: the childhood of Mary Everest, that extraordinary woman who eventually became the wife and helpmate of the great logician, George Boole. Mary's father was the devoted disciple of Hahnemann, the philosopher of homeopathic medicine; and he applied Hahnemann's principles, not merely to illness, but to the whole regimen of life. Following strictly the master's belief in cold baths and long walks before breakfast, the system-bound father practiced upon his children a form of daily torture that drove Mary Everest into a state of blank unfeelingness and irresponsiveness. She hated every item in the strict routine; and her whole affectional and sentimental life as a young girl, in relation to her parents, was warped by it. The resentment she felt against this inflexibility and this arbitrary disregard of natural disposition is indeed still evident in the account she wrote at the end of a long life.

Believing blindly in the system, Mary Everest's father never observed what was happening to his beloved children in actual life: for the sake of carrying through the doctrine, he disregarded the testimony of life and took no note of scores of indications in his children's conduct and health that should have warned him that he was working ruin. Every intellectually awakened parent who applied one or another of the rival systems in psychology and education that became fashionable during the last thirty years can testify out of his own experience, if he reflects upon it—or at least his children could testify—to the fallacy of oversimplification that is involved in the very conception and application of a system. Life cannot be reduced to a system: the best wisdom, when so reduced to a single set of insistent notes, becomes a cacophony; indeed, the more stubbornly one adheres to a system, the more violence one does to life.

Actual historic institutions, fortunately, have been modified by anomalies, discrepancies, contradictions, compromises: the older they are, the richer this organic compost. All these varied nutrients that remain in the social soil are viewed with high scorn by the believer in systems: like the advocates of old-fashioned chemical fertilizers, he has no notion that what makes the soil usable and nourishing is precisely the organic debris that remains. In most historic institutions, it is their weakness that is their saving strength. Czarism, for example, as practiced in Russia during the nineteenth century, was a hideous form of government: tyrannical, capricious, inwardly unified, severely repressive of anything but its own orthodoxy. But, as Alexander Herzen showed in his *Memoirs,* the system was made less intolerable by two things that had no lawful or logical part in it: bribery and corruption on one hand, which made it possible to get around regulations and to soften punishments; and skepticism from within, on the other, which made many of its officers incapable of carrying out with conviction and therefore with rigor the tasks imposed. In contrast, one may note in passing, the relative "purity" of the present Soviet Russian regime serves to buttress its inhumanity.

This tendency toward laxity, corruption, disorder, is the only thing that enables a system to escape self-asphyxiation: for a system is in effect an attempt to make men breathe carbon dioxide or oxygen alone, without the other components of air, with effects that are either temporarily exhilarating or soporific, but in the end must be lethal: since though each of these gases is necessary for life, the air that keeps men alive is a mixture of various gases in due proportion. So it is not the purity of the orthodox Christian doctrine that has kept the Eastern and Western churches alive and enabled them to flourish even in a scientific age, but just the opposite: the nonsystematic elements, seeping in from other cultures and from contradictory experiences of life; covert heresies that have given the Christian creed a vital buoyancy that seemingly tighter bodies of doctrine have lacked.

The fallacy of exclusive systems has become particularly plain during the last two centuries: never have their errors, in fact, proved more vicious than in our own time.

Since the seventeenth century we have been living in an age of system-makers, and what is even worse, system-appliers. The world has been divided first of all into two general parties, the conservatives and the radicals, or as Comte called them, the party of order and the party of progress—as if both order and change, stability and variation, continuity and novelty, were not equally fundamental attributes of life. People sought, conscientiously, to make their lives conform to a system: a set of limited, partial, exclusive principles. They sought to live by the romantic system or the utilitarian system, to be wholly idealist or wholly practical. If they were rigorously capitalist, in America, they glibly forgot that the free public education they supported was in fact a communist institution; or if they believed in communism, like the founders of the Oneida Community, they stubbornly sought to apply their communism to sexual relations as well as industry.

In short, the system-mongers sought to align a whole community according to some limiting principle, and to organize its entire life in conformity to the system, as if such wholesale limitations could do justice to the condition of man. Actually, by the middle of the nineteenth century, it had become plain that the most self-confident of the systems, capitalism, which had originally come in as a healthy challenge to static privilege and feudal lethargy, would, if unmodified by other social considerations, strangle life: maiming the young and innocent who toiled fourteen hours a day in the new factories, and starving adults wholesale, in obedience to the blind law of market competition, working in a manic-depressive business cycle. As a pure system, capitalism was humanly intolerable; what has happily saved it from violent overthrow has been the absorption of the heresies of socialism—public enterprises and social security—that have given it increasing balance and stability.

Now a system, being a conceptual tool, has a certain pragmatic usefulness: for the formulation of a system leads to intellectual clarification and therefore to a certain clean vigor of decision and action. The prescientific age of abstraction, as Comte originally characterized it, was a general period of unknotting and disentanglement: the numerous threads that formed the warp and woof of the whole social fabric were then isolated and disengaged. When the red threads were united in one skein, the green in another, the blue and purple in still others, their true individual texture and color stood out more clearly than when they were woven together in their original complex historic pattern. In analytic thinking one follows the thread and disregards the total pattern; and the effect of system-making in life was to destroy an appreciation of its complexities and any sense of its over-all pattern.

Such a sorting out of systems, with its corresponding division into parties, made it somewhat easier, no doubt, to introduce new threads of still different tones or colors on the social loom: it also encouraged the illusion that a satisfactory social fabric could be woven together of a single color and fiber. Unfortunately, the effort to organize a whole community, or indeed any set of living relations, on the basis of making every sector of life wholly red, wholly blue, or wholly green commits in fact a radical error. A community where everyone lived according to the romantic philosophy, for example, would have no stability, no continuity, no way of economically doing a thousand things that must be repeated every day of its life: left to spontaneous impulse, many important functions would not be performed at all. By whose spontaneous desires would garbage be collected or dishes washed? Necessity, social compulsion, solidarity play a part in real life that romanticism and anarchism take no account of.

Similarly, a community that lived on the radical principle, divorcing itself from its past and being wholly concerned with the future, would leave out as much of the richness of historic existence as John Stuart Mill's father left out of his education: by cutting off memory, it would even undermine hope. So, too, a thoroughly Marxian community, where no one had any life except that provided by the state on terms laid down by the state, would do away with the possibility of creating autonomous and balanced human beings: thus it would forfeit—as Soviet Russia has in fact forfeited—the generous core of all of Marx's own most noble dreams.

In short, to take a single guiding idea, like individualism or collectivism, stoicism or hedonism, aristocracy or democracy, and attempt to follow this thread through all of life's occasions, is to miss the significance of the thread itself, whose function is to add to the complexity and interest of life's total pattern. Today the fallacy of "either/or" dogs us everywhere: whereas it is in the nature of life to embrace and surmount all its contradictions, not by shearing them away, but by weaving them into a more inclusive unity. No organism, no society, no personality, can be reduced to a system or be effectually governed by a system. Inner direction or outer direction, detachment or conformity, should never become so exclusive that in practice they make a shift from one to the other impossible.

None of the existing categories of philosophy, none of the present procedures of science or religion, none of the popular doctrines of social action, covers the method and outlook presented here. Not personalism, not humanism, not materialism, not idealism, not existentialism, not naturalism, not Marxian Communism, not Emersonian individualism can comprehend the total view that, in the name of life, I have been putting forward in these pages. For the essence of the present philosophy is that many elements necessarily rejected by any single system are essential to develop life's highest creative potential; and that by turns one system or another must be invoked, temporarily, to do justice to life's endlessly varied needs and occasions.

Those who understand the nature of life itself will not, like Engels or Dewey or Whyte, see reality in terms of change alone and dismiss the fixed and the static as otiose; neither will they, like many Greek and Hindu philosophers, regard flux and movement and time as unreal or illusory and seek truth only in the unchangeable. Coming to the practical affairs of life, this philosophy of the whole does not overvalue any single system of property or production: just as Aristotle and the framers of the American Constitution wisely favored a mixed system of government, so one will favor a mixed economy, not afraid to invoke socialist measures when free enterprise leads to injustice or economic depression, or to favor competition and personal initiative when private monopolies or governmental organizations bog down in torpid security and inflexible bureaucratic routine. This is the philosophy of the open synthesis; and to make sure that it remains open I shall resist the temptation to give it a name. Those who think and act in its spirit may be identified, perhaps, by the absence of labels.

The skepticism of systems . . . has another name: the affirmation of organic life. If no single principle will produce a harmonious and well-balanced existence, for either the person or the community, then harmony and balance perhaps demand a degree of inclusiveness and completeness sufficient to nourish every kind of nature, to create the fullest variety in unity, to do justice to every occasion. That harmony must include and resolve discords: it must have a place for heresy as well as conformity; for rebellion as well as adjustment—and vice versa. And that balance must maintain itself against sudden thrusts and impulsions: like the living organism, it must have reserves at its command, capable of being swiftly mobilized, wherever needed to maintain a dynamic equilibrium.

II. THE REASON FOR BALANCE

Modern man, committed to the ideology of the machine, has succeeded in creating a lopsided world, which favors certain aspects of the personality that were long suppressed, but which equally suppresses whatever does not fit into its predominantly mechanical mold. Every effort to overcome the strains and distortions that have been set up in society by the general process of moral devaluation that has taken place during the last century, must have as its goal the restoration of the complete human personality.

All life rests essentially on the reconciliation of two opposite states, stability and change, security and adventure, necessity and freedom; for without regularity and continuity there would not be enough constancy in any process to enable one to recognize change itself, still less to identify it as good or bad, as life-promoting or life-destroying. The fixed structure of determined events—as Melville beautifully put it in the mat-weaving chapter in *Moby Dick*—is the warp on which the shuttle of free will weaves the threads of different colors and thicknesses which form the texture and pattern of life. Internal stability even of temperature, independent of a wide range of changes in the outside world, is a mark of the higher vertebrates; and since man, at the head of this vertebrate mammalian stock, has the widest range of responses of any organism, he likewise needs extra mechanisms, which he develops in mind and culture, for creating within himself the equilibrium that is essential for both survival and growth. To achieve balance without retarding growth, and to promote growth without permanently upsetting balance, are the two great aims of organic education.

Without balance there is defect of life; and if any proof were needed of that miscarriage, the increase of neuroses in our civilization, even apart from the number of people so ill that they are admitted to hospitals and asylums for the mentally unbalanced, would almost be sufficient. We have created an industrial order geared to automatism, where feeble-mindedness, native or acquired, is necessary for docile productivity in the factory; and where a pervasive neurosis is the final gift of the meaningless life that issues forth at the other end. More and more, our life has been governed by specialists, who know too little of what lies outside their province to be able to know enough about what takes place within it: unbalanced men who have made a madness out of their method. Our life, like medicine itself, has suffered from the dethronement of the general practitioner, capable of vigilant selection, evaluation, and action with reference to the health of the organism or the community as a whole. Is it not high time that we asked ourselves what constitutes a full human being, and through what modifications in our plan of life we can create him?

Now, the notion of balance has something of the simplicity and naturalness of the conception of the human body as most admirable and beautiful in its nakedness, which the ancient Greeks arrived at and made visible in their sculpture. Seemingly, that naked beauty was present from the beginning. But when we observe other cultures we see that the naked body in all its simplicity, developed in every part, undeformed and undisguised, is in fact a positive achievement. No small human effort, before and after the Greeks, has been spent on concealing the human body, on decorating it with garments, on mutilat-

15

ing it or scarifying it, on painting it or fantastically tattooing it, on altering the natural shape of the head, like the Peruvians, binding women's feet, like the Chinese, on carving the face or on creating fantastic ducklike lips, like the Ubangi, on covering the head with a wig like the Egyptians or the eighteenth-century Europeans, on exaggerating the nose or the ears or the buttocks.

In fine, the Greek notion of letting the body arrive at its full growth, without distortion and without concealment, finding beauty in its visible harmony and inner rightness, was a revolutionary conception. To delight in the human body without shame, to enjoy it without adulteration, is no simple human prerogative: it comes only at the summit of a high culture.

So with the notion of organic balance: both in the community and in the person. In the long history of civilizations the balanced personality, even as an ideal, stands forth as a similar rarity. Perhaps the reason for this rarity springs out of the peculiar nature of civilization: the fact that in origin it was based on the division of labor and on compulsory work: two measures that increased efficiency in production and multiplied the power of the ruling classes, at a general sacrifice of life: so that almost every people looked back to an earlier period of balance on a more primitive level as their veritable Golden Age. The conception of the balanced person, the Whole Man, first was put forth, perhaps, by the Chinese: in the person and teachings of Confucius, they beheld such an image and were profoundly affected by it.

But it was the Greeks of the fifth century who arrived at the fullest expression of the balanced person: first in life and then in reflection. Witness the living example of such a man as Sophocles, handsome in body and great of soul, capable of leading an army and writing a tragic drama, ready to move through every dimension of human experience, keeping every part of his life in interaction—here was the balanced person in its fullest development; and the culture of Athens, which produced such a man, also brought forth within two centuries a greater number of such men than history has shown anywhere else.

That balance and that fullness of life were not long maintained. As Plato recognized in *The Republic*, even Athens at her best had never found a place for half the human race, its women, in its plan of life: the inner conflict between romantic homosexual love and domestic heterosexual love produced a fissure that weakened this whole society. All the attempts to renew this society from Plato and Epicurus to Paul, from the early mystery religions to Christianity, sought to give woman a role the fifth-century Athenians had denied her; but by the time this was achieved, the conditions that had been so favorable to the balanced personality in the fifth century had been undermined: a Time of Trouble is, almost by definition, a time of imbalance and distortion.

But there was likewise a good reason for rejecting the classic doctrine of balance in its original form; and this is that the early formulation of it was a static one. From our insight into process throughout the universe, above all from our knowledge of the living body, we know that the stability we seek is not that of a closed system, which has achieved a fixed and final shape, like the stability of a crystal, and might remain the same for ten thousand years. All living creatures are open systems, constantly seizing energy, converting it into "work" and dissipating it and then replenishing it over again: so that the only form of balance that is truly conceivable or desirable in the human organism is a dynamic balance: that of the fountain, endlessly changing, though within the pattern of change retaining its form. Even the figure of the fountain is inadequate to describe organic forms, for dynamic balance itself undergoes shifts and changes through the cumulative effects of memory and through the further effects of time and fresh events and new purposes on maturation and growth.

As with walking, one achieves balance in life only by a series of lunges, which are in turn compensated by other lunges: to arrest that movement, in the interest of equilibrium, would be to paralyze the possibility of growth: the very condition that the equilibrium itself, in living organisms, exists to further. The events that most upset the balance of the personality in actual life, illness, misfortune, error, sin, grief—events that would deface any system of static perfection, as a blow with a hammer would deface a marble statue—have the effect of furthering spiritual growth and transcendence far more positively than any condition of effortless ease and freedom from sin would produce. The hothouse fruits of life, the product of the "best possible conditions," have perhaps a waxen beauty and freedom from surface imperfection that fruits grown in the open, susceptible to wind and weather, to worm and blight, do not possess: but the latter have the finer flavor, and, at least in the personality, the most interesting and significant marks of growth.

The classic notion of balance allowed no place for the negative moments of life: it dreamed of a timeless perfection that made no use of time itself, nor of the process of maturation, nor of trial and error, nor of sin and repentance: that is to say, it denied the processes of growth, which upset the possibility of static perfection in the act of enlarging the domains of beauty and significance. In this respect, the Christian understanding of the radical imperfection of life provided a better interpretation of man's essential biological as well as his personal nature than the classic one. Balance is valuable as an aid to growth: it is not the goal of growth.

But the ideal of balance is too central ever to disappear completely. In partial form it reappeared in the Benedictine monastery, with its life devoted to work, study, and prayer: a life whose concern for the manual arts rectified the bias of earlier leisure-class schemes. In the Renaissance, partly under the influence of Platonic ideas, the ideal came forth again in the dual conceptions of the gentleman and the artist. In both these personalities there was an effort to do justice to the whole man: the warrior, the priest, the philosopher, the athlete, the manual worker, were united, in nonspecialized forms, in a single human organism: the gentleman. Alberti, Leonardo da Vinci, Michelangelo, were equally developed on the side of thought, feeling, emotion, and action: the painting of the Sistine Chapel was not merely a work of imagination, but a gymnastic feat that demanded hardihood and daring. Among the aristocracy, during the Renaissance, women played a fuller part than they had done in Greece: and therefore the social balance was more effective. But neither slavery as practiced in Greece, nor the combination of feudalism and early capitalism that prevailed in Western Europe during the fifteenth century made it possible to extend the ideal of balance to every member of the community: so at the very moment that balance and unity became visible in the great personalities of this period, a paralyzing specialization and subdivision of labor made its way into the community at large: robbing the manual worker of such autonomy and balance as even the peasant once had at a low level in his daily life. Still, the ideal of the gentleman, fully cultivated in every aptitude of mind and body, lingered on into the nineteenth century: there was some of the Renaissance facility and roundedness in men like Goethe and Jefferson; and this was incarnated, in more democratic form, in a Thoreau, a Melville and a Whitman, with their capacity as gardener, surveyor, woodsman, farmer, printer, carpenter, sailor, as well as writer.

The growth of a mechanistic culture, during the last three centuries, has confirmed the older habits of caste division and specialization, by narrowing the province of the individual worker, by multiplying and refining the particular forms of specialization, by lessening the personal

significance of his task. Those who still sought for some sort of wholeness, balance, and autonomy were driven to the outskirts of Western
society: the pioneer alone preserved the qualities of the all-round man,
though he was forced to sacrifice many of the goods of a rich historic
tradition to achieve this. In general, the notion of the segmentation of
labor was carried from the factory to every other human province.

In accepting this partition of functions and this overemphasis of a
single narrow skill, men were content, not merely to become fragments
of men, but to become fragments of fragments: the physician ceased to
deal with the body as a whole and looked after a single organ, indeed,
even in Dr. Oliver Wendell Holmes's time, he remarked on specialists
in diseases of the right leg, who would not treat those of the left. In
similar fashion, each man tended to nourish in himself, not what made
him a full man, but what made him distinguishable from other men:
mental tattooing and moral scarification were supposed to have both
high decorative value and immense practical efficiency. Such people
cheerfully bartered the fullest possibilities of life in order to magnify
their power to think, to invent, to command.

As a result, the apparently simple notion of the balanced person, like
the notion of the naked body, symmetrically grown and harmoniously
developed, without the overemphasis or distortion of any organ, a person, not rigid and hard-shelled, but supple and capable of making the
fullest response to novel situations, unexpected demands, emergent
opportunities, almost dropped out of existence: repressed in life, rejected
in thought. Even groups and classes that had once espoused the aristocratic ideal of living a full and rounded life, shamefacedly dropped their
traditional aspirations and made themselves over into specialists, those
people Nietzsche pregnantly called *inverted cripples,* handicapped not
because they have lost a single organ, but because they have over-
magnified it. Upon the ancient Babel of tongues was erected a new
Babel of functions; and the human community tended to turn into a
secret society, in which no person was sufficiently developed as a man
to be able to guess what the other person, equally undeveloped as a man,
was thinking and feeling and premeditating. Naturally this is an exag-
geration: yet it hardly does justice to the loss of the facilities for communication and communion that has taken place. Only men who are
themselves whole can understand the needs and desires and ideals of
other men.

Historically speaking, the periods of highest vitality, fifth-century
Athens, thirteenth-century Florence, sixteenth-century London, early

nineteenth-century Concord, are those in which most men have been whole, and in which society has found the means of supporting and furthering their wholeness. In such cultures, organs and capacities and potentialities have been so generally developed that each person could, as it were, change places with any other person and still carry on his life and work: a general life-efficiency more than compensated for the special facilities derived from narrow concentration. I see no reason to think that Bacon wrote the plays of Shakespeare; but human potentialities were so evenly developed during this period that the hypothesis is not altogether absurd: not more absurd than to suppose that Shakespeare might have written *The New Atlantis* or *The Advancement of Learning*. In those periods of balance and completeness—and completeness is an essential attribute of the balanced person—Hegel's definition of an educated man still magnificently held: "He who is capable of doing anything any other man can do."

This view of human development contradicts the central dogma of modern civilization: that specialism is here to "stay." Rather, to the very extent that the perversions of specialism are accepted as inevitable, the civilization that clings to them is doomed. Our deepening insight into the needs of organisms, societies, and personalities supports just the opposite conclusion: specialism is hostile to life, for it is the nonspecialized organisms that are in the line of growth; and only by overcoming the tendency to specialization can the community or the person combat the rigidity which leads to inefficiency and a general failure to meet life's fresh demands. Let our overspecialized sluggards consider the ant: in sixty million years formic society has undergone no change and the experience of the ants has led to no further development, precisely because of the miracle of adaptive specialization that brought perfection and stability at the ant's level and closed every route to change and betterment.

The central effort in the renewal of life today must be to bring back the possibility of wholeness and balance, not indeed as goods in themselves, but as the conditions for renewal and growth and self-transcendence. We must break down the segregation of functions and activities, both within the personality and within the community as a whole: hence moral evaluations and decisions must not be intermittent acts, but constant ones, whose main purpose is to maintain the balance that is partly achieved and assist in those further developments, which, by upsetting balance, lead to growth and increasing fullness of life.

To this end, our sterile mechanistic culture must be exposed to an

20

even more thorough drenching of the emotions than the earlier romantists cists dared to dream of. Without re-establishing the capacity for strong expression, for erotic passion and love, for emotional exuberance and delight, we shall also be unable to establish the inhibitions and controls needed to escape automatism and to further autonomous activity; for inhibitions, imposed on life that is already tamped down and denied, are almost a sentence of death. Only those who have said Yes to life will have the courage to say No when the occasion demands it. Those who are starved will say Yes even to garbage—the current offal of the popular press, radio, television—because they have not yet tasted food.

Now the notion of balance in the personality is itself a many-sided one. Theoretically it derives primarily from a close study of organisms— internally, by physiologists, externally and socially by ecologists. Claude Bernard was the first to establish scientifically that a dynamic equilibrium in the internal environment was essential for the exercise of man's higher functions: he also proved that very small quantitative chemical changes could upset this balance and impair the higher functions. But the more thoroughly one studies both organisms and groups of organisms, the wider becomes the application of these leading ideas: in the diet, for example, even faint traces of copper or iodine may be essential to the proper functioning of the whole. Balance in other words is both quantitative and qualitative; and this general condition for effective life applies to every human activity. Balance in time, which is equally important, is established not by repetition but by rhythmic alternation, as of day and night, exertion and rest, expression and inhibition: small variations in rhythm may here prove to be as important for the full functioning of the organism as the presence of tracer elements in the diet; and a routine of work which ignores the need for rhythms and change may lead to frustration, impairment of function, and productive inefficiency.

. . . By our systematic scientific insight into balance today, we can carry the whole process much farther than was possible through the earlier Greek or Renaissance intuitions. But here I would emphasize one special aspect of balance that has a profound bearing upon the good life, all the more because it is an aspect that has, in our generation, been generally ignored: the balance that must be maintained between the expressive, life-asserting moments and the negative, inhibitive, nay-saying moments.

In reaction against the forbidding rigidity of feudalism, modern man sought to remove all boundaries and throw off all restraints. Blake's dictum, "Damn braces, bless relaxes," might have served as practical guide. Such freedom was mainly escapist: freedom from arbitrary coercion, from stagnant duties, from outworn obligations. But "freedom from," even when amply justified, must be attached to a positive ideal of "freedom for": and this by its nature involves a new restraint—fixation on a self-imposed goal. The freedom of the spoiled child, who has everything he might wish for and lacks only the power to wish or the patience to see his wish through, is the worst of slaveries. Freedom in love, for example, demands an inner readiness to *be* in love, freedom for commitment and continuity, not just for new erotic adventures. The Casanova who flits from lover to lover loses by that inconstancy one of the qualities of mature love: the totality of its attachment, the need, despite fluctuations of passion, for a long-continued union. There is no freedom in wandering unless one is equally free to stay home. So in other phases of life, inhibitions are as essential to freedom as to balance. Relaxes *and* braces, expressions *and* inhibitions, in a rhythmic interplay. That is a prime secret of balance.

Here I cannot improve on the observations of that wise woman, Mary Everest Boole, when she said:

The ordinary man thinks of physical temperance as a process of sacrificing the lower pleasures to the higher; he does not understand that the rhythm of temperance should be kept especially in what he calls the highest. The true prophet, on the contrary, knows that *nothing* is good except in rhythmic alternation. He is no more a glutton intellectually than physically; he no more desires the constant enjoyment of what is called realizing the Presence of God than he craves for unlimited brandy; he no more aspires to a heaven of constant rapture in the intercourse of Jesus and the Saints than to a Valhalla of everlasting mead-drinking in the company of ever lovely Valkyries. He desires, for every fibre of his body, and every convolution of his brain, and for all the faculties he may hereafter acquire that each may be the medium of an occasional revelation. . . . He no more desires for his children incessant health or prosperity than he desires for his vines a uniform temperature.

Actually, the imbalance between the organism and the environment, or more specifically, between the personality and the community, becomes increasingly fatal as we do one of two things: multiply the stimuli and pressures that come from without, or decrease the number of impulses and controls that originate from within. To achieve balance requires quantitative control on both sides; and the greater the means at our command, the greater becomes the need for continence, for discipline, for continued selectivity. Very definitely, therefore, the notion of quantitative restriction enters into the conception of even physiological balance, as it does with no less insistence into any scheme of positive morality: constancy and continence: the reduction of the maximum possible to the optimum assimilable. As we enlarge the sphere of interest and the field of operations, we automatically increase the number of shocks and stimuli that may throw the personality out of balance; and therefore we must counteract this tendency by building up protective inhibitory reactions, by lengthening the circuits of emotional response, and by slowing down the whole tempo of life.

But note: the ideal of balance must be applied in society before it can be fully effective in the life of the person. No amount of watchful self-discipline can create the necessary conditions for achieving equilibrium and growth within the life of the single individual or the isolated group: that is the fallacy of all fugitive and cloistered virtue. Even the Stoic boast, "Nothing can hurt me," was a piece of self-deception. Every system of moral or religious discipline that puts the whole weight of change upon the isolated individual does so by minimizing the actual influences and pressures that are at work in his life, and by voiding a large part of their significance. Profound transformations may and do take place first in the individual person: but they must come speedily to an end unless the condition for a more stable equilibrium is maintained by widening the social base.

The static balance of a life focused completely within itself and lived to itself, the balance of the self-absorbed and self-enclosed mystic or yogin is, in a sense, too easy to achieve; it is like walking firmly on a board laid on the ground: whereas the dynamic balance needed for spiritual growth is like that called into play by crossing a chasm on a single plank. The risk and the achievement of it are due to the constant operation of forces, within and without: the walker's giddy imaginative projection into space, his latent tendencies to suicide, weaknesses in the plank, the pull of gravity, the presence of another person treading on his heels, all give meaning to a process that would otherwise lack both tension and exhilaration. If a hermit's life is not more empty than it is, it is because he has internalized so many of the pressures of society: in fantasy he is still a social creature, tempted by lusts that do not have to have outward existence to be effective.

While the person, then, is an emergent from society, it is within society that he lives and functions; and it is for the purpose of sharing values and meanings with other persons that the moral life becomes something more than a lonely tight-rope walk in a private theater. Not merely are we, in the strict Pauline sense, members one of another;

23

but balance and purpose require for their sustenance a community whose activities and institutions work to the same end. . . . Without that constant support, without that interplay between the person and the group, only a meager and half-awakened life is possible. It is partly in other men's eyes that one sees one's true image; it is partly through other men's example and support that one fathoms one's own potentialities; and it is toward a purpose that we share increasingly, not merely with our immediate fellows, but with all mankind and with generations still unborn, that we rise as men to our utmost height.

Many thinkers of the nineteenth century, even before specialization had been carried to its present pitch, were quick to recognize these facts . . . this indeed is the one common element that brings together thinkers as diverse as Spencer and Marx and Kropotkin, artists as varied as Nietzsche and Ruskin and Walt Whitman and William Morris. Though the ideal of the balanced man has been less often stated during the last half-century, one can find it, once more, in the work of later thinkers, as individualized in their philosophies as Patrick Geddes and Havelock Ellis and A. N. Whitehead and Karl Mannheim, to mention only the dead. In the United States, the ideal of the balanced personality has been put forth by Professor F. S. C. Northrop, in his attempt to unify the ideas of the East and the West; and no less significantly, it has been restated, as an essential condition for overcoming the corrosions and devastations of our age, by such a rigorous psychologist as Edward Tolman, in his essay on "Drives Toward War."

After discussing the governing personality-images of Western culture in the past—the Spiritual Man of the Middle Ages, the Intellectual Man of the Enlightenment, the Economic Man of the Victorian Period, Tolman goes on to say:

The underlying thesis of the present essay will be that still a fifth myth (or, if you will, a fifth ideology) is now nearly ready to appear, and that it must be made to appear. I shall call it the myth of the Psychologically-adjusted Man. It will be the myth, the concept, that only when man's total psychology is understood and all his absolutely necessary psychological needs are allowed balanced satisfaction, will a society permitting relatively universal happiness and welfare be achieved and war be abolished. It is the myth (or rather, I dare hope, the ultimately true concept) that man is, societally speaking, not a spiritual, intellectual, economic, or heroic being, but rather an integrated complex, the entirety of whose psychological nature must be understood if general happiness and welfare are to result.

The chief changes my own analysis would lead me to make in Tolman's statement would be to add that it is not merely necessary to

24

understand man's complex wholeness, but as a further act of understanding, to create the positive channels through which it can be expressed. One of the road-blocks that halt this achievement is that we cannot achieve wholeness, either intellectual or personal, merely by uniting in their present specialized forms the existing body of men and institutions. Such an encyclopedic massing of specialisms—which H. G. Wells tirelessly advocated—will not produce synthesis in thought, any more than an assemblage of specialized functionaries within a community will produce a whole and balanced society. Such mechanical cohesion, whether promoted arbitrarily by the state or through more private initiative, can only produce a state of arrest: not to be confused with the state of dynamic integration. Hard though it may be for our age to accept the fact, we cannot become fully alive again without being prepared to sacrifice the overdevelopment of any particular valued function, and being ready to subordinate it to the dynamic good of the whole. This will mean, in almost every activity, a decrease in productiveness: happily that decrease will be offset, in the end, by an increasing fullness of life. Faced with the life of the ordinary machine-worker, for example, we must be ready, if necessary, to dismantle the assembly line in order to reassemble the human personality. In the interest of creating better citizens, better lovers and fathers, better men, we may have to lower the number of motor cars or refrigerators produced by the factory: balancing that loss by the higher output of men.

This same rule will apply to almost every specialized facility. Thus the scholar who values wholeness, who cultivates the ability to look around his subject, to include every aspect, to throw forth tentacles into related fields, will not be able to rival in quantitative productivity the work of his predecessors, who confined themselves to a narrow segment. In each case, something must be sacrificed: if not the man himself, then mechanical skill, refinement of detail, speed, output per man-hour or per lifetime. Though productivity may decrease, the durability of the product will go up. With our new standard in mind, it is apparent that a large part of the past two centuries' production, in both cities and institutions and books, will have to be done over—and done right.

—*The Conduct of Life*

III. THE "TERRIBLE SIMPLIFIERS"

Civilizations do not die of old age: they die of the complications of old age. Observing this process long ago, Burckhardt predicted the coming of the "terrible simplifiers": people who would reject all the goods modern man had acquired in order to restore the capacity to act. Those terrible simplifiers have appeared. They are the barbarians who renounce every part of our culture that makes a claim upon man's higher needs: avowed barbarians like the Nazis and more insidious barbarians who, by advertising, propaganda, and education, would turn every part of our life into the mean handiwork of coachman, cook, and groom, of beauty shop, assembly line, and roadhouse. We cannot save our culture from these barbarians, external or internal, by clinging to the habits that make us a prey to their corrupt vitality. To recover life and health again we must, like the Christians confronting the classic world, find a benign method of simplification. We must find a method that will assert the primacy of the person and that will re-endow the person with all its attributes, all its heritage, all its potentialities. But unlike the Christian, we must undertake this transformation before the barbarian has finally wrecked our civilization: only thus shall we be able to carry forward the many life-promoting activities that man has created since the breakup of the medieval synthesis.

The task for our age is to decentralize power in all its manifestations. To this end, we must build up balanced personalities: personalities that will be capable of drawing upon our immense stores of energy, knowledge, and wealth without being demoralized by them. On this point, Plato's words in *The Laws* cannot be improved: "If anyone gives too great power to anything, too large a sail to a vessel, too much food to the body, too much authority to the mind, and does not observe the mean, everything is overthrown, and in the wantonness of excess runs in the one case to disorders, and in the other to injustice, which is the child of excess."

If we are to control machines and organizations, then, we must make men; and our first task is that of self-examination, self-education, self-control. Those who fail at this point will be incapable of contributing to the political, economic, and social transformations that are now so long overdue.

IV. THE ORGANIC PERSON

The ideal personality for the opening age is a balanced personality: not the specialist but the whole man. Such a personality must be in dynamic interaction with every part of his environment and every part of his heritage. He must be capable of treating economic experiences and aesthetic experiences, parental experiences and vocational experiences, as the related parts of a single whole, namely, life itself. His education, his discipline, his daily routine must tend toward this wholeness. To achieve this, he must be ready to spurn the easy successes that come, in a dying culture, through self-mutilation.

Such a dynamic balance is not easily achieved: its consummations are precious and its stability is precarious: it demands a vigilance and an athletic readiness for new shifts and stresses that more specialized vocations do not habitually achieve. For balance is not a matter of allotting definite amounts of time and energy to each segment of life that requires attention: even our mechanical partition of functions does that. It means that the whole personality must be constantly at play, at least at ready call, at every moment of its existence and that no one part of life should be segregated from another part, incapable of influencing it or being influenced by it.

But qualitative balance is as important as quantitative balance: many kinds of experience have the role in life that vitamins have in the diet: quantitatively minute elements may be as important for spiritual health as the vitamins and minerals are for bodily health. Most of man's higher activities are in the latter category. No healthy person can look at pictures all day any more than he can make love all day. But for even the humblest person, a day spent without the sight or sound of beauty, the contemplation of mystery, or the search for truth and perfection is a poverty-stricken day; and a succession of such days is fatal to human life. That is why even the most superstitious forms of religion, which have at least kept alive some wraith of beauty or perfection, still contain for the mass of mankind something valuable that a bare scientific positivism has allowed to be lost both in thought and practice.

The importance of balance to both the community and the personality will come out more clearly, perhaps, if we call to mind the patent dangers that will attend stabilization: dangers that are already plainly visible in the bureaucratism and time-serving that have begun to infect every department of life: not alone government but business; and not alone business but education. Those who lack the creative capacity to establish a dynamic balance are already caught by its counterfeit and its negation: Alexandrianism or Byzantinism.

Organizations that have been stabilized for any length of time—the army is an excellent example—become embedded in routine and hostile to change: they are unable to meet fresh challenges, and their very "adjustment" becomes a profound cause of maladjustment. Scientific progress does not alter this fact, for scientific advances themselves tend to follow inflexible institutional forms, and they often seek perfection within a more and more obsolete frame of reference. Stability and security, pursued for their own sake, will result in a caste division of labor and in the denial of any changes that would upset an increasingly sessile routine: forms, precedents, stereotypes would supplant human needs, and the very attributes of life, its capacity for readjustment, for insurgence, for renewal, would be forfeited by these ill-conceived efforts to guard life more effectively.

These regressive forms of stabilization have already taken shape: they were seized upon by Nazi philosophers and leaders as the basis for enforcing permanent caste divisions. But the danger is not confined to the totalitarian reactionaries: many of those who talk loudest about rugged individualism prove themselves in their daily practice the upholders of a Byzantine rigidity and hollowness. The standard examination papers that have appeared in so many departments of American education under the guise of progressive method would, in a short generation, paralyze the acquisition and extension of fresh knowledge: this symbolizes a much wider menace to life and thought.

Precisely because stabilization brings with it these dangers, we must introduce into our conception of the type of personality needed the ability to touch life at many points, to travel light, and to keep every part of experience in a state of constant interplay and interaction: so that fresh challenges will appear at unexpected points, in unforeseeable circumstances. For the age of balance we need a new race of pioneers, of deliberate amateurs, in order to offset the tendency to harden practice into smooth molds and to sacrifice the growing personality to the machine. Such stereotyping of activity as will free the organism for its higher functions—like those human automatisms that put a large part of the burden of behavior on the vertebral column and the cerebellum—must not halt on its way to this destination.

In this respect the varied war experiences that people in many countries have undergone, as soldiers, air raid wardens, fire fighters, nurses, and so forth, must be regarded as essential contributions to the task of peacetime co-operation: typical of a new kind of citizenship and a more vivid routine of life. But we cannot afford to promote a war every generation to break up social fixations: that is burning down the house to roast the pig. We must erect these social and personal counterpoises to rigidity and fixity as the basic requirements for a maturing personality.

The custom of our time is to think no change worth even discussing unless it can be at once organized into a visible movement: the mass enlistment of thousands, preferably millions, of men and women. The very appearance of millions of men in black shirts and brown shirts gave Fascism publicity that made its rancid ideas seem important. Many of the actual movements that claim allegiance today are little better than devices of publicity: decorative devices that change nothing and move nothing. Such, even, would be a revolutionary movement, unless those who took part in it remodeled the instruments with which they work: first of all themselves.

Only in one place can an immediate renewal begin: that is, within the person; and a remolding of the self and the superego is an inescapable preliminary to the great changes that must be made throughout every community, in every part of the world. Each one, within his or her own field of action—the home, the neighborhood, the city, the region, the school, the church, the factory, the mine, the office, the union—must carry into his immediate day's work a changed attitude toward all his functions and obligations. His collective work cannot rise to a higher level than his personal scale of values. Once a change is effected in the person, every group will record and respond to it.

Today our best plans miscarry because they are in the hands of people who have undergone no inner growth. Most of these people have shrunk from facing the world crisis and they have no notion of the manner in which they themselves have helped to bring it about. Into every new situation they carry only a fossilized self. Their hidden prejudices, their glib hopes, their archaic desires and automatisms—usually couched in the language of assertive modernity—recall those of the Greeks in the fourth century B.C. or those of the Romans in the fourth century A.D. They are in a power dive and their controls have frozen. By closing their eyes they think they can avoid a crash.

Those who look for swift wholesale changes to take place in our institutions underrate the difficulties we now face: the inroads of barbarism and automatism, those twin betrayers of freedom, have been too deep. In their impatience, in their despair, such people secretly long to cast the burden of their own regeneration upon a savior: a president, a pope, a dictator—vulgar counterparts of a divinity debased or a corruption deified. But such a leader is only the mass of humanity writ small: the incarnation of our resentments, hates, sadisms, or of our cowardices, confusions, and complacencies. There is no salvation through such naked self-worship: God must work within us. Each man and woman must first silently assume his own burden.

We need not wait for bombs and bullets actually to strike us before

29

we strip our lives of superfluities: we need not wait for events to bend our wills to unison. Wherever we are, the worst has already happened and we must meet it. We must simplify our daily routine without waiting for ration cards; we must take on public responsibilities without waiting for conscription; we must work for the unity and effective brotherhood of man without letting further wars prove that the current pursuit of power, profit and all manner of material aggrandizement is treason to humanity: treason and national suicide. Year by year, we must persevere in all these acts, even though the restrictions are lifted and the urgencies of war have slackened. Unless we now rebuild our selves all our external triumphs will crumble.

There is no easy formula for this renewal. It is not enough for us to do all that is possible: we must do that which seems impossible. Our first need is not for organization but for orientation: a change in direction and attitude. We must bring to every activity and every plan a new criterion of judgment: we must ask how far it seeks to further the processes of life-fulfillment and how much respect it pays to the needs of the whole personality.

More immediately we must demand: What is the purpose of each new political and economic measure? Does it seek the old goal of expansion or the new one of equilibrium? Does it work for conquest or co-operation? And what is the nature of this or that industrial or social achievement—does it produce material goods alone or does it also produce human goods and good men? Do our individual life-plans make for a universal society, in which art and science, truth and beauty, religion and sanctity, enrich mankind? Do our public life-plans make for the fulfillment and renewal of the human person, so that they will bear fruit in a life abundant: ever more significant, ever more valuable, ever more deeply experienced and more widely shared?

If we keep this standard constantly in mind, we shall have both a measure for what must be rejected and a goal for what must be achieved. In time, we shall create the institutions and the habits of life, the rituals, the laws, the arts, the morals that are essential to the development of the whole personality and the balanced community: the possibilities of progress will become real again once we lose our blind faith in the external improvements of the machine alone. But the first step is a personal one: a change in direction of interest *toward* the person. Without that change, no great betterment will take place in the social order. Once that change begins, everything is possible.

—*The Condition of Man*

V. THE EXAMPLE OF SCHWEITZER

From many possible witnesses, in our own age, I shall turn to one whose long career affords a classic example of renewal and integration. I choose Albert Schweitzer because his life is in outline already familiar to many readers; and because his books, the conscious expression of his philosophy, are accessible in many languages. But it is on his life rather than on his writings that I shall concentrate; for his actions have transcended the limitations of his thought. Schweitzer's conscious philosophy, from my standpoint, is sometimes contradictory and inadequate: in the world of ideas, to speak with candor, he is not one of the greatest luminaries. But his intuitions are better integrated than his reasons; and the transformation effected in the life and work of Schweitzer is more profound and more widely significant than the best ideas he has yet formulated. From his actions, one may deduce a fuller philosophy than that which has consciously guided him. And through his masterly example, the task of formulation becomes an easier one.

Consider the course of Albert Schweitzer's life. He began as a student of philosophy who turned to Christian theology; and in his early twenties he did so brilliantly at his chosen career that honors and fame would have come to him rapidly, had he been content with the role of pastor and theologian. Within the theological world, he was plainly one of the olympians: he might have lived and died in that role, like so many other churchmen, preaching the doctrines of a religion he had never tested or practiced by any major act: the willing observer of outward forms and ceremonies, the happy recipient of worldly courtesies and worldly honors.

Fortunately, one of Schweitzer's early studies was an intimate examination of the life of Jesus, whom he rescued from the fashionable impugners and devaluators by a more rigorous use of the very historic method they had used for deflating him. This brought him to the conviction that a true believer in Jesus must, in the twentieth century, take up the cross himself and perform some redemptive work of sacrifice. Such a work would not bring fame and honor, but, more probably, neglect, ill-health, possibly death, if not also contumely and oblivion. Plainly many evils need to be abated: many sins Western society has committed cry for atonement. With a vigilant eye, Schweitzer picked a classic example: the degradation of primitive peoples through imperialist exploitation, often coming on top of a primitive life that in itself, by reason of its own ignorance, superstition, and brutality did violence to the human spirit.

Hence Schweitzer decided, like many another fervent Christian, to become a missionary. But since nothing could be more ironic than to carry the word of redemption to people too sunken in disease to be made whole, Schweitzer again followed Jesus' example: he would heal the sick while bringing the Gospel to them, and that healing should be no small part of his gospel. With that decision, the neophyte threw aside the honors of the theologian and settled down to the hard discipline of the medical student: the "Buddhist" gave place to the Promethean.

Those four years of medical preparation were doubtless difficult enough in themselves even to an able student of the humanities, trained in the rigorous scholarly discipline of a European university like Strasbourg; but they required a further intensity of concentration for the reason that Schweitzer, instead of closing up all the other channels of life, kept his emotions and feelings quick, by his cultivation of music as an organist. Through his special knowledge of Johann Sebastian Bach, Schweitzer brought into circulation again many precious scores that had been completely overlooked. As organist, as musicologist, above all as lover of music, Schweitzer served Dionysus as well as Christ: that constant concern with music, throughout his toilsome life, made his wholeness and balance an exemplary one.

In philosophy or theology, in medicine or in music, Schweitzer's talents were sufficient to guarantee him a career of distinction: as one of the eminent specialists of his time, in any of these departments, his success would have been prompt and profitable, just to the extent that he allowed himself to be absorbed in a single activity. But in order to remain a whole man, Schweitzer committed the typical act of sacrifice for the coming age: *he deliberately reduced the intensive cultivation of any one field, in order to expand the contents and the significance of his life as a whole.* Doubtless the humility that made it possible for him to entertain such a sacrifice derived directly from his Christian convictions: yet the result of that sacrifice was not the negation of his life but its fullest realization; for even in the humid jungles of Africa, where he finally made his home, he kept alive his highly cultivated interest in music: not merely having his organ by his side, but finding time, despite a lack of the usual scholarly apparatus, to write a life of Bach.

Both in his work as a medical missionary and in his public appearance as an organist, Schweitzer, who was a German by birth, performed another act of symbolic importance: an act perhaps easier, more natural, in the international world before 1914 than in our own day. For Schweitzer's field of action was less in his own original fatherland, among the people who spoke his preferred language, than in the country of its rival, and presently its active enemy, France: in that sense, he was another Jean-Christophe. So it was to an unattractive colony in French West Africa, in the steaming Equatorial jungle, that he turned for a field of endeavor. There, with occasional intervals abroad for lecturing and organ playing—including the interval he spent as a prisoner of war in France, in the very hospital at Saint Rémy where Van Gogh, another imitator of Jesus, had been confined—he has lived his life: serving a God who recognizes neither white nor black, neither French nor German.

Without that devaluation and renunciation of nationalism no life worthy of the name can now be built up. He who is one hundred per cent an American or a Russian, a German or a Frenchman, a European or an African or an Asiatic, is only half a man: the universal part of his personality, equally essential to his becoming human, is still unborn. Every act that softens the egoistic claims of nations and accentuates the unity of mankind, adds another foundation stone to the new world that we must now build.

—The Conduct of Life

III / OUTLOOK FROM A
BIOLOGIST'S LABORATORY

Professor J. B. S. (John Burdon Sanderson) Haldane, born November 5, 1892, at present professor of biometry at London University College, England, writes that he has "never had the impudence to sum up what I consider my most important thoughts for the benefit of humanity, but the enclosed ('Human Evolution: Past and Future') sums up some of them."

As the article embodies only a fraction of his views, Professor Haldane answered seven questions in the following responses:

"1. My personal philosophy has grown out of my professional work. I find the way of thinking (commonly called materialism) which satisfies me in science, satisfactory in other fields.

"2. I think the present is a very good time to live. I might have preferred Behar in the seventh century b.c., the time of Gautama (Buddha) and Vardhamura (Mahavira) or Athens in the early and middle fifth century b.c., or Iceland in the tenth century a.d.

"3. The present age will either be characterized as the mid-stage of the world revolution, or as the last few years of a historic period ended abruptly by a thermonuclear war. I do not know which.

"4. The most significant trend is scientific method (answering your question on what do I consider the most important trends of thinking today), and by this I include much of Marxism, and the opinions of Gandhi.

"5. Man's greatest social need is socialism.

"6. For me personally the future holds death. Before that, I should like to put in at least ten years of scientific research and teaching in India. If, as is very possible, the U.S.S.R. and the U.S.A. destroy one another, and Europe and China as well, there is about an even chance that biology may continue in India.

"I have found the most significant truths contributing to my personal philosophy in science, and after that, in history. I think that Darwin and Engels have influenced me more than any other writers."

Professor Haldane, who has written many books on biology, and essays on science and politics, worked during the Second World War on the physiology of diving and was partly responsible for methods used in clearing liberated ports. His work on genetics and evolution won him the Darwin Medal of the Royal Society in 1952. In 1945 he married Helen Spurway, his colleague in underwater work and his second wife. At sixty he "more or less retired from politics. . . . However, I would certainly be rated as a Red in the U.S.A.," he wrote in *Twentieth Century Authors,* "though in fact my opinions as to world politics are probably as near to those of Nehru as of any other well-known politician."

The Haldane selection is a paper delivered in 1947 at Princeton where the biologist asserted the duty to reform society is more urgent than that of attempting to control evolution and the task of the present is that of remodeling human society.

Human Evolution: Past and Future

BY J. B. S. HALDANE

I am asked to discuss one of the great problems of human biology. I do so gladly, but with one important reservation. I am going to treat of man from one point of view, the biological. This is wholly justifiable provided I do not leave you with the impression that this is the only point of view that matters. Only evil can come from forgetting that man must be considered from many angles. You can think of him as a producer and a consumer. This is fully justifiable provided that you do not think that the economic angle is the only angle. You can treat him as a thinker, as an individual, as a member of society, as a being capable of moral choice, as a creator and appreciator of beauty, and so on. Concentration on only one of these aspects is disastrous. I make these obvious remarks for the following reason. Hitler and his colleagues believed that the history of the human past could be interpreted, and the history of the human future created, on biological lines. Now the Nazis degraded most of the German people morally, and brought death and misery to a whole continent. Their biological ideas were grossly incorrect. But supposing they had been as accurate as any which we possess today or will possess a century hence, I believe that any attempt to reduce ethics and politics to biology would have involved a moral degradation.

A biologist can do two things besides discovering facts, such as the facts of human evolution and genetics. He can tell his fellows how to achieve ends which they desire already, such as the cure or prevention of a disease. He can tell them of possibilities at which they had not guessed, such as the possibility of making childbirth painless, or some of the possibilities of which I shall speak later. But he can never tell them what is worth doing. That is always an ethical, not a biological, question. In what follows, I shall say that I think certain things are worth doing, that it is better to be born with a normal mouth than a harelip, with a normal color sense rather than color-blind, and so on. These are my opinions as a human being. If you disagree with them, I cannot, as a biologist, persuade you to change your opinion. But if you agree, then, as a biologist, I may be able to help you to work for the ends on which we are agreed.

Perhaps you think I have taken too long over these preliminaries. But there are those who say that any attempt to apply biology to human affairs is mere Hitlerism. To my mind, that is as stupid as to say that when a tailor wants your measurement he is treating you as a mere lump of matter and no more. However that may be, I have felt it necessary to safeguard my rear. Now let us go forward.

We have been discussing evolution as something which has happened in the past, and is happening now. I may add in parentheses that we are all convinced that it has occurred, though we differ a good deal as to how, and still more as to why, it has occurred. The very first point I want to make is the time scale of the process. Forty years ago we knew the sequence of events in our evolutionary history, but could only guess at their dates. It is as if we knew that Washington lived before Lincoln, but did not know whether Washington was born two hundred or two thousand years ago. Now, thanks to the study of radioactive minerals, we know our dates with an error generally under 10 per cent when we are dealing with dates between about 30 million and 500 million years back. We know that somewhere around 350 million years ago our ancestors were fish, 270 million years ago amphibians somewhat like salamanders, 200 millions years ago reptiles not very like any living forms, and 70 million years ago, mammals something like shrews.

Curiously enough we cannot date the last few million years quite so accurately, until we get to the last 20,000, when we have layers of mud laid down each year in water from melting ice. But we can say that *Sinanthropus,* the so-called Pekin man, lived about half a million years ago, and almost surely less than a million and more than 200,000 years. Further we can say that at that time there were no men of the modern types; so our ancestors must have been a good deal less human than any existing race, even though, as they used tools, they probably deserved the name of man.

1. CONTROLLED EVOLUTION AS AN IDEAL

These Pekin men had queer-shaped heads, broadest about the level of the ears instead of much higher up, brow ridges, no chins, and so on. In half a million years we have changed a bit. Certainly the difference between *Sinanthropus* and modern man is as great as that which separates many nearly related animal species (for example the coyote and wolf). It is doubtful whether it is as great as that between two nearly related animal genera (for example dogs and wolves on the one hand, and various kinds of fox on the other). In fact it has taken about half a million years for a change large enough for zoologists to give it a name with full certainty. Other animals, such as horses and elephants, of whose ancestors we have a far better record, have been evolving at about the same rate.

These facts suggest that, if we did not try to control the evolutionary process in any way, our descendants half a million years hence might differ from us, for better or worse, about as much as we differ from Pekin man, or a cat from a puma. Now at present I do not think we know how to control our evolution, even if we wanted to, or if biologists were granted all the powers which Hitler exercised for twelve years. But supposing a thousand years hence we know how to direct our evolution, and further that the vast majority of men accept this ideal, as the vast majority of Americans accept the idea of sanitation today, what then?

The answer is rather curious. An unaided man can walk twenty miles a day with a fair load, and keep it up indefinitely. I have walked over fifty with a rifle and a few extras, but I couldn't keep it up. At present one can easily fly two thousand miles a day, but a five-thousand-mile flight is more difficult. Roughly speaking, science has increased our speed of travel a hundredfold. It is reasonable to hope that we might speed up evolution a hundredfold if we knew enough. If so, we might achieve a change as large as I have indicated in five thousand years, or two hundred generations. This is a long time. The earliest date in human history is 2283 B.C., or just over four thousand years ago. This is the date of a total eclipse of the sun which immediately preceded the capture and destruction of Ur by the Elamites. Five thousand years ago civilization had started in Egypt, Iraq, and maybe a few other areas, but most men were savages.

Is it worth while even talking about a change which we do not yet know how to bring about, and which would take five thousand years to accomplish if we did? Yes, it is worth while talking about it, for three reasons. In the first place we ought to discuss the right and wrong ways of using a power before we get it. The world would be a far safer and happier place today if we had discussed how to use nuclear, or so-called atomic, energy for a century, or even a generation, before we got it. If so, very likely almost all decent people would be agreed as to the rights and wrongs of this matter, which they certainly are not today. About twenty-five hundred years ago, the prophet Isaiah got the idea that one day all the nations of the earth would be at peace. Isaiah's idea of universal peace was something like a Jewish world empire. Ours is an association of friendly democracies. The ideal has only just become possible of accomplishment because world-wide transport has been achieved. But if visionaries had not been talking about it off and on since Isaiah's time, there would be no chance of achieving it now, when the alternative is, quite literally, destruction by fire from heaven. . . .

Secondly, we shall not get the required knowledge in a hurry. Even now we can do a little to alter the inborn capacities of the next generation. Let us begin to think about what sort of changes we want, and criticize one another's ideas, as democrats should.

Thirdly, if we put the ideal of controlling evolution before us, and try to accumulate the necessary knowledge, we may find out something even more important on the way. Columbus set out to find a sea route from Europe to China. A ship can get from Europe to China through the Panama Canal, but the discovery of America was a vastly more important result of his voyage than the opening of this route.

II. SLOW DEVELOPMENT AS A MAJOR EVOLUTIONARY TREND

Our first task will be to take a glance at human evolution, and to see how man differs from the other mammals, his nearest relatives, and how these differences have arisen. Man is an exceptionally brainy animal. The whale has a heavier brain, and the mouse has a brain which is a larger fraction of its body weight. But if we take a series of closely related animals, such as the cat, ocelot, puma, and lion, we find that their brain weight is roughly proportional to the square root of their body weight. If we rate animals on the ratio of brain weight to square root of body weight, the great and small cats, for example, are about equal, and man comes out well ahead of any other animal.

We use our brains for thinking, but it is a mistake to suppose that the brain is primarily a thinking organ. Thinking is mainly, if not wholly, performed with words and other symbols, as the Greeks recognized when they used the word logic—from *logos,* "a word"—for the study of thought processes. From the study of the effects of brain injuries we know what parts of the brain are most concerned in thought and language. These areas are usually in the left cerebral hemisphere in the neighborhood of the area which controls the right hand. The human brain has two superanimal activities, manual skill and logical thought. Manual skill appears to be the earlier acquisition of the two, and the capacity for language and thought has grown up around it. If we bred for qualities which involved the loss of manual ability, we should be more likely to evolve back to the apes than up to the angels.

We develop far more slowly than any other mammal. Most mammals are mature at one year or less, a chimpanzee at about seven years, a human being at fifteen or more, while growth is not complete till over twenty years, and the skull sutures are often open till nearly thirty, so that the brain can still grow. We are much more like baby monkeys than adult ones. In biological language we are neotenic, like the axolotl, a Mexican salamander which, unlike most salamanders, never comes out of the water, but breeds without shedding its larval gills. Since a little thyroid hormone will make it grow up, and for other reasons, we may be pretty sure that its ancestors came out of the water. An obvious advantage of this neotenic tendency has been that man has a very long period of learning. As regards behavior he is the most plastic of all the animals. His behavior patterns are less fixed by heredity than theirs and more dependent on his environment.

If this tendency continues, whether by natural processes or human design, we should expect our remote descendants to have an appearance which we should describe today as childish. We should expect their physiological, intellectual, and emotional development to be slower than our own. We should not expect them to be born with an overpowering urge to any particular kind of conduct, good or bad.

39

For example, some birds are monogamous, others polygamous. Monogamy is just one of a series of fairly stereotyped behavior patterns. Man has evolved away from stereotyped behavior patterns, and can be monogamous, polygamous, or celibate. How he will behave depends largely on the impact of society on him. Even a cat is comparatively plastic in its behavior. A kitten which is brought up with mice, and does not see other cats kill mice in its first few months of life, will rarely kill them. But a child's behavior is far less fixed in advance than a kitten's.

This feature, which is so highly developed in man, and which we call plasticity of behavior when we look at it from outside, is called the freedom of the will when we look at it from inside. In any evolution which could be called progressive we are likely to develop it still further. Bernard Shaw, in *Back to Methuselah,* shows us a young lady emerging from an egg some thousands of years hence, and spontaneously talking very good English. She is like those birds which, without education, produce a farily complex song characteristic of their species. I can imagine human beings bred for stereotyped behavior patterns. Perhaps if the Nazis had won they would have tried to do so. But any such step would be a step backward.

Man is not only the brainiest species of mammal. He is the most polymorphic and polytypic if we exclude domesticated species such as the dog. Let me explain these words. We say that a species is polymorphic when in the same area there are several different types breeding together, the differences being genetically determined. For example, the fox *Vulpes fulva* of eastern Canada has three color types: the red, cross and silver foxes. A polytypic species has different types in different areas. Your deer mouse, *Peromyscus maniculatus,* has a gray form inland, and nearly white forms on the white beaches of the Gulf of Mexico.

III. HUMAN DIVERSITY DESIRABLE

Man is polytypic. For example, the peoples of tropical Africa have very dark skins and kinky hair. Those of Europe have light skins and wavy or curly hair. The pre-Columbian peoples of North America have intermediate colored skins, but straighter hair than the Europeans. Man is polymorphic. And at least as regards to color, the European, the most successful of the human races at the present time, is also the most polymorphic. If anyone thinks that I am exaggerating this polymorphism, he will perhaps tell me of another mammalian species apart from domestic animals in which the hair color in a single geographical area ranges from black to pale yellow, the eye color from dark brown to pale blue.

This polymorphism is not necessarily, or even probably, due to race mixture in the past. For example, there is no reason to think that there was ever a race all of whose members had red hair. And the skull shape is as variable in cemeteries of six thousand years ago as in modern cemeteries.

Human polymorphism certainly extends to innate abilities as well as physical and chemical characters such as stature and hair color. For example, I am tone-deaf. I cannot distinguish between quite well-known tunes. I am pretty sure that this defect is congenital. I am also a better mathematician than the average, and have little doubt that I have abnormally high congenital ability for mathematics. No doubt I had good opportunities of learning mathematics, but so I had in the case of music. We know very little about the reasons for variation in human achievement, but we know enough to be reasonably sure that inborn differences play a great part in determining very high and low levels of achievement.

I believe that this psychological polymorphism has been a major reason for the success of the human species, and that a full recognition of this polymorphism and its implications is an essential condition for its success not only in the remote future but in our own lifetime. Let me make my meaning clearer. One of my colleagues, a man of greater manual ability than myself, and very likely of equal or greater intellectual ability, is also a musical executant who could have been a professional musician. If I had his musical gifts I might devote as much time as he does to music, at the expense of my scientific output. It is quite possible that my tone-deafness is an advantage not only for society but even for myself; though such a limitation would almost certainly be undesirable if my probable span of socially useful life were four hundred years instead of forty.

IV. THE POLITICAL IMPLICATIONS OF HUMAN DIVERSITY

I will now make a definition. Liberty is the practical recognition of human polymorphism. I hasten to add, because I recognize that your brains work differently from my own, that few of you will accept this definition. That society enjoys the greatest amount of liberty in which the greatest number of human genotypes can develop their peculiar abilities. It is generally admitted that liberty demands equality of opportunity. It is not equally realized that it demands a variety of opportunities, and a tolerance of those who fail to conform to standards which may be culturally desirable but are not essential for the functioning of society. If I lived in the Soviet Union I should not find its political and economic system irksome. I should be, and have been, irked by the assumption often made there that any cultured man enjoys listening to music and playing chess. If a nation were a pure line there would be little scope for liberty. Everyone between forty-five and fifty would want so many hours a week at the movies, so much (or so little) liquor per week, and so on. These would be provided by rationing, as our needed food calories are provided in England, and everyone would be equally happy. There would be no freedom, no deviants, and no progress.

We are polymorphic not only in our aesthetic but in our intellectual abilities. Ways of describing the world as different as analytical and projective geometry may be equally true, even if at present one human mind cannot accept more than one of them at a time. Last year I saw for the first time Rubens' and Breughel's great picture of Paradise at The Hague. As a geneticist I noted with interest that the guinea pig had been created with at least three genes recessive to the wild type. But I was even more struck by the fact that the Tree of Knowledge was infested by only one serpent but no fewer than four parrots. Maybe in the long run the parrots are more dangerous than the serpent. Certainly we must so far recognize polymorphism as to realize that our own formulations of knowledge are not unique.

Domesticated animals such as dogs are more polymorphic than man. But greyhounds and sheep dogs differ only because they are reproductively isolated. The Indian caste system was an attempt to divide society into a set of reproductively isolated groups each with its peculiar function. This system broke down, as I believe and hope that any such system would break down. I believe that when our descendants plan the genetical future of man they will have to plan for high polymorphism without reproductive isolation. I don't know how they will do it. Fortunately I shan't have to do the planning.

Man is also polytypic. This does not mean that any two races differ as much in intellectual, aesthetic, or moral potentialities as they do in color. The darkest European has lighter skin than the lightest Negro. There is no overlap. But even in a society where Negroes have poor opportunities of education the most cultured Negro is far more cultured than the average European, let alone the least cultured one. Nevertheless polytypicism has so far been an advantage to humanity. Without postulating any over-all superiority of one race to another, we can be fairly sure that some desirable genotypes are commoner in one people than in others and that this difference is to some extent reflected in its achievements. For example, the genotype needed for long-distance runners is relatively frequent among Finns, that needed for short-distance runners among American Negroes. Doubtless the same is true for the genotypes needed for cultural achievement.

In the past a given people at a given time has usually specialized in a few fields of culture. Thus, potential matematicians had little chance in medieval Europe, but potential architects had a good chance. Very likely the contributions of a people to our common culture depend considerably on the genotypes available in it. If so, it is certainly desirable that, until all peoples have reached such a stage of liberty that rare but desirable genotypes can develop their faculties everywhere, man should remain polytypic.

If, however, ten thousand years hence we combine extreme tolerance with a psychology which will enable us to pick out human abilities at an early age, then I can see no need to foster or preserve polytypicism—though it may be desirable to do so for reasons which are not obvious at the present time. In discussing polymorphism we must not forget sex dimorphism—that is to say, the innate differences between the sexes. It is curious that in our existing society most men try to diminish them by removing their beards, while women try to exaggerate them by the use of cosmetics and other devices. *Sinanthropus* and related types seem to have been much more sexually dimorphic than ourselves. So it looks as if men conformed better than women with the evolutionary trend. It is not clear whether this trend should be encouraged to go much further. It is essential that the sexes should understand each other, but a certain difference in intellectual and emotional reactions may well be socially desirable.

V. THE EVOLUTION OF THE MEEK

To sum up, I think that in the last million years man has become more cerebral, more neotenic, and more polymorphic. I think it probable that these are desirable evolutionary trends, while I suggest that judgment should be reserved concerning polytypicism and sexual dimorphism. Others will doubtless say that I have left out the one essential: namely, a bias toward their own canon of behavior, whether moral, religious, or political. However, I have at least given reasons why I believe that any hereditary fixation of behavior patterns is undesirable.

Even this moderate list of desirable qualities gives us food for thought. If it were shown, for example, that the median intellectual performance of English children at the age of fifteen were diminishing, and that this was not due to environmental changes, this fall could be due either to the fact that, on the whole, we were reaching a lower intellectual level at maturity, which would be undesirable; or that we were reaching the same level as our ancestors, or a higher one, but reaching it more slowly, which would be desirable.

How are we to achieve these ends? I do not know. We do not know in detail for what human characters we want to breed. The experience of animal husbandmen will not help us much, for several reasons. We do know that the domestic breeds have been selected for highly specialized performances. But in gaining desired qualities they have lost others which would be desirable in a different context. The greyhound cannot hunt by smell, the dachshund is a poor runner, the husky is ill adapted for city life and so on.

I also think that the history of man's ancestry, as revealed by the geological record, should make us a little cautious. If a Martian zoologist who knew no more than we do now about evolution had been asked to pick the most progressive vertebrate at any time in the past, I think he would very rarely have picked on the line which was destined to give rise to man. During most of the last quarter-billion years they have been pretty small, inconspicuous, and unspecialized animals. Looking at the Jurassic and Cretaceous mammals, and most of the Tertiary Primates, one might be inclined to summarize the evolutionary story as "Blessed are the meek, for they shall inherit the earth," and perhaps to suggest that peoples such as the British in the nineteenth century and the American in the twentieth, who have been successful in war, are dead ends from the evolutionary point of view.

However, if we go back to Permian, we find that our ancestors were large and progressive reptiles. No one who looks at the skeleton and particularly the teeth of such a beast as *Cynognathus,* which was not far from our own ancestral line, could possibly class it as meek. Why the descendants of large predatory theromorphs became small and vegetarian is very far from clear. It is possible that the giant forms discovered by Dr. von Koenigswald were actually our ancestors. If so, our ancestors a million years ago were monsters who could have torn up a tiger with their bare hands. In that case there was a second occasion on which our ancestral line tried physical dominance and gave it up again. It is also possible that the giants of Java and China were side branches from the human line, and represent an unsuccessful evolutionary experiment.

VI. NEGATIVE EUGENICS

After all this caution, I believe we can make a start. Whatever else we may want our descendants to be, we do not want them to be blind, deaf, paralyzed, or brittle-boned. Now these conditions are sometimes due to dominant genes, which can be prevented from spreading further by negative eugenics. At first sight it might be thought that these genes could be eliminated. For example, in many pedigrees of juvenile cataract, affected persons pass on the gene for cataract to about half their children, and it very rarely skips a generation. It has been said that were they all sterilized, these conditions would be abolished. This was one of the ideas behind Hitler's racial hygiene laws.

The idea is false, because these harmful genes constantly reappear as the result of mutation. Occasionally two normal parents will have a child with a harmful dominant gene, which is then handed on until natural selection or negative eugenics puts an end to its career. The two processes are roughly in equilibrium. Thus, achondroplastic dwarfs have about one-fifth the fitness of normal people. That is to say, they produce on an average about one-fifth as many children. So only one-fifth of the dwarfs alive at any time are the progeny of dwarfs, the others being the progeny of normal parents. If all dwarfs of this kind were sterilized we could only cut down the number of dwarfs by one-fifth.

With hemophilia we could cut down the frequency to about one-half by preventing the breeding of hemophilics and heterozygous women. With hereditary cataract we could cut down the frequency to much less than one-half—perhaps to one-tenth. Some, though not all, types of mental defect could be considerably reduced; so could harelip and many other physical defects. This would be well worth doing, but the battle would never be finally won, the race never finally purified.

We could, however, cut down the incidence of a great many congenital maladies to a large extent. Others, such as neonatal jaundice, or *erythroblastosis fetalis,* and perhaps mongoloid idiocy, are due to gene differences between father and mother. We could only abolish them by forbidding unions between people of different genotypes. A closed mating system based on skin color is bad enough, in the sense of making for the division and perhaps the instability of the community. One based on blood antigens, in which an Rh-negative woman might not marry an Rh-positive man, would perhaps be even worse. I should be the last to recommend it, even if it saved the lives of a few babies.

Nor at the present time can we do much to diminish the frequency of undesirable recessive conditions, whether they are lethal, like fetal ichthyosis, or merely a slight handicap, like albinism. The most efficient eugenic method is the introduction of good road transport into backward rural areas, thus encouraging outbreeding.

It may be that, if we knew enough, 1 per cent or even rather more of the population would be found to carry undesirable dominants or sex-linked recessives, which any sound eugenic policy would reduce. How should we do it? Many people believe that carriers should be sterilized, either voluntarily as in Denmark, or compulsorily, as in Nazi Germany. I do not, for the following reasons. Laws for compulsory sterilization are liable to gross abuse. Those for voluntary sterilization are only rather less so. I recall the case of a laborer in one of your Western states who was given an indeterminate sentence up to five years' imprisonment for theft. The judge suggested that he be voluntarily sterilized. He agreed and was not imprisoned. His agreement can only be called voluntary in a Pickwickian sense. However, I might be in favor of sterilization if it would finally rid us of these undesirable genes. But it would not.

There is another reason, perhaps worthy of consideration. If we are ever to control our evolution we shall certainly have to overhaul our whole mating system. By this I do not mean that we shall have to abolish marriage or adopt polygamy. I do not know what we shall have to do. We shall only do what is right if people realize that we have a duty to beget and bear the best-endowed children possible.

It is of the utmost importance that the idea should not be spread abroad that we can improve the human race to any serious extent by sterilizing individuals who do not come up to certain standards. In England we are already beginning to persuade people with harmful dominants to refrain from reproduction, either by chastity or by contraception. We shall not improve the human race by compulsion. A prerequisite for doing so is the moralization of our sexual behavior—that is to say, making it subordinate to ideal ends, not to impulse on the one hand or superstition on the other.

VII. DIFFICULTIES OF POSITIVE EUGENICS

What about positive eugenics? In many human societies those types which are most admired are bred out. The Middle Ages admired holiness and courage. The holy men and women were celibate, the courageous men killed one another. Our age admires money-making. The men who make most money have least children. I am less worried by this than many of my contemporaries. I am not convinced that a business executive is a higher type than a saint or even a feudal knight. In any case, a differential birth rate lasting over a century need no more permanently affect the gene frequencies of a race than selection of certain chromosome orders for a few months per year affects a *Drosophila* species. And in Sweden the tendency has already reversed itself, and the poor breed rather more slowly than the rich.

Why, it may be asked, should we not encourage the breeding of rare and desirable genes as we can discourage the breeding of rare and undesirable ones? The answer is that we do not know of a single rare gene in man whose frequency we should increase. I have no doubt that such exist. But our analysis of the genetic basis of human abilities is so utterly rudimentary that we know nothing of them. Their discovery will need a vast program of collaboration between geneticists, physiologists, and psychologists. Until even one such gene is known, it seems to me rather futile to talk about a program for positive eugenics.

I would, however, suggest that among the genes whose spread we would want to encourage are those for the nondevelopment of teeth, particularly wisdom teeth. Our cerebral development has caused a good deal of overcrowding of our teeth. I hope also that we shall do something about our noses, which are one of our weak points. (I have a nasal infection at the moment. No other organ lets me down so frequently.) The nose has of course been squashed out of shape by the growth of the brain. In consequence, while a sneeze takes a straight path in a dog or a horse, it has to take a hairpin bend in our own species. In a century or so we may know of detailed changes in our psychological make-up which are equally desirable.

In fact, while we can begin with negative eugenics, we cannot begin on postitive eugenics until we have got a great deal more knowledge and a wider diffusion of the eugenic attitude. Probably the first requisites for the development of this knowledge are, on the one hand, the mapping of the human chromosomes, a task to which I have devoted

47

some effort, and on the other, an attempt to analyze the psychological make-up of people judged to be exceptionally gifted, as Spearman in England and the Chicago school in America have tried to analyze that of more normal people. When these are accomplished it will be time to start research on the genetics of great intellectual or moral endowment. Much of it may turn out to be due to heterosis, and as unfixable as the good points of a mongrel dog, but I have little doubt that many rare and desirable genes for these characters exist.

So far I have assumed that our descendants will take over the control of evolution in an intelligent manner. Let us consider the other possibilities. In the next century the human race may largely destroy itself. From the genetic point of view a war using atomic energy would be worse than one using old-fashioned weapons, or even pestilences. For the survivors of Hiroshima and Nagasaki have been so affected that their descendants will show a variety of abnormalities. Some will appear in the first generation and disappear within ten or so. Others will be recessive, and first appear after several generations, their evil (and very rarely good) effects continuing for many thousand generations. The killing of 10 per cent of civilized humanity by atomic bombs might not end civilization. The vast crop of abnormalities produced by another irradiated 10 per cent might do so, and even render recovery very difficult.

I hope that we shall avoid such an international war, or, what seems to me just as likely, a civil war in which a small group get control of some atomic bombs and hold up a whole nation. If so, we may settle down to some peaceful world order, but do nothing about our evolution. In such a case we might stay put for a very long time. Sewall Wright has shown that, on certain assumptions, which seem to me thoroughly sound, evolution goes on quickest in a species divided up into many groups of a few score or hundred individuals nearly, but not quite, sexually isolated from other groups. This was the human condition for thousands of centuries during the Old Stone Age. With agriculture and industry the community has grown, and evolution has probably slowed down. For some time there was heavy selection against crowd diseases, but the progress of hygiene has checked this tendency.

I do not know what we are selecting for now. Let me take an example. Until two generations ago large families were respectable in my country. Anyone who voluntarily restricted his or her family was a deviant. Selection favored genes making for conformity to mores in this respect. Now it is a deviation from the norm to have a dozen children. We are selecting in favor of deviation, instead of against it.

We may be favoring genes which make for high sexual activity, low intelligence, or lack of susceptibility to propaganda, to mention only three possibilities. Most eugenists regard the parents of large families as, on the whole, undesirable genetically. This may well be true. It is certain that on the whole they are economically unsuccessful. Before we equate economic success and long-term biological value, however, it might be desirable to read the Sermon on the Mount or the record of the dinosaurs. I do not know if the trend described is desirable or not, and I contend that no else does.

Another possibility is that we shall control our evolution and choose the wrong path. If I had had to pick hopeful ancestors for a rational and skillful animal from past faunas I doubt if I should ever have got the right answer between the Pennsylvanian and the Miocene. I should certainly have picked *Struthiomimus,* a Cretaceous reptile like an ostrich, standing on its hind legs, but with arms in place of wings. I am equally sure that I should go wrong today. Dr. H. J. Muller has suggested a method for the radical improvement of the human race, involving the widespread use of artificial insemination. I guess that if I were made eugenic world dictator I should have one chance in a hundred of choosing the right path. Dr. Muller is ten times as good a geneticist as I, so he might have one chance in ten, but not, I think, much more.

I am convinced that the knowledge required, both of past evolution and present genetics and cytology, is considerably greater than the whole body of scientific knowledge on which our present civilization is based. We can get this knowledge if we want it. We may say that God is now enlarging the sphere of human choice, and therefore giving us new duties. Or we may say that the evolutionary process is now passing from the stage of unconsciousness to that of consciousness. But we have not yet got the knowledge.

Our immediate task is the remodeling of human society. This can be done in a few generations. The great men who founded your Republic based it on principles which had never before been applied to human societies but which nevertheless worked in practice. The great men behind the French and Russian revolutions made somewhat different but comparable experiments. No society is perfect, and the time scale of social change is so vastly less than that of evolutionary change that the duty to reform society is far more urgent than that to control evolution. The two duties must and will go together. But it would be fatal to

49

think of the man of the future as one who would fit into contemporary American, British, Russian, or Chinese society, or into any society which we can even imagine today.

If I am right he would probably be regarded as a physical, mental, and moral defective. As an adult he would probably have great muscular skill but little muscular strength, a large head, fewer teeth than we have, and so on. He would develop very slowly, perhaps not learning to speak till five years of age, but continuing to learn up to maturity at the age of forty, and then living for several centuries. He would be more rational and less instinctive than we are, less subject to sexual and parental emotions, to rage on the one hand and so-called herd instinct on the other. His motivation would depend far more than ours on education. In his own society he would be a good citizen, in ours perhaps a criminal or a lunatic. He would be of high general intelligence by our standards, and most individuals would have some special aptitude developed to the degree which we call genius.

But just as, were we transported to the past, we should be unlikely to win the admiration of *Sinanthropus,* so, were one of these products of planned evolution brought back to our own time, we should probably judge him an unpleasant individual. This thought need not distress us. We shall not meet him.

IV / A PHILOSOPHER IN THE JUNGLE

FORBIDDEN TO WORK IN HIS HOSPITAL WHEN HE WAS INTERNED AS A PRISONER of war and taken from Africa to France for imprisonment from 1914 to 1918, Albert Schweitzer, surgeon, theologian, musicologist, missionary and philosopher, began, on the second day of his internment, the first volume of his work, *The Philosophy of Civilization*. The war in Europe which interrupted his medical and missionary work with several thousand African natives in the area of Lambaréné, in French Equatorial Africa, thus turned him from the particular attention to man and his condition and ailments to a general study, and the Alsatian-born thinker set down his views against the opinion that mankind is constantly developing in the direction of progress. "My impression was that the fire of its ideals was burning low without anyone noticing it or troubling about it." In 1923 the first two volumes of his work appeared under the titles, *The Decay and Restoration of Civilization* and *Civilization and Ethics*. The only possible way out, he has said of his thinking then, was for man "to adopt a world-view which would bring him once more under the control of the ideals of true civilization which are contained in it." The world-view, he felt, consisted in an ethical affirmation of the world and of life. The man who has become a thinking being feels a compulsion to give to every will-to-live the same Reverence for Life that he gives to his own. The Reverence for Life therefore, he says, which has arisen in the thinking will-to-live contains world and life-affirmation and the ethical fused together. "Its aim is to create values, and to realize progress of different kinds which shall serve the material, spiritual, and ethical development of men and mankind."

Dr. Schweitzer's selection for this book is from his Autobiography, *Out of My Life and Thought*,[1] which appeared in 1933 and tells of his life, beginning in Alsace where he was born January 14, 1875, the son of a Lutheran minister. He was educated at the University of Strasbourg, the Sorbonne at Paris and the University of Berlin. At twenty-one Schweitzer decided he would consider himself justified in living until

[1] *London, George Allen and Unwin Ltd.*

he was thirty for science and art in order to devote himself from that time forward "to the direct service of humanity." At twenty-four his first book, on the religious philosophy of Kant, was published, and in 1905 he took up the study of medicine in order to spend the rest of his life as a doctor in Africa. In 1910 appeared his book, *The Quest for the Historical Jesus*. Most of his books have been written in the jungle mission and hospital which he founded, with his wife, when he reached Africa in 1913, where he has lived almost continuously ever since.

In 1952 Albert Schweitzer was awarded the Nobel Peace Prize, and in 1955, after a short visit to his old European home at Günsbach, France, he went to England where Queen Elizabeth II awarded him the Order of Merit. This is one of the most restricted orders the British sovereign can bestow, and only twenty-four living Britons are permitted to hold it at any time.

For help in reaching Dr. Schweitzer, the editor acknowledges the kind assistance of Dr. Emory Ross of the Board for Fundamental Education who is also connected with the Albert Schweitzer Fellowship, in New York. Dr. Schweitzer, asked to select something most representative of his thinking, felt that although this section of his autobiography was written in 1931, nothing has altered in his thinking to make him wish to alter or amend it. *"Dans mes idées annoncées dans mes livres je n'ai pas changé,"* he wrote the editor.

Dr. Schweitzer was in America in July, 1949, for a Goethe Festival at Aspen, Colorado, when Harvey Breit of the *New York Times* interviewed him. Mr. Breit found him "first of all, very large, very bulky, almost cumbersome in physique. His mustachios are dense and enormous. His head is bold and granite, his eyes are, in context, small and of a gentle intelligence. His hands resemble those weighted stones one sees in the fields (one wonders how the fingers manage the infinite nuances of a Bach trio-sonata); his wrists are massively square, connected without grace or curve to the huge hands. But Dr. Schweitzer is friendly (one had been led to expect an uncommunicative presence), engaging, jovial even; his talk is forceful and to the point; his attitude is kindly, simple and sympathetic (one might say beneficent if the word did not betray a natural gentleness into an overly pious significance)."

Five years later, John Gunther visited the doctor-philosopher at Lambaréné. "Schweitzer is too lofty, too manifold to grasp easily," he wrote in *Inside Africa,* "—a 'universal man' in the sense that Leonardo da Vinci and Goethe were universal men. . . . In Lambaréné, sitting in the garden by the river, I asked him which he thought himself to be most—French or German. His reply was quick, *'Homo sum!'* "

From Elemental Thinking:
Reverence for Life

(Epilogue to an Autobiography)

BY ALBERT SCHWEITZER

Two perceptions cast their shadows over my existence. One consists in my realization that the world is inexplicably mysterious and full of suffering; the other in the fact that I have been born into a period of spiritual decadence in mankind. I have become familiar with and ready to deal with each through the thinking which has led me to the ethical world- and life-affirmation of Reverence for Life. In that principle my life has found a firm footing and a clear path to follow.

I therefore stand and work in the world as one who aims at making men less shallow and morally better by making them think.

With the spirit of the age I am in complete disagreement, because it is filled with disdain for thinking. That such is its attitude is to some extent explicable by the fact that thought has never yet reached the goal which it must set before itself. Time after time it was convinced that it had clearly established a world-view which was in accordance with knowledge and ethically satisfactory. But time after time the truth came out that it had not succeeded.

Doubts, therefore, could well arise as to whether thinking would ever be capable of answering current questions about the world and our relation to it in such a way that we could give a meaning and a content to our lives.

But today in addition to that neglect of thought there is also prevalent a mistrust of it. The organized political, social, and religious associations of our time are at work to induce the individual man not to arrive at his convictions by his own thinking but to make his own such convictions as they keep ready made for him. Any man who thinks for himself and at the same is spiritually free, is to them something inconvenient and even uncanny. He does not offer sufficient guarantee that he will merge himself in their organization in the way they wish. All corporate bodies look today for their strength not so much to the spiritual worth of the ideas which they represent and to that of the

53

people who belong to them, as to the attainment of the highest possible degree of unity and exclusiveness. It is in this that they expect to find their strongest power for offense and defense.

Hence the spirit of the age rejoices, instead of lamenting, that thinking seems to be unequal to its task, and gives it no credit for what, in spite of imperfections, it has already accomplished. It refuses to admit, what is nevertheless the fact, that all spiritual progress up to today has come about through the achievements of thought, or to reflect that thinking may still be able in the future to accomplish what it has not succeeded in accomplishing as yet. Of such considerations the spirit of the age takes no account. Its only concern is to discredit individual thinking in every possible way, and it deals with that on the lines of the saying: "Whosoever hath not, from him shall be taken away even that which he hath."

Thus, his whole life long, the man of today is exposed to influences which are bent on robbing him of all confidence in his own thinking. The spirit of spiritual dependence to which he is called on to surrender is in everything that he hears or reads; it is in the people whom he meets every day; it is in the parties and associations which have claimed him as their own; it pervades all the circumstances of his life.

From every side and in the most varied ways it is dinned into him that the truths and convictions which he needs for life must be taken by him from the associations which have rights over him. The spirit of the age never lets him come to himself. Over and over again convictions are forced upon him in the same way as, by means of the electric advertisements which flare in the streets of every large town, any company which has sufficient capital to get itself securely established, exercises pressure on him at every step he takes to induce him to buy their boot polish or their soup tablets.

By the spirit of the age, then, the man of today is forced into skepticism about his own thinking, in order to make him receptive to truth which comes to him from authority. To all this constant influence he cannot make the resistance that is desirable because he is an overworked and distracted being without power to concentrate. Moreover, the manifold material trammels which are his lot work upon his mentality in such a way that he comes at last to believe himself unqualified even to make any claim to thoughts of his own.

His self-confidence is also diminished through the pressure exercised upon him by the huge and daily increasing mass of Knowledge. He is no longer in a position to take in as something which he has grasped all the new discoveries that are constantly announced; he has to accept them as fact although he does not understand them. This being his relation to scientific truth he is tempted to acquiesce in the idea that in matters of thought also his judgment cannot be trusted.

Thus do the circumstances of the age do their best to deliver us up to the spirit of the age.

The seed of skepticism has germinated. In fact, the modern man has no longer any spiritual self-confidence at all. Behind a self-confident exterior he conceals a great inward lack of confidence. In spite of his great capacity in material matters he is an altogether stunted being, because he makes no use of his capacity for thinking. It will ever remain incomprehensible that our generation, which has shown itself so great by its achievements in discovery and invention, could fall so low spiritually as to give up thinking.

In a period which regards as absurd and little worth, as antiquated and long ago left far behind, whatever it feels to be in any way akin to rationalism or free thought, and which even mocks at the vindication of inalienable human rights which were secured in the eighteenth century, I acknowledge myself to be one who places all his confidence in rational thinking. I venture to say to our generation that it must not think it has done with rationalism because the rationalism of the past had to give place first to Romanticism, and then to a *Realpolitik* which is coming to dominate the spiritual sphere as well as the material. When it has run the gauntlet of the follies of this universal *Realpolitik* and has thereby got itself into deeper and deeper misery, both spiritual and material, it will discover at last that there is nothing for it to do but trust itself to a new Rationalism, deeper and more efficient than the old, and in that seek its salvation.

Renunciation of thinking is a declaration of spiritual bankruptcy. Where there is no longer a conviction that men can get to know the truth by their own thinking, skepticism begins. Those who work to make our age skeptical in this way, do so in the expectation that, as a result of renouncing all hope of self-discovered truth, men will end by accepting as truth what is forced upon them with authority and by propaganda.

But their calculations are wrong. No one who opens the sluices to let a flood of skepticism pour itself over the land must expect to be able to bring it back within its proper bounds. Of those who let themselves get too disheartened to try any longer to discover truth by their own thinking, only a few find a substitute for it in truth taken from others. The mass of people remain skeptical. They lose all feeling for truth, and all sense of need for it as well, finding themselves quite comfortable in a life without thought, driven now here, now there, from one opinion to another.

But the acceptance of authoritative truth, even if that truth has both spiritual and ethical content, does not bring skepticism to an end; it merely covers it up. Man's unnatural condition of not believing that any truth is discoverable by himself, continues, and produces its natural results. The city of truth cannot be built on the swampy ground of skepticism. Our spiritual life is rotten throughout because it is permeated through and through with skepticism, and we live in consequence in a world which in every respect is full of falsehood. We are not far from shipwreck on the rock of wanting to have even truth organized.

Truth taken over by a skepticism which has become believing has not the spiritual qualities of that which originated in thinking. It has been externalized and rendered torpid. It does obtain influence over a man, but it is not capable of uniting itself with him to the very marrow of his being. Living truth is that alone which has its origin in thinking.

Just as a tree bears year after year the same fruit and yet fruit which is each year new, so must all permanently valuable ideas be continually born again in thought. But our age is bent on trying to make the barren tree of skepticism fruitful by tying fruits of truth on its branches.

It is only by confidence in our ability to reach truth by our own individual thinking, that we are capable of accepting truth from outside. Unfettered thought, provided it be deep, never degenerates into subjectivity. With its own ideas it stirs those within itself which enjoy any traditional credit for being true, and exerts itself to be able to possess them as knowledge.

Not less strong than the will to truth must be the will to sincerity. Only an age which can show the courage of sincerity can possess truth which works as a spiritual force within it.

Sincerity is the foundation of the spiritual life.

With its depreciation of thinking our generation has lost its feeling for sincerity and with it that for truth as well. It can therefore be helped only by its being brought once more onto the road of thinking.

Because I have this certainty I oppose the spirit of the age, and take upon myself with confidence the responsibility of taking my part in the rekindling of the fire of thought.

Thought on the lines of Reverence for Life is by its very nature peculiarly qualified to take up the struggle against skepticism. It is elemental.

Elemental thinking is that which starts from the fundamental questions about the relations of man to the universe, about the meaning of life, and about the nature of goodness. It stands in the most immediate connection with the thinking which impulse stirs in everyone. It enters into that thinking, widening and deepening it.

Such elemental thinking we find in Stoicism. When as a student I began going through the history of philosophy I found it difficult to tear myself away from Stoicism, and to pursue my way through the utterly different thinking which succeeded it. It is true that the results produced by Stoic thought were far from satisfying me, but I had the feeling that this simple kind of philosophizing was the right one, and I could not understand how people had come to abandon it.

Stoicism seemed to me great in that it goes straight for its goal; that it is universally intelligible, and is at the same time profound; that it makes the best of the truth which it recognizes as such, even if it is unsatisfying; that it puts life into such truth by the earnestness with which it devotes itself to it; that it possesses the spirit of sincerity; that it urges men to collect their thoughts, and to become more inward; and that it arouses in them the sense of responsibility. I felt, too, that the fundamental thought of Stoicism is true, namely that man must bring himself into a spiritual relation with the world, and become one with it. In its essence Stoicism is a nature philosophy which ends in mysticism.

Just as I felt Stoic thinking to be elemental, so I felt that of Lao-tse to be the same, when I became acquainted with his Tao-te-King. For him, too, the important thing is that man shall come, by simple thinking, into a spiritual relation to the world, and prove his unity with it by his life.

There is, therefore, an essential relationship between Greek Stoicism and Chinese. The only distinction between them is that the former had its origin in well-developed, logical thinking, the latter in intuitive thinking was undeveloped and yet marvelously profound.

This elemental thinking, however, which emerges in European as in extra-European philosophy, is unable to retain the leadership it has won; it must resign that position to the unelemental. It proves a failure because its results are not satisfying. It cannot see any meaning in the impulse to activity and to ethical deeds which is contained in the will-to-live of the spiritually developed man. Hence Greek Stoicism gets no further than the ideal of resignation, Lao-tse no further than the kindly inactivity which to us Europeans seems so curious.

The ultimate explanation of the history of philosophy is that the thoughts of ethical world- and life-affirmation which are natural to man can never acquiesce contentedly in the results of simple logical thinking about man and his relation to the universe, because they cannot fit themselves into it properly. They therefore compel thinking to take to roundabout roads, along which they hope to reach their goal. Thus there arises side by side with elemental thinking an unelemental, in various forms, which grows up round the other and often entirely conceals it.

These roundabout roads which thinking takes lead especially in the direction of an attempted explanation of the world which shall represent the will to ethical activity in the world as purposive. In the late Stoicism of an Epictetus and a Marcus Aurelius, in the Rationalism of the eighteenth century, and in that of Kung-tse (Confucius), Meng-tse (Mencius), Mi-tse (Micius), and other Chinese thinkers, the philosophy which starts from the elemental problem of the relation of man to the world reaches an ethical world- and life-affirmation by tracing the course of world-events back to a world-will with ethical aims, and claiming man for service to it. In the thinking of Brahmanism, and of the Buddha, as in the Indian systems generally, and in the philosophy of Schopenhauer, the opposite explanation of the world is put forward, namely that the Life which runs its course in space and time is purposeless, and must be brought to an end. The sensible attitude of man to the world is therefore to die to the world and to life.

Side by side with this form of thinking which, so far, at any rate, as its starting-point and its interests are concerned, has remained elemental, there enters the field, especially in European philosophy, another form which is completely unelemental in that it no longer has as its central point the question of man's relation to the world. It busies itself with the problem of the nature of knowledge, with logical speculations, with natural science, with psychology, with sociology, and with other things, as if philosophy were really concerned with the solution of all these questions for their own sake, or as if itself consisted merely in the sifting and systematizing of the results of the various sciences. Instead of urging man to constant meditation on himself and his relation to the world, this philosophy presents him with results of epistemology, of logical speculation, of natural science, of psychology, or of sociology, as matters according to which alone he is to shape his view of his life and his relation to the world. On all these things it discourses to him as if he were not a being who is in the world and lives his life in it, but one who is stationed near it, and contemplates it from the outside.

Because it approaches the problem of the relation of man to the universe from some arbitrarily chosen standpoint, or perhaps passes it by altogether, this unelemental European philosophy lacks unity and consistency, and shows itself more or less restless, artificial, eccentric, and fragmentary. At the same time, it is the richest and the most universal. In its systems, half-systems, and no-systems, which succeed and interpenetrate each other, it is able to contemplate the problem of world-view from every side, and in every possible perspective. It is also the most practical in that it deals with the natural sciences, history, and ethical questions more profoundly than the others do.

The world-philosophy of the future will owe its origin less to efforts to reconcile European and non-European thought, than to those made to reconcile elemental and unelemental thinking.

From the intellectual life of our time mysticism stands aside. It is in essence a form of elemental thinking, because it is directly occupied in enabling the individual man to put himself into a spiritual relation with the world. It despairs, however, of this being possible by means of logical thinking, and falls back on intuition, within which imagination can be active. In a certain sense, then, the mysticism also of the past goes back to a mode of thinking which tries roundabout routes. Since with us only that knowledge which is a result of logical thinking is accepted as truth, the convictions which make up the mysticism above described, cannot become our spiritual possession in the form in which they are expressed and declared to be proved. Moreover, they are not in themselves satisfying. Of all the mysticism of the past it must be said that its ethical content is too slight. It puts men on the road of inwardness, but not on that of a living ethic. The truth of a world-view must be proved by the fact that the spiritual relation to life and the universe into which that world-view brings us makes us into inward men with an active ethic.

Against the lack of thought, then, which characterizes our age nothing effective can be done either by the unelemental thinking which takes the roundabout route in the explanation of the world, or by mystical intuition. Power over skepticism is given only to that elemental thinking which takes up and develops the simple thinking which is natural in all men. The unelemental thinking on the other hand, which sets before men certain results of thinking at which it has in one way or another arrived, is not in a position to sustain their own thinking, but takes it from them in order to put another kind in its place. This acceptance of another kind of thinking means a disturbance and weakening of one's own. It is a step toward the acceptance of truth from outside, and thus a step toward skepticism. It was in this way that the great systems of German philosophy which when they appeared were taken up with such enthusiasm, prepared at the beginning of the nineteenth century the ground upon which later on skepticism developed.

To make men thinking beings once more, then, means to make them resort to their own way of thinking that they may try to secure that knowledge which they need for living. In the thinking which starts from Reverence for Life there is to be found a renewal of elemental thinking. The stream which has been flowing for a long distance underground comes again to the surface.

The belief that elemental thinking is now arriving at world- and life-affirmation, which it has hitherto vainly striven to reach, is no self-deception, but is connected with the fact that thinking has become thoroughly realistic.

It used to deal with the world as being only a totality of happenings. With this totality of happenings the only spiritual relation which man can reach is one in which, acknowledging his own natural subordination to it, he secures a spiritual position under it by resignation. To attribute any meaning and purpose to his own activities is impossible with such a conception of the world. He cannot possibly place himself at the service of this totality of happenings which crushes him. His way to world- and life-affirmation and to the ethical is barred.

It thereupon attempts, but in vain, to grasp by means of some sort of explanation of the world what elemental thinking, hindered by this lifeless and incomplete representation of the world, cannot reach in the natural way. This thinking is like a river which on its way to the sea is held up by a range of mountains. Its waters try to find a passage to the sea by roundabout ways. In vain. They only pour themselves into other valleys and fill them. Then, centuries later, the dammed-up waters manage to break through.

The world does not consist of happenings only; it contains life as well, and to the life in the world, so far as it comes within my reach, I have to be in a relation which is not only passive but active. By placing myself in the service of that which lives I reach an activity, exerted, upon the world which has meaning and purpose.

However simple and obvious a proceeding it may seem to be when once accomplished, to replace that lifeless idea of the world by a real world which is full of life, a long period of evolution was needed, nevertheless, before it became possible. Just as the solid rock of a mountain range which has risen from the sea first becomes visible when the layers of chalk which covered it have been eroded and washed away by the rain, so, in questions of world-view, is realist thinking overlaid by unrealistic.

The idea of Reverence for Life offers itself as the realistic answer to the realistic question of how man and the world are related to each other. Of the world man knows only that everything which exists is, like himself, a manifestation of the will-to-live. With this world he stands in a relation of passivity and of activity. On the one hand he is subordinate to the course of events which is given in this totality of life; on the other hand he is capable of affecting the life which comes within his reach by hampering or promoting it, by destroying or maintaining it.

The one possible way of giving meaning to his existence is that of raising his natural relation to the world to a spiritual one. As a being in a passive relation to the world he comes into a spiritual relation to it by resignation. True resignation consists in this: that man, feeling his subordination to the course of world-happenings, wins his way to inward freedom from the fortunes which shape the outward side of his existence. Inward freedom means that he finds strength to deal with everything that is hard in his lot, in such a way that it all helps to make him a deeper and more inward person, to purify him, and to keep him calm and peaceful. Resignation, therefore, is the spiritual and ethical affirmation of one's own existence. Only he who has gone through the stage of resignation is capable of world-affirmation.

As a being in an active relation to the world he comes into a spiritual relation with it by not living for himself alone, but feeling himself one with all life that comes within his reach. He will feel all that life's experiences as his own, he will give it all the help that he possibly can, and will feel all the saving and promotion of life that he has been able to effect as the deepest happiness that can ever fall to his lot.

Let a man once begin to think about the mystery of his life and the links which connect him with the life that fills the world, and he cannot but bring to bear upon his own life and all other life that comes within his reach the principle of Reverence for Life, and manifest this principle by ethical world- and life-affirmation expressed in action. Existence will thereby become harder for him in every respect than it would be if he lived for himself, but at the same time it will be richer, more beautiful, and happier. It will become, instead of mere living, a real experience of life.

Beginning to think about life and the world leads a man directly and almost irresistibly to Reverence for Life. Such thinking leads to no conclusions which could point in any other direction.

If the man who has once begun to think wishes to persist in his mere living he can do so only by surrendering himself, whenever this idea takes possession of him, to thoughtlessness, and stupefying himself therein. If he perseveres with thinking he can come to no other result than Reverence for Life.

Any thinking by which men assert that they are reaching skepticism or life without ethical ideals, is not thinking but thoughtlessness which poses as thinking, and it proves itself to be such by the fact that it is unconcerned about the mystery of life and the world.

Reverence for Life contains in itself Resignation, World- and Life-Affirmation, and the Ethical, the three essential elements in a world-view, as mutually interconnected results of thinking.

Up to now there have been world-views of Resignation, world-views of World- and Life-Affirmation, and world-views which sought to satisfy the claims of the Ethical. Not one has there been, however, which has been able to combine the three elements. That is possible only on condition that all three are conceived as essentially products of the universal conviction of Reverence for Life, and are recognized as being one and all contained in it. Resignation and World- and Life-Affirmation have no separate existence of their own by the side of the Ethical; they are its lower octaves.

Having its origin in realistic thinking, the ethic of Reverence for Life is realistic, and brings man to a realistic and steady facing of reality.

It may seem, at first glance, as if Reverence for Life were something too general and too lifeless to provide the content of a living ethic. But thinking has no need to trouble as to whether its expressions sound living enough, so long as they hit the mark and have life in them. Anyone who comes under the influence of the ethic of Reverence for Life will very soon be able to detect, thanks to what that ethic demands from him, what fire glows in the lifeless expression. The ethic of Reverence for Life is the ethic of Love widened into universality. It is the ethic of Jesus, now recognized as a necessity of thought.

Objection is made to this ethic that it sets too high a value on natural life. To this it can retort that the mistake made by all previous systems of ethics has been the failure to recognize that life as such is the mysterious value with which they have to deal. All spiritual life meets us within natural life. Reverence for Life, therefore, is applied to natural life and spiritual life alike. In the parable of Jesus, the shepherd saves not merely the soul of the lost sheep but the whole animal. The stronger the reverence for natural life, the stronger grows also that for spiritual life.

The ethic of Reverence for Life is found particularly strange because it establishes no dividing-line between higher and lower, between more valuable and less valuable life. For this omission it has its reasons.

To undertake to lay down universally valid distinctions of value between different kinds of life will end in judging them by the greater or lesser distance at which they seem to stand from us human beings— as we ourselves judge. But that is a purely subjective criterion. Who among us knows what significance any other kind of life has in itself, and as a part of the universe?

Following on such a distinction there comes next the view that there can be life which is worthless, injury to which or destruction of which does not matter. Then in the category of worthless life we come to include, according to circumstances, different kinds of insects, or primitive peoples.

To the man who is truly ethical all life is sacred, including that which from the human point of view seems lower in the scale. He makes distinctions only as each case comes before him, and under the pressure of necessity, as, for example, when it falls to him to decide which of two lives he must sacrifice in order to preserve the other. But all through this series of decisions he is conscious of acting on subjective grounds and arbitrarily, and knows that he bears the responsibility for the life which is sacrificed.

I rejoice over the new remedies for sleeping sickness, which enable me to preserve life, whereas I had previously to watch a painful disease. But every time I have under the microscope the germs which cause the disease, I cannot but reflect that I have to sacrifice this life in order to save other life.

I buy from natives a young fish eagle, which they have caught on a sand bank, in order to rescue it from their cruel hands. But now I have to decide whether I shall let it starve, or kill every day a number of small fishes, in order to keep it alive. I decide on the latter course, but every day I feel it hard that this life must be sacrificed for the other on my responsibility.

Standing, as he does, with the whole body of living creatures under the law of this dilemma (*Selbstentzweiung*) in the will-to-live, man comes again and again into the position of being able to preserve his own life and life generally only at the cost of other life. If he has been touched by the ethic of Reverence for Life, he injures and destroys life only under a necessity which he cannot avoid, and never from thoughtlessness. So far as he is a free man he uses every opportunity of tasting the blessedness of being able to assist life and avert from it suffering and destruction.

Devoted as I was from boyhood to the cause of the protection of animal life, it is a special joy to me that the universal ethic of Reverence for Life shows the sympathy with animals which is so often represented as sentimentality, to be a duty which no thinking man can escape. Hitherto ethics have faced the problem of man and beast either uncomprehending or helpless. Even when sympathy with the animal creation was felt to be right, it could not be brought within the scope of ethics, because ethics were really focused only on the behavior of man to man.

When will the time come when public opinion will tolerate no longer any popular amusements which depend on the ill-treatment of animals!

The ethic, then, which originates in thinking is not "according to reason," but nonrational and enthusiastic. It marks off no skillfully defined circle of duties, but lays upon each individual the responsibility for all life within his reach, and compels him to devote himself to helping it.

Any profound world-view is mysticism, in that it brings men into a spiritual relation with the Infinite. The world-view of Reverence for Life is ethical mysticism. It allows union with the infinite to be realized by ethical action. This ethical mysticism originates in logical thinking. If our will-to-live begins to think about itself and the world, we come to experience the life of the world, so far as it comes within our reach, in our own life, and to devote our will-to-live to the infinite will-to-live through the deeds we do. Rational thinking, if it goes deep, ends of necessity in the nonrational of mysticism. It has, of course, to deal with life and the world, both of which are nonrational entities.

In the world the infinite will-to-live reveals itself to us as will-to-create, and this is full of dark and painful riddles for us; in ourselves it is revealed as will-to-love, which will through us remove the dilemma (*Selbstentzweiung*) of the will-to-live.

The world-view of Reverence for Life has, therefore, a religious character. The man who avows his belief in it, and acts upon the belief, shows a piety which is elemental.

Through the active ethic of love with its religious character, and through its inwardness, the world-view of Reverence for Life is essentially related to that of Christianity. Hence there is a possibility that Christianity and thought may now meet in a new relation to each other which will do more than the present one to promote spiritual life.

Christianity has once already entered into a connection with thought, namely during the period of Rationalism in the eighteenth century. It did so because thought met it with an enthusiastic ethic which was religious in character. As a matter of fact, however, thought had not produced this ethic itself, but had, without knowing it, taken it over from Christianity. When, later on, it had to depend solely upon its own ethic, this latter proved to have in it so little life and so little religion that it had not much in common with Christian ethics. Then the bonds between Christianity and active thought were loosened, and the situation today is that Christianity has completely withdrawn into itself, and is concerned only with the propagation of its own ideas, as such. It no longer sees any use in proving them to be in agreement with thought, but prefers that they be regarded as something altogether outside it, and occupying a superior position. It loses, however, thereby its connection with the spiritual life of the time and the possibility of exercising any real influence upon it.

The emergence of the world-view of Reverence for Life now summons it to face once more the question whether it will or will not join hands with thought which is ethical and religious in character.

Christianity has need of thought that it may come to the consciousness of its real self. For centuries it treasured the great commandment of love and mercy as traditional truth without recognizing it as a reason for opposing slavery, witch-burning, torture, and all the other ancient and medieval forms of inhumanity. It was only when it experienced the influence of the thinking of the Age of Enlightenment (*Aufklärung*[1]) that it was stirred into entering the struggle for humanity. The remembrance of this ought to preserve it forever from assuming any air of superiority in comparison with thought.

Many people find pleasure today in talking continually of how

[1] *Aufklärung*=Illumination. The name given to the period of the eighteenth century made notable by the influence of the progressive thinkers: Montesquieu (1689–1755), Voltaire (1694–1778), Rousseau (1712–1778), Diderot (1713–1784), and others.— Translator.

"shallow" Christianity became in the age of Rationalism. Justice surely demands that we should find out and admit how much compensation was made for that "shallowness" by the services rendered by that Christianity. Today torture has been re-established. In many states the system of Justice acquiesces without protest in the most infamous tortures being applied, before and simultaneously with the regular proceedings of police and prison officials, in order to extract confessions from those accused. The sum total of misery thus caused every hour passes imagination. But to this renewal of torture the Christianity of today offers no opposition even in words, much less in deeds, and similarly it makes hardly any effort to counter the superstitions of today. And even if it did resolve to venture on resisting these things and on undertaking other things such as the Christianity of the eighteenth century accomplished, it would be unable to carry out its intention because it has no power over the spirit of the age.

To make up to itself for the fact that it does so little to prove the reality of its spiritual and ethical nature, the Christianity of today cheats itself with the delusion that it is making its position as a church stronger year by year. It is accommodating itself to the spirit of the age by adopting a kind of modern worldliness. Like other organized bodies it is at work to make good, by ever stronger and more uniform organization, its claim to be a body justified by history and practical success. But just in proportion as it gains in external power, it loses in spiritual.

Christianity cannot take the place of thinking, but it must be founded on it.

In and by itself it is not capable of mastering lack of thought and skepticism. The only age which can be receptive for the imperishable elements in its own thoughts is one animated by an elemental piety which springs from thinking.

Just as a stream is preserved from gradually leaking away, because it flows along above subsoil water, so does Christianity need the subsoil water of elemental piety which is the fruit of thinking. It can only attain to real spiritual power when men find the road from thought to religion no longer barred.

I know that I myself owe it to thinking that I was able to retain my faith in religion and Christianity.

The man who thinks stands up freer in the face of traditional religious truth than the man who does not, but the profound and imperishable elements contained in it he assimilates with much more effect than the latter.

66

The essential element in Christianity as it was preached by Jesus and as it is comprehended by thought, is this, that it is only through love that we can attain to communion with God. All living knowledge of God rests upon this foundation: that we experience Him in our lives as Will-to-Love.

Anyone who has recognized that the idea of Love is the spiritual beam of light which reaches us from the Infinite, ceases to demand from religion that it shall offer him complete knowledge of the suprasensible. He ponders, indeed, on the great questions: what the meaning is of the evil in the world; how in God, the great First Cause, the will-to-create and the will-to-love are one; in what relation the spiritual and the material life stand to one another, and in what way our existence is transitory and yet eternal. But he is able to leave these questions on one side, however painful it may be to give up all hope of answers to them. In the knowledge of spiritual existence in God through love he possesses the one thing needful.

"Love never faileth: but . . . whether there be knowledge it shall be done away," says St. Paul.

The deeper piety is, the humbler are its claims with regard to knowledge of the suprasensible. It is like a path which winds between the hills instead of going over them.

The fear that the Christianity which is favorably inclined to the piety originating in thought will step into pantheism is unreal. Every form of living Christianity is pantheistic in that it is bound to envisage everything that exists as having its being in the great First Cause of all being. But at the same time all ethical piety is higher than any pantheistic mysticism, in that it does not find the God of Love in Nature, but knows about Him only from the fact that He announces Himself in us as Will-to-Love. The First Cause of Being, as He manifests Himself in Nature, is to us always something impersonal. But to the First Cause of Being, who becomes revealed to us as Will-to-Love, we relate ourselves as to an ethical personality. Theism does not stand in opposition to pantheism, but emerges from it as the ethically determined out of what is natural and undetermined.

Unfounded, too, is the doubt whether the Christianity which has passed through a stage of thinking can still bring home his sinfulness to the consciousness of man with sufficient seriousness. It is not where sinfulness is most talked about that its seriousness is most forcibly taught. There is not much about it in the Sermon on the Mount. But thanks to the longing for freedom from sin and for purity of heart

D*   67 which Jesus has enshrined in the Beatitudes, these form the great call to repentance which is unceasingly working on man.

If Christianity, for the sake of any tradition or for any considerations whatever, refuses to have itself interpreted in terms of ethicoreligious thinking, it will be a misfortune for itself and for mankind.

What Christianity needs is that it shall be filled to overflowing with the spirit of Jesus, and in the strength of that shall spiritualize itself into a living religion of inwardness and love, such as its destined purpose should make it. Only as such can it become the leaven in the spiritual life of mankind. What has been passing for Christianity during these nineteen centuries is merely a beginning, full of weaknesses and mistakes, not a full-grown Christianity springing from the spirit of Jesus.

Because I am devoted to Christianity in deep affection, I am trying to serve it with loyalty and sincerity. In no wise do I undertake to enter the lists on its behalf with the crooked and fragile thinking of Christian apologetic, but I call on it to set itself right in the spirit of sincerity with its past and with thought in order that it may thereby become conscious of its true nature.

My hope is that the emergence of an elemental mode of thought which must lead us to the ethicoreligious idea of Reverence for Life, may contribute to the bringing of Christianity and thought closer to each other.

To the question whether I am a pessimist or an optimist, I answer that my knowledge is pessimistic, but my willing and hoping are optimistic.

I am pessimistic in that I experience in its full weight what we conceive to be the absence of purpose in the course of world-happenings. Only at quite rare moments have I felt really glad to be alive. I could not but feel with a sympathy full of regret all the pain that I saw around me, not only that of men but that of the whole creation. From this community of suffering I have never tried to withdraw myself. It seemed to me a matter of course that we should all take our share of the burden of pain which lies upon the world. Even while I was a boy at school it was clear to me that no explanation of the evil in the world could ever satisfy me; all explanations, I felt, ended in sophistries, and at bottom had no other object than to make it possible for men to share in the misery around them, with less keen feelings. That a thinker like Leibnitz could reach the miserable conclusion that though this world is, indeed, not good, it is the best that was possible, I have never been able to understand.

But however much concerned I was at the problem of the misery in the world, I never let myself get lost in broodings over it; I always held firmly to the thought that each one of us can do a little to bring some portion of it to an end. Thus I came gradually to rest content in the knowledge that there is only one thing we can understand about the problem, and that is that each of us has to go his own way, but as one who means to help to bring about deliverance.

In my judgment, too, of the situation in which mankind finds itself at the present time I am pessimistic. I cannot make myself believe that that situation is not so bad as it seems to be, but I am inwardly conscious that we are on a road which, if we continue to tread it, will bring us into "Middle Ages" of a new character. The spiritual and material misery to which mankind of today is delivering itself through its renunciation of thinking and of the ideals which spring therefrom, I picture to myself in its utmost compass. And yet I remain optimistic. One belief of my childhood I have preserved with the certainty that I can never lose it: belief in truth. I am confident that the spirit generated by truth is stronger than the force of circumstances. In my view no other destiny awaits mankind than that which, through its mental and spiritual disposition, it prepares for itself. Therefore I do not believe that it will have to tread the road to ruin right to the end.

If men can be found who revolt against the spirit of thoughtlessness, and who are personalities sound enough and profound enough to let the ideals of ethical progress radiate from them as a force, there will start an activity of the spirit which will be strong enough to evoke a new mental and spiritual disposition in mankind.

Because I have confidence in the power of truth and of the spirit, I believe in the future of mankind. Ethical world- and life-affirmation contains within itself an optimistic willing and hoping which can never be lost. It is, therefore, never afraid to face the dismal reality, and to see it as it really is.

In my own life anxiety, trouble, and sorrow have been allotted to me at times in such abundant measure that had my nerves not been so strong, I must have broken down under the weight. Heavy is the burden of fatigue and responsibility which has lain upon me without a break for years. I have not much of my life for myself, not even the hours I should like to devote to my wife and child.

But I have had blessings too: that I am allowed to work in the service of mercy; that my work has been successful; that I receive from other people affection and kindness in abundance; that I have loyal helpers, who identify themselves with my activity; that I enjoy a health which allows me to undertake most exhausting work; that I have a well-balanced temperament which varies little, and an energy which exerts itself with calmness and deliberation; and, finally, that I can recognize as such whatever happiness falls to my lot, accepting it also as a thing for which some thank-offering is due from me.

I feel it deeply that I can work as a free man at a time when an oppressive lack of freedom is the lot of so many, as also that though my immediate work is material, yet I have at the same time opportunities of occupying myself in the sphere of the spiritual and intellectual.

That the circumstances of my life provide in such varied ways favorable conditions for my work, I accept as something of which I would fain prove myself worthy.

How much of the work which I have planned and have in mind shall I be able to complete?

My hair is beginning to turn. My body is beginning to show traces of the exertions I have demanded of it, and of the passage of the years.

I look back with thankfulness to the time when, without needing to husband my strength, I could get through an uninterrupted course of bodily and mental work. With calmness and humility I look forward to the future, so that I may not be unprepared for renunciation if it be required of me. Whether we be workers or sufferers, it is assuredly our duty to conserve our powers, as being men who have won their way through to the peace which passeth all understanding.

—Translated by T. C. Campion, M. A., Oriel College, Oxford

V / AUTHOR WITH A PLANETARY VIEW

ALDOUS HUXLEY, WHO HAS BEEN DESCRIBED AT HIS NOVEL WRITING PERIOD'S peak as "Example No. 1 of the skeptical brilliance that burst forth after the First World War," but who has more or less deserted his fiction followers (looking for more in that particular vein) to preoccupy himself with essays, mysticism and "roads to salvation and roads to damnation," is represented in this book with an essay in which he feels man is committing himself to his own potential extinction by overpopulating the earth and by violating nature and its resources. His contribution is taken from *Themes and Variations.* The few years since its appearance in 1950 have done nothing to date the validity of the warnings; indeed, time has reinforced their pertinency to the extent that students of demography foresee that if present population trends continue the world population of 2.7 billion will be doubled to between 4 billion and 5.5 billions within fifty years, with unpredictable results. Man's violence to nature, involving, as Huxley points out, soil erosion and the destruction of irreplaceable natural resources—already reducing the available food supply for the world's present population—may create a world "explosion" long before the end of the century, say some demographers who have worked on population studies for the United Nations and other institutions.

Aldous Huxley, who was born July 26, 1894, in Surrey, England, is the brother of Julian Huxley, the English writer on science, whose studies in evolution are well known. The brothers are grandsons of Thomas Henry Huxley, the biologist, and grand-nephews of Matthew Arnold. Their father was Leonard Huxley, essayist. Whereas Julian Huxley's scientific studies led him to espouse an overt atheism, Aldous Huxley's later years have found him a student and expositor of religious and mystical thinking, some of which he has collected as commentary to the texts in a volume entitled *The Perennial Philosophy,* in which he tried to cull "the Highest Common Factor" in all philosophy and which he summarized as "the metaphysic that recognizes a divine Reality substantial to the world of things and lives and minds; the psychology that finds in the soul something similar to, or even identical with divine Reality; the ethic that places man's final end in the knowledge of the immanent and transcendent Ground of all being."

Mr. Huxley's intention as a young man was to become a doctor and he had begun to specialize in biology at Eton in 1908 when he contracted an eye disease which made him almost completely blind. He learned to read books and music in Braille and continued his studies with tutors. A scientific career out of the question, he turned to literature and philology.

"The most important single event in my life," he has written, "was unquestionably the onset of eye trouble. This had the effect of isolating me during my years of adolescence and forcing me to live largely on my own inner resources." In California, Huxley found a doctor who had discovered a method whereby through properly directed conscious effort the eye disability was remedied.

"This discovery," he writes in *Twentieth Century Authors,* "was for me a demonstration in one particular sphere, of the possibility of becoming the master of one's circumstances instead of the slave. The problem of freedom, in the psychological rather than the political sense of the word, is in large measure a technical problem. It is not enough to wish to become the master, it is not even enough to work hard at achieving such mastery. Correct knowledge as to the best means of achieving mastery is also essential. In one limited field of human disability, Dr. Bates had provided such knowledge. Similar techniques for controlling unfavorable circumstances in other isolated fields have been independently developed and are available for anyone who cares to learn them. All these techniques, however, are secondary and, so to stay, peripheral to a great central technique. This central technique, which teaches the art of obtaining freedom from the fundamental human disability of egotism, has been repeatedly described by the mystics of all ages and countries. It is with the problem of personal, psychological freedom that I now find myself predominantly concerned."

Mr. Huxley lives, with his wife, in California.

The Double Crisis

BY ALDOUS HUXLEY

The human race is passing through a time of crisis, and that crisis exists, so to speak, on two levels—an upper level of political and economic crisis, and a lower level of demographic and ecological crisis. That which is discussed at international conferences and in the newspapers is the upper-level crisis—the crisis whose immediate causes are the economic breakdown due to the war and the struggle for power between national groups possessing, or about to possess, the means of mass extermination. Of the low-level crisis, the crisis in population and world resources, hardly anything is heard in the press, on the radio or at the more important international conferences. The Big Threes and Big Fours do not deign to discuss it; leaving the matter to the subaltern and unauthoritative delegations to conferences on health or food, they devote their entire energies to the question of who shall bully whom. And yet the low-level crisis is at least as serious as the crisis in the political and economic field. Moreover, the problems on the upper level cannot be solved without reference to the problems that are shaping up in the cosmic and biological basement. If it is ignored, the low-level crisis is bound to exacerbate the crisis on the political and economic levels. At the same time, a concentration of attention and energy on power politics and power economics will make a solution of the low-level problems not merely difficult, but impossible. In what follows I propose to discuss certain aspects of the low-level crisis and to point out how the obscure happenings in the basement have affected and are likely to go on affecting the lives of private individuals, the policies of statesmen and the conduct of nations.

It has been fashionable for some time past to talk about "poverty in the midst of plenty." The phrase implies that the planet possesses abundant resources to feed, clothe, house and provide amenities for its existing population and for any immediately foreseeable increase in that population, and that the present miseries of the human race are due entirely to faulty methods of production and, above all, of distribution. Given currency reform, socialism, Communism, unrestricted capitalism, distributism or whatever the favorite remedy may be, humanity, like

73

the prince and princess in the fairy stories, will be able to live happily ever after. Want and hunger will be transformed into abundance and the whole earth will become one vast Land of Cockayne.

Such are the miracles to be achieved by political and economic planning. But when we pass from these high-level considerations to a study of what is going on at the biological and ecological levels, our optimism is apt to seem a little premature, to say the least. Instead of poverty in the midst of plenty, we find that there is poverty in the midst of poverty. World resources are inadequate to world population. At the present time, our planet supports a little less than two and a quarter billions of human beings, and the area of food-producing land is in the neighborhood of four billion acres. It has been calculated that two and a half acres of land are needed to provide a human being with a diet which nutritionists would regard as adequate. Thus, even if all the available productive land were good—and much of it is of very poor quality— the existing population could not be assured of an adequate diet. Actually, in order to guarantee an adequate diet for all of the world's two and a quarter billions of men, women and children, the present food supply would have to be doubled. But this cannot be accomplished overnight. In the words of Dr. Thomas Parran, former U. S. Surgeon-General, "The greatest possible increase in food production will not for decades be enough to meet the minimum adequate diet." And meanwhile world population is rising. It is rising at the rate of about two hundred millions every ten years. This means that, by the time the food supply is doubled, there will be, not two and a quarter billions of mouths to feed, but well over three billions. In spite of all that may have been achieved in the interval, malnutrition will be just as serious and just as widespread as it is today.

Moreover, while population goes up, the fertility of the soil declines. "Modern man," writes Ward Shepard in his *Food or Famine,* "has perfected two devices, either of which is capable of annihilating civilization. One is atomic war, the other is world soil-erosion. Of the two, soil-erosion is the more insidiously destructive. War disrupts or destroys the social environment, which is the matrix of civilization. Soil-erosion destroys the natural environment, which is its foundation." In other words, atomic war may destroy one particular civilization—the Western-Industrial variety, for example; soil erosion, if unchecked, can put an end to the possibility of any civilization whatsoever.

The catalogue of man's crimes against his environment is long and dismal. In Africa the Sahara is advancing; the habitable mountains and tablelands of the Equator are rapidly eroding; the Southern plains are overgrazed dust bowls. Central America is in process of becoming a desert. Much of South America is being washed down unterraced mountain slopes into the sea. With every drought vast areas of Australia and the United States turn into wind-blown dust. In Asia it is the same lamentable story. As population goes up, the fertility of the ever more ruthlessly exploited land goes down. There is spreading and deepening human poverty in the midst of spreading and deepening natural poverty.

In certain respects the European picture is decidedly brighter. Thanks to sound agricultural practices and a climate that is without extremes, the farmers of Western Europe can produce good crops, and go on producing them, without, in the process, ruining their land. But however good these crops may be, they are insufficient to provide the present population of the territory with its minimum food requirements. In relation to the local resources, Western Europe is overpopulated. In England, Belgium, Holland, Italy and the Western zones of Germany, there is less than one acre of food-producing land for each inhabitant. And even where the density of population is lower than in these countries, the productive land available is still insufficient to provide a full diet (to say nothing of the necessary timber and fibers) for the local inhabitants. According to some competent authorities, even Russia is overpopulated. The short northern summer severely limits the size of the crops, and the long northern winter severely limits the number of animals that can be kept alive on stored-up fodder. And over the greater part of the country precipitation is low and irregular. In these circumstances even a low population density may be excessive. And the birth-rate is high, modern hygiene and medicine are prolonging the expectation of life, numbers are rapidly increasing. But meanwhile new methods of arctic agriculture have been devised; ambitious schemes of irrigating Central Asia are under study; and, having abolished the laws of "reactionary genetics," Lysenko promises a revolution in plant breeding. Will the tundras, the deserts and ideologically correct science be able to feed and clothe the 250 millions who will inhabit the U.S.S.R. in 1970? Let us hope so; for the alternative is a crusade for more *Lebensraum*.

Since 1800 Western Europe has more than trebled its population. This huge increase was made possible by elementary hygiene and the exploitation of the virgin territories of the New World. Today hygiene and medicine are keeping more Europeans alive; but the New World has a large and rapidly increasing population of its own and, after more than a century of abuse, not a little of its soil has lost or is in process of losing its fertility. In a good year there is still a very large exportable surplus. But not every season is a good season. During the lean years of the thirties, the United States had very little to sell abroad. And here we may remark that the success of the Marshall Plan and, indeed, the whole outcome of the Cold War depend, among other things, on the weather. Consider, for example, this by no means impossible contingency: for three years in succession Russia has bumper wheat crops, while the harvests of Western Europe, North America, Australia and the Argentine are ruined by drought or excessive rains. In these circumstances, who will control the world—the people with the atomic bombs, or the people with bread? Obviously, the people with bread.

Up to the present, Western Europe has contrived to pay for the food imported from the New World by selling manufactured articles and technical services. With the industrialization of the New World, these are becoming less and less acceptable. Europe will find it increasingly difficult to pay for supplies which, as the population pressure on the New World's eroded soils increases, are bound to diminish. And this will happen at a time when Asia, newly industrialized and overcrowded as never before, will be desperately competing for whatever surpluses of food the New World can still make available to the Old.

Food is a renewable commodity. If the soil is not abused, this year's harvest will be succeeded next year by another harvest no less bountiful. But the vein of tin or copper, which was the source of this year's supply of ore, will not be renewed in years to come. When the lode has been worked out, the miner must move on to another deposit of the mineral. And if he can find no other deposits? *Aprés moi le déluge*. Industrialism is the systematic exploitation of wasting assets. In all too many cases, the thing we call progress is merely an acceleration in the rate of that exploitation. Such prosperity as we have known up to the present is the consequence of rapidly spending the planet's irreplaceable capital.

How long can the accelerating dissipation of capital go on? How soon will the wasting assets of the world be exhausted? We do not know. All that is certain is that the supplies of many hitherto essential commodities are limited and that, in many places, very rich and easily available deposits of those commodities have been, or are in process of being, worked out. And this is happening at a time when a rising population with steadily improving methods of production is calling for ever-increasing quantities of consumer goods—in other words, is making ever heavier demands on the limited reserves of our planetary capital.

Up to this point, I have dealt with world population as a single undifferentiated whole. The problem thus posed is that of increasing pressure upon diminishing resources. But this basic problem of our time is deepened and complicated by the fact that rates of increase are not uniform throughout the world's population. Differential birthrates as between the various peoples of the earth, and as between classes within a people, are rapidly engendering a host of new problems.

In Western Europe and North America, the over-all birth-rate has sharply declined in the course of the last fifty or sixty years. Because of the lowered death-rate and the relatively large numbers of persons within the reproductive age groups, this decline in the birth-rate has not yet manifested itself in a net decline of population. But the onset of such a decline is close at hand. For example, by 1970 the population of France and Great Britain will have declined by about four millions apiece, and the number of persons over sixty-five will be approximately equal to the number of those under fifteen. Similar declines are due, at a slightly later date, in the other countries of Western Europe and in the New World (except South America). Meanwhile, in spite of much higher death-rates, the population of Eastern Europe and of Asia is destined to go on increasing. By the end of the present century, Asia alone will have a population of about two billions. And in 1970, when Western Europe will have some nine million fewer inhabitants than it possesses today, Russia will have gained upwards of fifty millions.

Within any nation whose birth-rate is declining, there is a tendency for the decline to be most rapid among the most accomplished and gifted members of the population, least rapid among those whose hereditary and educational endowment is the lowest. The higher the Intelligence Quotient and the level of education, the smaller the family, and vice versa. The future population of Western Europe and North America will be constituted, in the main, by the descendants of the least intelligent persons now living in those areas. Among the lower animals, biological degeneration, involving the heritable qualities of whole populations, is a slow and gradual process. But human beings differ from other animals in possessing self-consciousness and a measure of free will, and in being the inhabitants of a man-made universe within the greater natural order. Reacting to what goes on in this man-made universe, they use their free will to modify their basic patterns of animal behavior. And when the nature of the human universe is such as to

77

discourage the more sensitive, intelligent and prudent individuals from reproducing their kind, the deterioration of entire societies comes about with an almost explosive rapidity. Thus an eminent English authority, Sir Cyril Burt, foresees that by the end of the present century there will be, in Great Britain, half as many children of scholarship ability as there are at present, and twice as many defectives, while the average intelligence of the population as a whole will have declined by five IQ points. And the case of Britain is not unique. Throughout Western Europe and, a little later, in North America, the decline in numbers is destined to be accompanied by a rapid deterioration in the quality of the population.

We have now to consider the ways in which these untoward biological happenings have affected, or are likely in the future to affect, our behavior on the levels of domestic and international politics.

The nature of the low-level crisis is such that it must necessarily take a very long time to remove its underlying causes. The best we can do is to palliate the more dangerous symptoms and to draw up plans for a genuinely etiological treatment.

Differential birth-rates within any national community lead, as we have seen, to a qualitative deterioration of the population as a whole. The effects of such a deterioration have not yet made themselves felt, and it is hard to foresee in detail what they will be. We must be content merely to pose a question. Is it possible for democratic institutions to flourish in a community in which the incidence of outstanding ability is falling while that of mental defect is rising? Fifty years from now our grandchildren will know the answer. In the interval it will be necessary to develop new types of training designed to get the best out of worsening human material and to find means for inducing the congenitally gifted to reproduce their kind.

Where the birth-rate of an entire nation declines sharply, while that of its neighbors remains high, we must expect, in the world as it is now constituted, a more or less serious threat to peace. Regardless of what faith may currently be professed, the real and effective religion of twentieth-century man is nationalistic idolatry. Nominally we may be Christians or Buddhists or Hindus or Moslems or Jews; but in actual fact we worship, not one God, but fifty or sixty godlets each of whom is, by definition, the enemy, actual or potential, of all the rest. In every country where there is no established church, the only religion taught in the public schools is some local variant of Shintoism—a saluting of flags, a cult of the State and, very often, of the men who control its machinery, a glorification of the national prowess, as set forth in the official history books. Entities which are the accidental and transient products of history are treated as though they were divine, as though they embodied principles of eternal and universal validity. From childhood the citizen is taught that his highest duty is to work for the greater glory of the local idol. But since this glory is expressed mainly in terms of political and military power, it follows that no individual can do his nationalistic duty without inflicting harm on some at least of his fellow men. In the context of nationalistic idolatry, any shift in the balance of power constitutes a temptation to wage war, aggressive on the part of those nations which are becoming stronger, defensive or preventive on the part of those whose situation is changing for the worse. Such a shift will take place wherever the birth-rates of two equally industrialized nations change in such a way that one has an increasing and predominantly youthful population, while the other has a population that is growing smaller, older and perhaps also less intelligent.

Populations increase and decrease relatively, not only to one another, but also to natural resources. In most parts of the world, as we have seen, the relation between population and resources is already unfavorable and will probably become even more unfavorable in the future. This growing poverty in the midst of growing poverty constitutes a permanent menace to peace. And not only to peace, but also to democratic institutions and personal liberty. For overpopulation is not compatible with freedom. An unfavorable relationship between numbers and resources tends to make the earning of a living almost intolerably difficult. Labor is more abundant than goods, and the individual is compelled to work long hours for little pay. No surplus of accumulated purchasing power stands between him and the tyrannies of unfriendly Nature or of the equally unfriendly wielders of political and economic power. Democracy is, among other things, the ability to say No to the boss. But a man cannot say No to the boss unless he is sure of being able to eat when the boss's favor has been withdrawn. And he cannot be certain of his next meal unless he owns the means of producing enough wealth for his family to live on, or has been able to accumulate a surplus out of past wages, or has a chance of moving away to virgin territories, where he can make a fresh start. In an overcrowded country, very few people own enough to make them financially independent; very few are in a position to accumulate purchasing power; and there is no free land. Moreover, in any country where population presses hard upon natural resources, the general economic situation is apt to be so

79

precarious that government control of capital and labor, production and consumption, becomes inevitable. It is no accident that the twentieth century should be the century of highly centralized governments and totalitarian dictatorships; it had to be so for the simple reason that the twentieth century is the century of planetary overcrowding. It is childish to imagine that we can "plant democratic institutions" in India, or China, or "teach the Germans to take their place among the democratic nations of the world." So long as the relationship between population and natural resources remains as hopelessly unfavorable as it now is throughout Asia and in the greater part of Europe, above all in defeated Germany, it will be for all practical purposes impossible for democratic institutions to take root and develop. Wherever Malthus' nightmare has come true, political institutions tend inevitably toward totalitarianism. In Western Europe, where the tradition of democracy is still strong, the new totalitarianism will be for some time benevolent and humane. It remains to be seen how long it will be before their almost absolute power corrupts the politicians who wield it.

In the political field, the greatest enemy to liberty is war. That is why, from time immemorial, all tyrants have been so fond of war or at least of the preparation for war. Universal military conscription puts every individual at the mercy of the central government. An aggressive foreign policy evokes reactions in kind, and these reactions are then used as an excuse for more militarism and a further curtailment of civil and personal liberties. Dictators can always consolidate their tyranny by an appeal to patriotism. Meanwhile, the danger of war is made a pretext for a policy, not of reducing, but actually of increasing the birth-rate— a policy which was vigorously pursued by Hitler and Mussolini and is being even more vigorously pursued today by the rulers of Soviet Russia. More babies mean more cannon fodder, more colonists for conquered territories, and also more misery, more need for centralized "planning" and more power for the political bosses, less liberty for the masses. Overcrowding and militarism are the guarantees of dictatorship.

In our days war on any considerable scale can be waged only by a highly industrialized nation. There can be no successful aggression without the copious and complicated armaments which are the modern means of aggression. Lacking these means, the people of an over-populated country are confronted with only two alternatives. They can either stop breeding, and so reduce the population. Or else, they can go on breeding until famine, disease, political unrest and civil war combine to raise the death-rate to the point where a decreased population can re-establish a favorable relationship with natural resources. But some overpopulated countries are also industrialized; and for these, there is a third alternative: to enslave or exterminate their neighbors, and so acquire more land, food, raw materials and markets.

It should be added that, though they cannot themselves wage large-scale war, industrially weak nations can provoke and assist in the waging of war by industrially powerful nations. An unfavorable relationship between numbers and resources is experienced, by the less fortunate citizens of an overpopulated nation, as chronic hunger, low wages, long hours, lack of freedom and opportunity. The resulting discontent is apt to be expressed in political unrest and revolt against constituted authority. At the present time all political unrest, whatever its cause, tends to be rationalized in terms of Communist theory and organized in terms of Communist power politics. But at this moment of history Communism is, among other things, the instrument of Russian nationalism, and Russia is an industrialized country, capable of waging large-scale war and committed in advance to a permanent crusade against the West.

Let us consider a concrete example. Throughout Asia a misery, whose basic cause is the unfavorable relation between numbers and resources, finds its expression in political unrest. Canalized by professional Communists, this unrest may be expected to result in the setting up of governments which will do everything in their power to aid Russia and to thwart the plans of the Western powers. Merely by withholding essential raw materials, a Communist Asia could delay or even completely prevent European recovery. The West would then find itself confronted by the alternatives of surrender or preventive war. Thus we see that the overpopulation even of industrially feeble nations may constitute a grave threat to world peace.

In the world as we know it nation A will collaborate wholeheartedly with nation B only when both are menaced by C. During a war that is being waged to preserve their national sovereignty, a group of allies will consent to sacrifice a part of that sovereignty for the sake of victory. But as soon as victory has been achieved, the allied nations return to their normal conditions of more or less hostile symbiosis, ready, however, to collaborate again, either with the same or with some other partners, against the same or another enemy.

On the international level, union here is always the product of disunion somewhere else; there is no unrestricted mutual aid except against a third party. Hence the old despairing jest to the effect that

81

those who desire peace on earth should pray for an invasion from Mars. But, fortunately in one respect, unfortunately in another, we do not have to wait for an attack across interplanetary space. Man is his own Martian, at war against himself. Overbreeding and extractive agriculture are his weapons and, though he may not know it, his war aims are the ravaging of his planet, the destruction of his civilization and the degradation of his species.

That the nations have not yet united against this common enemy within their own ranks is due partly to the distracting influence of nationalistic idolatry, partly to ignorance and partly to men's habit of thinking about the problem in wholly inappropriate terms. Time, energy and money that could be better spent are everywhere devoted to power politics and preparations for war. And meanwhile, throughout the more fortunate regions of the earth, most persons are still unaware of the fact that the general condition of mankind is one of poverty in the midst of growing poverty; and in the less fortunate regions, where the harsh facts are inescapable, there is a tendency to believe that the remedy for such poverty is a violent and radical change of government. The inhabitants of countries in which there is an unfavorable relationship between numbers and resources can easily be persuaded that the causes of their misery are political and that, as soon as their present rulers are replaced by others, trained in Moscow, all will be well. But one-party government is no cure for overpopulation, and the collectivization of agriculture will not increase the area of productive land.

It has been fashionable for a long time past to maintain that the reformer's primary concern is with questions of ownership and distribution. And, in effect, distribution is often inefficient and unfair, and there can be no moral or utilitarian justification for that outright and irresponsible ownership of land which permits a man to withhold or destroy at his pleasure the natural resources upon which the life of a whole society depends.

We need a new system of money that will deliver us from servitude to the banks and permit people to buy what they are able to produce; and we need a new system of ownership that will check the tendency toward monopoly in land and make it impossible for individuals to lay waste to planetary resources which belong to all mankind. But changes in social and economic organization are not enough, of themselves, to solve our problem. Production is inadequate to present population, and population, over large areas, is rapidly rising. A change in the laws governing the ownership of land will not change its quantity or quality. The equitable distribution of too little may satisfy men's desire for justice; it will not stay their hunger. In a world where population is growing at the rate of about 56,000 a day, and where erosion is daily ruining an equal or perhaps greater number of productive acres, our primary concern must be with reducing numbers and producing more food with less damage to the soil.

Sooner or later mankind will be forced by the pressure of circumstances to take concerted action against its own destructive and suicidal tendencies. The longer such action is postponed, the worse it will be for all concerned. To delay is to risk the spread and intensification of misery, to invite revolution, war and tyranny. But if we start at once to resolve the low-level crisis, there is at least a chance that we may escape the most disastrous consequences of nationalistic idolatry and power politics.

The history of the League of Nations and of the United Nations Organization proves conclusively that, on the basis of nationalistic idolatry and power politics, there cannot possibly be co-operation between all the world's sovereign states; there can only be co-operation of one group against another group. Overpopulation and erosion constitute a Martian invasion of the planet. Against this invasion the alliance can be world-wide and the fight can be waged without war. This is the first reason why the low-level crisis should take its place at the top of the agenda of every international conference.

Here is another reason. There is nobody who does not wish to have enough to eat. In the face of this universal agreement any government which, for merely political or ideological reasons, refuses to join the crusade against the Martian in our midst is likely to become exceedingly unpopular.

A third good reason is to be found in the fact that this crusade is mainly a technological affair. Differences of opinion over technological problems rarely result in bloodshed; differences of opinion over political and ideological problems have been the cause of uncounted murders, feuds, wars and revolutions. Here violence is in direct proportion to ignorance. About technological problems we either know enough already, or if we do not, we know how to set about acquiring the necessary knowledge. But where politics and ideologies are concerned the case is very different. For example, nobody knows enough to be able to decide whether a certain theory of history is true or false or meaningless. And nobody knows enough to be able to say which among all the possible alternatives is the form of government best suited to human societies. In regard to the theory of history it seems very unlikely that the necessary knowledge will ever be accumulated. And in regard to any given form of government, knowledge can come only with the passage of time. Future events in the material universe can, to some extent, be foreseen; but our ability to predict psychological events is practically nonexistent. How will our children and grandchildren react to forms of organizations which, to ourselves, seem the last word in beneficent efficiency? Will they like what we like, or will they detest it? Will an arrangement which works well enough for us work equally well for them? We do not and we cannot know. That is why we must never take the practical application of a principle as seriously as the principle which is being applied. Thus, we may take very seriously the principle that the State exists in order to make possible the development of individuals as free and responsible persons. But we must not take too seriously any particular plan for applying that principle in political and economic practice. The mere passage of time may demonstrate the unsoundness of any particular application of first principles. To treat political expedients as though they were sacred and inviolable is to commit an idolatry that can only result in totalitarian coercion. Thus, in our ignorance, we do not know whether the Webbs were right in advocating centralized planning as the best means to the desired end, or whether Belloc was right in warning us against the evils of the Servile State. Time alone will show; and when it begins to show, we must be ready, in the name of our principles, to modify the policy which, in our ignorance, we once regarded as the most effective application of those principles. Unfortunately there are very many persons to whom the admission of ignorance is intolerable. Laying claim to certainty in spheres where certainty is impossible, to infallibility concerning matters where even a Pope admits that he can err, they rationalize faith, passion and self-interest into a simulacrum of knowledge. Hence the wars, the revolutions, the tyrannies, the wholesale enslavement of political heretics. A pseudo knowledge compounded of faith, passion and self-interest cannot convince doubters, or the exponents of another system of pseudo knowledge, except by force. Real knowledge is based upon observation and experiment; and those who possess such knowledge are always able to appeal to facts and the tested rules of scientific procedure. In the technological sphere there can be unforced agreement and persuasion without resort to threats or open violence. We should therefore give approval to any international project which may distract the attention of the world's rulers from the insoluble and war-provoking problems of power politics in order to focus it upon problems which, being technological, admit of some solution and do not necessarily commit all those concerned to fratricide and self-destruction. And in the case of a project which cannot be delayed except at grave risk to the entire human species, our approval should be whole-hearted and enthusiastic.

That the Russians have been "winning the peace" is due, at least in part, to the fact that they profess and teach, as absolutely true, a clear-cut philosophy of man and Nature. This philosophy permits them to predict the future and to affirm (with a confidence which, though un-justified and baseless, is nonetheless deeply impressive) that, if a certain kind of political and economic revolution is made, general well-being will inevitably follow. In the West we neither impose, nor have we voluntarily accepted, any coherent conception of the world; we lay no claims to understand History from the inside; we do not profess to know in advance what is going to happen fifty or a hundred years from now; and when we are called upon to frame world policies, we find it easier, because of our lack of a philosophy, to be *against* the Russians than to be *for* anything which the great masses of suffering humanity are likely to find either plausible or attractive. The Western refusal to assert an infallibility or to impose an orthodoxy is something of which we need not be ashamed. Less creditable, however, is the fact that we have failed to develop a generally acceptable philosophy for ourselves and for those whom we would like to draw to our side; and still more discreditable is our failure to formulate any policy sensible and beneficent enough to seem more attractive than the policies of Communism. The nearest approach to such a positive policy was the Marshall Plan. But the Marshall Plan was overlaid, by 1949, by military alliances, and military alliances seem attractive only to those imme-diately involved and (in view of the past history of military alliances) not wildly attractive even to them.

The positive, realistic and universally attractive policy of which the Western powers are so desperately in need can easily be found. It is a policy aimed at palliating the effects and removing the causes of that low-level crisis through which the entire human species is passing. If the Russians are willing to co-operate in the framing and carrying out of this policy, so much the better. If they refuse and the Cold War is to persist, this policy can be made into a powerful diplomatic and prop-agandist weapon in the hands of the democracies. Its adoption will not, of course, guarantee peace in our time; but it may perhaps decrease the probabilities of war in the immediate and, still more, in the remoter future. Let us consider in detail the lines along which our policy should be framed.

The world's economic and political crisis has its origin, at least in part, in the underlying demographical crisis. In most countries the relationship between numbers and resources is unfavorable. Nature has her own methods for re-establishing a favorable balance; but, applied to human beings living under twentieth-century conditions, such methods involve not merely intense and widespread misery, but also the gravest threat to civilization. Stated in its most general terms, the problem is to reconcile biological facts with human values.

Our first task is to create a general awareness of the danger. At every opportunity we must insist upon the fact that man is his own Martian, that the invasion of the planet is already under way and that fresh cohorts are constantly arriving to swell the ranks simultaneously of the enemy and of his victims. At the same time we have to proclaim no less insistently that the miseries resulting from this Martian invasion cannot be removed by any revolution, however radical. Overpopulation and erosion do their destructive work on a plane which is not that of politics. A concerted attempt to cope with events on the demographical and agricultural plane may indirectly exercise a salutary effect upon international politics. But an attempt to impose one kind of political system upon all the peoples of the earth will do nothing whatever to resolve the low-level crisis, but on the contrary will prevent men from doing anything about it and thereby increase the sum and intensity of preventable misery. The low-level crisis can be resolved in only two ways—by controlling world population and by increasing food production, while restoring and preserving the earth's fertility.

Man cannot live by bread alone; but still less can he live exclusively by idealism. To talk about the Rights of Man and the Four Freedoms in connection, for example, with India is merely a cruel joke. In a country where two-thirds of the people succumb to the consequences of malnutrition before they reach the age of thirty, but where, nonetheless, the population increases by fifty millions every decade, most men possess neither rights nor any kind of freedom. The "giant misery of the world" is only aggravated by mass violence and cannot be mitigated by inspirational twaddle. Misery will yield only to an intelligent attack upon the causes of misery.

It is, of course, a great deal easier to talk about a world-population policy than it is to get such a policy accepted by the various national

86

governments; and it will be easier to get the policy accepted than to get it implemented. Moreover, even if it should, by some miracle, come to be accepted and implemented immediately, the beneficent results could not, in the nature of things, be apparent for several generations. Let us elaborate a little on this depressing theme.

So long as idolatrous nationalism remains the effective religion of mankind, and so long as it is taken for granted that war is right, proper and inevitable, no government of a country with a high birth-rate will pledge itself to the reduction of that rate; and no government of a country with a low birth-rate will forego in advance the privilege of trying to increase that rate with a view to increasing the size of its armed forces.

Assuming now, for the sake of argument, that, in spite of nationalism and militarism, a world-population policy should be agreed upon, how easy would it be to get that policy implemented? The answer is that, in the countries where its immediate implementation would be most desirable, it would be exceedingly difficult, indeed almost impossible, to do so. For a variety of reasons, material and psychological, birth control cannot be practiced by persons whose standard of living falls below a level which, for the great majority of Asiatics and even of Eastern Europeans, is unattainably high. To obtain any conscious or deliberate reduction of the high birth-rates prevailing in the East would be a task requiring many years of education and technological advance.

Finally, even if a substantial cut in the present high birth-rates of the world were to be agreed upon and successfully implemented tomorrow, the number of persons in the reproductive age groups is at present so large that, despite the reduced birth-rate, over-all population would continue to increase until at least the end of the present century. In the most favorable circumstances we can reasonably imagine, world population is bound to rise to at least three billions before it starts to decline. This means that, whatever happens, the next half-century will be a time of the gravest political and economic danger. If a world-population policy should be agreed upon and implemented in the near future, this danger may be expected to grow less acute after about the year 2000. If no such policy is adopted, the crisis is likely, unless something startlingly good or something startlingly bad should happen in the interval, to persist for many years thereafter. So far as we can now judge, the human situation is likely to be more than ordinarily difficult and precarious for at least two generations, and perhaps for much longer. The sooner we can get a reasonable population policy adopted and imple-

87

mented, the shorter will be the period of special danger through which, it would seem, mankind must inevitably pass.

Here a brief parenthesis is in order. In this matter of population we are on the horns of a dilemma. For what is good for us in one way is bad in another; and what is bad in one way, in another is good. Biologically and historically speaking, the large family is more normal than the small. A woman who has borne five or six children is "nearer to Nature" than one who has artificially restricted the number to one or two. In countries where the birth-rate is sharply declining, there has been, during the last forty years, a marked increase in the incidence of neurosis and even of insanity. In part this increase is attributable to the industrialization and urbanization with which, in modern times, a falling birth-rate has always been associated; in part, to the fact that birth control has created patterns of sexual and familial life which are in some way profoundly unsatisfactory to adults and children alike. Wherever biologically normal behavior has been sacrificed to modern civilization, we tend to become maladjusted and unbalanced. But wherever biologically normal behavior patterns have not been sacrificed to modern civilization, we find ourselves growing hungrier, less free and in acuter danger of being involved in war and revolution. On which of these two horns shall we choose to be impaled? To my mind, the first is the lesser evil. Overpopulation, with its accompaniments of extractive agriculture, tyranny and mass murder, can cause irreparable disasters. Of the bad psychological consequences of birth control some perhaps may yield to appropriate medication, others may be prevented, by appropriate social arrangements, from ever arising. Departure from biologically normal behavior is always dangerous; but the dangers involved in birth control are not so great as those which arise when individuals retain their natural breeding habits in a world where hygiene, insecticides, antibiotics and false teeth have radically changed their natural dying habits. If we interfere with the forces that bring death, we must also interfere with those that bring life. Otherwise we shall have overpopulation, an unfavorable relationship between man and his environment, wholesale destruction of planetary resources, hunger, revolution, war and wholesale extermination. Given sewage systems, aureomycin and plastic dentures, contraception becomes a necessity and the adoption of a world-population policy, a matter of the most urgent importance. Unfortunately, as we have seen, a world-population policy cannot be expected to show results for many years to come. But while we are waiting for it to take effect we can set to work immediately on the task of checking erosion, preserving the fertility of the soil and increasing the production of food.

At the present time most nations are quite incapable of undertaking this task singlehanded. They live from hand to mouth; and the mouth is forever growing larger, the hand, as it desperately tries to extract more food from a limited area of exhausted soil, becomes increasingly destructive. For these nations there is no margin of time, or land, or resources. Everything, and more than everything, that their territory can produce has to be used up now. Future fertility must be sacrificed to present hunger. In a country where population presses heavily upon resources, self-preservation results in self-destruction.

If the Western powers had a positive instead of a mainly negative international policy, they would come forward with a plan to check this rake's progress toward human and planetary bankruptcy. Or rather they would come forward with several plans. First, a plan to repair the damage already done to the earth's cultivated lands; second, a plan to replace destructive methods of farming and forestry by methods more in harmony with the laws of Nature; and, third, a plan to discover and develop new sources of supply.

The cost of carrying out the first two plans would be high—though certainly no higher than the cost of preparing to win the Third World War and crush the First World Revolution. It would be high because, in order to give eroded land a chance to recover its fertility, it would be necessary for a period of years to relieve the pressure imposed upon it by an excessive population. In other words, it would be necessary to provide overcrowded countries with an amount of food equal to the difference between what they might have extracted from the soil by ruinous exploitation and what, under the plan, they are able to extract while checking erosion and preparing the shift to better agricultural methods. It would also be necessary to subsidize the migration to safer areas of those persons now living on specially vulnerable watersheds. Additional funds would have to be found for supplying experts to technologically backward countries, for training nationals of those countries in sound agriculture and the theory and practice of conservation, and for undertaking a world-wide survey of soils, climates and natural resources.

The third plan would be in the nature of a vast international project for research and experimentation. To men of science and technicians recruited from every part of the world would be assigned the task of discovering new ways, not of murdering their fellows, but of feeding

89

and clothing them. Let us consider a few of the more obvious possibilities that will have to be explored.

Large areas of the earth's surface are uninhabited because, under present conditions, they are uninhabitable. But in some of these areas the expenditure of much capital and hard work might render the land productive. At present the development of deserts, tundras and tropical forests is prohibitively costly; but as population rises and the demand for food and fibers yet further outstrips supply, what is now uneconomic may come to be a "business proposition." It will be the business of our hypothetical board of experts to decide which areas are to be developed, when the development shall take place, and at what expenditure of international funds.

It is desirable that the world's total food supply should be increased, and increased in any way whatsoever. But let us always remember that, from a political point of view, the most satisfactory kind of increase is one which does not involve a natural monopoly by specially favored nations. In the context of nationalism, a natural monopoly in food surpluses can become an instrument by means of which one nation, or group of nations, may coerce other nations, less fortunate than themselves. Ideally, the world's food supply should be increased in such a way that the increase shall not strengthen existing natural monopolies, or create new ones, but shall permit every nation to live on supplies grown on its own land or coming from sources equally available to all mankind. Under existing circumstances, international trade is as much of a curse as a blessing. It will become an unmitigated blessing only when nationalistic idolatry shall have ceased to be the effective religion of mankind.

Meanwhile we should do everything in our power to foster national, or at least regional, self-sufficiency in the prime necessities of existence. A step in this direction would be taken if we could develop means for getting more food from the sea. At the present time most of the seas in the neighborhood of densely populated areas are being overfished. More effort has to be put forth in order to obtain a diminishing harvest of fish—and this at a time when we need more food to satisfy the growing population. Can the oceans be made to yield new sources of supply? Can seaweeds be processed into fodder and manure? What about plankton? What about the enclosure and fertilizing of landlocked bays and inlets?

But some countries have no access to the sea. Even salt water is a natural monopoly. Our international board of researchers must consider yet other ways of achieving regional self-sufficiency. What about the transformation of poor land into productive fish ponds? What about the cultivation of fresh-water algae for fodder? What about the conversion of sawdust and vegetable wastes into sugar solutions for the cultivation of edible yeasts? And the bacteria with their tremendous capacity for bringing about chemical transformations—can any of these be domesticated and set to work producing food for man?

Natural monopolies in minerals are perhaps even more dangerous, politically speaking, than natural monopolies in food surpluses. When located in the territory of a strong nation with a culture orientated toward aggressive enterprise, deposits of coal, petroleum and the metals necessary to heavy industry are a standing temptation to imperialist expansion. When located in the territory of a weak nation, they are a standing invitation to aggression from abroad. Research should be systematically directed to the development of universally available surrogates for the present sources of power and industrial production—for example, wind power and sun power, in combination with an efficient storage battery, as a supplement and partial substitute for power derived from coal and petroleum; glass, plastics, light metals derived from clay and sea water as partial substitutes for the capriciously distributed minerals upon which industry at present depends. By these means we might perhaps succeed in breaking the natural monopolies which are so politically dangerous; and at the same time we should be doing something to shift our industrial civilization from its precarious basis in the exploitation of rapidly wasting assets to a more secure, a more nearly permanent foundation.

We now come to the henceforth inescapable fact of nuclear fission. For us the question is simple: How can nuclear fission help us in resolving the low-level crisis? In the immediate future its greatest contribution will probably be made in the field of genetics. By exposing seeds to the gamma rays emanating from an atomic pile, we can produce large numbers of unprecedented mutations. The overwhelming majority of these mutations will be harmful; but a few may result in varieties not merely viable, but even economically useful—varieties yielding more of this or that food element, varieties capable of maturing under climatic conditions which would be fatal to the parent strain, varieties resistant to certain diseases and parasites, and so forth.

Theoretically and ideally, nuclear fission should provide cheap power for developing territories too arid, or too cold, or too rugged, or too remote from the conventional sources of power to be worth exploiting

E

under present conditions. In practice, however, atomic power is likely to remain for some time to come a very expensive luxury. Twenty years from now it may be that the dream of almost costless power will have been realized. It will be none too soon; for twenty years from now the planet will have to support a population greater by 400 millions than its population today. And meanwhile every lunatic in a position of power, every fanatic, every idealist, every patriot will be under chronic temptation to use the new source of energy for political purposes, in a war of aggression, or prevention, or defense. To purchase advantages which, in the short and middle run, are not likely to be very great, we must run risks so enormous as to be incommensurable with a conceivable gain. One is reminded of Pascal's wager. We are betting on a strictly finite good against the far from remote possibility of an evil that, for practical purposes, may be regarded as infinite.

In a world where nationalism is axiomatic and where the differences between politico-religious ideologies are as irreconcilable as they were in the days of the Crusades, an international project for the relief of hunger and the conservation of our planetary resources seems to offer the best and perhaps the only hope for peace and international co-operation. At this point, the sponsors of world federation will object that our project cannot be carried out except by a world government. Political union, they will say, must come first; economic and technological collaboration will then follow as a matter of course. But at the present time, unfortunately, the governments of most nations do not want union. Or, to be more accurate, they want union, but do not want the means to union. For the means to political union entail immediate sacrifices which it would not be pleasant to make. For example, in a politically federated Europe many local industries, which have been fostered and protected by national tariffs, would prove to be redundant and would either have to be suppressed by government fiat or would find themselves ruined by the competition of industries more efficiently managed or more favorably situated in relation to raw materials and markets. The suppression of redundant industries would cause much hardship among owners, managers and workers alike. And this is only one of the costs of political union. Enormous advantages in the long run can be secured only by a number of rather painful sacrifices in the short run. Political union can be imposed by force, under a military dictatorship, or under the pressure of circumstances. During periods of "normalcy" the political union of sovereign, democratic states is much harder to achieve. Men and women will not vote for a policy which entails the immediate loss of their jobs and a disturbing change in their habits. As a general rule, it is only in times of crisis that people are willing to make sacrifices now for the sake of a good in the future. All the higher religions are, among other things, devices for convincing human beings that their every moment is a moment of crisis, involving matters of spiritual life and death, and that therefore it is reasonable as well as right to make certain sacrifices. On quite another level, every moment in the life of human beings on an overcrowded and eroding planet is also a moment of crisis. To explain the nature of man's Martian aggression against himself and to convince the masses of the necessity of concerted action against the invasion should not be too difficult, all the more so as the immediate sacrifices involved will not be excessive and the advantages to be expected in the long and middle run are so concrete, evident and appealing. Once established, this primarily technological alliance against the Martian forces of overpopulation and erosion can be expected to develop into a political and economic collaboration which, in its turn, may prove to be the precursor of genuine world federation under a single authority. If, in the meantime, federation can be achieved by purely political means, so much the better. It does not matter which comes first, the political chicken or the technological egg. What is important is that, in some way or other, we should get both, and get them with the least possible delay.

VI / POETRY FOR THE HISTORIAN

GEORGE MACAULAY TREVELYAN, IN HIS AUTOBIOGRAPHY OF AN HISTORIAN, describes himself as a "traditional kind of historian. . . . The best that can be said of me is that I tried to keep up to date a family tradition as to the relation of history to literature, in a period when the current was running strongly in the other direction towards history exclusively 'scientific.' " The author of more than twenty books, he is perhaps best known for his *History of England* and for his *English Social History*. "I already knew," he writes, "at the turn of the century exactly the sort of thing I wanted to do, and I spent the next forty years (barring war-time) in doing it. . . . I never had dreams of being a general, or a statesman or an engine-driver, like other aspiring children. I wanted to be an historian. I never remember desiring to be anything else."

Son of Sir George Otto Trevelyan, the nephew and biographer of Macaulay and author of a four-volume history of the American Revolution, Trevelyan, who was born in 1876, came of a family where tradition was apparent. His childhood was passed in Shakespeare's Warwickshire, "a goodly heritage for a boy who soon came to think that poetry, history and solitary walking across country were the three best things in life." Later, on travels and walks with his father, "there was no one like him to make history vivid to boys."

The youngest "history specialist" at Harrow, where he studied under the same Robert Somervell who Sir Winston Churchill has said taught him the mastery of English, Trevelyan went up to Cambridge at seventeen, where his father had gone before him. He lectured and taught later at Cambridge but left to devote more time to his writing. In 1928 he was made regius professor of modern history at Cambridge, a Crown appointment, and near the age limit of sixty-five and retirement, he was made Master of Trinity. For many years he was active in the National Trust, which aims to protect an area of some two hundred thousand acres in its natural state against the inroads of English "destruction and progress."

"The English poets have supplied me throughout my life with the

94

sacred books of my eclectic philosophy and religion. Love of poetry has affected the character, and in places the style of my historical writings, and in part dictated my choice of subjects—for instance Garibaldi attracted me because his life seemed to me the most poetical of all true stories, and I tried to preserve a little of this quality in telling the tale in prose. . . . More generally, I take delight in history, even its most prosaic details, because they become poetical as they recede into the past."

Stray Thoughts on History

BY G. M. TREVELYAN

History is read by different people for various reasons; it has many uses and values. To me, its chief but not its only value is poetic. Its poetic value depends on its being a true record of actual happenings in the past. For the mystery of time past continually enthralls me. Here, long before us, dwelt folk as real as we are today, now utterly vanished, as we in our turn shall vanish. History can miraculously restore them to our vision and understanding, can tell us a little of what were their hopes and fears, their words and works. The curtain of cloud that hides the scenes of the past is broken here and there, and we have magic glimpses into that lost world, which is as actual as our own, though placed on another step of the moving staircase of time. Forward we cannot see at all; backward we can see fitfully and in part. In that strange relation of past and present, poetry is always inherent, even in the most prosaic details, in Greek potsherds and Roman stones, in Manor rolls and Parliamentary reports, all hallowed in our imagination by the mere passage of the years.

And apart from this consecration by time which envelops all the past, so many of the things which history reveals belong by their own nature to the stuff of poetry, the passions and aspirations of men and even of nations, their dramatic failures and successes, the action of chance the disposer, the wonderful creativeness of man, the brief life of his best creations and hopes and systems, above all his indomitable spirit, always beaten down and rising again in some new, utterly unpredictable form. As a great poem, as an epic without beginning or end, I read history and never tire.

But I can find in it no "philosophy of history." Philosophy must be brought to history, it cannot be extracted from it. And I have no philosophy of my own to bring, beyond a love of things good and a hatred of things evil.

On the last page of his *Philosophy of History* Hegel thus sums up: "The History of the World is nothing but the development of the idea of Freedom," of which he finds the best or at least the latest expression in the Protestant Monarchical States of Germany about 1830. Whatever the freedom of the individual was worth in the Germany of that period —and it was worth a good deal, I think—where is it now?[1] Clearly it was not the one far-off divine event to which the whole Creation moved!

Acton contemplated writing a history of Freedom growing up through the balance of opposing forces. That idea might indeed have been made to cover much of the political and religious history of Europe from the sixteenth to the nineteenth centuries, but it would not have covered all the aspects of that period, for politics and religion are not everything; and it would not have gone far to explain the story of the century in which we live.

A larger lead is given by our own contemporary, Mr. Toynbee. With a scope of historial knowledge deeper than Hegel's and wider than Acton's, he treats the history of man as a series of episodes, of outbursts of activity first in one region then in another, and tries to detect the causes of such outbursts, the circumstances conducive to great movements of human energy and achievement. "Challenges and responses," he writes (I, p. 329), "is the factor that counts above all others."

Mr. Toynbee's *Study of History* is indeed very suggestive, but it does not pretend to be a complete explanation of the past. For "challenges" are so often made that meet no "response"; circumstances so often make a call on a portion of mankind and the call is not answered. Sometimes indeed it is answered, and then as often as not in some utterly unexpected and novel manner. The life of a great man has often diverted the course of history. How are you to make a "philosophy of history" out of such a casual affair? The rise of Christianity was either the result of the special intervention of God, or else of a series of chances. In either case it was not the consequence of a law of human affairs to be explained by "your philosophy." It is easy to show how the ground

[1] 1948.

was prepared for a world-wide religion, by the Roman Empire, the Roman roads, the Stoic philosophy and so forth. Such was the field, but whence the seed? The particular world-wide religion that actually came was the outcome of the lives of Jesus Christ and Paul of Tarsus. Their advent was not "inevitable"—unless indeed it was miraculously provided. History can record the facts, but neither philosophy nor science can tell us why they occurred, nor why Caesar, Mohammed and Shakespeare were born in their appropriate times.

"History repeats itself" and "History never repeats itself" are about equally true. The question, in any given case, is which part of history is going to repeat itself. We never know enough about the infinitely complex circumstances of any past event to prophesy the future by analogy. The best informed and perhaps the wisest of our statesmen in 1792 was William Pitt. In reducing the armed forces of the Crown that February he argued that it would be safe to do so because of the state to which France had been brought by her Revolutionary troubles. "Unquestionably," he told the House of Commons, "there never was a time in the history of this country, when from the situation of Europe, we might more reasonably expect fifteen years of peace than at the present moment."

That was one of the world's worst prophecies. Yet Pitt was no fool. I presume that his error arose from too confident a use of historical analogy. The fighting power of nations had often been weakened by internal faction. England, as Pitt knew, had been of little importance in Europe during the fierce political struggles of the reigns of Charles I and II. But then there had been the spisode of Cromwell which Pitt's calculation overlooked. No one ever knows which part of the past is going to "repeat itself." It is not even true that a violent political and social revolution is always followed by a military despotism: George Washington was not a military despot.

What opportunities, what stimulants, what liberties for the development of a man's faculties and for his enjoyment of life, were available to folk in the various regions and epochs of the past? My curiosity on such points draws me to what is called social history. The question is not completely answered by political history, by recording the presence or absence of civil and religious freedom. It is true that in a totalitarian state there can be little chance for the development of a man's best individual self. But if we contrast, let us say, medieval England with

97

present-day England, it is not easy to decide which gave most freedom and stimulus to the development of a man's power to be himself, to exert his talents, to enjoy and enlarge his life. In the Middle Ages there was a great deal of civil liberty of a local and privileged kind for some individuals and corporations; but there was, legally at least, no religious liberty at all. People whose best thoughts and instincts led them to be heretics, were liable to be crushed by power; and the serf bound to the manor had to accept the village life to which he was born.

And yet, I suspect there were then certain kinds of opportunity and freedom that have diminished in our modern city life. I mean the liberties and opportunities that result from isolation. Absence of means of communication did more for human freedom than Magna Carta. The badness of the roads, the want of mechanical transport, diminished the tyrant's power; restricted the range of bureaucracy; exalted local differences into the main rule of life; limited even the supposedly ubiquitous powers of the Church; left every man free to look about him at the world God made, and say what he himself thought and felt, without first looking in the daily paper to find out what they were thinking and feeling in London. The shepherd watching his flocks on the Downs, alone by himself all day, may or may not have been a serf, but he enjoyed a particular kind of spiritual freedom unknown to the trade union workman, the bank clerk or the civil servant of today. Which was the freer on the whole, is a difficult question. The knight in the manor house, the baron in his castle, though restrained by royal laws and local customs, was so much the cock of his own walk that his individual idiosyncrasy in speech and character developed freely whether for good or for bad. "The world is too much with us," complained Wordsworth, and it is a vast deal more with us in our day than it was in his. But in the Dark and Middle Ages "the world" was much less "with" people, for the simple reason that a very thin population was widely scattered over a land of woods and marshes only half redeemed from nature. Men living amid such surroundings were not all of a pattern.

These conditions still held good to a large extent in Tudor and Stuart times. The liberty due to isolation was gradually diminishing but was not lost until the Industrial Revolution. The intellectual stimulus of the Reformation and its controversies, the new learning, the new sense of nationhood, the discovery of the world beyond the ocean, impinging on a people still bred in more or less of rural isolation, gave us the age of Shakespeare. The Forest of Arden lay at his door in boyhood and youth; it was cut down to feed the furnaces in Stuart times. That freedom of the forest was one sort of freedom, well known to the English of old, the freedom of Robin Hood and Maid Marian, of the Nutbrown Maid, of Rosalind and the man who made her.

Chaucer and Shakespeare both give an impression of their English contemporaries, as rough but for the most part good-natured men and women, each markedly individual, inconsequent in their moral judgments, with a great zest for life, not looking far ahead nor expecting much from the future, using their tongues with amazing force and freedom, molding that wonderful new instrument, the English language, to express the humor and passion of each passing hour.

Only such occasional gleams of light reveal to us the texture of the minds of ordinary folk in England from the twelfth to the sixteenth century. But there is one unpremeditated achievement of theirs which tells us much about them; I mean the creation of the English language, their living monument. In the twelfth century, different parts of the community spoke Anglo-Saxon, French and Latin respectively. Gradually, in the wear and tear of social intercourse, a new language was roughed out by the shaping and welding together of these three elements, until in Chaucer's time it was already said:

> Learned and lewid, old and young
> All understanden English tongue.

But if the new language had been made by the time of Chaucer, it was not perfected till the time of Shakespeare. The people who could fashion such a vehicle for their common, daily thoughts in castle and cottage, in field and market, must have possessed wit, humor and imagination, more I think than their descendants, whose minds, molded by science, newspapers and films, have different merits and different defects. No people since the ancient Greeks had evolved so rich a vocabulary and phraseology as that which we find in Chaucer, the English Bible and Shakespeare.

Even in small things the words they coined indicate the quality of their minds. The obscure country folks who, in forgotten centuries, found the names for our birds and wild flowers,—buttercup, day's eye and marigold, ousel and thrush, robin redbreast, tom-tit, and a hundred more—had minds simpler and in some ways sweeter than ours. In other ways indeed they were more coarse and more cruel than their descendants. Being a race of craftsmen, not mass producers, their average artistic sense was greatly superior to ours; as their architecture and masonry, and all their "utility" articles of common use incontestably prove.

But to think thus of our ancestors is not to regard the medieval period as an age of gold. War, pestilence and famine were perpetually destroying human happiness. Greed, cruelty and hypocrisy characterized the holders of power, ecclesiastical, monarchical and feudal. In certain respects the eighteenth and nineteenth centuries had a right to look back with pity and contempt on the Middle Ages, but the twentieth century with its world wars and totalitarian governments has lost even that right.

All through the Middle Ages and long afterward, the fact of local isolation, due to badness of communications, protected many things individual and excellent, permitted to survive not on principle but by neglect. Moreover, on the positive side, medieval folk had one supreme merit; they rejoiced to create privileged autonomous societies to perform special functions: beginning with clerical corporations, they went on to craft-guilds, and self-governing cities; Parliaments and Inns of Court; universities and grammar schools; all of these proved invaluable "pockets" for the development of civilization, for they could perform their special functions freely in their own way.[2] And so the Middle Ages prepared the Renaissance and the Reformation, the Tudor, Stuart and Hanoverian epochs, because in medieval times there had been so many "pockets" guarded, either by privilege or by neglect, from the surrounding tyranny and barbarism.

In a totalitarian State all "pockets" are eliminated. In present-day England our still surviving love of political liberty protects "pockets" to a certain extent, but the centralizing tendency of the age and modern means of locomotion destroy them apace. Without "pockets" any civilization soon becomes stale. Those who desire uniformity in all things lose sight of this important principle. Where there is nothing with independent life outside the State machine, civilization must lose all power of healthy growth. It is from minorities, small groups and individuals that fresh life has always come.

The mixture of good and evil in historical events is very difficult to disentangle. Later medieval England and therefore modern England were the outcome of the impact of the Norman Conquest on the Anglo-

[2] An exception that proves the rule is found in the violent suppression of the "liberties" of Oxford University by Church and State in 1382 on account of Wycliffe's influence there, with the result of sterilizing intellectual life for most of the ensuing century.

Saxons. Harold's Anglo-Saxons were in fact largely mixed with Scandinavians in the East and North, and with Britons in the West. The Norman Conquest made relatively little difference to the racial strains, but a great difference to the type of civilization. Instead of remaining a part of Norse or Scandinavian Europe, England became for some centuries a part of French and Latin Europe.

Was this change good or bad? We cannot say with certainty, because we cannot have it over again the other way and compare results. It is utterly impossible to say what power of self-development the Anglo-Saxons would have shown if they had not been first subjected to the Norman-French and then merged with their conquerors.

If William's invasion had failed as it so nearly did, could an independent England, affiliated to Scandinavia, have evolved a civilization as valuable and as powerful as that which was produced under the Plantagenet kings. My personal sympathies are with Harold, but that does not answer the question. I would not take the responsibility of asking the Fates to reverse the decision of Hastings. If Harold had beaten William, there would never have been the plays of Shakespeare, and I should never have been here to read them. It is difficult to vote for the nonexistence of oneself and everyone and everything one knows. Things might indeed have been better if Harold had won, but they might so easily have been less good in the end.

I say "in the end." For a century after the Conquest the evils of the subjection of the island to cruel foreign taskmasters must have appeared to outweigh any benefits already accruing, though no doubt the deep foundations of English power and government were being laid. But what a price to pay for future security and civilization! The French-speaking adventurers whom William had enlisted by the promise of the lands of the Anglo-Saxons, everywhere replaced the easygoing, kindly native landlords. In fact the English were treated as they themselves treated the Irish five hundred years later. The able Norman Kings exercised some restraint over the feudal hierarchy they had installed, but as late as the reign of Stephen (1135-54), these foreign devils were behaving with revolting cruelty to the inhabitants of the land. Indeed William himself had subdued the North by depopulating whole districts. And in the richest part of England, East Anglia, many Scandinavian freemen had been, by the time of the Domesday survey, reduced to the position of unfree villeinage.

Those who feel sure of the ultimate benefit of Norman-Angevin rule in developing the many-sided civilization of later medieval England may well be right. But they must all the more stand astonished at such mixture of evil with good. How can the two strands be separated? However we read it, this affair of the Norman Conquest is at once the most fascinating drama and the most bewildering enigma of all our long history[3]

What, similarly, are we to say of another event, even greater than the Norman Conquest of England, the fall of the Roman Empire in the West? Bury, who knew the facts better than any other modern historian, said once that its fall was due to a chance concatenation of circumstances, and was not inevitable. In the East the Byzantine form of the Roman Empire survived for another millennium, in a fossilized sort of way. I doubt whether such fossilization would have been possible in the livelier West of Europe. At any rate it did not occur. As Macaulay put it, "It cost Europe a thousand years of barbarism to escape the fate of China."

There is no doubt the Dark Ages meant "barbarism," though it did not last for quite a thousand years. But in the course of centuries this vigorous barbarism, helped in the early stages by the discipline and tradition of Roman Christianity, gave birth to an entirely new civilization of astonishing vigor and variety, which lasted and grew into ever new shapes from the twelfth century until our own day. No such new civilization was the child of the Eastern Empire that survived.

It is impossible not to mourn with Gibbon over the destruction of the outward form and fabric of Ancient Rome and its appendages— the hundreds of magnificent cities; the thousands of marble temples and palaces; the scores of thousands of gracious Graeco-Roman statues; the literature and philosophy; and the *Pax Romana* itself, which the world has in vain been seeking to replace ever since. But not only did the *Pax Romana* rest on a totalitarian system of politics, but the art and elegance, the towers and temples, the wealth and comfort, the leisure and luxury of it all rested on the slavery of white populations, as completely as the much inferior civilization of the Southern States of the American Union rested on the slavery of Negroes. The conquests that created the Roman Empire, not excepting Caesar's conquest of Gaul, had been a series of colossal slave raids. The basic economy of Roman society in the first centuries after Christ was a slave basis. So firmly rooted was the system that even the Christian Church did not demand the manumission but only the kindlier treatment of slaves.

[3] The dramatic aspect has been finely brought out by Miss Hope Muntz in her *Golden Warrior*, the saga of Harold and William. (Scribner, 1949.)

For my part I cannot wish such a society, for all its splendor, to have survived. Nor do I believe that the slaves would ever have got free except by the destruction of that society. At any rate that was how they did get free. The breakup of the *Pax Romana,* the invasion of Gaul and Italy by the barbarian hosts, gave the slaves the opportunity of emancipating themselves which they eagerly seized. War and anarchy opened the doors of the *ergastula.* The slave society "agonized, dissolved and sank." Upon its ruins "medieval" society was gradually formed on the feudal basis. The craftsman of the town became a freeman, the tiller of the soil a freeman or a serf—no longer at any rate a slave. And political power, formerly concentrated in the Roman Emperor, was divided between ten thousand ever-shifting local centers, between innumerable individuals and corporations, clerical and lay. Feudal anarchy and priestcraft, local war and constant change, vigor and independence, everywhere the pulse of life! Not a pleasant time for quiet folk, and no culture to be had! Yet these Dark Ages proved a fine seedbed for a future civilization, such as no totalitarian system, ancient or modern, can supply, except at the price of its own disruption.

The difficulty of forming judgments about the past is that every historical approval or condemnation (say of the French Revolution) is based on the assumption that if things had gone differently they would have been better—or worse. But this is just what we can never find out. And so, though we may each of us have his opinions, let us hold them with a modest diffidence.

The endlessly attractive game of speculating on the might-have-beens of history can never take us far with sense or safety. For if one thing had been different, everything would thenceforth have been different— and in what way we cannot tell. Out of a million, or rather out of an infinite number of possible lines that human affairs might have taken, only one materialized under the impulsion of chance. And this arbitrary choice of Fate is constantly repeating itself every moment of Time.

As serious students of history, all we can do is to watch and to investigate how in fact one thing led to another in the course actually taken. This pursuit is rendered all the more fascinating and romantic because we know how very nearly it was all completely different. Except perhaps in terms of philosophy, no event was "inevitable." But, for good or for bad, it happened so, and wears forever the inviolable sacredness of the accomplished fact. The statue has taken its shape and can never go back into the quarry.

VII / VIEWS OF A NUCLEAR PHYSICIST

J. ROBERT OPPENHEIMER, DIRECTOR OF THE INSTITUTE FOR ADVANCED Study at Princeton, New Jersey, since 1947, and between 1943 and 1945 director of the laboratory at Los Alamos in New Mexico where the first atomic bombs were perfected, believes "an indispensable, perhaps *the* indispensable, element in giving meaning to the dignity of man, and in making possible the taking of decision on the basis of honest conviction, is the openness of men's minds, and the openness of whatever media there are for communion between men, free of restraint, free of repression, and free even of that most pervasive of all restraints, that of status and hierarchy." Adviser to the Atomic Energy Commission, the White House, and the Departments of State and Defense from 1945 through 1953, he was denied security clearance in 1954.

Professor Oppenheimer was for eighteen years professor of physics at the University of California and at the California Institute of Technology. He was born in New York, New York, April 22, 1904, and took his arts degree at Harvard in 1925, later studying at Cambridge and Göttingen universities. He is married and has a son and a daughter. Author of many papers on physics, he is also author of the books, published by Simon & Schuster, *Science and the Common Understanding* and *The Open Mind,* eight recent lectures, four of which concern the relationship between "science as an intellectual activity and the wider culture of our times" and four dealing with atomic weapons and related questions of policy.

Man's probings into the mysteries of the universe within the atom have led to a "maze of findings that cannot be reduced to an orderly concept of the physical world," he told the twenty-fifth anniversary meeting of the American Institute of Physics in 1956. "But always in the past," he said, "there has been an explanation of immense sweep and simplicity and in it vast detail has been comprehended as necessary. Do we have the faith that this is inevitably true of man and nature? Do we even have the confidence that we shall have the wit to discover it? For some odd reason, the answer to both questions is Yes." The new explanation, however, he believes, must await the coming of a new Einstein, and that might not happen in this generation.

As a teacher of physicists, Dr. Oppenheimer believes "we must make more humane what we tell the young physicist and must seek ways to make more robust and more detailed what we tell the man of art or letters or affairs if we are to contribute to the integrity of our common cultural life."

"Prospects in the Arts and Sciences" was delivered as the concluding lecture at the Columbia University's Bicentennial celebration in 1955 and was broadcast by the Columbia Broadcasting System.

Prospects in the Arts and Sciences

BY J. ROBERT OPPENHEIMER

The words "prospects in the arts and sciences" mean two quite different things to me. One is prophecy: What will the scientists discover and the painters paint, what new forms will alter music, what parts of experience will newly yield to objective description? The other meaning is that of a view: What do we see when we look at the world today and compare it with the past? I am not a prophet; and I cannot very well speak to the first subject, though in many ways I should like to. I shall try to speak to the second, because there are some features of this view which seem to me so remarkable, so new and so arresting, that it may be worth turning our eyes to them; it may even help us to create and shape the future better, though we cannot foretell it.

In the arts and in the sciences, it would be good to be a prophet. It would be a delight to know the future. I had thought for a while of my own field of physics and of those nearest to it in the natural sciences. It would not be too hard to outline the questions which natural scientists today are asking themselves and trying to answer. What, we ask in physics, is matter, what is it made of, how does it behave when it is more and more violently atomized, when we try to pound out of the stuff around us the ingredients which only violence creates and makes manifest? What, the chemists ask, are those special features of nucleic acids and proteins which make life possible and give it its characteristic endurance and mutability? What subtle chemistry, what arrangements, what reactions and controls make the cells of living organisms differentiate so that they may perform functions as oddly diverse as transmitting information throughout our nervous systems or covering our heads with hair? What happens in the brain to make a record of the past, to hide it from consciousness, to make it accessible to recall? What are the physical features which make consciousness possible?

All history teaches us that these questions that we think the pressing ones will be transmuted before they are answered, that they will be replaced by others, and that the very process of discovery will shatter the concepts that we today use to describe our puzzlement.

It is true that there are some who profess to see in matters of culture, in matters precisely of the arts and sciences, a certain macrohistorical pattern, a grand system of laws which determines the course of civilization and gives a kind of inevitable quality to the unfolding of the future. They would, for instance, see the radical, formal experimentation which characterized the music of the last half-century as an inevitable consequence of the immense flowering and enrichment of natural science; they would see a necessary order in the fact that innovation in music precedes that in painting and that in turn in poetry, and point to this sequence in older cultures. They would attribute the formal experimentataion of the arts to the dissolution, in an industrial and technical society, of authority—of secular, political authority, and of the catholic authority of the church. They are thus armed to predict the future. But this, I fear, is not my dish.

If a prospect is not a prophecy, it is a view. What does the world of the arts and sciences look like? There are two ways of looking at it: One is the view of the traveler, going by horse or foot, from village to village to town, staying in each to talk with those who live there and to gather something of the quality of its life. This is the intimate view, partial, somewhat accidental, limited by the limited life and strength and curiosity of the traveler, but intimate and human, in a human compass. The other is the vast view, showing the earth with its fields and towns and valleys as they appear to a camera carried in a high-altitude rocket. In one sense this prospect will be more complete; one will see all branches of knowledge, one will see all the arts, one will see them as part of the vastness and complication of the whole of human life on earth. But one will miss a great deal; the beauty and warmth of human life will largely be gone from that prospect.

It is in this vast high-altitude survey that one sees the general surprising quantitative features that distinguish our time. This is where the listings of science and endowments and laboratories and books published show up; this is where we learn that more people are engaged in scientific research today than ever before, that the Soviet world and the free world are running neck and neck in the training of scientists, that more books are published per capita in England than in the United States, that the social sciences are pursued actively in America, Scandinavia, and England, that there are more people who hear the great music of the past, and more music composed and more paintings painted. This is where we learn that the arts and sciences are flourishing. This great map, showing the world from afar and almost as to a stranger, would show more: It would show the immense diversity of culture and life, diversity in place and tradition for the first time clearly manifest on a world-wide scale, diversity in technique and language, separating science from science and art from art, and all of one from all of the other. This great map, world-wide, culture-wide, remote, has some odd features. There are innumerable villages. Between the villages there appear to be almost no paths discernible from this high altitude. Here and there passing near a village, sometimes through its heart, there will be a superhighway, along which windy traffic moves at enormous speed. The superhighways seem to have little connection with villages, starting anywhere, ending anywhere, and sometimes appearing almost by design to disrupt the quiet of the village. This view gives us no sense of order or of unity. To find these we must visit the villages, the quiet, busy places, the laboratories and studies and studios. We must see the paths that are barely discernible; we must understand the superhighways and their dangers.

In the natural sciences these are and have been and are likely to continue to be heroic days. Discovery follows discovery, each both raising and answering questions, each ending a long search, and each providing the new instruments for a new search. There are radical ways of thinking unfamiliar to common sense and connected with it by decades or centuries of increasingly specialized and unfamiliar experience. There are lessons of how limited, for all its variety, the common experience of man has been with regard to natural phenomena, and hints and analogies as to how limited may be his experience with man. Every new finding is a part of the instrument kit of the sciences for further investigation and for penetrating into new fields. Discoveries of knowledge fructify technology and the practical arts, and these in turn pay back refined techniques, new possibilities of observation and experiment.

In any science there is harmony between practitioners. A man may work as an individual, learning of what his colleagues do through reading or conversation; he may be working as a number of a group on problems whose technical equipment is too massive for individual effort. But whether he is a part of a team or solitary in his own study, he, as a professional, is a member of a community. His colleagues in his own branch of science will be grateful to him for the inventive or creative thoughts he has, will welcome his criticism. His world and work will be objectively communicable; and he will be quite sure that if there is error in it, that error will not long be undetected. In his own line of work he lives in a community where common understanding combines with common purpose and interest to bind men together both in freedom and in co-operation.

This experience will make him acutely aware of how limited, how inadequate, how precious is this condition of his life; for in his relations with a wider society, there will be neither the sense of community nor of objective understanding. He will sometimes find, in returning to practical undertakings, some sense of community with men who are not expert in his science, with other scientists whose work is remote from his, and with men of action and men of art. The frontiers of science are separated now by long years of study, by specialized vocabularies, arts, techniques, and knowledge from the common heritage even of a most civilized society; and anyone working at the frontier of such science is in that sense a very long way from home, a long way too from the practical arts that were its matrix and origin, as indeed they were of what we today call art.

The specialization of science is an inevitable accompaniment of progress; yet it is full of dangers, and it is cruelly wasteful, since so much that is beautiful and enlightening is cut off from most of the world. Thus it is proper to the role of the scientist that he not merely find new truth and communicate it to his fellows, but that he teach, that he try to bring the most honest and intelligible account of new knowledge to all who will try to learn. This is one reason—it is the decisive organic reason—why scientists belong in universities. It is one reason why the patronage of science by and through universities is its most proper form; for it is here, in teaching, in the association of scholars and in the friendships of teachers and taught, of men who by profession must themselves be both teachers and taught, that the narrowness of scientific life can best be moderated, and that the analogies, insights, and harmonies of scientific discovery can find their way into the wider life of man.

In the situation of the artist today there are both analogies to and differences from that of the scientist; but it is the differences which are the most striking and which raise the problems that touch most on the evil of our day. For the artist it is not enough that he communicate with others who are expert in his own art. Their fellowship, their understanding, and their appreciation may encourage him; but that is not the end of his work, nor its nature. The artist depends on a common sensibility and culture, on a common meaning of symbols, on a community of experience and common ways of describing and interpreting it. He need not write for everyone or paint or play for everyone. But his audience must be man; it must be man, and not a specialized set of experts among his fellows. Today that is very difficult. Often the artist has an aching sense of great loneliness, for the community to which he addresses himself is largely not there; the traditions and the culture, the symbols and the history, the myths and the common experience, which it is his function to illuminate, to harmonize, and to portray, have been dissolved in a changing world.

There is, it is true, an artificial audience maintained to moderate between the artist and the world for which he works: the audience of the professional critics, popularizers, and advertisers of art. But though, as does the popularizer and promoter of science, the critic fulfills a necessary present function and introduces some order and some communication between the artist and the world, he cannot add to the intimacy and the directness and the depth with which the artist addresses his fellow men.

To the artist's loneliness there is a complementary great and terrible barrenness in the lives of men. They are deprived of the illumination, the light and tenderness and insight of an intelligible interpretation, in contemporary terms, of the sorrows and wonders and gaieties and follies of man's life. This may be in part offset, and is, by the great growth of technical means for making the art of the past available. But these provide a record of past intimacies between art and life; even when they are applied to the writing and painting and composing of the day, they do not bridge the gulf between a society, too vast and too disordered, and the artist trying to give meaning and beauty to its parts.

In an important sense this world of ours is a new world, in which the unity of knowledge, the nature of human communities, the order of society, the order of ideas, the very notions of society and culture have changed and will not return to what they have been in the past. What is new is new not because it has never been there before, but because it has changed in quality. One thing that is new is the prevalence of newness, the changing scale and scope of change itself, so that the world alters as we walk in it, so that the years of man's life measure not some small growth or rearrangement or moderation of what he learned in childhood, but a great upheaval. What is new is that in one generation our knowledge of the natural world engulfs, upsets, and complements all knowledge of the natural world before. The techniques, among which and by which we live, multiply and ramify, so that the whole world is bound together by communication, blocked here and there by the immense synapses of political tyranny. The global quality of the world is new: our knowledge of and sympathy with remote and diverse peoples, our involvement with them in practical terms, and our commitment to them in terms of brotherhood. What is new in the world is the massive character of the dissolution and corruption of authority, in belief, in ritual, and in temporal order. Yet this is the world that we have come to live in. The very difficulties which it presents derive from growth in understanding, in skill, in power. To assail the changes that have unmoored us from the past is futile, and in a deep sense, I think, it is wicked. We need to recognize the change and learn what resources we have.

Again I will turn to the schools and, as their end and as their center, the universities. For the problem of the scientist is in this respect not different from that of the artist or of the historian. He needs to be a part of the community, and the community can only with loss and peril be without him. Thus it is with a sense of interest and hope that we see a growing recognition that the creative artist is a proper charge on the university, and the university a proper home for him; that a composer or a poet or a playwright or painter needs the toleration, understanding, the rather local and parochial patronage that a university can give; and that this will protect him from the tyranny of man's communication and professional promotion. For here there is an honest chance that what the artist has of insight and of beauty will take root in the community, and that some intimacy and some human bonds can mark his relations with his patrons. For a university rightly and inherently is a place where the individual man can form new syntheses, where the accidents of friendship and association can open a man's eyes to a part of science or art which he had not known before, where parts of human life, remote and perhaps superficially incompatible, can find in men their harmony and their synthesis.

These, then, in rough and far too general words, are some of the things we see as we walk through the villages of the arts and of the sciences and notice how thin are the paths that lead from one to another, and how little in terms of human understanding and pleasure the work of the villages comes to be shared outside.

The superhighways do not help. They are the mass media—from the loudspeakers in the deserts of Asia Minor and the cities of Communist China to the organized professional theater of Broadway. They are the purveyors of art and science and culture for the millions upon millions—the promoters who represent the arts and sciences to humanity and who represent humanity to the arts and sciences; they are the means by which we are reminded of the famine in remote places or of war or trouble or change; they are the means by which this great earth and its peoples have become one to one another, the means by which the news of discovery or honor and the stories and songs of today travel and resound throughout the world. But they are also the means by which the true human community, the man knowing man, the neighbor understanding neighbor, the schoolboy learning a poem, the women dancing, the individual curiosity, the individual sense of beauty are being blown dry and issueless, the means by which the passivity of the disengaged spectator presents to the man of art and science the bleak face of unhumanity.

For the truth is that this is indeed, inevitably and increasingly, an open and, inevitably and increasingly, an eclectic world. We know too much for one man to know much, we live too variously to live as one. Our histories and traditions—the very means of interpreting life—are both bonds and barriers among us. Our knowledge separates as well as it unites; our orders disintegrate as well as bind; our art brings us together and sets us apart. The artist's loneliness, the scholar despairing because no one will any longer trouble to learn what he can teach, the narrowness of the scientist—these are unnatural insignia in this great time of change.

For what is asked of us is not easy. The openness of this world derives its character from the irreversibility of learning; what is once learned is part of human life. We cannot close our minds to discovery; we cannot stop our ears so that the voices of far-off and strange people can no longer reach them. The great cultures of the East cannot be

III

walled off from ours by impassable seas and defects of understanding based on ignorance and unfamiliarity. Neither our integrity as men of learning nor our humanity allows that. In this open world, what is there, any man may try to learn.

This is no new problem. There has always been more to know than one man could know; there have always been modes of feeling that could not move the same heart; there have always been deeply held beliefs that could not be composed into a synthetic union. Yet never before today have the diversity, the complexity, the richness so clearly defied hierarchical order and simplification; never before have we had to understand the complementary, mutually not compatible ways of life and recognize choice between them as the only course of freedom. Never before today has the integrity of the intimate, the detailed, the true art, the integrity of craftsmanship and the preservation of the familiar, of the humorous and the beautiful stood in more massive contrast to the vastness of life, the greatness of the globe, the otherness of people, the otherness of ways, and the all-encompassing dark.

This is a world in which each of us, knowing his limitations, knowing the evils of superficiality and the terrors of fatigue, will have to cling to what is close to him, to what he knows, to what he can do, to his friends and his tradition and his love, lest he be dissolved in a universal confusion and know nothing and love nothing. It is at the same time a world in which none of us can find hieratic prescription or general sanction for any ignorance, any insensitivity, any indifference. When a friend tells us of a new discovery we may not understand, we may not be able to listen without jeopardizing the work that is ours and closer to us; but we cannot find in a book or canon—and we should not seek—grounds for hallowing our ignorance. If a man tells us that he sees differently than we, or that he finds beautiful what we find ugly, we may have to leave the room, from fatigue or trouble; but that is our weakness and our default. If we must live with a perpetual sense that the world and the men in it are greater than we and too much for us, let it be the measure of our virtue that we know this and seek no comfort. Above all, let us not proclaim that the limits of our powers correspond to some special wisdom in our choice of life, of learning, or of beauty.

This balance, this perpetual, precarious, impossible balance between the infinitely open and the intimate, this time—our twentieth century— has been long in coming; but it has come. It is, I think, for us and our children, our only way.

This is for all men. For the artist and for the scientist there is a special problem and a special hope, for in their extraordinarily different ways, in their lives that have increasingly divergent character, there is still a sensed bond, a sensed analogy. Both the man of science and the man of art live always at the edge of mystery, surrounded by it; both always, as the measure of their creation, have had to do with the harmonization of what is new with what is familiar, with the balance between novelty and synthesis, with the struggle to make partial order in total chaos. They can, in their work and in their lives, help themselves, help one another, and help all men. They can make the paths that connect the villages of arts and sciences with each other and with the world at large the multiple, varied, precious bonds of a true and world-wide community.

This cannot be an easy life. We shall have a rugged time of it to keep our minds open and to keep them deep, to keep our sense of beauty and our ability to make it, and our occasional ability to see it in places remote and strange and unfamiliar; we shall have a rugged time of it, all of us, in keeping these gardens in our villages, in keeping open the manifold, intricate, casual paths, to keep these flourishing in a great, open, windy world; but this, as I see it, is the condition of man; and in this condition we can help, because we can love, one another.

VIII / A PHILOSOPHER
AMONG SOULS

"THE PSYCHE IS THE WORLD'S PIVOT: NOT ONLY IS IT THE ONE GREAT condition for the existence of a world at all, it is also an intervention in the existing natural order, and no one can say with certainty where this intervention will finally end . . . the psyche not only disturbs the natural order but, if it loses its balance, actually destroys its own creation. Therefore the careful consideration of psychic factors is of importance in restoring not merely the individual's balance, but society's as well, otherwise the destructive tendencies gain the upper hand. In the same way that the atom bomb is an unparalleled means of physical mass destruction, so the misguided development of the soul must lead to psychic mass destruction. The present situation is so sinister that one cannot suppress the suspicion that the Creator is planning another deluge that will finally exterminate the existing race of men."

This, from Dr. Jung, is placed here for him who runs while he reads. In fact, the general reader might well read the eighth section of "The Spirit of Psychology" first. For the reader who has more time (and he will need plenty) Dr. Jung's contribution follows, the longest piece in this book and one which will probably be started more times, dropped more times, and resumed more times, than any other contribution in the volume. Here for the first time in a general trade book, Carl Gustav Jung, founder of "analytical psychology" and the exponent of a theory of the "collective unconscious," has presented his whole philosophy of the soul. It is, he says, a résumé of his "last thoughts and insights." He views the unconscious in historical perspective, treats the significance of the unconscious in psychology, goes into the dissociation or dissociability of the psyche, treats instinct and will, the unconscious as a multiple consciousness, and defines patterns of behavior and archetypes.

Dr. Jung, who lives in Switzerland, where he heads the C. G. Jung Institute for Analytical Psychology, was eighty years old in 1955. Associated with Sigmund Freud in the pioneer days of psychoanalysis, he took his own direction in later years, minimizing sex in his studies and emphasizing present complexes rather than childhood complexes in the explanation of neuroses. He spent some time among African natives and American Indians in the study of primitive traits of mind.

Scholars, seeking *all* the footnotes and authorities cited, must refer to a volume entitled *Spirit and Nature, Papers from the Eranos Yearbooks,* copyright 1954 by the Bollingen Foundation Inc., New York, in the translation by R. F. D. Hull, Bollingen Series XXX-1, published by Pantheon Press.

The Spirit of Psychology

BY CARL GUSTAV JUNG

1. THE UNCONSCIOUS IN HISTORICAL PERSPECTIVE

More clearly, perhaps, than any other science psychology demonstrates the spiritual transition from the classical age to the modern. The history of psychology up to the seventeenth century consists essentially in the enumeration of doctrines concerning the soul, without the soul's being able to get a word in edgeways as the object investigated. As the immediate datum of experience it seemed so completely known to every thinker that he was convinced there could be no need of any further, let alone objective, experience. This attitude is totally alien to the modern standpoint, for today we are of the opinion that, over and above all subjective certainty, objective experience is needed to establish an opinion that lays claim to be scientific. Notwithstanding this, however, it is still difficult, even today, to apply the purely empirical or phenomenological standpoint consistently in psychology, because the original naïve idea that the soul, being the immediate datum of experience, was the best known of all knowables is one of our most deeply rooted convictions. Not only does every layman presume to an opinion, but every psychologist too—and not merely with reference to the subject but, what is of greater consequence, with reference also to the object. He knows, or rather he thinks he knows, what is going on in another individual, and what is good for him. This is due less to a sovereign disregard of differences than to a tacit assumption that all individuals are the same. As a result, people incline unconsciously to a belief in the universal validity of subjective opinions. I mention this fact only to show that in spite of the growing empiricism of the last three hundred years the original attitude has by no means disappeared. Its continued existence only goes to prove how difficult is the transition from the old philosophical view to the modern empirical one.

Naturally it never occurred to the representatives of the old view that their doctrines were nothing but psychic phenomena, for it was naïvely assumed that with the help of intelligence or reason man could as it were climb out of his psychic condition and remove himself to one that was suprapsychic and rational. People had not yet begun to question whether the statements of the human spirit might not in the end be symptoms of certain psychic conditions. This question would be entirely natural, but it has such far-reaching and revolutionary consequences that we can understand only too well why both past and present have done their best to ignore it. We are still very far today from Nietzsche's view of philosophy, and indeed of theology, as an *"ancilla psychologiae,"* for not even the psychologist is prepared to regard his statements outright as a subjectively conditioned confession. We can speak of a uniformity of individual subjects only insofar as they are in large measure unconscious—unconscious, that is, of their actual differences. The more unconscious a man is, the more he will conform to the general canon of psychic behavior. But the more conscious he becomes of his individuality, the more pronounced will be his difference from other subjects and the less he will come up to common expectations. Further, his reactions are much less predictable. This is due to the fact that an individual consciousness is always more highly differentiated and more extensive. But the more extensive it becomes the more differences it will perceive, and the more it will emancipate itself from the collective rules, for the empirical freedom of the will grows in proportion to the extension of consciousness.

As the individual differentiation of consciousness proceeds, so the objective validity of its views decreases and their subjectivity increases. It is no longer taken for granted that one's own preconceptions are applicable to others. This logical development had the consequence that in the seventeenth century—a century of great importance for the growth of science—psychology began to rise up by the side of philosophy, and it was Christian von Wolff (1679-1754) who was the first to speak of "empirical" or "experimental" psychology, thus acknowledging the need to put psychology on a new footing. Psychology had to forgo the philosopher's rational definition of truth, because it gradually became clear that no philosophy had sufficient general validity to be uniformly fair to the diversity of individual subjects. And since on questions of principle, too, an indefinitely large number of different subjective statements was possible, whose validity in their turn could be maintained only subjectively, it naturally became necessary to abandon philosophical argument and to replace it by experience. Psychology thereupon turned into a natural science.

For the time being, however, philosophy retained its grip on the wide field of "rational" or "speculative" psychology, and only with the passage of the centuries could the latter gradually develop into a natural science. This process of change is not complete even today. Psychology, as a subject, still comes under the Philosophical Faculty in most universities, and "medical" psychology has to seek refuge with the Medical Faculty. So officially the situation is still largely medieval, since even the natural sciences are only admitted as "Phil. II," under the cloak of Natural Philosophy. Although it has been obvious for at least two hundred years that philosophy above all is dependent on psychological premises, everything possible was done to obscure the autonomy of the empirical sciences when the discovery of the earth's rotation and the moons of Jupiter could no longer be suppressed. Of all the natural sciences, psychology has been the least able to win its independence.

This backwardness seems to me significant. The position of psychology is comparable with that of a psychic function which is inhibited by the conscious mind: only such components of it are admitted to exist as accord with the prevailing trend of consciousness. Whatever fails to accord is actually denied existence, in defiance of the fact that there are numerous phenomena or symptoms to prove the contrary. Anyone acquainted with these psychic processes knows with what subterfuges and self-deceiving maneuvers one sets about splitting off the inconvenience. It is precisely the same with empirical psychology: as the discipline subordinate to a general philosophical psychology, experimental psychology is admitted as a concession to the empiricism of natural science, but is cluttered up with technical philosophical terms. As for psychopathology, it stays put in the Medical Faculty as a curious appendix to psychiatry. "Medical" psychology, as might be expected, finds little or no recognition in the universities.

If I express myself somewhat drastically in this matter, it is with intent to throw into relief the position of psychology at the turn of the nineteenth and the beginning of the twentieth century. Wundt's standpoint is entirely representative of the situation as it then was—representative also because there emerged from his school a succession of notable psychologists who set the tone at the beginning of the twentieth century. In his *Outlines of Psychology,* Wundt says:

Any psychical element that has disappeared from consciousness is to be called unconscious in the sense that we assume the possibility of its renewal, that is, its reappearance in the actual interconnection of psychical processes. Our knowledge of an element that has become unconscious does not extend beyond this possibility of its renewal. . . . Therefore it has no meaning except as a disposition for the rise of future components. . . . Assumptions as to the state of the "unconscious" or as to "unconscious processes" of any kind . . . are *entirely unproductive for psychology.* There are, of course, physical concomitants of the psychical dispositions mentioned, of which some can be directly demonstrated, some inferred from various experiences.

A representative of the Wundt school opines that "a psychic state cannot be described as psychic unless it has reached at least the threshold of consciousness." This argument assumes, or rather asserts, that only the conscious is psychic and that therefore everything psychic is conscious. The author happens to say a "psychic" state: logically he should have said a "state," for whether such a state is psychic is precisely the point at issue. Another argument runs: the simplest psychic fact is sensation, since it cannot be analyzed into simpler facts. Consequently, that which precedes or underlies a sensation is never psychic, but only physiological. *Ergo,* there is no unconscious.

J. F. Herbart once said: "When a representation [idea] falls below the threshold of consciousness it goes on living in a latent way, continually striving to recross the threshold and to displace the other representations." As it stands the proposition is undoubtedly incorrect, for unfortunately anything genuinely forgotten has no tendency to recross the threshold. Had Herbart said "complex" in the modern sense of the word instead of "representation," his proposition would have been absolutely right. We shall hardly be wrong in assuming that he really did mean something of the sort. In this connection a philosophical opponent of the unconscious makes the very illuminating remark: "Once this be admitted, one finds oneself at the mercy of all manner of hypotheses concerning this unconscious life, hypotheses which cannot be controlled by any observation." It is evident that this thinker is not out to recognize facts, but that for him the fear of running into difficulties is decisive. And how does he know that these hypotheses cannot be controlled by observation? For him this is simply an a priori. But with Herbart's observation he does not deal at all.

I mention this incident not because of its positive significance but only because it is so thoroughly characteristic of the antiquated philosophical attitude toward empirical psychology. Wundt himself is of the opinion that as regards the "so-called unconscious processes it is not a question of unconscious psychic elements, but only of more dimly *conscious* ones," and that "for hypothetical unconscious processes we could substitute actually demonstrable or at any rate less hypothetical conscious processes." This attitude implies a clear rejection of the unconscious as a psychological hypothesis. The cases of "double consciousness" he explains as "modifications of individual consciousness which very often occur continuously, in steady succession, and for which, by a violent misinterpretation of the facts, a plurality of individual consciousnesses is substituted." The latter, so Wundt argues, "would have to be simultaneously present in one and the same individual." This, he says, "is admittedly not the case." Doubtless it is hardly possible for two consciousnesses to express themselves simultaneously in a single individual in a blatantly recognizable way. That is why these states usually alternate. Pierre Janet has shown that while the one consciousness controls the head, so to speak, the other simultaneously puts itself into communication with the observer by means of a code of expressive manual movements. Double consciousness may therefore very well be simultaneous.

Wundt thinks that the idea of a double consciousness, and hence of a "superconsciousness" and "subconsciousness" in Fechner's sense, is a "survival from the psychological mysticism" of the Schelling school. He obviously boggles at an unconscious representation being one which nobody "has." In that case the word "representation" would naturally be obsolete too, since it suggests a subject to whom something is present or "presented." That is the basic reason for Wundt's rejection of the unconscious. But we can easily get round this difficulty by speaking, not of "representations" or "perceptions," but of *contents,* as I usually do. Here I must anticipate a point with which I shall be dealing at some length later on, namely the fact that something very like "representedness" or consciousness does attach to unconscious contents, so that the possibility of an unconscious subject becomes a serious question. Such a subject, however, is not identical with the ego. That it was principally the "representations" which were Wundt's bête noire is clear also from his emphatic rejection of "inborn ideas." How literally he takes this can be seen from the following: "If the newborn animal really had an idea beforehand of all the actions it purposes to do, what a wealth of anticipated life experiences would lie stored in the human and animal instincts, and how incomprehensible it would seem that not man alone, but animals too, acquire most things only through experience and practice!" There is nevertheless an inborn "pattern of behavior" and just such a treasure house, not indeed of anticipated, but of accumulated, life experiences; only, it is not a question of "representations" but of sketches, plans, or images which, though not actually "presented" to the ego, are yet just as real as Kant's hundred thalers, which had been sewn into the lining of a jacket and forgotten by the owner. Wundt might have remembered Christian von Wolff, whom he himself mentions, and his distinction with regard to "unconscious" states which "can be inferred only from what we find in our consciousness."

To the category of "inborn ideas" also belong Adolf Bastian's "elementary ideas," by which we are to understand the fundamentally analogous forms of perception that are to be found everywhere, hence more or less what we know today as "archetypes." Wundt, of course, poohpoohs this notion, still under the delusion that he is dealing here with "representations" and not with "dispositions." He says: "The origination of one and the same phenomenon in different places is not absolutely impossible, but, from the standpoint of empirical psychology, it is in the highest degree unlikely." He denies a "common psychic heritage of humanity" in this sense and repudiates the very idea of an intelligible myth symbolism with the characteristic pronouncement that the supposition of a "system of ideas" hiding behind the myth is impossible. The pedantic assumption that the unconscious is, of all things, a system of ideas would not hold water even in Wundt's day, let alone before or afterward.

It would be incorrect to assume that the rejection of the idea of the unconscious in academic psychology at the turn of the century was anything like universal. That is by no means the case, for Fechner, and after him Theodor Lipps, had given the unconscious a place of decisive importance. Although for Lipps psychology is a "science of consciousness," he nevertheless speaks of "unconscious" perceptions and representations, which he regards as processes. "The nature or, more accurately, the idea of a 'psychic' process is not so much a conscious content or conscious experience as the psychic reality which must necessarily be thought to underlie the existence of such a process." "Observation of conscious life persuades us that not only are unconscious perceptions and representations . . . at times to be found in us, but that psychic life *is therein principally enacted all the time, and only occasionally, at special points, does that which operates within us reveal its presence directly, in appropriate images.*" "Thus psychic life always goes far beyond the bounds of what is or may be present in us in the form of conscious contents or images."

Theodor Lipp's remarks in no wise conflict with our modern views, on the contrary they form the theoretical basis for the psychology of the unconscious in general. Nevertheless resistance to the hypothesis of the unconscious persisted for a long time afterward. For instance it is characteristic that Max Dessoir, in his history of modern German psychology, does not even mention C. G. Carus and Eduard von Hartmann.

II. THE SIGNIFICANCE OF THE UNCONSCIOUS IN PSYCHOLOGY

The hypothesis of the unconscious puts a large question mark after the idea of the psyche. The soul, as hitherto postulated by the philosophical intellect and equipped with all the necessary faculties, threatened to emerge from its chrysalis as something with unexpected and uninvestigated properties. It no longer represented anything immediately known, about which nothing more remained to be discovered except a few more or less satisfying definitions. Rather it now appeared in strangely double guise, as both known and unknown. In consequence, the old psychology was thoroughly unseated and as much revolutionized[1] as classical physics had been by the discovery of radioactivity. These first experimental psychologists were in the same predicament as the mythical discoverer of the numerical sequence, who strung peas together in a row and simply went on adding another unit to those

[1] I reproduce here what William James says about the importance of the discovery of the unconscious psyche (*Varieties of Religious Experience,* New York, 1902, p. 233): "I cannot but think that the most important step forward that has occurred in psychology since I have been a student of that science is the discovery, first made in 1886, that . . . there is not only the consciousness of the ordinary field, with its usual center and margin, but an addition thereto in the shape of a set of memories, thoughts, and feelings, which are extramarginal and outside of the primary consciousness altogether, but yet must be classed as conscious facts of some sort, able to reveal their presence by unmistakable signs. I call this the most important step forward because, unlike the other advances which psychology has made, this discovery has revealed to us an entirely unsuspected peculiarity in the constitution of human nature. No other step forward which psychology has made can proffer any such claim as this." The discovery of 1886 to which James refers is the positing of a "subliminal consciousness" by Frederic W. H. Myers. See note 20.

already present. When he contemplated the result, it looked as if there were nothing but a hundred identical units; but the numbers he had thought of only as names unexpectedly turned out to be peculiar entities with irreducible properties. For instance, there were even, uneven, and primary numbers; positive, negative, irrational, and imaginary numbers, etc.[2] So it is with psychology: if the soul is really only an idea, this idea has an alarming air of unpredictability about it—something with qualities no one would ever have imagined. One can go on asserting that the soul is consciousness and its contents, but that does not prevent, in fact it hastens, the discovery of a background not previously suspected, a true matrix of all conscious phenomena, a preconsciousness and a postconsciousness, a superconsciousness and a subconsciousness. The moment one forms an idea of a thing and successfully catches one of its aspects, one invariably succumbs to the illusion of having caught the whole. One never considers that a total apprehension is right out of the question. Not even an idea posited as total is total, for it is still an entity on its own with unpredictable qualities. This self-deception certainly promotes peace of mind: the unknown is named, the far has been brought near, so that one can lay one's finger on it. One has taken possession of it, and it has become an inalienable piece of property, like a slain creature of the wild that can no longer run away. It is a magical procedure such as the primitive practices upon objects and the psychologist upon the soul. He is no longer at its mercy, but he never suspects that the very fact of grasping the object conceptually gives it a golden opportunity to display all those qualities which would never have made their appearance had it not been imprisoned in a concept (remember the numbers!).

The attempts that have been made, during the last three hundred years, to grasp the soul are all part and parcel of that tremendous expansion of knowledge which has brought the universe nearer to us in a way that staggers the imagination. The thousandfold magnifications made possible by the electron microscope vie with the 500 million light-year distances which the telescope travels. Psychology is still a long way from a development similar to that which the other natural sciences have undergone; also . . . it has been much less able to shake off the trammels of philosophy. All the same, every science is a function of the soul and all knowledge is rooted in it. The psyche is the greatest of all cosmic wonders and the *sine qua non* of the world as an object. It is

[2] A mathematician once remarked that everything in science was man-made except numbers, which had been created by God Himself.

in the highest degree odd that Western man, with but very few—and ever fewer—exceptions, apparently pays so little regard to this fact. Swamped by the knowledge of external objects, the subject of all knowledge has been temporarily eclipsed to the point of seeming nonexistence.

The soul was a tacit assumption that seemed to know itself in every particular. With the discovery of a possible unconscious psychic realm, man had the opportunity to embark upon a great adventure of the spirit, and one might have expected that a passionate interest would be turned in this direction. Not only was this not the case at all, but there arose on all sides an outcry against such an hypothesis. Nobody drew the conclusion that if the subject of knowledge, the psyche, were in fact a veiled form of existence not immediately accessible to consciousness, then all our knowledge must be incomplete, and moreover to a degree that we cannot determine. The validity of conscious knowledge was questioned in an altogether different and more menacing way than it had ever been by the critical procedures of epistemology. The latter put certain bounds to human knowledge in general, from which post-Kantian German Idealism struggled to emancipate itself; but natural science and common sense accommodated themselves to it without much difficulty, if they condescended to notice it at all. Philosophy fought against it in the interests of an antiquated pretension of the human mind to be able to pull itself up by its own bootstrings and know things that were right outside the range of human understanding. The victory of Hegel over Kant dealt the gravest blow to reason and to the further spiritual development of the German and then of the European mind, all the more dangerous as Hegel was a psychologist in disguise who projected great truths out of the sphere of the subject into a cosmos he himself had created. We know how far Hegel's influence extends today. The forces compensating this calamitous development personified themselves partly in the later Schelling, partly in Schopenhauer and Carus,[3] while on the other hand that unbridled "bacchantic God" whom Hegel had already scented in nature finally burst upon us in Nietzsche.

Carus' hypothesis of the unconscious was bound to hit the then prevailing trend of German philosophy all the harder, as the latter had apparently just got the better of Kantian criticism and had restored, or rather reinstated, the well-nigh godlike sovereignty of the human spirit —Spirit with a capital S. The spirit of medieval man was, in good and bad alike, still the spirit of the God whom he served. Epistemological criticism was on the one hand an expression of the modesty of medi-

[3] C. G. Carus.

F

eval man, and on the other a renunciation of, or abdication from, the spirit of God, and consequently a modern extension and reinforcement of human consciousness within the limits of reason. Wherever the spirit of God is extruded from our human calculations, an unconscious substitute takes its place. In Schopenhauer we find the unconscious Will as the new definition of God, in Carus the unconscious, and in Hegel identification and inflation, the practical equation of philosophical reason with Spirit, thus making possible that intellectual juggling with the object which achieved such a horrid brilliance in his philosophy of the State. Hegel offered a solution of the problem raised by epistemological criticism in that he gave ideas a chance to prove their unknown power of autonomy. They induced that hybris of reason which led to Nietzsche's superman and hence to the catastrophe that bears the name of Germany. Not only artists, but philosophers too, are sometimes prophets.

I think it is obvious that all philosophical statements which transgress the bounds of reason are anthropomorphic and have no validity beyond that which falls to psychically conditioned statements. A philosophy like Hegel's is a self-revelation of the psychic background and, philosophically, a presumption. Psychologically, it amounts to an invasion by the unconscious. The peculiar high-flown language Hegel uses bears out this view: it is reminiscent of the megalomaniac language of schizophrenics, who use terrific spellbinding words to reduce the transcendent to subjective form, to give banalities the charm of novelty, or pass off commonplaces as searching wisdom. So bombastic a terminology is a symptom of weakness, ineptitude, and lack of substance. But that does not prevent the latest German philosophy from using the same crackpot power words and pretending that it is not unintentional psychology.

In face of this elemental inrush of the unconscious into the Western sphere of human reason, Schopenhauer and Carus had no solid ground under them from which to develop and apply their compensatory effect. Man's salutary submission to a benevolent Deity, and the *cordon sanitaire* between him and the demon of darkness—the great legacy of the past—remained unimpaired with Schopenhauer, at any rate in principle, while with Carus it was hardly touched at all, since he sought to tackle the problem at the root by leading it away from the overpresumptuous philosophical standpoint toward that of psychology. We have to close our eyes to his philosophical allure if we wish to give full weight to his essentially psychological hypothesis. He had at least come a step nearer to the conclusion we mentioned earlier, by trying to construct a world picture that included the dark part of the soul. This structure still lacked something whose unprecedented importance I would like to bring home to the reader.

For this purpose we must first make it quite clear to ourselves that all knowledge is the result of imposing some kind of order upon the reactions of the psychic system as they flow into our consciousness—an order which reflects the behavoir of a *metapsychical* reality, of that which is in itself real. If, as certain modern points of view, too, would have it, the psychic system coincides and is identical with our conscious mind, then, in principle, we are in a position to know everything that can be known, i.e., everything that lies within the limits of the theory of knowledge. In that case there is no cause for disquiet beyond that felt by anatomists and physiologists when contemplating the function of the eye or the organ of hearing. But should it turn out that the psyche does *not* coincide with consciousness, and, what is more, that it functions unconsciously in a way similar to, or *different* from, the conscious portion of it, then our disquiet must rise to the point of agitation. For it is then no longer a question of general epistemological limits, but of a flimsy threshold that separates us from the unconscious contents of the psyche. The hypothesis of the threshold and of the unconscious means that the indispensable raw material of all knowledge—namely psychic reactions—and perhaps even unconscious "thoughts" and "insights" lie close beside, above, or below consciousness, separated from us by the merest "threshold" and yet apparently unattainable. We have no knowledge of how this unconscious functions, but since it is conjectured to be a psychic system it may possibly have everything that consciousness has, including perception, apperception, memory, imagination, will, affectivity, feeling, reflection, judgment, etc., all in subliminal form.[4]

---

[4] G. H. Lewes (*The Physical Basis of Mind*, London, 1877) takes all this for granted. For instance, on p. 358, he says: "Science has various modes and degrees, such as Perception, Ideation, Emotion, Volition, which may be conscious, subconscious, or unconscious." On p. 363: "Consciousness and Unconsciousness are correlatives, both belonging to the sphere of Sentience. Every one of the unconscious processes is operant, changes the general state of the organism, and is capable of at once issuing in a discriminated sensation when the force which balances it is disturbed." On p. 367: "There are many involuntary actions of which we are distinctly conscious, and many voluntary actions of which we are at times subconscious and unconscious. . . . Just as the thought which at one moment passes unconsciously, at another consciously, is in itself the same thought . . . so the action which at one moment is voluntary, and at another involuntary, is itself the same action." Lewes certainly goes too far when he says (p. 373): "There is no real and essential distinction between voluntary and involuntary actions." Occasionally there is a world of difference.

Here we are faced with Wundt's objection that one cannot possibly speak of unconscious "perceptions," "representations," "feelings," much less of "volitional actions," seeing that none of these phenomena can be represented without an experiencing subject. Moreover the idea of a threshold presupposes a mode of observation in terms of energy, according to which consciousness of psychic contents is essentially dependent upon their intensity, that is, their energy. Just as only a stimulus of a certain intensity is powerful enough to cross the threshold, so it may with some justice be assumed that other psychic contents too must possess a higher energy potential if they are to get across. If they possess only a small amount of energy they remain subliminal, like the corresponding sense perceptions.

As Lipps[5] has already pointed out, the first objection is nullified by the fact that the psychic process remains essentially the same whether it is "represented" or not. Anyone who takes the view that the phenomena of consciousness comprise the whole psyche must go a step further and say that "representations which we do not have"[6] can hardly be described as "representations." He must also deny any psychic quality to what is left over. For this rigorous point of view the psyche can only have the phantasmagoric existence that pertains to the ephemeral phenomena of consciousness. This view does not square with common experience, which speaks in favor of a possible psychic activity without consciousness. Lipps' idea of the existence of psychic processes *an sich* does more justice to the facts. I do not wish to waste time in proving this point, but will content myself with saying that never yet has any reasonable person doubted the existence of psychic processes in a dog, although no dog has, to our knowledge, ever expressed consciousness of its psychic contents.[7]

III. THE DISSOCIABILITY OF THE PSYCHE

There is no a priori reason for assuming that unconscious processes must inevitably have a subject, any more than there is for doubting the reality of psychic processes. Admittedly the problem becomes difficult when we suppose unconscious acts of the will. If this is not to be just

[5] Theodor Lipps.

[6] Gustav Theodor Fechner, *Elemente der Psychophysik* (2nd ed., Leipzig, 1889), Vol. II, pp. 438 ff.

[7] I am not counting "Clever Hans" and other "talking" animals. ("Clever Hans" was one of the famous trained horses of Elberfeld who tapped out answers to mathematical questions with his hoof.—Translator.)

a matter of "instincts" and "inclinations," but rather of considered "choice" and "decision" which are peculiar to the will, then one cannot very well get round the need for a controlling subject to whom something is "represented." But that, by definition, would be to lodge a consciousness in the unconscious, though this is a conceptual operation which presents no great difficulties to the psychopathologist. He is familiar with a psychic phenomenon that seems to be quite unknown to "academic" psychology, namely the dissociation or dissociability of the psyche. This peculiarity arises from the fact that the connecting link between the psychic processes themselves is a very conditional one. Not only are unconscious processes sometimes strangely independent of the experiences of the conscious mind, but the conscious processes, too, show a distinct loosening or discreteness. We all know of the absurdities which are caused by complexes and are to be observed with the greatest accuracy in the association experiment. Just as the cases of double consciousness doubted by Wundt really do happen, so the cases where not the whole personality is split in half, but only smaller fragments are broken off, are much more probable and in fact more common. They constitute one of the age-old experiences of mankind which is reflected in the universal supposition of a plurality of souls in one and the same individual. As the plurality of psychic components felt at the primitive level shows, the original state is one where the psychic processes are very loosely knit and by no means form a self-contained unity. Moreover psychiatric experience indicates that it often takes only a little to shatter the unity of consciousness so laboriously built up in the course of development and to resolve it back into its original elements.

This dissociability also enables us to set aside the difficulties that flow from the logically necessary assumption of a threshold of consciousness. If it is correct to say that conscious contents become subliminal through loss of energy, and conversely that unconscious processes become conscious through accretion of energy, then, if unconscious acts of volition are to be possible, it follows that these must possess an energy which enables them to achieve consciousness, or at any rate to achieve a state of secondary consciousness which consists in the unconscious process being "represented" to a subliminal subject who chooses and decides. This process must necessarily possess the amount of energy required for it to achieve such a consciousness; in other words, it is bound eventually to reach its "bursting point."[8] If that is so, the question arises as to why the unconscious process does not go right over the threshold

[8] James, *Varieties of Religious Experience*, p. 232.

and become perceptible to the ego? Since it obviously does not do this, but apparently remains suspended in the domain of a subliminal secondary subject, we must now explain why this subject, which is *ex hypothesi* charged with sufficient energy to become conscious, does not in its turn push over the threshold and articulate with the primary ego consciousness. Psychopathology has the material needed to answer this question. This secondary consciousness represents a personality component which has not been separated from ego consciousness by mere accident, but which owes its separation to definite causes. Such a dissociation has two distinct aspects: in the one case there is an originally conscious content that became subliminal because it was repressed on account of its incompatible nature; in the other case the secondary subject consists essentially in a process that never entered into consciousness at all because no possibilities exist there of apperceiving it. That is to say, ego consciousness cannot accept it for lack of understanding, and in consequence it remains for the most part subliminal, although, from the energy point of view, it is quite capable of becoming conscious. It owes its existence not to repression, but to subliminal processes that were never themselves conscious. Yet because there is in both cases sufficient energy to make it potentially conscious, the secondary subject does in fact have an effect upon ego consciousness—indirectly or, as we say, "symbolically," though the expression is not a particularly happy one. The point is that the contents that appear in consciousness are at first *symptomatic*. Insofar as we know, or think we know, what they refer to or are based on, they are *semiotic,* even though Freudian literature constantly uses the term "symbolic," regardless of the fact that in reality symbols always express what we do *not* know. The symptomatic contents are in part truly symoblic, being the indirect representatives of unconscious states or processes whose nature can be only imperfectly inferred and realized from the contents that appear in consciousness. It is therefore possible that the unconscious harbors contents so powered with energy that under other conditions they would be bound to become perceptible to the ego. In the majority of cases they are not repressed contents, but simply contents that are not yet conscious and have not been subjectively realized, like the demons and gods of the primitives or the "isms" so fanatically believed in by modern man. This state is neither pathological nor in any way peculiar; it is on the contrary the original norm, whereas the psychic wholeness comprehended in the unity of consciousness is an ideal goal that has never yet been reached.

Not without justice we connect consciousness, by analogy, with the sense functions, from the physiology of which the whole idea of a "threshold" is derived. The sound frequencies perceptible to the human ear range from 20 to 20,000 vibrations per second; the wave lengths of light visible to the eye range from 7700 to 3900 angstrom units. This analogy makes it conceivable that there is a lower as well as an upper threshold for psychic events, and that consciousness, the perceptive system par excellence, may therefore be compared with the perceptible scale of sound or light, having like them a lower and upper limit. Maybe this comparison could be extended to the psyche in general, which would not be an impossibility if there were "psychoid" [soul-like] processes at both ends of the psychic scale. In accordance with the principle "*natura non facit saltus,*" such an hypothesis would not be altogether out of place. . . . If I make use of the term "psychoid" I do so with three reservations: firstly, I use it as an adjective, not as a noun; secondly, no psychic quality in the proper sense of the word is implied, but only a "quasi-psychic" one such as the reflex processes possess; and thirdly, it is meant to distinguish a category of events from merely vitalist phenomena on the one hand and from specifically psychic processes on the other. The latter distinction also obliges us to define more closely the nature and extent of the psyche, and of the unconscious psyche in particular.

If the unconscious can contain everything that is known to be a function of consciousness, then we are faced with the possibility that it too, like consciousness, possesses a subject, a sort of ego. This conclusion finds expression in the common and ever-recurring use of the term "subconsciousness." The latter term is certainly open to misunderstanding, as either it means what is "below consciousness," or it postulates a "lower" and secondary consciousness. At the same time this hypothetical "subconsciousness," which is immediately associated with a "superconsciousness,"[9] brings out the real point of my argument: the fact, namely, that a second psychic system coexisting with consciousness—no matter what qualities we suspect it of possessing—is of absolutely revolutionary significance in that it could radically alter our view of the world. Even if no more than the perceptions taking place in such a second psychic system were carried over into ego consciousness, we should have the possibility of enormously extending the bounds of our mental horizon.

Once we give serious consideration to the hypothesis of the uncon-

[9] Especial exception is taken to this "superconsciousness" by people who have come under the influence of Indian philosophy. They usually fail to appreciate that their objection only applies to the hypothesis of a "subconscious," which ambiguous term I avoid using. On the other hand my concept of the *unconscious* leaves the question of "above" or "below" completely open, as it embraces both aspects of the psyche.

scious, it follows that our view of the world can be but a provisional one; for if we effect so radical an alteration in the subject of perception and cognition as this dual focus implies, the result must be a world view very different from any known before. This holds true only if the hypothesis of the unconscious holds true, which in turn can only be verified if unconscious contents can be changed into conscious ones— if, that is to say, the disturbances emanating from the unconscious, the effects of spontaneous manifestations, of dreams, fantasies, and complexes, can successfully be integrated into consciousness by the interpretative method.

IV. INSTINCT AND WILL

Whereas, in the course of the nineteenth century, the main concern was to put the unconscious on a philosophical footing,[10] toward the end of the century various attempts were made in different parts of Europe, more or less simultaneously and independently of one another, to understand the unconscious experimentally or empirically. The pioneers in this field were Pierre Janet[11] in France and Sigmund Freud[12] in the old Austria. Janet made himself famous for his investigation of the formal aspect, Freud for his researches into the content of psychogenic symptoms.

I am not in a position here to describe in detail the transformation of unconscious contents into conscious ones, so must content myself with hints. In the first place the structure of psychogenic symptoms was successfully explained on the hypothesis of unconscious processes. Freud, starting from the symptomatology of the neuroses, made out a plausible case for dreams as the mediators of unconscious contents. What he elicited as contents of the unconscious seemed, on the face of it, to consist of elements of a personal nature that were quite capable of consciousness and had therefore been conscious under other conditions. It seemed to him that they had "got repressed" on account of their morally incompatible nature. Hence, like forgotten contents, they had

[10] Cf. in particular Eduard von Hartmann, *Philosophie des Unbewussten* (1869; tr., *Philosophy of the Unconscious*, London and New York, 1931).

[11] An appreciation of his achievement is to be found in Jean Paulus, *Le Problème de l'hallucination et l'évolution de la psychologie d'Esquirol à Pierre Janet* (Paris, 1941).

[12] In this connection we should also mention the important Swiss psychologist Théodore Flournoy and his chef d'oeuvre *Des Indes à la Planète Mars* (Paris and Geneva, 1900; tr., *From India to the Planet Mars*, New York, 1900.) Other pioneers were W. B. Carpenter (*Principles of Mental Physiology*, London, 1874) and G. H. Lewes (*Problems of Life and Mind*, London, 1872–79). For Frederic W. H. Myers see note 20.

once been conscious and had become subliminal, and more or less unrecoverable, owing to a countereffect exerted by the attitude of the conscious mind. By suitably concentrating the attention and letting oneself be guided by associations—that is, by the pointers still existing in consciousness—the associative recovery of lost contents went forward as in a mnemotechnical exercise. But whereas forgotten contents were unrecoverable because of their lowered threshold value, repressed contents owed their relative unrecoverability to a check exercised by the conscious mind.

This initial discovery logically led to the interpretation of the unconscious as a phenomenon of repression which could be understood in personalistic terms. Its contents were lost elements that had once been conscious. Freud later acknowledged the continued existence of archaic vestiges in the form of primitive modes of functioning, though even these were explained personalistically. On this view the unconscious psyche appears as a subliminal appendix to the conscious mind.

The contents that Freud raised to consciousness are those which are the most easily recoverable because they have the capacity to become conscious and were originally conscious. The only thing they prove with respect to the unconscious psyche is that there is a psychic limbo somewhere beyond consciousness. Forgotten contents which are still recoverable prove the same. This would tell us next to nothing about the nature of the unconscious psyche did there not exist an undoubted link between these contents and the instinctual sphere. We think of the latter as physiological, as in the main a function of the glands. The modern theory of internal secretions and hormones lends the strongest support to this view. But the theory of human instincts finds itself in a rather delicate situation, because it is uncommonly difficult not only to define the instincts conceptually, but even to establish their number and their limitations.[13] In this matter opinions diverge. All that can be ascertained with any certainty is that the instincts have a physiological and a psychological aspect.[14] Of great use for descriptive purposes is

[13] This indistinctness and blurring of the instincts may, as E. N. Marias has shown in his experiments with apes (*The Soul of the White Ant*, London, 1937, p. 429 [tr. from Afrikaans]), have something to do with the superior learning capacity prevailing over the instincts, as is obviously the case with man too.

[14] "The instincts are physiological and psychic dispositions which . . . cause the organism to move in a clearly defined direction" (W. Jerusalem, *Lehrbuch der Psychologie*, 3rd ed., Vienna and Leipzig, 1902, p. 188). From another point of view Oswald Külpe describes instinct as "a fusion of feelings and organic sensations" (*Grundriss der Psychologie*, Leipzig, 1895, p. 333).

Pierre Janet's view of the *"partie supérieure et inférieure d'une fonction."*[15]

The fact that all the psychic processes accessible to our observation and experience are somehow bound to an organic substrate indicates that they are articulated with the life of the organism as a whole and therefore partake of its dynamism—in other words, they must have a share in its instincts or be in a certain sense the results of the action of those instincts. This is not to say that the psyche derives exclusively from the instinctual sphere and hence from its organic substrate. The psyche as such cannot be explained in terms of physiological chemistry, if only because, together with "life" itself, it is the only "natural factor" capable of converting statistical organizations which are subject to natural law into "higher" or "unnatural" states, in opposition to the rule of entropy that runs throughout the inorganic realm. How life produces complex organic systems from the inorganic we do not know, though we have direct experience of how the psyche does it. Life therefore has a specific law of its own which cannot be deduced from the known physical laws of nature. Even so the psyche is to some extent dependent upon processes in the organic substrate. At all events it is highly probable that this is so. The instinctual base governs the *partie inférieure* of the function, while the *partie supérieure* corresponds to its predominantly "psychic" component. The *partie inférieure* proves to be the relatively unalterable, automatic part of the function, and the *partie supérieure* the voluntary and alterable part.[16]

The question now arises: when are we entitled to speak of "psychic" and how in general do we define the "psychic" as distinct from the "physiological"? Both are life phenomena, but they differ in that the functional component characterized as the *partie inférieure* has an unmistakably physiological aspect. Its existence or nonexistence seems to be bound up with the hormones. Its functioning has a compulsive character: hence the designation "drive." Rivers asserts that the "all-

[15] *Les Névroses* (1909), pp. 384 ff.

[16] Janet says (*ibid.*, p. 384): "Il me semble nécessaire de distinguer dans toute fonction des parties inférieures et des parties supérieures. Quand une fonction s'exerce depuis longtemps elle contient des parties qui sont très anciennes, très faciles, et qui sont réprésentées par des organes très distincts et très spécialisés . . . ce sont là les parties inférieures de la fonction. Mais je crois qu'il y a aussi dans toute fonction des parties supérieures consistant dans l'adaptation de cette fonction à des circonstances plus récentes, beaucoup moins habiteulles, qui sont réprésentées par des organes beaucoup moins différenciés." But the highest part of the function consists "dans son adaptation à la circonstance particulière qui existe au moment présent, au moment où nous devons l'employer."

or-none reaction,"[17] is natural to it, i.e., the function acts altogether or not at all, which is specific of compulsion. On the other hand the *partie supérieure,* which is best described as psychic and is moreover sensed as such, has lost its compulsive character, can be subjected to the will[18] and even applied in a manner contrary to the original instinct.

From these reflections it appears that the psychic is an emancipation of function from its instinctual form and so from the compulsiveness which, as sole determinant of the function, causes it to harden into a mechanism. The psychic condition or quality begins where the function loses its outer and inner determinism and becomes capable of more extensive and freer application, that is, where it begins to show itself accessible to a will motivated from other sources. At the risk of anticipating my program, I cannot refrain from pointing out that if we delimit the psyche from the physiological sphere of instinct at the bottom, so to speak, a similar delimitation imposes itself at the top. For, with increasing freedom from sheer instinct the *partie supérieure* will ultimately reach a point at which the intrinsic energy of the function ceases altogether to be oriented by instinct in the original sense, and attains a so-called "spiritual" form. This does not imply a substantial alteration of the motive power of instinct, but merely a different mode of its application. The meaning or purpose of the instinct is not unambiguous, as the instinct may easily mask a sense of direction other than biological, which only becomes apparent in the course of development.

Within the psychic sphere the function can be deflected through the action of the will and modified in a great variety of ways. This is possible because the system of instincts is not truly harmonious in composition and is exposed to numerous internal collisions. One instinct disturbs and displaces the other, and although, taken as a whole, it is the instincts that make individual life possible, their blind compulsive character affords frequent occasion for mutual injury. Differentiation of function from compulsive instinctuality, and its voluntary application, are of paramount importance in the maintenance of life. But this increases the possibility of collision and produces cleavages—the very dissociations which are forever putting the unity of consciousness in jeopardy.

In the psychic sphere, as we have seen, the will influences the func-

[17] W. H. R. Rivers, "Instinct and the Unconscious," *British Journal of Psychology* (Cambridge), Vol. X (1919–20), pp. 1-7.

[18] This formulation is purely psychological and has nothing to do with the philosophical problem of indeterminism.

tion. It does this by virtue of the fact that it is itself a form of energy and has the power to overcome another form. In this sphere which I define as psychic the will is in the last resort motivated by instincts, not of course absolutely, otherwise it would not be a will, which by definition must have a certain freedom of choice. "Will" implies a certain amount of energy freely disposable by the psyche. There must be such amounts of disposable libido (or energy), or modifications of the functions would be impossible, since the latter would then be chained to the instincts—which are in themselves extremely conservative and correspondingly unalterable—so exclusively that no variations could take place, unless it were organic variations. As we have already said, the motivation of the will must in the first place be regarded as essentially biological. But at the (permitting such an expression) upper limit of the psyche where the function breaks free from its original goal, the instincts lose their influence as movers of the will. Through having its form altered the function is pressed into the service of other determinants or motivations which apparently have nothing further to do with the instincts. What I am trying to make clear is the remarkable fact that the will cannot transgress the bounds of the psychic sphere: it cannot coerce the instinct, nor has it power over the spirit, insofar as we understand by this something more than the intellect. Spirit and instinct are by nature autonomous and both limit in equal measure the applied field of the will. Later I shall show what constitutes the relation of spirit to instinct.

Just as, in its lower reaches, the psyche loses itself in the organic-material substrate, so in its upper reaches it resolves itself into a "spiritual" form about which we know as little as we do about the functional basis of instinct. What I would call the psyche proper extends to all functions which can be brought under the influence of a will. Pure instinctuality allows no consciousness to be conjectured and needs none. But because of its empirical freedom of choice the will needs a superordinate authority, something like a consciousness of itself, in order to modify the function. It must "know" of a goal different from the goal of the function. Otherwise it would coincide with the driving force of the function. Driesch rightly emphasizes: "There is no willing without knowing."[19] Volition presupposes a choosing subject who envisages different possibilities. Looked at from this angle, psyche

[19] *Die "Seele" als elementarer Naturfaktor* (Leipzig, 1903), p. 80. "Individualized stimuli inform . . . the 'primary knower' of the abnormal state, and now this 'knower' not only *wants* a remedy but *knows* what it is" (p. 82).

is essentially conflict between blind instinct and will (freedom of choice). Where instinct predominates, *psychoid* processes set in which pertain to the sphere of the unconscious as elements incapable of consciousness. The psychoid process is not the unconscious as such, for this has a far greater extension. Apart from psychoid processes there are in the unconcious ideas and volitional acts, hence something akin to conscious processes; but in the instinctual sphere these phenomena retire so far into the background that the term "psychoid" is probably justified. If, however, we restrict the psyche to acts of the will, we arrive at the conclusion that psyche is more or less identical with consciousness, for we can hardly conceive of will and freedom of choice without consciousness. This apparently brings us back to where we always stood, to the axiom *psyche = consciousness*. What, then, has happened to the postulated psychic nature of the unconscious?

V. CONSCIOUS AND UNCONSCIOUS

This question, regarding the nature of the unconscious, brings with it the extraordinary intellectual difficulties with which the psychology of the unconscious confronts us. Such difficulties must inevitably arise whenever the mind launches forth boldly into the unknown and invisible. Our philosopher sets about it very cleverly, since, by his flat denial of the unconscious, he clears all complications out of his way at one sweep. A similar quandary faced the physicist of the old school, who believed exclusively in the wave theory of light and was then led to the discovery that there are phenomena which can only be explained by the corpuscular theory. Happily, physics has shown the psychologist that it too can cope with an apparent *contradictio in adiecto*. Encouraged by this example, the psychologist may be emboldened to tackle this controversial problem without having the feeling that he has dropped out of the world of natural science altogether.

Before we scrutinize our dilemma more closely, I would like to clarify one aspect of the concept of the unconscious. The unconscious is not simply the unknown, it is rather the *unknown psychic;* and this we define on the one hand as all those things in us which, if they came to consciousness, would presumably differ in no respect from the known psychic contents, with the addition, on the other hand, of the psychoid system. So defined, the unconscious depicts an extremely fluid state of affairs: everything of which I know, but of which I am not at the moment thinking; everything of which I was once conscious but have now forgotten; everything perceived by my senses, but not noted by my conscious mind; everything which, involuntarily and without paying attention to it, I feel, think, remember, want, and do; all the future things that are taking shape in me and will sometime come to the consciousness: all this is the content of the unconscious. These contents are all more or less capable, so to speak, of consciousness, or were once conscious and may become conscious again the next moment. Thus far the unconscious is "a fringe of consciousness," as William James puts it.[20] To this marginal phenomenon, which is born of alternating shades of light and darkness, there also belong the Freudian findings we have already noted.

We now come to the question: in what state do psychic contents find themselves when not related to the conscious ego? (This relation constitutes all that can be called consciousness.) In accordance with "Occam's razor," *entia praeter necessitatem non sunt multiplicanda* ("principles are not to be multiplied beyond the necessary"), the most cautious conclusion would be that, except for the relation to the conscious ego, nothing is changed when a content becomes unconscious. For this reason I reject the view that momentarily unconscious contents are only physiological. The evidence is lacking, and apart from that the psychology of neurosis provides striking proofs to the contrary. One has only to think of the cases of double personality, *automatisme ambulatoire,* etc. Both Janet's and Freud's findings indicate that everything goes on functioning in the unconscious state just as though it were conscious. There is perception, thinking, feeling, volition, and intention, just as though a subject were present; indeed, there are not a few cases— e.g., the double personality above mentioned—where a second ego actu-

---

[20] James speaks also of a "transmarginal field" of consciousness and identifies it with the "subliminal consciousness" of F. W. H. Myers, one of the founders of the British Society for Psychical Research (cf. *Proceedings, S.P.R.,* Vol. VII, 1891–92, p. 305, and William James, "Frederic Myers' Services to Psychology," *Proceedings S.P.R.,* Vol XLII, May, 1901). Concerning the "field of consciousness" James says (*Varieties of Religious Experience,* p. 232): "The important fact which this 'field' formula commemorates is the indetermination of the margin. Inattentively realized as is the matter which the margin contains, it is nevertheless there, and helps both to guide our behavior and to determine the next movement of our attention. It lies around us like a 'magnetic field' inside of which our center of energy turns like a compass needle as the present phase of consciousness alters into its successor. Our whole past store of memories floats beyond this margin, ready at a touch to come in; and the entire mass of residual powers, impulses, and knowledges that constitute our empircal self stretches continuously beyond it. So vaguely drawn are the outlines between what is actual and what is only potential at any moment of our conscious life, that it is always hard to say of certain mental elements whether we are conscious of them or not."

ally appears and vies with the first. Such findings seem to show that the unconscious is in fact a "subconscious." But from certain experiences—some of them known even to Freud—it is clear that the state of unconscious contents is not quite the same as the conscious state. For instance, feeling-toned complexes in the unconscious do not change in the same way that they do in consciousness. Although they may be enriched by associations, they are not corrected, but are conserved in their original form, as can easily be ascertained from the continuous and uniform effect they have upon the conscious mind. Similarly, they take on the uninfluenceable and compulsive character of an automatism, of which they can be divested only if they are made conscious. This latter procedure is rightly regarded as one of the most important therapeutic factors. In the end such complexes—presumably in proportion to their distance from consciousness—assume, by self-amplification, an archaic and mythological character and hence a certain numinosity, as is perfectly clear in schizophrenic dissociations. Numinosity, however, is wholly outside conscious volition, for it transports the subject into the state of rapture, which is a state of will-less surrender.

These peculiarities of the unconscious state contrast very strongly with the way complexes behave in the conscious mind. Here they can be corrected: they lose their automatic character and can be essentially transformed. They slough off their mythological envelope, and, by entering into the adaptive process going forward in consciousness, they personalize and rationalize themselves to the point where a dialectical discussion becomes possible.[21] Evidently the unconscious state is different after all from the conscious. Although at first sight the process continues in the unconscious as though it were conscious, it seems, with increasing dissociation, to sink back to a more primitive (archaic-mythological) level, to approximate in character to the underlying instinctual pattern, and to assume the qualities which are the hallmarks of instinct: automatism, nonsusceptibility to influence, all-or-none reaction, and so forth. Using the analogy of the spectrum, we could compare the lowering of unconscious contents to a displacement toward the red end of the color band, a comparison which is especially edifying in that red, the blood color, has always signified emotion and instinct.[22]

[21] In schizophrenic dissociation there is no such change in the conscious state, because the complexes are received not into a complete but into a fragmentary consciousness.

[22] Red had a *spiritual* significance for Goethe, but that was in accord with his creed of feeling. Here we may conjecture the alchemical and Rosicrucian background, e.g., the red tincture and the carbuncle. Cf. *Psychology and Alchemy* (*Collected Works,* Vol. 12, New York and London, 1953), p. 449.

The unconscious is accordingly a different medium from the conscious. In the near-conscious areas there is not much change, because here the alternation of light and shadow is too rapid. But it is just this no man's land which is of the greatest value in supplying the answer to the burning question of whether psyche=consciousness. It shows us how relative the unconscious state is, so relative, indeed, that one feels tempted to make use of a concept like "the subconscious" in order to define the darker part of the psyche. But consciousness is equally relative, for it embraces not only consciousness as such, but a whole scale of intensities of consciousness. Between "I do this" and "I am conscious of doing this" there is a world of difference, amounting sometimes to outright contradiction. Consequently there is a consciousness in which unconsciousness predominates, as well as a consciousness in which self-consciousness predominates. This paradox becomes immediately intelligible when we realize that there is no conscious content which can with absolute certainty be said to be totally conscious, for that would necessitate an unimaginable totality of consciousness, and that in turn would presuppose an equally unimaginable wholeness and perfection in the human mind. So we come to the paradoxical conclusion that there is no conscious content which is not in some other respect unconscious. Maybe, too, there is no unconscious psychism which is not at the same time conscious.[23] The latter proposition is more difficult to prove than the first, because our ego, which alone could verify such an assertion, is the point of reference for all consciousness and has no such association with unconscious contents as would enable it to say anything about their nature. So far as the ego is concerned they are, for all practical purposes, unconscious, which is not to say that they are not conscious to it in another respect, for the ego may know these contents under one aspect, but not know them under another aspect, when they cause disturbances of consciousness. Besides, there are processes with regard to which no relation to the conscious ego can be demonstrated and which yet seem to be "represented" or "quasi-conscious." Finally, there are cases where an unconscious ego and hence a second consciousness are present, as we have already seen, though these are the exceptions.

In the psychic sphere the compulsive pattern of behavior gives way to variations of behavior which are conditioned by experience and by volitional acts, that is, by conscious processes. With respect to the

[23] With the explicit exception of the psychoid unconscious, as this includes things which are not capable of consciousness and are only "quasi-pyschic."

psychoid, reflective-instinctive state, therefore, the psyche implies a loosening of bonds and a steady recession of mechanical processes in favor of "selected" modifications. This selective activity takes place partly inside consciousness and partly outside it, i.e., without reference to the conscious ego, and hence unconsciously. In the latter case the process is "quasi-conscious," *as if* it were "represented" and conscious.

As there are no sufficient grounds for assuming that a second ego exists in every individual or that everyone suffers from dissociation of personality, we have to discount the idea of a second ego consciousness as a source of voluntary decisions. But since the existence of highly complex, quasi-conscious processes in the unconscious has been shown, by the study of psychopathology and dream psychology, to be uncommonly probable, we are for better or worse driven to the conclusion that although the state of unconscious contents is not identical with that of conscious ones, it is somehow very "like" it. In these circumstances there is nothing for it but to suppose something midway between the conscious and unconscious state, namely an approximative consciousness. As we have immediate experience only of a reflected state, which is *ipso facto* conscious and known because it consists essentially in relating ideas or other contents to an ego complex that represents our empirical personality, it follows that any other kind of consciousness—either without an ego or without contents—is virtually unthinkable. But there is no need to frame the question so absolutely. On a somewhat more primitive human level ego consciousness loses much of its meaning, and consciousness is accordingly modified in a characteristic way. Above all it ceases to be reflected. And when we observe the psychic processes in the higher vertebrates and particularly in domestic animals, we find phenomena resembling consciousness which nevertheless do not allow us to conjecture the existence of an ego. As we know from direct experience, the light of consciousness has many degrees of brightness, and the ego complex many gradations of emphasis. On the animal and primitive level there is a mere "luminosity," differing hardly at all from the glancing fragments of a dissociated ego. Here, as on the infantile level, consciousness is not a unity, being as yet uncentered by a firmly-knit ego complex, and just flickering into life here and there wherever outer or inner events, instincts, and effects happen to call it awake. At this stage it is still like a chain of islands, or an archipelago. Nor is it a fully integrated whole even at the higher and highest stages; rather, it is capable of indefinite expansion. Gleaming islands, and indeed whole continents, can still add themselves to our modern consciousness—a phenomenon that has become the daily experience of the psychotherapist. Therefore we would do well to think of ego consciousness as being surrounded by a multitude of little luminosities.

VI. THE UNCONSCIOUS AS A MULTIPLE CONSCIOUSNESS

The hypothesis of multiple luminosities rests partly, as we have seen, on the near-conscious state of unconscious contents, and partly on the incidence of certain images which must be regarded as symbolical. These are to be found in the dreams and visual fantasies of modern individuals, and can also be traced in historical records. As the reader may be aware, one of the most important sources for symbolical ideas in the past is alchemy. From this I take, first and foremost, the idea of the *scintillae*—sparks—which appear as visual illusions in the "arcane substance." Thus the *Aurora Consurgens,* Part II, says: *"Scito quod terra foetida cito recipit scintillulas albas"* (Know that the foul earth quickly receives white sparks). These sparks Khunrath explains as *"radii atque scintillae"* of the *"anima catholica,"* the world soul, which is identical with the spirit of God.[24] From this interpretation it is clear that certain of the alchemists had already divined the psychic nature of these luminosities. They were seeds of light broadcast in the chaos, which Khunrath calls *"mundi futuri seminarium"* (the seed plot of a world to come).[25] One such spark is the human mind.[26] The arcane substance—the watery earth or earthly water (*limus:* mud) of the World Essence—is "universally animated" by the "fiery spark of the soul of the world," in accordance with the Wisdom of Solomon 1:7: "For the Spirit of the Lord filleth the world." In the "Water of the Art," in "our Water," which is also the chaos, there are to be found the "fiery sparks of the soul of the world as pure *Formae Rerum essen-*

---

[24] "Its divers rays and sparks are dispersed and dissipated throughout the immense bulk of the whole mass of the *prima materia:* the sparks of the one universal soul now inhabiting those disunited parts of the world which were later separated from the place and mass of the body, and even from its circumference." Heinrich Conrad Khunrath, *Amphitheatrum sapientiae aeternae solius verae, Christiano-kabalisticum, divino-magicum . . . Tertriunum, Catholicon* (Hanau, 1604), pp. 195 f., 198.

[25] *Ibid.,* p. 197. Cf. the Gnostic doctrine of the Seeds of Light harvested by the Virgin of Light, and the Manichaean doctrine of the light particles which have to be taken into one's body as ritual food, at a sort of Eucharist when melons were eaten. The earliest mention of this idea seems to be the χαοπιστής (Ireanaeus, *Contra haereses,* I, 2, 4).

[26] *"Mens humani animi scintilla altior et lucidior"* (The mind of the human soul is a higher and more luminous spark). *Amphitheatrum,* p. 63.

tiales." These *formae*[27] correspond to the Platonic Ideas, from which one could equate the *scintillae* with the archetypes on the assumption that the Forms "stored up in some heavenly place" are a philosophical version of the latter. One would have to conclude from these alchemical visions that the archetypes have about them a certain effulgence, and that numinosity entails luminosity. Paracelsus seems to have had an inkling of this. The following is taken from his *Philosophia Sagax*: "And as little as aught can exist in man without the divine numen, so little can aught exist in man without the natural lumen. A man is made perfect by numen and lumen and these two alone. Everything springs from these two, and these two are in man, but without them man is nothing, though they can be without man." In confirmation of this Khunrath writes: "There be . . . *Scintillae Animae Mundi igneae, Luminis nimirum Naturae,* fiery sparks of the world soul, i.e., of the light of nature . . . dispersed or sprinkled in and throughout the structure of the great world into all fruits of the elements everywhere." The sparks come from the "Ruach Elohim," the Spirit of God. From among the *scintillae* he distinguishes a *"scintilla perfecta Unici Potentis ac Fortis,"* which is the elixir and hence the arcane substance itself. If we may compare the sparks to the archetypes, it is evident that Khunrath lays particular stress on one of them. This One is also described as the Monad and the Sun, and they both indicate the Deity. A similar image is to be found in the letter of Ignatius of Antioch to the Ephesians, where he writes of the coming of Christ: "How, then, was he manifested to the ages? A star shone forth in heaven above all the other stars, the light of which was inexpressible, while its novelty struck men with astonishment. And all the rest of the stars, with the sun and moon, formed a chorus to this star. . . ."[28] Psychologically, the One Scintilla or Monad is to be regarded as a symbol of the self—an aspect I mention only in passing.

The sparks have a clear psychological meaning for Dorn.[29] This light is the *lumen naturae* which illuminates consciousness, and the *scintillae*

[27] The *"formae scintillaeve Animae Mundi"* (forms or sparks of the world soul) are also called by Khunrath (p. 189) *"rationes seminariae Naturae specificae"* (the seed-ideas of Nature, the origin of species), thus reproducing an ancient idea. In the same way he calls the *scintilla "Entelechia"* (p. 65).

[28] Ch. XIX, 1 ff. (tr. in *The Writings of the Apostolic Fathers,* Ante-Nicene Christian Library, I; Edinburgh, 1883).

[29] "Thus he will come to see with his spiritual eyes a number of sparks shining through day by day and more and more and growing into such a great light that thereafter all things needful to him will be made known." Gerhard Dorn, "De speculativa philosophia," in *Theatrum chemicum* (Ursel, 1602), Vol. I, p. 275.

are germinal luminosities shining forth from the darkness of the unconscious. Dorn, like Khunrath, owes much to Paracelsus, with whom he concurs when he supposes "an invisible sun unknown to many."[30] Of this natural light innate in man Dorn says: "For the life shineth in us, albeit dimly, as the light of men, and as though in darkness. It is not to be extracted from us, yet it is in us and not of us, but of Him to Whom it belongs, and Who hath deigned to make us his dwelling place. . . . He has implanted that light in us that we may see in its light the light of Him Who dwells in the inaccessible light, and that we may excel His other creatures; in this wise we are made like unto Him, for He has given us a spark of His light. Thus the truth is to be sought not in ourselves, but in the image of God which is in us."[31]

Thus the one archetype emphasized by Khunrath is known also to Dorn as the *sol invisibilis* or *imago Dei*. In Paracelsus the *lumen naturae* comes primarily from the "*astrum*" or "*sydus,*" the "star" in man. The "firmament" (a synonym for the star) is the natural light. Hence the "cornerstone" of all truth is "Astronomia," which is "a mother to all the other arts. . . . After her beginneth the divine wisdom, after her beginneth the light of nature," even the "most excellent Religiones" hang upon Astronomia. For the star "desireth to drive man toward great wisdom . . . that he may appear wondrous in the light of nature, and the mysteria of God's wondrous work be discovered and revealed in their grandeur." Indeed, man himself is an "Astrum": "not by himself alone, but for ever and ever with all apostles and saints; each and every one is an astrum, the heaven a star . . . therefore saith also the Scripture: ye are lights of the world." "Now as in the star lieth the whole natural light, and from it man taketh the same like food from the earth into which he is born, so too must he be born into the star." Also the animals have the natural light which is an "inborn spirit." Man at his birth is "endowed with the perfect light of nature." Paracelsus calls it "*primum ac optimum thesaurum, quem naturae Monarchia in se claudit*" (the first and best treasure which the monarchy of nature hides within itself), in this concurring with the world-wide descriptions of the One as the pearl of great price, the hidden treasure, the "treasure hard to attain," etc. The light is given to the "inner man" or the inner body (*corpus subtile,* breath-body). . . . Man is "a prophet of the natural light." He "learns" the *lumen naturae* through dreams,

[30] "*Sol est invisibilis in hominibus, in terra vero visibilis, tamen ex uno et eodem sole sunt ambo*" (The sun is invisible in men, but visible in the world, yet both are of one and the same sun.) Ibid., p. 308.

[31] "De philosophia meditativa," *Theatrum chemicum,* Vol. I, p. 460.

among other things. "As the light of nature cannot speak, it buildeth shapes in sleep from the power of the word" (of God).

I have allowed myself to dwell at some length on Paracelsus and to cite a number of authentic texts, because I wanted to give the reader a rough idea of the way in which this author conceives the *lumen naturae*. It strikes me as significant, particularly in regard to our hypothesis of a multiple consciousness and its phenomena, that the characteristic alchemical vision of sparks scintillating in the blackness of the arcane substance should, for Paracelsus, change into the spectacle of the "interior firmament" and its stars. He beholds the darksome psyche as a star-strewn night sky, whose planets and fixed constellations represent the archetypes in all their luminosity and numinosity. The starry vault of heaven is in truth the open book of cosmic projection, in which are reflected the mythologems, i.e., the archetypes. In this vision astrology and alchemy, the two classic functionaries of the psychology of the collective unconscious, join hands.

Paracelsus was directly influenced by Agrippa of Nettesheim, who supposes a "*luminositas sensus naturae*." From this "gleams of prophecy came down to the four-footed beasts, the birds, and other living creatures," and enabled them to foretell future things. He bases the *sensus naturae* on the authority of Gulielmus Parisiensis, who is none other than William of Auvergne (G. Alvernus; d. 1249), bishop of Paris from about 1228; author of many works, which influenced Albertus Magnus among others. Alvernus says that the *sensus naturae* is superior to the perceptive faculty in man, and he insists that animals also possess it. The doctrine of the *sensus naturae* is developed from the idea of the all-pervading world soul with which another Gulielmus Parisiensis was much concerned, a predecessor of Alvernus by name of Guillaume de Conches (1080–1154), a Platonist scholastic who taught in Paris. He identified the *anima mundi,* this same *sensus naturae,* with the Holy Ghost, just as Abelard did. The world soul is a natural force which is responsible for all the phenomena of life and the psyche. As I have shown elsewhere, this view of the *anima mundi* ran through the whole tradition of alchemy insofar as Mercurius was interpreted now as *anima mundi* and now as the Holy Ghost. In view of the importance of alchemical ideas for the psychology of the unconscious it may be worth our while to devote a little time to a very illuminating variant of this spark symbolism.

Even more common than the spark motif is that of the fish's eyes, which have the same significance.

THIS IS MY PHILOSOPHY

From Ignatius Loyola's autobiography, which he dictated to Loys Gonzales, we learn that he used to see a bright light, and sometimes this apparition seemed to him to have the form of a serpent. It appeared to be full of shining eyes, which were yet no eyes. At first he was greatly comforted by the beauty of the vision, but later he recognized it to be an evil spirit. This vision sums up all the aspects of our optic theme and presents a most impressive picture of the unconscious with its disseminated luminosities. One can easily imagine the perplexity which a medieval man would be bound to feel when confronted by such an eminently "psychological" intuition, especially as he had no dogmatic symbol and no adequate patristic allegory to come to his rescue. But, as a matter of fact, Ignatius was not so very wide of the mark, for multiple eyes are also a characteristic of Purusha, the Hindu Cosmic Man. . . .

Such visions must be understood as introspective intuitions that somehow capture the state of the unconscious and, at the same time, as amalgams of the central Christian idea. Naturally enough, the motif has the same meaning in modern dreams and fantasies, where it appears as the star-strewn heavens, as stars reflected in dark water, as nuggets of gold or golden sand scattered in black earth, as a regatta at night, with lanterns on the dark surface of the sea, as a solitary eye in the depths of the sea or earth, as a parapsychic vision of luminous globes, and so on. Since consciousness has always been described in terms derived from the behavior of light, it is in my view not too much to assume that these multiple luminosities correspond to tiny conscious phenomena. If the luminosity appears in monadic form as a single star, sun, or eye, it readily assumes the shape of a mandala and must then be interpreted as the self. It has nothing whatever to do with "double consciousness," because there is no indication of a dissociated personality. On the contrary, the symbols of the self have a "uniting" -character.

VII. PATTERNS OF BEHAVIOR AND ARCHETYPES

We have stated that the lower reaches of the psyche begin at the moment when the function emancipates itself from the compulsive force of instinct and becomes amenable to the will, and we have defined the will as disposable energy. But that, as said, presupposes a disposing subject, capable of judgment and endowed with consciousness. In this way we arrived at the position of proving, as it were, the very thing that we started by rejecting, namely the identification of psyche with consciousness. This dilemma resolves itself once we realize how very relative consciousness is, since its contents are conscious and unconscious at the same time, i.e., conscious under one aspect and unconscious under another. As is the way of paradoxes, this statement is not immediately comprehensible. We must, however, accustom ourselves to the thought that conscious and unconscious have no clear demarcations, the one beginning where the other leaves off. It is rather the case that the psyche is a conscious-unconscious whole. As to the no man's land which I have called the "personal unconscious," it is fairly easy to prove that its contents correspond exactly to our definition of the psyche. But—as we define "psychic"—is there a psychic unconscious that is not a "fringe of consciousness" and not personal?

. . . Freud established the existence of archaic vestiges and primitive modes of functioning in the unconscious. Subsequent investigations have confirmed this result and brought together a wealth of observational material. In view of the structure of the body it would be astonishing if the psyche were the only biological phenomenon not to show clear traces of its evolutionary history, and it is altogether probable that these marks are closely connected with the instinctual base. Instinct and the archaic mode meet in the biological conception of the "pattern of behavior." There are in fact no amorphous instincts, as every instinct bears in itself the pattern of its situation. Always it fulfills an image, and the image has fixed qualities. The instinct of the leaf-cutting ant fulfills the image of ant, tree, leaf, cutting, transport, and the little ant garden of fungi. If any one of these conditions is lacking, the instinct does not function, because it cannot exist without its total pattern, without its image. Such an image is an *a priori* type. It is inborn in the ant prior to any activity, for there can be no activity at all unless an instinct of corresponding pattern initiates and makes it possible. This schema holds true of all instincts and is found in identical form in all individuals of the same species. The same is true also of man: he has in him these *a priori* instinct types which provide the occasion and the pattern for his activities, in so far as he functions instinctively. As a biological being he has no choice but to act in a specifically human way and fulfill his pattern of behavior. This sets narrow limits to his possible range of volition, the more narrow the more primitive he is, and the more his consciousness is dependent upon the instinctual sphere. Although from one point of view it is quite correct to speak of the pattern of behavior as a still existing archaic vestige, as Nietzsche did in respect of the function of dreams, such an attitude does scant justice to the biological and psychological meaning of these types. They are not just relics or residues of earlier functional modes; they are the ever-present and biologically necessary regulators of the instinctual sphere, whose range of action covers the whole realm of the psyche and only loses its absoluteness when limited by the relative freedom of the will. We may say that the image represents the *meaning* of the instinct.

Although the existence of an instinctual pattern in human biology is probable, it seems very difficult to prove the existence of distinct types empirically. For the organ with which we might apprehend them —consciousness—is not only itself a transformation of the original instinctual image, but also its transformer. It is therefore not surprising that the human mind finds it impossible to classify man into precise types similar to those we know in the animal kingdom. I must confess that I can see no direct way to solve this problem. And yet I have succeeded, or so I believe, in finding at least an indirect way of approach to the instinctual image.

In what follows I would like to give a brief description of how this discovery took place. I had often observed patients whose dreams pointed to a rich store of fantasy material. Equally, from the patients themselves, I got the impression that they were stuffed full of fantasies, without their being able to tell me just where the inner pressure lay. I therefore took up a dream image or an association of the patient's, and, with this as a point of departure, set him the task of elaborating or developing his theme by giving free rein to his fantasy. This, according to individual taste and talent, could be done in any number of ways, dramatic, dialectic, visual, acoustic, or in the form of dancing, painting, drawing, or modeling. The result of this technique was a vast number of complicated patterns whose diversity puzzled me for years, until I was able to recognize that in this method I was witnessing the spontaneous manifestation of an unconscious process which was merely assisted by the technical ability of the patient, and to which I later gave the name "individuation process." But long before this recognition dawned upon me I had made the discovery that this method often diminished, to a considerable degree, the frequency and intensity of the dreams, thus reducing the inexplicable pressure exerted by the unconscious. In many cases this brought a large measure of therapeutic success, which encouraged both myself and the patient to press forward despite the baffling nature of the results.[32] I felt bound to

[32] Cf. "Aims of Modern Psychotherapy" in *The Practice of Psychotherapy, Coll. Works,* Vol. 16, pars. 101 ff.; and *Two Essays on Analytical Psychology, Coll. Works,* Vol 7, pars. 343 ff. (Both New York and London, resp. 1954 and 1953.)

insist that they were baffling, if only to stop myself from framing, on the basis of certain theoretical assumptions, interpretations which I felt were not only inadequate but liable to prejudice the ingenuous patterns of the patient. The more I suspected these patterns of harboring a certain purposefulness, the less inclined I was to risk any theories about them. This reticence was not made easy for me, since in many cases I was dealing with patients who needed an intellectual *point d'appui* if they were not to get totally lost in the darkness. I had to try to give provisional interpretations at least, so far as I was able, interspersing them with innumerable "perhapses" and "ifs" and "buts" and never stepping beyond the bounds of the pattern lying before me. I always took good care to let the interpretation of each image tail off into a question whose answer was left to the free fantasy activity of the patient.

The chaotic assortment of images that at first confronted me reduced itself in the course of the work to certain well-defined themes and formal elements which repeated themselves in identical or analogous form with the most varied individuals. I mention, as the most salient characteristics, chaotic multiplicity and order, dualism, the opposition of light and dark, of upper and lower, right and left, the union of opposites in a third, the quaternity (square, cross), rotation (circle, sphere), and finally the centering process and a radial arrangement that usually followed some quaternary system. Triadic formations, apart from the *complexio oppositorum* in a third, were relatively rare and formed notable exceptions which could be explained by special conditions.[33] The centering process is, in my experience, the never-to-be-surpassed climax of the whole development,[34] and is characterized as such by the fact that it brings with it the greatest possible therapeutic effect. The distinctive features listed above go to the limits of abstraction, yet at the same time they are the simplest expressions of the formative principles here at work. In actual reality the patterns are infinitely more variegated and far more concrete. Their variety defies description. I can only say that there is probably no motif in any known mythology that does not at some time appear in these configurations. If there was any conscious knowledge of mythological motifs worth mentioning in my patients, it is left far behind by the ingenuities of creative fantasy.

These facts show in an unmistakable manner how fantasies guided by unconscious regulators coincide with the memorials of man's

---

[33] The same applies to the pentadic figures.
[34] So far as the development can be ascertained from the objective material.

spiritual activity as known to us from tradition and ethnological research. All the abstract features I have mentioned are in a certain sense conscious: everyone can count up to four and knows what a circle is and a square, but, as formative principles, they are unconscious and by the same token their psychological meaning is not conscious either. My most fundamental views and ideas derive from these experiences. First I made the observations, and only then did I hammer out my views. And so it is with the hand that guides the crayon or brush, the foot that executes the dance step, with the eye and the ear, with the word and the thought: a dark impulse is the ultimate arbiter of the pattern, an unconscious *a priori* precipitates itself into plastic form, and one has no inkling that another person's consciousness is being steered by the same principles at the very point where one feels utterly exposed to the boundless subjective vagaries of chance. Over the whole procedure there seems to reign a dim foreknowledge not only of the pattern, but of its meaning.[35] Image and meaning are identical; and as the first takes shape, so the latter becomes clear. Actually the pattern needs no interpretation: it portrays its own meaning. There are cases where I can let interpretation go as a therapeutic requirement. Scientific knowledge, of course, is another matter. Here we have to elicit from the sum total of our experience certain concepts of the greatest possible general validity, which are not given *a priori*. This particular work entails a translation of the timeless, ever-present operative archetype into the scientific language of the present.

These experiences and reflections lead me to believe that there are certain collective unconscious conditions which act as regulators and stimulators of creative fantasy activity and call forth corresponding formations by availing themselves of the existing conscious material. They behave exactly like the motive forces of dreams, for which reason active imagination, as I have called this method, to some extent takes the place of dreams. The existence of these unconscious regulators—I sometimes refer to them as "dominants"[36] because of their mode of functioning—seemed to me so important that I based upon it my hypothesis of an impersonal collective unconscious. The most remarkable thing about this method, I felt, was that it did not involve a *reductio in primam figuram,* but rather a synthesis—supported by an attitude voluntarily adopted, though for the rest wholly natural—

[35] Cf. *Psychology and Alchemy,* pp. 211 ff.
[36] Cf. *Two Essays on Analytical Psychology,* par. 151.

of passive conscious material and unconscious influences, hence a kind of spontaneous amplification of the archetypes. The images are not to be thought of as a reduction of conscious contents to their simplest denominator, as this would be the direct road to the primordial images which I said previously was unimaginable; they only make their appearance in the course of amplification.

On this natural amplification process I also base my method of eliciting the meaning of dreams, for dreams behave in exactly the same way as active imagination, only the support of conscious contents is lacking. To the extent that the archetypes intervene in the shaping of conscious contents by regulating, modifying, and motivating them, they act like the instincts. It is therefore very natural to suppose that these factors are connected with the instincts and to inquire whether the typical situational patterns which these collective form-principles apparently represent are not in the end identical with the instinctual patterns, namely, with the patterns of behavior. I must admit that up to the present I have not got hold of any argument that would finally refute this possibility.

Before I pursue my reflections further, I must stress one aspect of the archetypes which will be obvious to anybody who has practical experience of these matters. That is, the archetypes have, when they appear, a distinctly numinous character which can only be described as "spiritual," if "magical" is too strong a word. Consequently this phenomenon is of the utmost significance for the psychology of religion. In its effects it is anything but unambiguous. It can be healing or destructive, but never indifferent, provided of course that it has attained a certain degree of clarity.[37] This aspect deserves the epithet "spiritual" above all else. It not infrequently happens that the archetype appears in the form of a *spirit* in dreams or fantasy products, or even comports itself like a ghost. There is a mystical aura about its numinosity, and it has a corresponding effect upon the emotions. It mobilizes philosophical and religious convictions in the very people who deemed themselves miles above any such fits of weakness. Often it drives with unexampled passion and remorseless logic toward its goal and draws

[37] Occasionally it is associated with synchronistic or parapsychic effects. I mean by synchronicity, as I have explained elsewhere, the not uncommonly observed "coincidence" of subjective and objective happenings, which just cannot be explained causally, at least in the present state of our knowledge. On this premise astrology is based and the methods of the *I Ching*. These observations, like the astrological findings, are not generally accepted, though as we know this has never hurt the facts. I mention these special effects solely for the sake of completeness and solely for the benefit of those readers who have had occasion to convince themselves of the reality of parapsychic phenomena.

the subject under its spell, from which despite the most desperate resistance he is unable, and finally no longer even willing, to break free, because the experience brings with it a depth and fullness of meaning that was unthinkable before. I fully appreciate the resistance that all rooted convictions are bound to put up against psychological discoveries of this kind. With more foreboding than real knowledge most people feel afraid of the menacing power that lies fettered in each of us, only waiting for the magic word to release it from the spell. This magic word always rhymes with "ism" and works most successfully with those who have the least access to their interior selves and have strayed the furthest from their instinctual roots into the truly chaotic world of *collective consciousness.*

In spite or perhaps because of its affinity with instinct the archetype represents the authentic element of spirit, but a spirit which is not to be identified with the human intellect, since it is the latter's *spiritus rector.* The essential content of all mythologies and all religions and all isms is archetypal. The archetype is spirit or pseudo spirit: what it ultimately proves to be depends on the attitude of the human mind. Archetype and instinct are the most polar opposites imaginable, as can easily be seen when one compares a man who is ruled by his instinctual drives with a man who is seized by the spirit. But, just as between all opposites there obtains so close a bond that no position can be established or even thought of without its corresponding negation, so in this case also *"les extrêmes se touchent."* They belong together as correspondences, which is not to say that the one is derivable from the other, but that they subsist side by side as reflections of the opposition that underlies all psychic energy. Man finds himself simultaneously driven to act and free to reflect. This contrariety in his nature has no moral significance, for instinct is not in itself bad any more than spirit is good. Both can be both. Negative electricity is as good as positive electricity: first and foremost it is electricity. The psychological opposites, too, must be regarded from a scientific standpoint. True opposites are never incommensurables; if they were they could never unite. All contrariety notwithstanding, they do show a constant propensity to union, and the Cusan defined God Himself as a *complexio oppositorum.*

Opposites are extreme qualities in any state, by virtue of which that state is perceived to be real, for they form a potential. The psyche is made up of processes whose energy springs from the equilibration of all kinds of opposites. The spirit: instinct antithesis is only one of the commonest formulations, but it has the advantage of reducing the greatest number of the most important and most complex psychic processes to a common denominator. So regarded, psychic processes seem to be balances of energy flowing between spirit and instinct, though the question of whether a process is to be described as spiritual or as instinctual remains shrouded in darkness. Such evaluation or interpretation depends entirely upon the standpoint or state of the conscious mind. A poorly developed consciousness, for instance, which because of massed projections is inordinately impressed by concrete or apparently concrete things and states, will naturally see in the instinctual drives the source of all reality. It remains blissfully unaware of the spirituality of such a philosophical surmise, and is convinced that with this opinion it has established the essential instinctuality of all psychic processes. Conversely, a consciousness that finds itself in opposition to the instincts can, in consequence of the enormous influence then exerted by the archetypes, so subordinate instinct to spirit that the most grotesque "spiritual" complications may arise out of what are undoubtedly biological happenings. Here the instinctuality of the fanaticism needed for such an operation is ignored.

Psychic processes therefore behave like a scale along which consciousness "slides." At one moment it finds itself in the vicinity of instinct, and falls under its influence; at another, it slides along to the other end where spirit predominates and even assimilates the instinctual processes most opposed to it. These counterpositions, so fruitful of illusion, are by no means symptoms of the abnormal; on the contrary they form the twin poles of that psychic one-sidedness which is typical of the normal man of today. Naturally this does not manifest itself only in the sphere of the spirit: instinct antithesis; it assumes many other forms, as I have shown in my *Psychological Types*.

This "sliding" consciousness is thoroughly characteristic of modern man. But the one-sidedness it causes can be removed by what I have called the "realization of the shadow." A less "poetic" and more scientific-looking Greco-Latin neologism could easily have been coined for this operation. In psychology, however, one is to be dissuaded from ventures of this sort, at least when dealing with eminently practical problems. Among these is the "realization of the shadow," the growing awareness of the inferior part of the personality, which should not be twisted into an intellectual activity, for it has far more the meaning of a suffering and a passion that implicate the whole man. The essence of that which has to be realized and assimilated has been expressed so trenchantly and so plastically in poetic language by the word "shadow" that it would be almost presumptuous not to avail oneself of this linguistic heritage. Even the term "inferior part of the personality" is inadequate and misleading, whereas "shadow" presumes nothing that would rigidly fix its content. The "man without a shadow" is statistically the commonest human type, one who imagines he actually is only what he cares to know about himself. Unfortunately neither the so-called religious man nor the man of scientific pretensions forms any exception to this rule.[38]

Confrontation with an archetype or instinct is an *ethical* problem of the first magnitude, the urgency of which is felt only by people who find themselves faced with the need to assimilate the unconscious and integrate their personalities. This only falls to the lot of the man who realizes that he has a neurosis, or that all is not well with his psychic constitution. These are certainly not the majority. The "common man," who is preponderantly a mass man, acts on the principle of realizing nothing, nor does he need to, because for him the only thing that commits mistakes is that vast anonymity conventionally known as the "State" or "Society." But once a man knows that he is, or should be, responsible, he feels responsible also for his psychic constitution, the more so the more clearly he sees what he would have to be in order to become healthier, more stable, and more efficient. Once he is on the way to assimilating the unconscious he can be certain that he will escape no difficulty that is an integral part of his nature. The mass man, on the other hand, has the privilege of being at all times "not guilty" of his social and political catastrophes in which the whole world s engulfed. His final balance is thrown out accordingly; whereas the other at least has the possibility of finding a spiritual point of vantage, a kingdom that "is not of this world."

It would be an unpardonable sin of omission were one to overlook the *feeling value* of the archetype. This is extremely important both theoretically and therapeutically. As a numinous factor the archetype determines the manner of the structuring and the course it will follow, with seeming foreknowledge, or as though it were already in possession of the goal to be circumscribed by the centering process.[39] I would like

[38] This was the truth upon which Philip Wylie based his vehement attack on modern civilization, here leveled exclusively at the United States (*Generation of Vipers*, New York, 1942). With few variations, however, it applies equally to Europeans. The development of consciousness in civilized man has its attendant and very serious dangers, which are still apparently not recognized for what they are, and are often misinterpreted in the most disastrous way.

[39] Cf. *Psychology and Alchemy*, Part II, for evidence of this.

to make the way in which the archetype functions clear from this simple example: While sojourning in Equatorial East Africa, on the southern slopes of Mount Elgon, I found that the natives used to step out of their huts at sunrise, hold their hands before their mouths, and spit or blow into them vigorously. Then they lifted their arms and held their hands with the palms toward the sun. I asked them the meaning of what they did, but nobody could give me an explanation. They had always done it like that, they said, and had learnt it from their parents. The medicine man, he would know what it meant. So I asked the medicine man. He knew as little as the others, but assured me that his grandfather had still known. It was just what people did at every sunrise, and at the first phase of the new moon. For these people, as I was able to show, the moment when the sun or the new moon appeared was *"mungu,"* which corresponds to the Melanesian words *"mana"* or *"mulungu"*[40] and is translated by the missionaries as "God." Actually the word *"athista"* in Elgonyi means sun as well as God, although they deny that the sun is God. Only the moment when it rises is *mungu* or *athista*. Spittle and breath mean soul-substance. Hence they offer their soul to God, but do not know what they are doing and never have known. They do it, motivated by the same pre-conscious archetype which the ancient Egyptians, on their monuments, also ascribed to the sun-worshiping dog-headed baboon, albeit in full knowledge that this ritual gesture was in honor of God. The behavior of the Elgonyi certainly strikes us as exceedingly primitive, but we forget that the educated Westerner behaves no differently. What the meaning of the Christmas tree might be our forefeathers knew even less than ourselves, and it is only quite recently that we have bothered to find out at all.

The archetype is pure, unvitiated nature,[41] and it is nature that causes man to utter words and perform actions whose meaning is unconscious to him, so unconscious that he no longer gives it a thought, even if he were capable of thinking, like the Westerner. A later, more conscious humanity, faced with such meaningful things whose meaning none could declare, hit upon the idea that these must be the last vestiges of a Golden Age, when there were men who knew all things and taught wisdom to the nations. In the degenerate days that followed, these teachings were forgotten and were now only repeated as mindless mechanical gestures. In view of the findings of modern psychology it cannot be doubted that there are preconscious

---

[40] (*Mulungu*="spirit, soul, daemonism, magic, prestige": *Two Essays*, par. 108.—ED.)
[41] "Nature" here means simply that which is, and always was, given.

archetypes which were never conscious and can be established only indirectly through their effects upon the conscious contents. There is in my opinion no tenable argument against the hypothesis that all the psychic functions which today seem conscious to us were once unconscious and yet worked as if they *were* conscious. We could also say that all the psychic phenomena to be found in man were already present in the natural unconscious state. To this it might be objected that it would then be far from clear why there is such a thing as consciousness at all. I would however remind the reader that, as we have already seen, all unconscious functioning has the automatic character of an instinct, and that the instincts are always coming into collision or, because of their compulsiveness, pursuing their courses unaltered by any influence even under conditions that may positively endanger the life of the individual. As against this, consciousness enables him to adapt in an orderly way and to check the instincts, and consequently cannot be dispensed with. Man's capacity for consciousness alone makes him man.

The achievement of a synthesis of conscious and unconscious contents, and the conscious realization of the archetype's effects upon the conscious contents, represents the climax of a concentrated spiritual and psychic effort, insofar as this is undertaken consciously and of set purpose. That is to say, the synthesis can also be prepared in advance and brought to a certain point—James's "bursting point"—unconsciously, whereupon it irrupts into consciousness of its own volition and confronts the latter with the formidable task of assimilating the contents that have burst in upon it, yet without damaging the viability of the two systems, i.e., of ego consciousness on the one hand and the irrupted complex on the other. Classical example of this process are Paul's conversion and the Trinity vision of Nicholas of Flüe.

By means of "active imagination" we are put in a position of advantage, for we can then make the discovery of the archetype without sinking back into the instinctual sphere, which would only lead to blank unconsciousness or, worse still, to some kind of intellectual substitute for instinct. This means—to employ once more the simile of the spectrum—that the instinctual image is to be located not at the red end but at the violet end of the color band. The dynamism of instinct is lodged as it were in the infrared part of the spectrum, whereas the instinctual image lies in the ultraviolet part. If we remember our color symbolism, then, as I have said, red is not such a bad match for instinct. But for spirit, as might be expected,[42] blue would be a better match than violet. Violet is the "mystic" color, and it certainly reflects the indubitably "mystic" or paradoxical quality of the archetype in a most satisfactory way. Violet is a compound of blue and red, although in the spectrum it is a color in its own right. Now, it is unfortunately rather more than just an edifying thought if we feel bound to emphasize that the archetype is more accurately characterized by violet, for, as well as being an image in its own right, it is at the same time a *dynamism* which makes itself felt in the numinosity and fascinating power of the archetypal image. The realization and assimilation of instinct never take place at the red end, i.e., by absorption into the instinctual sphere, but only through integration of the image which signifies and at the same time evokes the instinct, although in a form quite different from the one we meet on the biological level. When Faust remarks to Wagner: "You are conscious only of the single urge / O may you never learn to know the other!" this is a saying that could equally well be applied to instinct in general. It has two aspects: on the one hand it is experienced as physiological dynamism, while on the other hand its multitudinous forms enter into consciousness as images and groups of images, where they develop numinous effects which offer, or appear to offer, the strictest possible contrast to instinct physiologically regarded. For anyone acquainted with religious phenomenology it is an open secret that although physical and spiritual passion are deadly enemies, they are nevertheless brothers in arms, for which reason it often needs the merest touch to convert the one into the other. Both are real, and together they form a pair of opposites, which is one of the most fruitful sources of psychic energy. There is no point in deriving one from the other in order to give primacy to one of them. Even if we know only one at first, and do not notice the other until much later, that does not prove that the other was not there all the time. Hot cannot be derived from cold, nor high from low. An opposition either exists in its binary form or it does not exist at all, and a being without opposites is completely unthinkable, as it would be impossible to establish its existence.

Absorption into the instinctual sphere, therefore, does not and cannot lead to conscious realization and assimilation of instinct, be-

---

[42] This expectation is based on the experience that blue, the color of air and sky, is most readily used for depicting spiritual contents, whereas red, the "warm" color, is used for feelings and emotions.

cause consciousness struggles in a regular panic against being swallowed up in the primitivity and unconsciousness of sheer instinctuality. This fear is the eternal burden of the hero myth and the theme of countless taboos. The closer one comes to the instinct world, the more violent is the urge to shy away from it and to rescue the light of consciousness from the murks of the sultry abyss. Psychologically, however, the archetype as an image of instinct is a spiritual goal toward which the whole nature of man strives; it is the sea to which all rivers wend their way, the prize which the hero wrests from the fight with the dragon.

Because the archetype is a formative principle of instinctual power, its blue is contaminated with red: it appears to be violet, or again, we could interpret the simile as an apocatastasis of instinct raised to a higher frequency, just as we could easily derive instinct from a latent (i.e., transcendent) archetype that manifests itself on a longer wave length.[43] Although it can admittedly be no more than an analogy, I nevertheless feel tempted to recommend this violet image to my reader as an illustrative hint of the archetype's affinity with its own opposite. The creative fantasy of the alchemists sought to express this abstruse secret of nature by means of another, no less visual, symbol: the Uroboros, or tail-eating serpent.

I do not want to drive this simile to death, but, as the reader will understand, one is always delighted, when discussing difficult problems, to find support in a helpful analogy. In addition this simile helps to throw light on a question we have not yet asked ourselves, much less answered, the question regarding the *nature* of the archetype. The archetypal ideas mediated to us by the unconscious should not be confused with the archetype as such. They are very varied structures which all point back to one essentially nonvisual basic form. The latter is characterized by certain formal elements and by certain fundamental meanings, although these can be grasped only approximately. The archetype as such is a psychoid factor that belongs, as it were, to the invisible, utraviolet end of the spectrum. It does not appear, in itself, to be capable of reaching consciousness. I venture this hypothesis because everything archetypal which is perceived by consciousness seems to represent a set of variations on a ground theme. One is most impressed by this fact when one studies the endless variations of the mandala motif. This is a relatively simple ground form

[43] Sir James Jeans (*Physics and Philosophy*, Cambridge, 1942, pp. 282 ff.) points out that the shadows on the wall of Plato's cave are just as real as the invisible figures that throw them and whose presence can only be inferred mathematically.

whose meaning can be said to be "central." But although it looks like the structure of a center, it is still uncertain whether within that structure the center or the periphery, division or nondivision, is the more accentuated. Since other archetypes give rise to similar doubts, it seems to me probable that the real nature of the archetype is not capable of being made conscious, that it is transcendent, on which account I call it psychoid. Moreover every archetype, as a visual phenomenon, is already conscious and therefore differs to an indeterminable extent from the cause of the vision. As Theodore Lipps has stressed, the nature of the psychic is unconscious. Anything conscious is part of the phenomenal world which—so modern physics teaches—does not supply explanations of the kind that objective reality requires. Objective reality requires a mathematical model, and experience shows that this is built up of invisible and nonvisual—noumenal—factors. Psychology cannot evade the universal validity of this fact, the less so as the observing psychic is already included in any formulation of objective reality. Nor can psychological theory be formulated mathematically, because we have no measuring rod with which to measure psychic quantities. We have to rely solely upon qualities, that is, upon perceptible phenomena. Consequently psychology is incapacitated from making any valid statement about unconscious states, or to put it another way, there is no hope that the validity of any statement about unconscious states or processes will ever be verified scientifically. Whatever we say about the archetypes, they remain visualizations or concretizations which pertain to the field of consciousness. But—we cannot speak about archetypes in any other way. We must, however, constantly bear in mind that what we mean by "archetype" is intrinsically nonvisual and noumenal and has as much to do with the physical continuum as this has with it. Just as mathematical physics, in its psychological aspect, can do no more than establish the presence of an observer without being able to assert anything about the nature of that observer, so, thanks to the phenomenon of synchronicity, psychology can at least indicate a peculiar relation to the space-time continuum, though without being able to make out the least thing concerning its nature. For all we know, psychology might itself be the mathematically indeterminable, qualitative nature of that continuum. Certainly our present knowledge permits us no more than the comparison with two cones whose apices, meeting in an absolutely unextended point, a real zero point, touch and do not touch.

In my previous writings I have always treated archetypal phenomena as psychic, because the material to be expounded or investigated was concerned solely with ideas. The psychoid nature of the archetype, as put forward here, does not contradict these earlier formulations; it only means a further degree of conceptual differentiation, which became inevitable as soon as I saw myself obliged to undertake a more general analysis of the nature of the psyche and to clarify the empirical concepts concerning it, and their relation to one another.

Just as the "psychic infrared," the biological instinctual psyche, gradually passes over into the physiology of the organism and thus merges with its chemical and physical conditions, so the "psychic ultraviolet," the archetype, describes a field which exhibits none of the peculiarities of the physiological and yet, in the last analysis, can no longer be regarded as psychic, although it manifests itself psychically. But physiological processes behave in the same way, without on that account being declared psychic. Although there is no form of existence that is not mediated to us psychically and only psychically, it would hardly do to say that everything is merely psychic. We must apply this argument logically to the archetypes as well. Since their essential being is unconscious to us, and yet they are experienced as spontaneous agencies, there is probably no alternative at present but to describe their nature, in accordance with their chiefest effect, as "spirit. . . ." If so, the position of the archetype would be located beyond the psychic sphere, analogous to the position of physiological instinct, which is immediately rooted in the stuff of the organism and, with its psychoid nature, forms the bridge to matter in general. In archetypal conceptions and instinctual perceptions, spirit and matter confront one another on the psychic plane. Matter as well as spirit appear in the psychic realm as distinctive qualities of conscious contents. The ultimate nature of both is transcendent, that is, noumenal, since the psyche and its contents are the only reality which is given to us *without a medium*.

VIII. GENERAL CONSIDERATIONS AND PROSPECTS

The problems of analytical psychology, as I have tried to outline them here, led to conclusions that astonished even me. I fancied I was working along the best scientific lines, establishing facts, observing, classifying, describing causal and functional relations, only to discover in the end that I had involved myself in a net of reflections which extend far beyond natural science and ramify into the fields of philosophy, theology, comparative religion, and the humane sciences in general. This transgression, as inevitable as it was suspect, has caused me no little worry. Quite apart from my personal incompetence in these fields, it seemed to me that my reflections were suspect also in principle, because I am profoundly convinced that the "personal equation" has a telling effect upon the results of psychological observation. The tragic thing is that psychology has no self-consistent mathematics at its disposal, but only a calculus of subjective prejudices. Also, it lacks the immense advantage of an Archimedean point such as physics enjoys. The latter observes the physical world from the psychic standpoint and can translate it into psychic terms. The psyche, on the other hand, observes itself and can only translate the psychic back into the psychic. Were physics in this position, it could do nothing except leave the physical process to its own devices, because in that way it would be most plainly itself. There is no medium for psychology to reflect itself in: it can only portray itself in itself, and describe itself. That, logically, is also the principle of my own method: it is, at bottom, a purely experiential process in which hit and miss, interpretation and error, theory and speculation, doctor and patient, form a *symptosis* (σύμπτωσις) or a *symptoma* (σύμπτωμα)—a coming together—and at the same time are symptoms of a certain process or run of events. What I am describing, therefore, is basically no more than an outline of psychic happenings which exhibit a certain statistical frequency. We have not, scientifically speaking, removed ourselves to a plane in any way "above" the psychic process, nor have we translated it into another medium. Physics, on the other hand, is in a position to detonate mathematical formulas—the product of pure psychic activity—and kill 78,000 persons at one blow.

This literally "devastating" argument is calculated to reduce psychology to silence. But we can, in all modesty, point out that mathematical thinking is also a psychic function, thanks to which matter can be organized in such a way as to burst asunder the mighty forces that bind the atoms together—which it would never occur to them to do in the natural course of things, at least not upon this earth. The psyche is a disturber of the natural laws of the cosmos, and should we ever succeed in doing something to Mars with the aid of atomic fission, this too will have been brought to pass by the psyche.

The psyche is the world's pivot: not only is it the one great condition for the existence of a world at all, it is also an intervention in the existing natural order, and no one can say with certainty where this intervention will finally end. It is hardly necessary to stress the dignity of the soul as an object of natural science. With all the more urgency, then, we must emphasize that the smallest alteration in the psychic factor, if it be an alteration of principle, is of the utmost significance as regards our knowledge of the world and the picture we make of it. The integration of unconscious contents into consciousness, which is the main endeavor of analytical psychology, is just such an alteration of principle, in that it does away with the sovereignty of the subjective ego and of collective consciousness and confronts the latter with collective unconscious contents. Accordingly the ego seems to be dependent on two factors: firstly, the conditions of collective, i.e., the social, consciousness, and secondly the collective unconscious dominants or archetypes. The latter fall phenomenologically into two categories: instinctual and archetypal. The first includes the natural impulses, the second the dominants that emerge into consciousness as universal ideas. Between the contents of collective consciousness, which purport to be generally accepted truths, and those of the collective unconscious there is so pronounced a contrast that the latter are rejected as totally irrational, not to say meaningless, and are most unjustifiably excluded from the scientific purview as though they did not exist. However, psychic phenomena of this kind exist with a vengeance, and if they appear nonsensical to us, that only proves that we do not understand them. Once their existence is recognized they can no longer be banished from our world picture, especially as the prevailing conscious *Weltanschauung* proves to be incapable of grasping the phenomena in question. A conscientious study of these phenomena quickly reveals their uncommon significance, and we can hardly avoid the conclusion that between collective consciousness and the collective unconscious there is an almost unbridgeable gulf over which the subject finds himself suspended.

As a rule collective consciousness wins hands down with its "reasonable" generalities that cause the average intelligence no difficulty whatever. It still believes in the necessary connection of cause and effect and has scarcely taken note of the fact that causality has become relative. The shortest distance between two points is still, for it, a straight line, although physics has to reckon with innumerable shortest distances, which strikes the educated Philistine of today as exquisitely absurd. Nevertheless the impressive explosion at Hiroshima has induced an awestruck respect for even the most abstruse alembications of modern physics. The explosion which we recently had occasion to witness in

Europe, though far more terrible in its repercussions, was recognized as an unmitigated psychic disaster only by the few. Rather than do this, people prefer the most preposterous political and economic theories, which are about as useful as explaining the Hiroshima explosion as the chance hit of a large meteorite.

If the subjective consciousness prefers the ideas and opinions of collective consciousness and identifies with them, then the contents of the collective unconscious are repressed. The repression has typical consequences: the energy charge of the repressed contents adds itself to that of the repressing factor, whose operational significance is increased accordingly. The higher its charge mounts, the more the repressive attitude acquires a fanatical character and the nearer it comes to conversion into its opposite, i.e., an enantiodromia. And the more highly charged the collective consciousness, the more the ego forfeits its practical importance. It is as it were absorbed by the opinions and tendencies of collective consciousness, and the result of that is the mass man, the ever-ready victim of some wretched "ism." The ego keeps its integrity only if it does not identify with one of the opposites, and if it understands how to hold the balance between them. This is only possible if it remains conscious of both at once. However, the necessary insight is made exceedingly difficult not by one's social and political leaders alone, but also by one's religious mentors. They all want decision in favor of one thing, and therefore the utter identification of the individual with a necessarily onesided "truth." Even if it were a question of some great truth, identification with it would still be a catastrophe, as it arrests all further spiritual development. Instead of knowledge one then has only belief, and sometimes that is more convenient and therefore more attractive.

If on the other hand the content of the collective unconscious is realized, if the existence and efficacy of archetypal ideas are made known, then a violent conflict usually breaks out between what Fechner has called the "daytime and the nighttime view." Medieval man (and modern man too in so far as he has kept the attitude of the past) lived fully conscious of the discord between worldliness, which was subject to the *princeps huius mundi* (St. John 12:31 and 16:11[44]), and the will of God. For centuries this contradiction was demonstrated before his very eyes by the struggle between imperial and papal power. On

[44] Although both passages hint that the devil was cast out during the lifetime of Jesus, in the Apocalypse the business of rendering him harmless is deferred until Doomsday (Rev. 20:2ff.).

the moral plane the conflict swelled to the everlasting cosmic tug of war between good and evil in which man was implicated on account of original sin. This medieval man had not yet fallen such a helpless victim to worldliness as the contemporary mass man, for, to offset the notorious and so to speak tangible powers of this world, he still acknowledged the equally influential metaphysical potencies which demanded to be taken into account. Although in one respect he was politically and socially unfree and without rights—e.g., as a serf—and also found himself in the extremely disagreeable situation of being tyrannized over by black superstition, he was at least biologically nearer to that unconscious wholeness which primitive man enjoys in even larger measure, and the wild animal possesses to perfection. Looked at from the standpoint of modern consciousness, the position of medieval man seems as deplorable as it is in need of improvement. But the much needed broadening of the mind by science has only replaced medieval one-sidedness—namely that age-old unconsciousness which once predominated and has gradually become defunctive—by a new one-sidedness, the overvaluation of "scientifically" attested views. These each and all relate to knowledge of the external object and in a chronically one-sided way, so that nowadays the backwardness of psychic development in general and of self-knowledge in particular has become one of the most pressing contemporary problems. As a result of the prevailing one-sidedness and in spite of the terrifying optical demonstration of an unconscious that has become alienated from the conscious, there are still vast numbers of people who are the blind and helpless victims of these conflicts, and who apply their scientific scrupulosity only to external objects, never to their own psychic condition. Yet the psychic facts are as much in need of objective scrutiny and acknowledgement. There are objective psychic factors which are every bit as important as radios and automobiles. Ultimately everything (particularly in the case of the atom bomb) depends on the uses to which these factors are put, and that is always conditioned by one's state of mind. The current "isms" are the most serious threat in this respect, because they are nothing but dangerous identifications of the subjective with the collective consciousness. Such an identity infallibly produces a mass psyche with its irresistible urge to catastrophe. Subjective consciousness must, in order to escape this doom, avoid identification with collective consciousness by recognizing its shadow as well as the existence and the importance of the archetypes. These latter are an effective defense against the brute force of collective consciousness and the mass psyche that goes with it.

Talking of effectiveness, the religious outlook of medieval man corresponds roughly to the attitude induced in the ego by the integration of unconscious contents, with the difference that in the latter case suggestibility to environmental influences and unconsciousness are replaced by scientific objectivity and self-consciousness. But so far as religion, for the contemporary consciousness, still means, if anything, a creed, and hence a collectively accepted system of religious statements neatly codified as potted dogmatic precepts, it has more affinities with collective consciousness even though its symbols express the once operative archetypes. So long as the communal consciousness presided over by the Church is objectively present, the psyche, as said, continues to enjoy a certain equilibrium. At all events it constitutes a sufficiently effective defense against inflation of the ego. But once Mother Church and her motherly Eros fall into abeyance, the individual is at the mercy of any passing collectivism and the attendant mass psyche. He succumbs to social or national inflation, and the tragedy is that he does so with the same psychic attitude which had once bound him to a church.

But if he is independent enough to recognize the bigotedness of the social "ism," he may then be threatened with subjective inflation, for usually he is not capable of seeing that religious ideas do not, in psychological reality, rest solely upon tradition and faith, but originate with the archetypes, the "careful consideration" of which—*religere!*—constitutes the essence of religion. The archetypes are continuously present and active; as such they need no believing in, but only an intuition of their meaning and a certain sapient awe, a δεισιδαιμονία, which never loses sight of their import. A consciousness sharpened by experience knows the catastrophic consequences that disregard of this entails for the individual as well as for society. Just as the archetype is partly a spiritual factor, and partly like a hidden meaning immanent in the instincts, so the spirit, as I have shown in another Eranos lecture, is two-faced and paradoxical: a great help and an equally great danger.[45] It seems as if man were destined to play a decisive role in solving this uncertainty, this doubt which arose eons before the birth of mankind, and to solve it moreover by virtue of his consciousness, which once started up like a light in the murk of the primeval world. Nowhere do we know for sure about these matters, but least of all where "isms"

[45] Aptly put in the logion cited by Origen (*Homiliae in Jeremiam*, XX, 3): "He who is near unto me is near unto the fire. He who is far from me is far from the kingdom." This "unclaimed saying of the Master" refers to Isaiah 33:14.

flourish, for they are only a sophisticated substitute for the lost link with psychic reality. The massing of the soul that infallibly results destroys the meaning of the individual and of culture generally.

From this it is clear that the psyche not only disturbs the natural order but, if it loses its balance, actually destroys its own creation. Therefore the careful consideration of psychic factors is of importance in restoring not merely the individual's balance, but society's as well, otherwise the destructive tendencies gain the upper hand. In the same way that the atom bomb is an unparalleled means of physical mass destruction, so the misguided development of the soul must lead to psychic mass destruction. The present situation is so sinister that one cannot suppress the suspicion that the Creator is planning another deluge that will finally exterminate the existing race of men. But if anyone imagines that a healthy belief in the existence of archetypes can be inculcated from outside, he is as simple as the people who want to outlaw war or the atom bomb. Such measures remind one of the bishop who excommunicated the cockchafers for their unseemly proliferation. Change of consciousness begins at home; it is a secular matter that depends entirely on how far the psyche's capacity for development extends. All we know at present is that there are single individuals who are capable of developing. How great their total number is we do not know, just as we do not know what the suggestive power of an extended consciousness may be, or what influence it may have upon the world at large. Effects of this kind never depend on the reasonableness of an idea, but far more on the question (which can only be answered *ex effectu*): is the time ripe for change, or not?

As I have said, the psychology of complex phenomena finds itself in an uncomfortable situation compared with the other natural sciences because it lacks a base outside its object. It can only translate itself back into its own language, or fashion itself in its own image. The more it extends its field of research and the more complicated its objects become, the more it feels the lack of a point which is distinct from those objects. And once the complexity has reached that of empirical man, his psychology inevitably merges with the psychic process itself. It can no longer be distinguished from the latter, and so turns into it. But the effect of this is that the process attains to consciousness. In this way psychology actualizes the unconscious urge to consciousness. It is in fact the coming to consciousness of the psychic process, but it is not, in the deeper sense, an explanation of this process, for no explanation of the psychic can be anything other than the living process of the psyche itself. Psychology is doomed to cancel itself out as a science and therein precisely it reaches its scientific goal. Every other science has so to speak an outside; not so psychology, whose object is the inside of all science.

Psychology therefore culminates of necessity in a developmental process which is peculiar to the psyche and consists in integrating the unconscious contents into consciousness. This means that the psychic human being becomes a whole, and becoming whole has remarkable effects on ego consciousness which are extremely difficult to describe. I doubt my ability to give a proper account of the change that comes over the subject under the influence of the individuation process; it is a relatively rare occurrence which is experienced only by those who have gone through the wearisome but, if the unconscious is to be integrated, indispensable business of coming to terms with the unconscious components of the personality. Once these unconscious components are made conscious, it results not only in their assimilation to the already existing ego personality, but in a transformation of the latter. The main difficulty is to describe the manner of this transformation. Generally speaking the ego is a hard-and-fast complex which, because tied to consciousness and its continuity, cannot easily be altered, and should not be altered unless one wants to bring on pathological disturbances. The closest analogies to an alteration of the ego are to be found in the field of psychopathology, where we meet not only with neurotic dissociations but also with the schizophrenic fragmentation, or even dissolution, of the ego. In this field, too, we can observe pathological attempts at integration—if such an expression be permitted. These consist in more or less violent irruptions of unconscious contents into consciousness, the ego proving itself incapable of assimilating the intruders. But if the structure of the ego complex is strong enough to withstand their assault without having its structure fatally dislocated, then assimilation can take place. In that event there is an alteration of the ego as well as of the unconscious contents. Although it is able to preserve its structure, the ego is ousted from its central and dominating position and thus finds itself in the role of a passive observer who lacks the power to assert his will under all circumstances, not so much because it has been weakened in any way, as because certain considerations give it pause. That is, the ego cannot help discovering that the afflux of unconscious contents has vitalized the personality, enriched it and created a figure that somehow dwarfs the ego in scope and intensity.

This experience paralyzes an overegocentric will and convinces the ego that in spite of all difficulties it is better to be taken down a peg than to get involved in a hopeless struggle in which one is invariably handed the dirty end of the stick. In this way the will, as disposable energy, gradually subordinates itself to the stronger factor, namely to the new totality figure I call the *self*. Naturally in these circumstances there is the greatest temptation simply to follow the power instinct and to identify the ego with the self outright, in order to keep up the illusion of the ego's mastery. In other cases the ego proves too weak to offer the necessary resistance to the influx of unconscious contents and is thereupon assimilated by the unconscious, which produces a blurring or darkening of ego consciousness and its identification with a preconscious wholeness. Both these developments make the realization of the self on the one hand, and the existence of empirical ego consciousness on the other, impossible. They amount therefore to pathological effects. The psychic phenomena recently observable in Germany fall into this category. It is abundantly clear that such an *abaissement du niveau mental,* i.e., the overpowering of the ego by unconscious contents and the consequent identification with a preconscious wholeness, possesses a prodigious psychic virulence, or power of contagion, and is capable of the most disastrous effects. Developments of this kind should therefore be watched very carefully and require the closest control. I would recommend anyone who feels himself threatened by such tendencies to hang a picture of St. Christopher on the wall and to meditate upon it. For the self has a functional meaning only when it can act compensatorily to ego consciousness. If the ego is dissolved in identification with the self, it gives rise to a sort of nebulous superman with a puffed up ego and a deflated self. Such a personage, however saviorlike or baleful his demeanor, lacks the *scintilla,* the soul spark, the little wisp of divine light that never burns more brightly than when it has to struggle against the invading darkness. What would the rainbow be were it not limned against the lowering cloud?

This simile is intended to remind the reader that pathological analogies of the individuation process are not the only ones. There are spiritual monuments of quite another kind, and they are positive illustrations of our process. Above all I would mention the *koans* of Zen Buddhism, those sublime paradoxes that light up, as with a flash of lightning, the inscrutable interrelations between ego and self. In very different language St. John of the Cross has made the same problem more readily accessible to the Westerner in his account of the "dark night of the soul." That we find it needful to draw analogies from psychopathology and from Eastern and Western mysticism is only to be expected: the individuation process is, psychically, a borderline phenomenon which requires special conditions in order to become conscious. Perhaps it is the first step along a path of development to be trodden by the men of the future—a path which for the time being has taken a pathological turn and landed Europe in catastrophe.

To one familiar with our psychology, it may seem a waste of time to keep harping on the old established difference between becoming conscious and the coming-to-be of the self (individuation). But again and again I note that the individuation process is confused with becoming conscious of the ego and that the ego is in consequence identified with the self, which naturally produces a hopeless conceptual muddle. Individuation is then nothing but egocenteredness and autoeroticism. But the self comprises infinitely more than a mere ego, as the symbolism has shown from of old. It is as much one's self, and the other selves, as the ego. Individuation does not shut one out from the world, but gathers the world to oneself.

—Translation by R. F. D. Hull

IX/ DEFINITIONS FROM A BUILDER

SON OF A MUSICIAN AND PREACHER ON HIS FATHER'S SIDE AND OF A MOTHER who was a teacher who wanted him to become an architect, Frank Lloyd Wright, one of the three or four great architects of today, was born in Richland Center, Wisconsin, June 8, 1869. As this book was under way, the bubbling, energetic, white-haired artist—for it is not enough to describe him only as a builder—was as characteristically active at eighty-seven as at any other period of his life; he was traveling, lecturing, writing, and when momentarily aground at one spot or the other, busy directing the apprentices who flock, in summer, to his studio-workshop home at Taliesin, Spring Green, Wisconsin, or in the winter at Taliesin West, Paradise Valley, Phoenix, Arizona. (Taliesin, which is Welsh, for his lineage is Welsh, is named, according to Mr. Wright, after the Taliesin who was a Druid and a member of King Arthur's Round Table and as a sixth-century bard sang the glories of fine art. The name means "Shining Brow," and Taliesin in Wisconsin is built on the brow of a hill.)

Frank Lloyd Wright says that very early in his architectural career he had the choice of "honest arrogance or hypocritical humility" and he chose arrogance. Anyone who has ever heard him talk, condemning American architecture as nonexistent, deriding appliances and machines when used as ends rather than means, and sprinkling his discourse with as much insult as wit, will know what he means.

The architect's only apprenticeship was between 1887 and 1893, when he set up his independent practice. His first professional tasks in Chicago were under Dankmar Adler and Louis Sullivan of the firm Adler and Sullivan. Sullivan, he admits, left an impression on him. Louis Sullivan was the first American architect to create the building that is purposefully "tall," the present-day skyscraper, which Wright has later called a city block set on end. But just as important, he has said, is the man who invented the elevator, without which no skyscraper would be practicable.

Mr. Wright is given credit for many innovations. His style brought

168

into use the word "streamlined," he created the "open floor plan" in which, in a building, "the outside gradually came in more and more and the inside went out more." He emphasized "tenuity and flexibility" instead of rigidity, and built a hotel in Tokyo which floated on a cushion of soft mud and proved itself an indestructible survivor of a disastrous earthquake.

He used "gravity heating" (floor heating), indirect lighting (more than fifty years ago) and corner windows which "went around the world," but, he adds, "the idea of the thing I intended never followed it. The liberation of space became merely a window instead of the release of an entire sense of structure, a radical change in the idea of a building."

Mr. Wright has been three times married. He has written a number of books on architecture as well as his autobiography.

Concerning the future of his profession, Mr. Wright has written: "A future for architecture depends upon a new sense of reality, a different success ideal, a deeper social consciousness, a finer integrity of the individual—that there may be promoted the integration of a whole people with their own soil or ground. This will in turn bring about freedom from a false economy. It will bring about the end of labor, money, ground and buildings as speculative commodities. It will bring about the rise of cultured sentiment to take the place of educated sentimentality. It will abolish commercial standards that are only profit-taking. It will close institutes, museums and universities until new ones may be created to bring culture to youth by way of action in an atmosphere of truth and beauty. It will train youth to want and utilize its own ground. There is also necessary a new type of architect and a new structure of government that governs only where individuality may not exist. Such a government will function as a business of the whole people in matters common to the whole people, and only so, instead of as a policeman and a politician. A further essential is a popular realization of organic structure as the basis of all culture in the development of the whole life of a whole people. Such a future as this must grow slowly. Finally the abandonment of ultra-urban life is necessary. A new type of city must be realized. There will be organic structure in government, organic structure in society, organic structure in the economics of both."[1]

[1] "Some Aspects of the Future of Architecture," from *Architecture and Modern Life* by Baker Brownell and Frank Lloyd Wright. Copyright 1937 by Harper & Brothers, and reprinted in *The Future of Architecture*, by Frank Lloyd Wright, copyright 1953 by Horizon Press, Inc.

The Language of an Organic Architecture

BY FRANK LLOYD WRIGHT

Organic (or intrinsic) architecture is the free architecture of ideal democracy. To defend and explain whatever I have myself built and written on the subject I here append a nine-word lexicon needed, world-wide, at this moment of our time.

The words.

1. NATURE. Why? As in popular use this word is first among abuses to be corrected.

2. ORGANIC. Ignorant use or limitation of the word organic.

3. FORM FOLLOWS FUNCTION. Too many foolish stylistic constructions are placed upon the slogan.

4. ROMANCE. A universal change is taking place in the use of this word, a change to which organic architecture has itself given rise. No longer sentimental.

5. TRADITION. Confusion of all eclectics, especially critics, concerning the word.

6. ORNAMENT. The grace or perdition of architecture; for the past five hundred years "appliqué."

7. SPIRIT. Any version or subversion of the word by the so-called international style or by any fashion promoted by experts.

8. THIRD DIMENSION. Where and why the term was original. What it now means in architecture.

9. SPACE. A new element contributed by organic architecture as style.

When the nine words I have listed here are added together (they often are) a degradation of original form and intent which no vitality can bear, is widespread. Due to much prevalent imposition the gutter seems the only visible destination of an original idea of architecture that is basic to democratic culture: an ideal that might become the greatest constructive creative philosophy of our day if only understood and well practiced. That philosophy is surely the center line of integral or democratic culture in these United States if and when we awaken to the true meaning and intent not only of organic architecture but also of the American democracy we are founded as a nation to maintain. So I shall try to explain these nine terms. All are on the center line of both architecture and democracy. Current trends of standardized education today tend to turn young lives more and more toward sterility. Elimination of creation in favor of any cliché that will best serve mechanization. Mediocrity serves it best because mechanization best serves the mediocre. Present tendencies toward the mediocre international style not only degrade organic American architecture but will eventually destroy the creative architect in America, as elsewhere.

DEFINITIONS

1. NATURE means not just the "out-of-doors," clouds, trees, storms, the terrain and animal life, but refers to their nature as to the nature of materials or the "nature" of a plan, a sentiment, or a tool. A man or anything concerning him, *from within*. Interior nature with capital N. Inherent PRINCIPLE.

2. The word ORGANIC denotes in architecture not merely what may hang in a butcher shop, get about on two feet or be cultivated in a field. The word "organic" refers to *entity*, perhaps "integral" or "intrinsic" would therefore be a better word to use. As originally used in architecture, organic means *part-to-whole-as-whole-is-to-part*. So *entity as integral* is what is really meant by the word "organic." INTRINSIC.

3. FORM FOLLOWS FUNCTION. This is a much abused slogan. Naturally form does so. But on a lower level, and the term is useful only as indicating the platform upon which architectural form rests. As the skeleton is no finality of human form any more than grammar is the "form" of poetry, just so function is to architectural form. Rattling the bones is not architecture. Less is only more where more is no good.

Form *is* predicated by function but, so far as poetic imagination can go with it without destruction, transcends it. "Form follows function" has become spiritually insignificant: a stock phrase. Only when we say or write *"form and function are one"* is the slogan significant. It is now the password for sterility. Internationally.

4. ROMANCE, like the word BEAUTY, refers to a *quality*. Reactionary use of this honorable but sentimentalized term by critics and current writers is confusing. Organic architecture sees actuality as the intrinsic romance of human creation or sees essential romance as actual in

creation. *So romance is the new reality.* Creativity *divines* this. No teamwork can conceive it. A committee can only receive it as a gift from the inspired individual. In the realm of organic architecture human imagination must render the harsh language of structure into becomingly humane expressions of form instead of devising inanimate façades or rattling the bones of construction. Poetry of form is as necessary to great architecture as foliage is to the tree, blossoms to the plant or flesh to the body. Because sentimentality ran away with this human need and negation is now abusing it is no good reason for taking the abuse of the thing for the thing.

Until the mechanization of building is in the service of creative architecture and not creative architecture in the service of mechanization we will have no great architecture.

5. TRADITION may have many traditions just as TRUTH may have many truths. When we of organic architecture speak of truth we speak of generic principle. The genus "bird" may fly away as flocks of infinitely different birds of almost unimaginable variety: all of them merely derivative. So in speaking of tradition we use the word as also a *generic* term. Flocks of traditions may proceed to fly from generic tradition into unimaginable many. Perhaps none have creative capacity because all are only derivative. Imitations of imitation destroy an original tradition.

TRUTH is a divinity in architecture.

6. ORNAMENT. Integral element of architecture, ornament is to architecture what efflorescence of a tree or plant is to its structure. *Of* the thing, not *on* it. Emotional in its nature, ornament is—if well conceived—not only the *poetry* but *is the character of structure revealed and enhanced.* If not well conceived, architecture is destroyed by ornament.

7. SPIRIT. What is spirit? In the language of organic architecture the "spiritual" is never something descending upon the thing from above as a kind of illumination *but exists within the thing itself as its very life. Spirit* grows upward from within and outward. Spirit does not come down from above to be suspended there by skyhooks or set up on posts.

There are two uses of nearly every word or term in usual language but in organic sense any term is used in reference to the inner not the outer substance. A word, such as "nature" for instance, may be used to denote a material or a physical means to an end. Or the same word may be used with spiritual significance but in this explanation of the use of terms in organic architecture the spiritual sense of the word is uppermost in use in every case.

8. The THIRD DIMENSION. Contrary to popular belief, the third dimension is not *thickness* but is *depth*. The term "third dimension" is used in organic architecture to indicate the sense of depth which issues as *of* the thing not *on* it. The third dimension, depth, exists as intrinsic to the building.

9. SPACE. The continual becoming: invisible fountain from which all rhythms flow to which they must pass. Beyond time or infinity.

The new reality which organic architecture serves to employ in building.

The breath of a work of art.

If what I have myself written upon the subject of architecture and any one of the 560 buildings I have built are studied with this nine-word lexicon in mind, I am sure we will have far less of the confusion and nonsensical criticism upon which inference, imitation, doubt and prejudice have flourished. "Isms," "ists" and "ites" defeat the great hope we are still trying to keep alive in our hearts in face of prevalent expedients now sterilizing the work of young American architects and rendering our schools harmful to the great art of architecture although perhaps profitable to science commercialized. If organic (intrinsic) architecture is not to live, we of these United States of America will never live as a true culture. Architecture must first become basic to us as creative art, therefore beneficent the world over. Present tendencies in education are so far gone into reverse by way of museum factotums, various committees and university regents spending millions left behind by hard-working millionaires that owing to fashions of internationalism promoted by the internationalite we will have seen the last of the architecture of great architects not only in our democracy but all over the world beside where there is danger of the machine becoming a pattern of life instead of life using the machine as a tool.

Because our Declaration of Independence saw democracy as the gospel of individuality and saw it as above polemics or politics, probably a definition of the word democracy should be added to this lexicon of nine words. Therefore a tenth:

DEMOCRACY is our national ideal . . . not yet well understood by ourselves so not yet realized. But we are a new republic professing this ideal of freedom for growth of the individual. Why not cherish it? Freedom is not to be conceived as numbered freedoms. If true, freedom is never to be conceived in parts. Freedom is of the man and is not accorded to him or ascribed to him except as he may require protection. For that purpose government—as protection—exists, not as a policy maker. Democracy is thus the highest form of aristocracy ever seen. Aristocracy intrinsic.

A gentleman? No longer chosen and privileged by autocratic power he must rise from the masses by inherent virtue. His qualities as a man will give him title and keep it for him. Individual conscience will rule his social acts. By love of quality as against quantity he will choose his way through life. He will learn to know the difference between the curious and the beautiful. Truth will be a divinity to him. As his gentlehood cannot be conferred, so it may not be inherited. This gentleman of democracy will be found in any honest occupation at any level of fortune, loving beauty, doing his best and being kind.

Anyone may see by our own absurd acts and equivocal policies how confused we are by our own ideal when we proceed to work it out. But the principles of organic architecture are the center line of our democracy in America when we do understand what both really mean.

Only by the growth and exercise of *individual conscience* does the man earn or deserve his "rights." Democracy is the opposite of totalitarianism, Communism, Fascism or mobocracy. But democracy is constantly in danger from mobocracy—the rising tide of as yet unqualified herd-instinct. Mechanized mediocrity. The *conditioned* mind instead of the *enlightened* mind.

INTEGRITY IN ARCHITECTURE

What is needed most in architecture today is the very thing that is most needed in life—Integrity. Just as it is in a human being, so integrity is the deepest quality in a building; but it is a quality not much demanded of any building since very ancient times when it was natural. It is no longer the first demand for a human being either, because "success" is now so immediately necessary. If you are a success, people will not want to "look the gift horse in the mouth." No. But then if "success" should happen today something precious has been lost from life.

Somebody has described a man of this period as one through the memory of whom you could too easily pass your hand. Had there been true *quality* in the man the hand could not so easily pass. That quality

174

in the memory of him would probably have been "integrity."

In speaking of integrity in architecture, I mean much the same thing that you would mean were you speaking of an individual. Integrity is not something to be put on and taken off like a garment. Integrity is a quality *within* and *of* the man himself. So it is in a building. It cannot be changed by any other person either, nor by the exterior pressures of any outward circumstances; integrity cannot change except from within because it is that in you which *is you*—and due to which you will try to live your life (as you would build your building) in the best possible way. To build a man or building from within is always difficult to do because deeper is not so easy as shallow.

Naturally should you want to really live in a way and in a place which is true to this deeper thing in you, which you honor, the house you build to live in as a home should be (so far as it is possible to make it so) integral in every sense. Integral to site, to purpose, and to you. The house would then be a home in the best sense of that word. This we seem to have forgotten if ever we learned it. Houses have become a series of anonymous boxes that go into row on row upon row of bigger boxes either merely negative or a mass nuisance. But now the house in this interior or deeper organic sense may come alive as organic architecture.

We are now trying to bring *integrity* into building. If we succeed, we will have done a great service to our moral nature—the psyche— of our democratic society. Integrity would become more natural. Stand up for *integrity* in your building and not only do you stand for integrity in the life of those who did the building but socially a reciprocal relationship is inevitable. An irresponsible, flashy, pretentious or dishonest individual would never be happy in such a house as we now call organic because of this quality of integrity. The one who will live in it will be he who will grow with living in it. So it is the "job" of any true architect to envision and make this human relationship—so far as lies in his power—a reality.

If one lives within a house wherein everything is genuine and harmonious, a new sense of freedom gives one a new sense of life—as contrasted with the usual existence in the house indiscriminately planned and where life is *contained* within a series of confining boxes, all put within the general box. Such life is bound to be inferior to life lived in this new integrity—the Usonian Home.

In designing the Usonian house, as I have said, I have always pro-portioned it to the human figure in point of scale; that is, to the scale of the human figure to occupy it. The old idea in most buildings was to make the human being feel rather insignificant—developing an in-feriority complex in him if possible. The higher the ceilings were then, the greater the building was. This empty grandeur was considered to be human luxury. Of course, great, high ceilings had a certain utility in those days, because of bad planning and awkward construction. (The volume of contained air was about all the air to be had without violence.)

The Usonian house, then, aims to be a *natural* performance, one that is integral to site; integral to environment; integral to the life of the inhabitants. A house integral with the nature of materials—wherein glass is used as glass, stone as stone, wood as wood—and all the elements of environment go into and throughout the house. Into this new in-tegrity, once there, those who live in it will take root and grow. And most of all belonging by nature to the nature of its being.

Whether people are fully conscious of this or not, they actually derive countenance and sustenance from the "atmosphere" of the things they live in or with. They are rooted in them just as a plant is in the soil in which it is planted. For instance, we receive many letters from peo-ple who sing praises for what has happened to them as a consequence; telling us how their house has affected their lives. They now have a certain dignity and pride in their environment; they see it has a mean-ing or purpose which they share as a family or feel as individuals.

We all know the feeling we have when we are well dressed and like the consciousness that results from it. It affects our conduct and you should have the same feeling regarding the home you live in. It has a salutary effect morally, to put it on a lower plane than it deserves, but there are higher results above that sure one. If you feel yourself becom-ingly housed, know that you are living according to the higher demands of good society, and of your own conscience, then you are free from embarrassment and not poor in spirit but rich—in the right way. I have always believed in being careful about my clothes; getting well dressed because I could then forget all about them. That is what should happen to you with a good house that is a *home*. When you are con-scious that the house is right and is honestly becoming to you, and feel you are living in it beautifully, you need no longer be concerned about it. It is no tax upon your conduct, nor a nag upon your self-respect, because it is featuring you as you like to see yourself.

THE GRAMMAR OF YOUR HOUSE

Every house worth considering as a work of art must have a grammar of its own. "Grammar," in this sense, means the same thing in any construction—whether it be of words or of stone or wood. It is the shape-relationship between the various elements that enter into the constitution of the thing. The "grammar" of the house is its manifest articulation of all its parts. This will be the "speech" it uses. To be achieved, construction must be grammatical.

Your limitations of feeling about what you are doing, your choice of materials for the doing (and your budget of course) determine largely what grammar your building will use. It is largely inhibited (or expanded) by the amount of money you have to spend, a feature only of the latitude you have. When the chosen grammar is finally adopted (you go almost indefinitely with it into everything you do) walls, ceilings, furniture, etc., become inspired by it. Everything has a related articulation in relation to the whole and all belong together, look well together because all together are speaking the same language. If one part of your house spoke Choctaw, another French, another English, and another some sort of gibberish, you would have what you mostly have now—not a very beautiful result. Thus, when you do adopt the "grammar" of your house, it will be the way the house is to be "spoken," "uttered." You must be consistently grammatical for it to be understood as a work of Art.

X/ A PHILOSOPHER OF LOVE
AT HARVARD

"EVENTFULNESS HAS POSSIBLY BEEN THE MOST SIGNIFICANT FEATURE OF MY life-adventure. In sixty-eight years I have passed through several cultural atmospheres: the pastoral-hunter's culture of the Komi, the agricultural, and then the urban culture of Russia and Europe, and, finally, the megalopolitan technological culture of the United States. Starting my life as a son of an itinerant artisan and peasant mother, I have been a farm hand, itinerant artisan, factory worker, clerk, teacher, conductor of a choir, revolutionary, political prisoner, journalist, student, editor of a metropolitan paper, member of Kerensky's cabinet, an exile, professor in Russian, Czech and American universities, and a scholar. No less eventful has been the range of my life. I experienced six imprisonments—three under the Czarist and three under the Communist regimes; the unforgettable experience of a man condemned to death and daily, during six weeks, expecting his execution by the Communist firing squad. . . .

"These life-experiences have taught me more than the books I have read and lectures to which I have listened.

"Born and reared among the Komi, Ugro-Finnish people in the north of Russia, up to my eleventh year, I did not see even a small town. Incidentally I learned to read and write; incidentally I became a pupil of a 'normal school,' and at the age of ten, father and mother dead, I became 'independent,' penniless, but free to chart my life-course. Earning my living, I was a student of a teachers college; arrested and imprisoned four months before graduation for my political activities in 1906; then a starving and hunted revolutionary; student of a night school, of the Psycho-Neurological Institute, and of the University of St. Petersburg. Two more imprisonments gave to me a firsthand experience in criminology and penology, the field of my graduate study and then of my first professorship. Besides several papers, in my junior year I published by first volume: *Crime and Punishment, Service and Reward* (1913). In 1916 I received a Magister's degree in criminal law;

in 1922, the degree of Doctor of Sociology from the University of St. Petersburg. With the Russian Revolution I became one of the founders of the Russian Peasant Soviet (dispersed by the Communists); editor of a metropolitan paper: *The Will of the People;* member of the Council of the Russian Republic; a secretary to Prime Minister Kerensky; and a member of the Russian Constituent Assembly (dispersed by the Communist government). From the beginning of the Revolution I fought Lenin, Trotsky, Kamenev and other Communist leaders. For this I was arrested on January 3, 1918, and imprisoned for four months in the Fortress of Peter and Paul. Released, I resumed my struggle with the Communists, and was one of the group which engineered the overthrow of the Communist government in Archangel in 1918. In October, 1918, I was again arrested and condemned to death by the Communist government of Vologda Province. After six weeks of waiting to be shot, by Lenin's order I was freed and returned to my academic activity at the University of St. Petersburg. There I became the founder, first professor, and chairman of the department of sociology. Between 1920-22 I published five volumes on law and sociology. In 1922 I was again arrested and, finally, banished by the Soviet government. A few days after my arrival in Berlin, my good friend, President Masaryk, invited me to be a guest of Czechoslovakia. I stayed there for nine months. On invitation from the universities of Illinois and Wisconsin to lecture on the Russian Revolution, in November, 1923, I came to the United States, and in 1924 was offered a professorship by the University of Minnesota. After six years I was made the first professor and chairman of the sociology department at Harvard. Since 1930 (in which year I became a naturalized American citizen) I have been living and working in this great university.

"In 1948 Mr. Eli Lilly and the Lilly Endowment on their own initiative offered $120,000 for my studies on how to make human beings less selfish and more creative. This generous offer led to the establishment of the Harvard Research Center in Creative Altruism in 1949, which I am directing now.

"During the years of my being in America, honorary memberships in several academies of science and arts, presidency in the International Institute of Sociology, honorary doctorships and similar distinctions have been granted to me. During the same years I have published, besides many scientific papers, twenty-eight books, among them *Contemporary Sociological Theories,* translated into eleven languages, and *Crisis of Our Age,* into eight.

"In 1917 I was married and have two sons—one a graduate and the other a medical student at Harvard."

—PITIRIM A. SOROKIN
In a letter to the editor

Integralism Is My Philosophy

BY PITIRIM A. SOROKIN

I.

Integralism is its name. It views the total reality as the infinite X of numberless qualities and quantities: spiritual and material, momentary and eternal, ever-changing and unchangeable, personal and super-personal, temporal and timeless, spatial and spaceless, one and many, the littlest than the little, and the greatest than the great. In this sense it is the veritable *mysterium tremendum et fascinosum* and the *coincidentia oppositorum* (reconciliation of the opposites). Its highest center is the Infinite Creative X that passes all human understanding.

In its inexhaustible plenitude the total reality is inaccessible to the finite human mind. However, its main aspects can roughly be grasped by us because we are also its important part. Of its innumerable modes of being three forms or differentiations appear to be most important: (1) empirical-sensory, (2) rational-mindful, and (3) supersensory-superrational. The empirical aspect of the total reality is perceived by us through our sense organs and their extensions: microscopes, telescopes, etc. Science is especially (though not exclusively) preoccupied with a cognition of this sensory aspect. The rational aspect of the reality is comprehended mainly by our reason: mathematical and logical thought in all its rational forms. Mathematics, logic, and rational philosophy concentrate at a cognition of this form of being of the X. Finally, the glimpses of its superrational and supersensory aspect are given to us by truly creative-supersensory and superrational intuition, or "divine inspiration," or "flash of enlightenment" of all the creative geniuses: founders of great religions, sages, seers and prophets, giants of philosophy and ethics, by great scientists, artists, moral leaders, and other eminent creators in all fields of culture. These geniuses unanimously testify the fact that their discoveries or the creation of their master-pieces has been started and then guided by the grace of the intuition, and that they have been but a mere instrumentality of this creative force far transcending their human capacity. In a limited form every one of us is now and then visited by this grace of "the supreme enlighten-ment."

The truth obtained through integral use of all three channels of cog-nition—senses, reason, and intuition—is a fuller and more valid truth than that received only through the channel of either sensory percep-tion, or of logico-mathematical reasoning, or of intuition. The history of human knowledge is a cemetery filled with wrong empirical observa-tions, false reasonings, and pseudo intuitions. In the integral use of these three channels of cognition, they supplement as well as check one an-other. Integral cognition means also that we learn about the reality not only from empirical scientists and logical thinkers, but also from great religious and ethical leaders like Buddha and Jesus, Confucius and Lao-tse, and from the creators in the fine arts, like Beethoven and Bach, Homer and Shakespeare, Phidias and Michelangelo. They reveal to us, in Richard Wagner's words, *universalia ante rem*. So much for the total reality and its cognition.

II.

In this integral conception of the total reality man is also conceived as a marvelous integral being. He is not only an empirical organism of the *homo sapiens* species, and not only rational thinker and doer; in addition he is a supersensory and superrational being, an active partic-ipant in the supreme, creative X of the total cosmos. Man has become one of the important creative centers of the total reality. Contrary to today's prevalent opinion, man is not only an unconscious and conscious creature, but he is also a superconscious master-creator capable of con-trolling and transcending his unconscious and conscious energies and actually doing so in the moments of his "divine inspiration," in the periods of his intensest and best creativity. Man's greatest discoveries, inventions, and creative achievements have been largely due to man as the superconscious master-creator, assisted by man as a rational thinker and by man as en empirical observer and experimenter.

181

III.

In spite of the comparatively short period of man's creative history on this planet, the total result of his creativity is truly astounding. Man has created a new realm of reality in the cosmos known to us. Besides the two basic classes of reality—inorganic and organic phenomena—which existed on this planet before the emergence of man, he has built a third basic class of phenomena: the superorganic or cultural, quite different from the inorganic and organic. In contradistinction to inorganic phenomena that have only one physicochemical component, and to organic phenomena that have two components—physical and vital (life)—the cultural phenomena have the "immaterial" component of *meaning* (as idea, as value, as artistic pattern or moral norm of conduct) that is superimposed upon the physical and/or vital components. This component of meaning radically changes the nature of the inorganic and organic phenomena which it permeates and upon which it is superimposed. Without its meaning, a book, say, Plato's *Republic* or a printed score of Bach's Mass in B Minor is but a mere physical (paper) object of certain geometric form and physicochemical properties. With its meaning, it turns into the superorganic system of the greatest ideas or musical values for which its physical properties (paper) become quite irrelevant, because this system of ideas or values can be "incarnated and objectified" in different physical media: recorded on a record, written on a papyrus, spoken or sung (through use of air waves), and so on. A cheap piece of cloth attached to a stick is transformed by meaning into a national flag, embodying the honor and majesty of a nation, for which lives are sacrificed and persons are murdered. Without the component of meaning there is little difference between the acts of shooting, as in the crime of homicide, in the execution of a criminal, and in the shooting of a war-enemy, because the physical act of shooting may be identical in all cases. Culturally, these acts are profoundly different from one another. Deprived of its meaning, Venus of Milo turns into a mere piece of marble of certain form and chemical composition. Biologically, the organism of a monarch or dictator may be much weaker than that of his subjects; culturally, the authority and power of a monarch or dictator are incomparably greater than those of his biologically strongest subjects. Biologically and physically, there are no human organisms that are "kings," "popes," "generals," "criminals," "heroes," "saints," "farmers," and so on. These and millions of other "meanings" are superimposed upon the human organisms by the superorganic culture.

These examples show the specific nature of the cultural or superorganic phenomena and the astounding role of meanings in the transformation of biophysical phenomena into something quite different from their biological and physical nature. At the present time this cultural realm consists of: (a) an infinitely rich *ideological* universe of *meanings* unified into systems of language, science, technology, religion, philosophy, law, ethics, literature, painting, sculpture, architecture, music, drama, economic, political and social theories, and so on; (b) the totality of so-called "*material culture*," representing "an incarnation and objectification" of all these meanings in biophysical media, beginning with the simplest tool and ending with the most complex machinery and gadgets, books, paintings, sculptures, buildings, highways and airways, villages and cities, and so forth; (c) the totality of *individuals as sociocultural persons* ("kings," "farmers," "criminals," "saints," "husbands," "wives," "prostitutes," "citizens," "debtors," "masters," "slaves," "Frenchmen," "Americans," "Catholics," "Socialists," etc.) and of *sociocultural groups* (political, scientific, religious, economic, occupational, national, artistic, etc.); and (d) the totality of the *overt actions, ceremonies, rituals, proceedings,* in which the individuals and groups actualize, realize, and practice this or that set of meanings. The total superorganic universe made of the above—*ideological, material, personal, and behavioral*—cultural phenomena has become the most powerful environment that immediately envelops, conditions, determines, and molds every individual and group in its own image. This cultural universe has already grown to such an extent in its dynamic and creative power that it has harnessed, to a notable extent, the inorganic and organic forces, subjected them to its own control, has greatly changed the surface of the whole earth and is progressively extending its control beyond the earth-limits into an ever-extended outer space. And there seems to be no fixed limit to the growth of this superorganic reality and to its creative power and control. Since this new class of reality has been created by man, man can proudly call himself a master-creator of the superorganic cosmos, and can justifiably view himself as one of the creative centers in the infinite world of the total reality. Herein lies the answer to the ancient question: "What is man, that thou shouldst magnify him?"

IV.

Among all the meaningful values of the superorganic world there is the supreme integral value—the veritable *summum bonum*. It is the indivisible unity of Truth, Goodness, and Beauty. Though each member of this supreme Trinity has a distinct individuality, all three are inseparable from one another, like the members of the Christian Trinity of God-Father, God-Son, and the Holy Ghost. The genuine Truth is always good and beautiful; the true Goodness is always true and beautiful; and the pure Beauty is invariably true and good. These greatest values are not only inseparable from one another, but they are transformable into one another, like one form of physical energy, say, heat, is transformable into other kinds of energy, electricity or light or mechanical motion. Each newly discovered truth contributes also to the values of beauty and goodness. Each act of unselfish creative love (goodness) enriches the realms of truth and beauty; and each masterpiece of beauty morally ennobles and mentally enlightens the members of the human universe. (The same cannot, of course, be said about any sham truth, sham goodness, and sham beauty.) For these reason the main historical mission of mankind consists in an unbounded creation, accumulation, refinement, and actualization of Truth, Beauty, and Goodness in the nature of man himself, in man's mind and behavior, in man's superorganic universe and beyond it, and in man's relationships to all human beings, to all living creatures, and to the total cosmos. By discharging this task man is fulfilling in the best and most faithful way his duty toward the Supreme Cosmic Creator. Any step in a successful realization of this goal brings man nearer, and makes him more similar to this Supreme Creator. Man becomes a veritable son of God created in God's own image. Any important achievement in this supreme mission represents a real progress of man and of the human universe. Any failure in it becomes a regressive step in human history. This mission thus gives us the true measure of human progress or regress. Other measures of progress and regress are uncertain and often misleading.

V.

At the present juncture of human history, a notable increase of an unselfish, creative love (goodness) in the superorganic world is the paramount need of humanity. Mankind can survive and continue its creative mission, if during the next few decades no new important truth is discovered and no new masterpiece of beauty is created. But mankind's survival and the progress of its creative activity become highly uncertain if the "production, accumulation and actualization" of an unselfish love in the human universe are not increased. Out of many reasons for this statement two can be mentioned here. First is the fact that for the last four centuries or so, creativity in the fields of Truth and Beauty has somewhat outrun that in the field of Goodness. During this period man's knowledge and control of the inorganic and organic phenomena have increased more than during the total preceding history of mankind. Likewise, during these centuries man's creativity in the field of sensate or secular fine arts has also been marvelous. Preoccupied with the discoveries, inventions, and creations in the field of empirical truth and secular beauty, man has somehow neglected a deeper study of goodness and of his own moral—rational and superrational—nature. As a result, he has failed in inventing new, efficacious ways and means for moral ennoblement of himself, for a spiritual transfiguration of his superorganic world, and for control of his own physical and animal propensities. During these centuries he has remained uncreative and "unreformed" morally—as selfish and as much controlled by the biological forces of the "struggle for existence," of sex, and of quest for pleasures and material values, as he was before this period. Even more: morally he has possibly regressed from the high level of goodness reached by him in some of the previous periods of his historical existence. Such a disequilibrium in the supreme Trinity of his greatest values has resulted, as it always does, in an explosion of the individual and group selfishness with ensuing intensification and brutalization of interhuman and intergroup conflicts: wars, revolutions, revolts, crime, and other manifestations of moral anarchy.

In the twentieth century this interhuman strife assumed the catastrophic proportions of two world wars and many oher wars, of endless bloody revolutions and revolts, not to mention crimes and milder forms of the "struggle for existence." At present, due to the discovery of the intra-atomic secrets and to the invention of Apocalyptic means of destruction, this moral anarchy begins to threaten the survival of mankind and especially the continuation of its creative mission. This situation explains why a notable increase of unselfish, creative love in the total human universe is the paramount present need of humanity.

This reason is reinforced by another one. Roughly, beginning with the end of the nineteenth century the Western part of the superorganic world has entered a transitional period from one basic form of its culture and social organization—sensate or secular—to another form, profoundly different from the previous one: a new ideational (religious) or integral form. The magnificent house of sensate culture, built by Western man during the last five centuries, has begun to disintegrate while the new house of the basically different culture and society is not yet built. Such transitional periods from one of the main modes of sociocultural reality to another always result in the greatest—total—crisis of respective society and culture. In my works, especially in my *Social and Cultural Dynamics* and its abbreviated version, *The Crisis of Our Age,* this and similar sociocultural transitions and crises were analyzed in detail and, on the basis of this analysis, already in the 1920's I diagnosed the crisis and predicted the coming of bigger and more terrible wars, revolutions, and anarchy, with all the horrible attendants of these: gigantic destruction, misery, bestiality, insanity, and many other phenomena, up to the shift of the creative center of history from Europe, where it has been for the last five centuries, to the Pacific, with the Americas, and the reawakened great cultures of India, China, Japan, Russia, and Europe (as one of the partners but not monopolistic leader) as the main actors and the bearers of the torch of creativity in the future acts of human drama. A quotation from *Social and Culture Dynamics* tells a part of this diagnosis and forecastings.

Every important aspect of life, organization, and the culture of the Western society is in the extraordinary crisis. . . . Its body and mind are sick and there is hardly a spot on its body which is not sore, nor any nervous fibre which functions soundly. . . . We are seemingly between two epochs: the dying Sensate of our magnificent yesterday, and the coming Ideational or Idealistic culture of the creative tomorrow. We are living, thinking, and acting at the end of a brilliant six-hundred-year-long Sensate day. The oblique rays of the sun still illumine the glory of the passing epoch. But the light is fading, and in the deepening shadows it becomes more and more difficult to see clearly and to orient ourselves safely in the confusions of the twilight. The night of the transitory period begins to loom before us, with its nightmares, frightening shadows, and heartrending horrors. Beyond it, however, the dawn of a new great culture is probably waiting to greet the men of the future.

When these statements were written, there was no war, no revolution, not even an economic depression of 1929. The horizon of the sociocultural life looked clear and unclouded. Everything on the surface seemed to be excellent and hopeful. The prevalent opinion of the leaders of thought as well as of the masses was optimistic. They believed in a "bigger and better" prosperity and the disappearance of war and bloodshed; in international co-operation and good will led by the League of Nations; in the econmic, mental, and moral improvement of mankind and in "streamlined progress." In such a mental atmosphere my statements and warnings were naturally a voice in the wilderness. They were sharply criticized as impossible or disdainfully dismissed as "loony."

Within a decade or so, these "loony" forecastings have come to pass; the crisis has been developing according to "the schedule" of my diagnosis and predictions.

Situated between two epochs, with the old values crumbling and the new values not consolidated and "interiorized" as yet, man of today finds himself utterly confused and lost in the debris of the disintegrating sensate world and society. He acts as a rudderless boat thrown about by the winds of his animal propensities, largely freed from the control of man's rational and superrational forces. In such conditions, according to the old observation of Plato and Aristotle, man is liable to become "the worst of the beasts." And he has morally regressed indeed to the level of a sophisticated human animal that justifies by highfalutin ideologies the worst of his actions.

This demoralization and its suicidal consequences can be stopped only through an increased production, accumulation, and circulation of an unselfish, creative love in man and in today's human universe. The studies of the Harvard Research Center in Creative Altruism show

that none of the prevalent prescriptions against international and civil wars and other forms of interhuman bloody strife can eliminate or notably decrease these conflicts. By these popular prescriptions I mean, first, elmination of wars and strife by political changes, especially by democratic political transformations. Tomorrow the whole world could become democratic, and yet wars and bloody strife would not be eliminated because democracies happen to be no less belligerent and strife-infected than autocracies. Still less pacification can be expected from autocracies. Neither the United Nations nor the World Government can give a lasting internal and international peace if the establishment of these bodies is not reinforced by notable altruization of persons, groups, institutions, and culture.

The same goes for education in its present form as a panacea against war and bloody strife. Tomorrow all grown-up persons in the world could become Ph.D.'s, and yet this enormous progress in education would not eliminate wars and bloody conflicts. Since the tenth century to the present century education has made enormous progress—the number of schools of all kinds, the per cent of literacy, the number of scientific discoveries and inventions have greatly and almost systematically increased, and yet the international wars, the bloody revolutions, and the grave forms of crime have not decreased. On the contrary, in the most scientific and most educated twentieth century they have reached an unrivaled height and made this century the bloodiest among all the preceding twenty-five centuries of Graeco-Roman and European history.

The same goes for religious changes, if by religion is meant a purely ideological belief in God or in the credo of any of the great religions. One of the evidences for that is given by our investigation of seventy-three Boston converts "brought to Jesus" by two popular evangelical preachers. Of these seventy-three converts only one changed his overt behavior in an altruistic direction after his conversion. Thirty-seven converts slightly changed their speech reactions; after their conversion they began to repeat more frequently the words, "Our Lord Jesus Christ" and similar utterances, but their overt behavior did not change tangibly. The remaining converts changed neither their actions nor their speech-reactions. If by religious revival and "moral rearmament" are meant this sort of ideological and speech-reactional transformation, it would not bring peace or decrease interhuman strife, because it represents mainly a cheap self-gratification for psychoneurotics and sham-religious persons.

The same goes for Communist, Socialist, or Capitalist economic remedies: for scientific, artistic, legal, or other ways of establishing and maintaining lasting peace in the human universe when these are not backed by increased altruization of persons and groups. Without a notable increase of unselfish, creative love (as ideally formulated in the *Sermon on the Mount*) in overt behavior, in over interindividual and intergroup relationships, in social institutions and culture, there is no chance for a lasting peace and for interhuman harmony, internal or external.

Our studies show also that this unselfish, creative love, about which we still know very little, potentially represents a tremendous power. (a) It can stop aggressive interindividual and intergroup attacks; (b) it can transform inimical relationships into amicable ones; (c) love begets love, and hate generates hate; (d) love can tangibly influence international policy and pacify international conflicts. In addition to these effects an unselfish and wise (adequate) love manifests itself (e) as a life-giving force, necessary for physical, mental, and moral health; (f) altruistic persons live longer than egoistic individuals, (g) children deprived of love tend to become morally and socially defective; (h) love is a powerful antidote against criminal, morbid, and suicidal tendencies, against hate, fear, and psychoneuroses; (i) love performs important cognitive and aesthetic functions; (j) it is the loftiest and most effective educational force for enlightenment and moral ennoblement of humanity; (k) it is the heart and soul of freedom and of all main moral and religious values; (l) its minimum is absolutely necessary for the durable existence of any society, and especially, for a harmonious social order and creative progress; (m) finally, at the present catastrophic moment of human history an increased "production, accumulation, and circulation of love-energy," or a notable altruization of persons and groups, institutions and culture, especially an extension of unselfish love of everyone for everyone in mankind, is a necessary condition for the prevention of new wars and for the alleviation of enormously increased interindividual and intergroup strife.

With a notable increase of our knowledge of love, its potentialities can be used for the service of mankind in immeasurably greater proportions.

These considerations explain why, in my opinion, to increase creative, unselfish love is at the present moment of human history the paramount task of humanity. If the task is successfully solved—and it can be solved if mankind undertakes it most earnestly—then the extremely dangerous crisis of our age can be overcome and man's creative mission can be resplendently continued. Then a "new heaven and a new earth" —integrally creative, harmonious, and happy—will greet the coming generations.

XI / PHILOSOPHER IN
DEFENSE OF PHILOSOPHY

KARL JASPERS, GERMAN-BORN FOLLOWER OF THE DANISH PHILOSOPHER Kierkegaard, now head of the department of philosophy at the University of Basel, Switzerland, has been characterized as a "Christian existentialist" in his preoccupation with the individual and the individual's attempt to meet the situations of life, change, struggle, guilt and death. Some of his works have been translated, including *Man in the Modern Age* and the more recent volume *The Perennial Scope of Philosophy*. Professor Jaspers' contribution to *This Is My Philosophy* appears here in its first translation from the German by Edith A. Daechsler and Annie Taffs. Professor Jaspers was born in 1883 and lives at Basel, where he is teaching that "philosophy must not abdicate —least of all today. Precisely because of the catastrophe that has over-taken the Western world, philosophical thought," he says, "can regain full independence only by discovering its relation to the very origin of humanity."

The Task of Philosophy in Our Day

BY KARL JASPERS

What is the task of philosophy today? We hear this answer: It has none, for it lacks reality, constituting merely the out-of-the-way occupation of a group of specialists. Incumbents of chairs of philosophy, the origin of which dates back to the Middle Ages, meet in vain in conventions which represent the modern method of seeking recognition. A comprehensive literature testifies to their monologues, seldom read and rarely purchased, except in a few faddist periodicals for snobs. True, the press, as the organ of public opinion, takes some notice of these publications gathering dust on library shelves; but it does so without genuine interest. In short, philosophy might be considered superfluous, a petrified relic of time gone by, awaiting dissolution; it no longer has a task to fulfill.

In the face of this rejection it may well be said in the first place that not everything bearing the name of philosophy is to be mistaken for the genuine article. Philosophy exists wherever man becomes conscious of his being through thought. It is omnipresent without being called by name. A man who thinks is at the same time philosophizing, correctly or falsely, superficially or profoundly, fleetingly or with slow deliberation. In a world where standards are valued and judgments expressed, we find philosophy. It is seen no less in the consistent dogma of the Church than in the independent thinking of conscious philosophy; it exists in the convictions of the unbeliever, in the destructive ideas of nihilism, in Marxism, in psychoanalysis and in the many theories of life prevalent today. The rejection of philosophy is itself the result of a kind of philosophy unaware of itself as such. The task of philosophy, as represented by professionals at universities, is to bring to light this ubiquitous, inescapable philosophy, particularly through the teachings of the great philosophers known to history. This is a service of no mean value.

Yet how ineffectual these explanations sound when we think of the fundamental realities surrounding mankind today!

The two powerful forces now reigning on the globe are the free world and the world of totalitarianism. Keeping both of these in mind is a matter of vital importance to our philosophic consciousness. For they determine the true nature of philosophy today. Philosophic thought has helped to produce these realities, and through strength or weakness will help to determine the nature of the world of tomorrow.

On the one hand there are the possibilities offered by freedom; on the other, absolute control by one mind; on one side, research, discussion and constant struggle of mind and matter; on the other, so-called total knowledge and the machinations of intrigue; on the one hand, individual planning within the limits of the possible; on the other, total planning without recognition of limits; on one side, variety bordering on anarchy; on the other, uniformity bordering on the organization of the ant-state composed of human beings no longer themselves but devoured alike as a substance of indifferent value by party, bureaucracy, police and army.

Totalitarian systems operate on the assumption of complete cognizance of the course of history and the workings of nature. On the basis of this total knowledge they do their total planning. But as no one can, either through knowledge or action, grasp the whole world, he who nevertheless attempts to do so may indeed conquer the world, by force, but he would seize it as a murderer might seize a corpse, not as a man entering into relationship with other human beings to build a common world. He who takes possession of the whole through his supposedly total knowledge philosophizes in a kind of inverted way. He thinks with logical dialectic intensity in formal sequence, but without critical judgment. For he is not touched by reality, therefore cannot be refuted by it, and he does not elucidate the premise of his own convictions, such as his belief in a state of future salvation (an idea quite without substance), for the realization of which even lies become an indispensable factor, while supposedly it is produced automatically by the magic process of dialectic history.

In the realm of totalitarianism, philosophy is patently finished. National Socialism pronounced it liquidated. It was replaced (in Germany) by racial anthropology and political science. Bolshevism on the other hand substituted Marxism. At the universities of Eastern Germany the fundamental subject for all students is therefore not philosophy but Marxist sociology. National Socialism and Bolshevism claim absolute truth for their teachings. Whoever resists this truth is to be exterminated. Their reason for not accepting this truth can only be ill will, inferior origin, wrong class-consciousness or false convictions.

What task can possibly be undertaken by thinking men under such a reign of terror? History knows the martyr and the exile who withdrew into forest and desert. But up to now the activities of such men were known to and recognized by the world they lived in. Today the situation is radically different. Great numbers of individuals simply disappear and are never heard of again. The helplessness of the individual is complete. While his existence endures he can indeed withdraw into the inmost secrecy of his being, provided he is able to find there the memory of a completely reliable friend, wife or husband—in the sense of Nietzsche's words, "Truth begins with two." Complete solitude may cause a man to lose confidence in his self; doubts as to the truth of his beliefs may infect him when he is left to face them alone, cut off from communication with others. An individual seems capable of believing the most absurd ideas, if compelled to do so by the constant and overpowering pressure of his surroundings. Under this suggestive coercion, and the threat of soundless annihilation, there remains for his philosophy only that truth which, though invisible, is the only true reality, the truth that materialists call illusion, imagination or dreams, namely the transcendence of God. What may continue to exist besides is the consciousness of self-preservation, a readiness for the improbable but still possible moment of liberation. The task of philosophy is to strengthen the inner resistance to the cynical propaganda of a one-sided public, as well as to guard against one's falling prey to absurd beliefs such as those which reach their climax in the "confessions" at mock trials.

What a difference we see in the free world! Here no one takes possession of a man's world as if from the outside. Here man tries to conquer the world together with his fellow men. Here he strives through competition within the framework of law and order to maintain his existence and influence. Here he attempts the journey through time by combining forces with all others without an absolute supreme authority all-knowing and planning on a total scale, set up and usurped by man. The still remaining unjust conditions he seeks to transform by better laws and more favorable opportunities for all. He pursues his course, advancing in a spirit of reverent discontent. Should there appear in the free world a vision of totalitarianism as the final outcome, such a possibility would seem unthinkable as a permanent state; it would have to explode, leaving behind it a wasteland from which it would be impossible to reconstruct the past; only something entirely new and utterly different could follow.

In the domain of freedom philosophic thinking takes place in a great variety of ways owing to the multiplicity of possibilities. Here too we find nowadays the feeling of helplessness on the part of the individual, he being one among millions, effaced as to the effect of his individual achievements. But this consciousness of weakness is fundamentally different from that experienced under the pressure of totalitarianism. Just as a single vote seems of no importance at elections and yet the sum total of such votes decides the outcome, despite the apparent insignificance of the individual ballots, so all the individual activities in the realm of freedom appear as of no significance in the course of events. The will-to-power turns with distaste from this state of affairs. The truly human will, on the other hand, conscious of its alliance with all, accepts with dignity and a sense of responsibility the importance of the single ballot as a small but decisive factor. Thus the free individual spends his entire life as the minute particle helping to sustain the whole. Such realization keeps the spirit of freedom alive.

In the domain of freedom there exist, however, all the spiritual forces that tend to destroy freedom without conscious intent or deliberate motive. Many a man who condemns totalitarianism yet furthers it by his thinking, because his spiritual attitude is not rooted in the reality of his individual being but secretly urges him to force and obedience and in a crisis quite naturally causes him to take sides with the latter. Suddenly the veil is drawn and his true identity is revealed.

Many a professor of philosophy has been of the opinion that there should be only one professor of philosophy at a university—more than one would confuse the minds of the students. Some, believing only one philosophy to be the true one, have even voiced the desirability of having only one philosopher for the whole nation, aspiring, of course, to this honor themselves. Whatever the content of the philosophy of these claimants may be, their mode of thinking is the same. They are paving the way for totalitarianism.

One great task of philosophy today lies in the realization of the forces which seek to take it unawares and destroy it. So alluring on the surface, so devious in their workings, these forces, containing some truth but always distorting it, seize control of the most talented. One may call them diabolic. Their complete unreliability, capable of anything, may dazzle by brilliance, be it in literature or art, through the power of expression, at once realistic and mystifying. They may compel by their extreme cynicism, whether reveling in a nature myth unbounded in its vitality or gloating in a wild nomenclature of horror, or indulging in the language of radical truth. At the core there is always deception, resorting even to the use of truth for fraudulent ends. They make use of the intellect to destroy the meaning of words, falsifying language itself, speaking not to convey meaning but to dupe. Falsehoods stimulate, but lead with disciplined technique to nothingness, where, in horror at monstrous ideas, the cessation of thought engenders a willingness to submit. All these phenemena are practice for the readiness to yield to totalitarianism.

It is the task of philosophy to combat these forces by spiritual means. Freedom of thought can only be achieved for each one of us by the constant mastery of these forces in ourselves or when they are met in public. Therefore all activity of the mind today is tied up with the responsibility for the freedom of mankind. This responsibility, however, can only be realized through freedom of judgment on the part of each individual in public discussion, without the arrogant censorship of a power that selects and forbids. But the struggle being waged against the "nonphilosophy" of totalitarianism carries within itself a great danger: The enemy I am fighting forces me to use weapons foreign to my nature. In the struggle against the spirit of a violent, dictatorial mode of thought, the liberal communicative attitude may be forced to abandon its own tolerance in the face of total intolerance. In its desire for communication, it may face complete lack of communication if the opponent continually sidesteps, is silent, changes the subject, diverts, and deceives. The enemy dictates the tactics of the fight. Through these the nature of the combatant is itself changed. Freedom would lose its battle, even in victory, if it allowed this transmutation to take place.

The idea of chivalrous combat maintained the relations between opponents in accord with common standards. Total warfare regards all opponents as idiots, deceivers, or criminals, and forces them to apply similar terms to the functionaries of totalitarianism. Total warfare recognizes no obligation deriving from a superior common source. The cleavage resulting between men has terrifying consequences: the state of beasts fighting unconditionally for their existence is restored. In the methods of psychological warfare used, this state of affairs is prepared for and anticipated. In the face of such experiences, terror may well assail us. In the apparent artlessness of partners in discussion and the manner of their polemics, we sense the presence of potential propagandists and henchmen of totalitarianism, without knowing what is actually to be expected from them.

An essential factor of this spiritual evil today is domination by confused scientific thinking. We believe in knowledge. Knowledge is to be the authority to which we appeal.

To cite some examples: Russell, the famous English philosopher and logician, anticipates, at the conclusion of his total picture of Occidental philosophy, the union of mankind through knowledge. Curiously enough, men are united by knowledge only in matters of intellect, not as living, historically evolved, integrated beings. Community of knowledge, as far as the effect of unity of understanding in the realm of the physical is concerned, may indeed be brought about—a common knowledge, from the stone hatchet to the atom bomb, for its use as a weapon of destruction. For agreement on scientific matters engenders no community of sentiment. We are making unreasonable demands when we expect such an achievement from science alone.

In the oath of the Modernists of the year 1910, we find the sentence, "I believe that God can be recognized and proved with certainty by the visible works of His creation as a cause can be recognized by its effect." Strange indeed! The proof of God's existence is to be taken on faith. What can be proved, however, makes no demand on faith. A confession of faith is not necessary where the intellect can establish a matter with finality.

A third example is the mode of thought of totalitarian regimes. They base their claims on knowledge, yet demand faith for the acceptance of this knowledge. For example, we are told: There exists nothing but the universe and that which man can achieve. Instead of on revelation, man is to take his stand on knowledge. But, strangely enough, this knowledge is absolute in its tenets. It is omniscient. I am to *believe* it, therefore I must raise no objections, express no doubts, seek no proof, in short I am no longer to investigate scientifically, except in the field of technical inventions which can be put to immediate practical use.

But Russell and the authors of the Modernists' oath, as well as the exponents of totalitarian science, have something other than *knowledge* in mind. They mean a sort of thinking that is in itself already a kind of faith. Russell believes in the strength of integrity in the sciences as the one unifying form of the Reason of mankind. The author of the Modernists' oath has a type of philosophic belief that reassures itself in forms of thought which recognize nothing but which elucidate a believing consciousness. The Marxist dogmatist believes in the inevitable course of history, the National Socialist in the survival of the fittest, both want only to expedite what will happen in any event, and this by the act of exterminating "inferior" individuals, groups or races that resist the order of things, beings predestined to annihilation. Both dogmatists submit in confident obedience to a premise mistaken for knowledge.

These examples, however much they may differ, focus attention on one point from which modern consciousness is brought to confusion. The involuntary assumption is that we may know through knowledge what is really a matter of faith. But faith is that absolute essence of man's being which can never be replaced by knowledge, though here falsely represented as such. I am to expect from science what it can never achieve. I am to accept by "faith" even what it seems I already can comprehend as knowledge. Absurd doctrines are declared to be sound conclusions reached by science. All of these proclaim something that transcends scientific knowledge as if it were no more than more scientific knowledge. Such dogmatists are under the influence of the modern overestimation of the potentialities of science; they indulge a sort of scientific superstition.

It is the great, and by no means completed, task of philosophy today to clarify the relation of science to philosophy, indeed to clarify all ways of thinking and comprehending. This task, in its fundamental and comprehensive future realization, constitutes a matter for experts; in the striving for a simpler solution, it is the concern of all. This solution would lead to liberation from scientific superstition, and consequently to the establishment of meaning and boundaries for the marvels of our indispensable modern sciences; it would also increase confidence in the potentialities of philosophy itself.

The problem of science is one of the great subjects for factual investigation on the part of philosophy. An entirely different task arises for philosophy today in the new state of society in the free world, growing out of the fact that the masses now play a decisive role in elections, not only through the utilization of their powers by a will not their own, but also through their own knowledge and volition. Philosophic thinking can bring about results in the world of today only if it reaches the majority of individuals. For the situation today is as follows: The masses of the population can read and write, without yet attaining the full measure of Western culture. But they share in its knowledge, thought and actions. They can profit increasingly by the new opportunities to the degree in which they penetrate into the far reaches of lofty ideas and discriminating judgments. It is therefore necessary for the hours of consciousness of mankind that essential truths be made as simple, as clearly comprehensible as possible without sacrificing their depths. Today many people do not know what they really want. Propaganda takes possession of unthinking, defenseless souls, utilizing interests and influences without regard for right or wrong. It is inevitable today that truth itself must take the shape of propaganda in order to reach the ears of men. The great task of active intelligence therefore must be to effect simple presentations of truth so that the truth will find an echo in the intrinsically inherent faculty of human reason. Essential for this purpose are simple thoughts that by their clarity may reach man in his reflections at that point where he not only knows but where his inmost being is active, that is, where Reason is fully awake.

As opposed to the view set forth at the beginning of this paper declaring philosophy to be at an end, I believe I have here pointed to various tasks which make philosophy today the responsibility of man as Man. In opposition to supposedly total knowledge, philosophy is charged with the duty of keeping awake the faculty of independent thought and therewith the independence of the individual which totalitarian powers seek to extinguish. Philosophy must remind every individual that he *can* be *himself,* and that he ceases to be a man if he relinquishes this privilege. For our common future it is of decisive importance that thinking, proceeding from the deepest sense of responsibility, guided by reason and a lucid will, attain realization. We who are commissioned to deal with philosophy professionally as material for instruction, are far from accomplishing what is required of us in this situation. What little, however, is being attempted by countless men with the best of good will, should not be lightly dismissed as of no consequence.

A NOTE ON EXISTENZPHILOSOPHIE AND EXISTENTIALISM

The mood of the actualities of modern life which precedes all specific thinking was shown by Nietzsche: "I am describing what will come to pass, what is now inevitable, the rise of nihilism." Since this extremity was overpoweringly real to both Nietzsche and Kierkegaard, philosophy now takes its direction from them. As the finality of this conception challenged all original philosophy from the outset, it became possible for our philosophy once more to apprehend ancient philosophy almost as if it were modern. The term "philosophy of existence" (*Existenzphilosophie*) owes its origin to Kierkegaard's idea of existence. The name could be dispensed with, for what is essential in it is the one perennial philosophy, seeking form and utterance under the conditions of our time. The philosophy of existence may be looked upon as the attempt to overcome nihilism.

Either nihilism is seized upon with a bravery that, being bravery, is no longer nihilism; or else an independent philosophy, which has passed through the cleansing fire of nihilism, is seeking realization and is regaining from the origin of tradition those ideas by which man truly exists. But such a philosophy cannot end merely with evolving the idea of human existence. It reaches beyond man. It comprehends what in the first place makes man himself possible. For man is not himself in his freedom without the power by which he exists. There is no existence without transcendence.

Now this word "existence" denotes a common element in modern

198

philosophy which has led to almost all philosophy, with the exception of logic and positivism, being called "philosophy of existence." In the mind of the public a sort of specter has thus been created which does not exist.

It seems to me that the origin of the term "existentialism" stems from Sartre. He is the man whose work has found the most far-reaching echo in the world. Without Sartre the whole matter would presumably have remained confined to narrower circles and would hardly have been understood as one in idea, seeing that the philosophies that go by this name today are very different, even radically diverse, in their fundamentals. Because Sartre became widely known as a poet through his novels and dramas and gained further recognition more as a philosopher by reason of an important philosophic work, *"L'être et le Néant,"*[1] all the others must be content with being classed as more or less his followers. A few years ago I saw in an American newspaper a cartoon: In the center was a large picture of Sartre, smiling, content; surrounding him, as smaller satellites, were Kierkegaard, Nietzsche, Pascal, and the writer of these lines. What a reversal of values! The great men, to be named only with reverence, were here ranged beside our own small likenesses. Thus in the game of the world, transforming everything into puppet form, a picture is made. In a French newspaper there appeared a wittily conceived celestial letter from Pascal, which ended with "I am no existentialist."

In spite of all this, one may perhaps hope that even amid the noise of all this confusion, some truth is stirring, an independent philosophy which stripped of illusions yet is establishing itself in the tradition of millenniums. Perhaps some unifying element is at work here which unites us in all our heterogeneity, because in a certain sense it impels toward the earnest realities of existence.

To define, limit and classify, definitively and systematically, as from a superior standpoint, all philosophies and philosophers, I consider as unjust as it is impossible, and lacking in understanding.
—Translation by Edith A. Daechsler and Annie Taffs

[1] *Being and Nothingness.*

XII / PHILOSOPHY OF A SCIENTIST IN THE CITADEL OF LEARNING

DR. WERNER HEISENBERG, WHO HAS BEEN SINCE 1941 DIRECTOR OF THE Max Planck Institute for Physics in Göttingen, Germany, is the author of a number of papers and books on nuclear physics and the quantum theory. He was born in 1901 and educated at the Universities of Munich and Göttingen. He obtained his doctorate at Munich and has taught at the Universities of Leipzig, Copenhagen and Berlin. He is married and lives at Göttingen in the British zone of occupation, Germany.

Science and International Understanding

BY WERNER HEISENBERG

It has often been said that science should be a bridge between peoples and should help to better international understanding. It has also repeatedly been stressed, with full justification, that science is international and that it directs man's thoughts to matters which are understood by all peoples and in whose solution scientists of the most diverse languages, races or religions can participate equally. In speaking to you[1] about this role of science at this particular time it is important that we should not make things too easy for ourselves. We must also discuss the opposite thesis, which is still fresh in our ears, that science is national and that the ideas of the various races are fundamentally different. It was held that science had to serve one's own people in the first instance

[1] Speech delivered before students of Göttingen University on July 13, 1946.

200

and help to secure one's own political power: that science forms the basis of all technical developments, and hence of all progress, as well as of all military power. It was also held that the task of the pure sciences as well as of philosophy was to support our *Weltanschauung* and our beliefs. These in turn were regarded as the foundations of political power among our own people. I should like to discuss which of these two views is correct and what are the relative merits of the arguments that can be produced in their favor.

1

To gain clarity on this question we shall have to discover, in the first instance, how science is carried on, how an individual is brought into contact with scientific problems and how these problems excite his interest. Since I know only my own science well, you will not misunderstand me if I first speak about atomic physics and if I recall my own experiences as a student.

When I left school in 1920 in order to attend the University of Munich, the position of our youth as citizens was very similar to what it is today. Our defeat in the First World War had produced a deep mistrust of all the ideals which had been used during the war and which had lost us that war. They seemed hollow now and we wanted to find out for ourselves what was of value in this world and what was not: we did not want to rely on our parents or our teachers. Apart from many other values we rediscovered science in this process. After having studied a few popular books I began to take an interest in the branch of science concerned with atoms, and wanted to form an opinion of the peculiar statements which were being made about space and time in the theory of relativity. In this way I came to attend the lectures of my later teacher, Sommerfeld, who fanned this interest and from whom I learnt, in the course of the term, how a new and deeper understanding of atoms had developed as a result of the researches of Röntgen, Planck, Rutherford, and Bohr. I came to know that the Dane, Niels Bohr, and the Englishman, Lord Rutherford, imagined an atom to be a planetary system in miniature and that it was likely that all the chemical properties of the elements would, in future, be predictable with the help of Bohr's theory, by making use of the planetary orbits of the electrons. At that time, however, this had not been achieved. This last point naturally interested me most and every new work of Bohr was discussed at the Munich Seminar with vigor and passion. You can well imagine what it meant for me when Sommerfeld invited me, in the summer of 1921, to accompany him to Göttingen to hear a series of lectures given by Niels Bohr about his atomic theory. It was held in this very "Collegienhaus." This cycle of lectures in Göttingen, which in future was always to be referred to as the "Bohr Festival," has in many ways determined my future attitude to science and especially to atomic physics.

First of all, we could sense in Bohr's lectures the power of the ideas of a man who had seriously grappled with these problems and who understood them better than anyone else in the whole world. Secondly, there were some points on which I had previously formed an opinion different from that expounded by Bohr. These questions were fought out during long walks to the Rohn and to the Hainberg.

These conversations left a deep impression on me. First I learnt that when trying to understand atomic structure it was obviously quite immaterial whether one was German, Danish or English. I also learnt something perhaps even more important, namely, that in science a decision can always be reached as to what is right and what is wrong. It was not a question of belief, or *Weltanschauung,* or hypothesis; but a certain statement could either be simply right and another statement simply wrong. Neither origin nor race decides this question: it is decided by nature, or if you prefer, by God, in any case not by man.

Very much enriched by these experiences, I returned to Munich and continued, under Sommerfeld's direction, with my own experiments on atomic structures. When I had completed my doctor's examination I went to Copenhagen, in the autumn of 1924, with the aid of a so-called Rockefeller Grant, in order to work with Bohr. There I came into a circle of young people of the most diverse nationalities—English, American, Swedish, Norwegian, Dutch and Japanese—all of whom wanted to work on the same problem, Bohr's atomic theory. They nearly always joined together like a big family for excursions, games, social gatherings and sports. In this circle of physicists I had the opportunity of really getting to know people from other nations and their ways of thought. The learning and speaking of other languages which this necessitated was the best way of becoming really familiar with other ways of life, foreign literatures and foreign art. I could see more and more clearly how little mattered the diversity of nations and races when there was common effort centered on a difficult scientific problem. The differences of thought which were so clearly shown in art seemed to me more of an enrichment of one's own possibilities than a disturbing factor.

With this background I arrived in Cambridge in the summer of 1925, and spoke about my work to a small circle of theoreticians in a college, in the study of the Russian physicist Kapitza. Among those present, there was an unusually gifted student hardly twenty-three years old who took my problems and constructed, within a few months, a comprehensive theory of the atomic shell. His name was Dirac and he was a man of outstanding mathematical ability. His methods of thought were vastly different from mine, his mathematical methods more elegant and more unusual than those to which we were used at Göttingen. However, in the end, he arrived at the same results as Born, Jordan and I, at least on all points of importance. This confirmation and the fact that the results were so beautifully complementary served as further proof of the "objectivity" of science and its independence of language, race or belief.

As well as Copenhagen and Cambridge, Göttingen remained a center for this international family of atomic physicists. The work was directed by Franck, Born and Pohl and many of the scientists about whom you read in the newspapers in connection with the atom bomb, such as Oppenheimer and Blackett, as well as Fermi who studied in Göttingen at that time.

I have quoted these personal reminiscences only in order to give an example of the internationalism of the community of science. It has, of course, been the same for centuries in many other sciences and this family of atomic physicists was in no way out of the ordinary. I could quote many international groups of "savants" from the history of science who were linked through the frontiers of nations by common work.

Perhaps I might mention one other group of scientists who, in the seventeenth century, founded mathematical science in Europe. It is especially appropriate to do so because the memory of Leibnitz is being celebrated this year as well as the foundation of the Scientific Academies. I should like to quote a few sentences of Dilthey's description of that epoch.

A bond, unhampered by any limitations of language or nationality, linked the few individuals who devoted their lives to this new science. They formed a new aristocracy and were conscious of it, just as before in the days of the Renaissance, humanists and artists had felt themselves to be such an aristocracy. The Latin and, later on, the French language rendered the easiest mutual understanding possible and they became the instrument of a scientific world literature. Already around the middle of the seventeenth century, Paris had become the center of collaboration between philosophers and scientists. There Gassendi, Marsenne and Hobbes exchanged ideas and even the proud recluse Descartes joined their circle for a time. His presence made an unforgettable impression on Hobbes and later Leibnitz; for it was there that both became devoted to the ideas of mathematical science. Later, London became another center.

We can see then that science has been carried on in this way throughout history and that the "Republic of Sages" has always played an important part in the life of Europe. It has always been considered self-evident that adherence to such an international circle would not prevent the individual scientist from devotedly serving his own people and feeling himself one of them. On the contrary, such a broadening of one's horizon frequently enhances esteem for the best aspects of the life of one's own country. One learns to love it and feels indebted to it.

II

Having said all this I must now also deal with the question of why all this scientific collaboration, all these real human relationships, seemingly do so little in preventing animosity and war.

First of all it must be stressed that science represents only a small part of public life and that only very few people in each country are really connected with science. Politics, however, are shaped by stronger forces. They have to take into account the actions of large masses of people, their economic position and the struggle for power of a few privileged groups favored by tradition. These forces have, so far, always overpowered the small number of people who were ready to discuss disputed questions in a scientific way—that is, objectively, dispassionately and in the spirit of mutual understanding. The political influence of science has always been very small, and this is understandable enough. It does, however, frequently place the scientist in a position which is in some ways more difficult than that of any other group of men. For science has, in its practical applications, a very great influence on the life of the people. Prosperity and political power depend on the state of science and the scientist cannot ignore these practical consequences even if his own interest in science is of a less practical nature. Thus, the action of an individual scientist often carries far more weight than he would wish and he frequently has to decide, according to his own conscience, whether a cause is good or bad. When the differences between nations can no longer be reconciled he is therefore often faced with the painful decision either of cutting himself off from his own people or from those friends who are linked with him by their common work. The position in the various science is here somewhat different. The medical practitioner, who helps people irrespective of their nationality, can more easily reconcile his actions to the demands of the state and of his own conscience than the physicist, whose discoveries may lead to the manufacture of weapons of destruction. But, by and large, there always remains this tension; there are on the one hand the demands of the state, which wants to enlist science particularly for the benefit of its own people and hence the strengthening of its own political power. On the other hand there is the duty owed by the scientist to his work which links him to people of other nations.

The relations between the scientist and the State have changed in a characteristic way during the past decades. During the First World War the scientists were so closely tied to their states that academies frequently expelled scientists of other countries or signed resolutions in favor of their own cause and against the cause of the other nation. This hardly happened at all during the Second World War. The link between the scientists was frequently much stronger, even to the extent, in many countries, of difficulties arising between them and their own governments. Scientists claimed the right to judge the policies of their governments independently and without ideological bias. The State, on its side, viewed the international relations of scientists with deep mistrust so that eventually scientists were sometimes even treated like prisoners in their own country and their international relations considered almost immoral. Conversely it has now become almost a matter of course that scientists will help their colleagues wherever possible, even though they belong to the enemy country. This development may lead to a fortunate strengthening of international, as against national, relations, but care will have to be taken that it does not become the origin of a dangerous wave of mistrust and enmity of large masses of people against the profession of science itself.

There have been such difficulties in previous centuries when men of science stood up for the principle of tolerance and independence from dogma against the current political power. We need only think of a

Galileo or a Giordano Bruno. That these difficulties have assumed even greater importance today may be because the practical effects of science can directly decide the fate of millions of people.

This brings me to a frightening aspect of our present-day existence which has to be clearly recognized so that the correct action can be taken. I am not only thinking of the new sources of energy which physics has mastered during the last year and which could lead to unimaginable destruction. New possibilities of interfering with nature are threatening us in many other fields, though it is true that chemical means of destroying life have hardly been used in this last war. In biology, too, we have gained such insight into the processes of heredity and into the structure and chemistry of large albumen molecules that it has become a practical possibility to produce infectious diseases artificially, and perhaps worse, even the biological development of man may be influenced in the direction of some predetermined selective breeding. Finally, the mental and spiritual state of people could be influenced and, if this were carried out from a scientific point of view, it could lead to terrible mental deformations of great masses of people. One has the impression that science approaches on a broad front a region in which life and death of humanity at large can become dependent on the actions of a few, very small groups of people. Up to now these things have been discussed in a journalistic and sensational way in the newspapers and most people have not realized the terrible danger which threatens them as a result of further inevitable scientific developments. It is certainly the task of science to rouse humanity to these dangers and to show them how important it is that all mankind, independent of national and ideological views, should unite to meet the peril. Of course, this is more easily said than done, but it is certainly a task which we can no longer escape.

For the individual scientist there remains, however, the necessity of deciding according to his own conscience and free from all ties, whether a cause is good or even which of two causes is less bad. We cannot escape the fact that large masses of people, and with them those who hold the power of government, often act senselessly and with blind prejudice. By giving them the scientific knowledge the scientist can easily be maneuvered into a position which Schiller describes in these verses:

Woe to those who bestow the light of heaven on him who is forever blind, it sheds no light for him, it can but char and blacken lands and cities.

Can science really contribute to understanding between the peoples when it is faced with such a situation? It has the power to release great forces, greater than have ever before been in the control of man, but these forces will lead into chaos unless they are sensibly used.

III

This leads me to the real inherent task of science. The development which I have just described and which has apparently turned against himself those forces which man controls and which can lead to the most terrible destruction, this development must certainly be closely connected with some spiritual processes of our time, and it is necessary to speak briefly about these.

Let us look back a few centuries. At the end of the Middle Ages man discovered, apart from the Christian reality centered round the divine revelation, yet another reality of material experience. That was "objective" reality which we experience through our senses or by experiment. But in this advance into a new field certain methods of thought remained unchanged. Nature consisted of things in space which changed in time according to cause and effect. Outside of this there was the world of spirit, that is, the reality of one's own mind which reflected the external world like a more or less perfect mirror. Much as the reality determined by the sciences differed from the Christian reality, it nevertheless represented also a divine world order with man's action based on a firm foundation, and in which there could be little doubt about the purpose of life. The world was infinite in space and time, it had in a way replaced God or had at least become, by its infinity, a symbol of the divine.

But this view of nature has also become undermined during our century. Fundamental attitudes of thought lost their absolute importance as concrete action moved more and more into the center of our world. Even time and space became a subject of experience and lost their symbolic content. In science we realize more and more that our understanding of nature cannot begin with some definite cognition, that it cannot be built on such a rocklike foundation, but that all cognition is, so to speak, suspended over an unfathomable depth.

This development of science corresponds probably to the increasingly relative assessment of all values in the life of man, an assessment which has been noticeable for some decades and which can easily end up in a generally skeptical attitude capped by the desperate question "for what purpose?" Thus develops the attitude of unbelief which we call "nihilism." From this point of view life appears to be purposeless or, at best, an adventure which we have to endure while having had no say in it. We find this attitude in many parts of the world today and its most unpleasant form is illusionary nihilism, as v. Weizsäcker recently called it. It is a nihilism disguised by illusion and self-deception.

The characteristic trait of every nihilist attitude is the lack of a solid belief which can give direction and strength to all the reactions of an individual. Nihilism shows itself in the life of an individual by his lack of an unerring instinct for right and wrong, for what is an illusion and what is a reality. In the life of nations it leads to a change of direction in which the immense forces, which have been gathered for the achievement of a certain aim, have the very opposite result and this can cause great destruction. People are often so blinded by hatred that they cynically watch this change and dispose of it with a shrug of the shoulder.

I said a little earlier that this development in the outlook of men may have some relation to the development of scientific thought. We must therefore ask whether science too has lost its solid beliefs. I am very anxious to make it quite clear that there can be no question of this. The very opposite is true. The present situation of science is probably the strongest argument we possess for a more optimistic attitude to the great problems of the world.

For in *those* branches of science in which we have found that our knowledge is "suspended in mid-air," in *just those* branches have we achieved a crystal-clear understanding of the relevant phenomena. This knowledge is so transparent and carries such force of conviction that scientists of the most diverse peoples and races have accepted it as the undoubted basis of all further thought and cognition. Of course, we also make mistakes in science and it may take some time before these are found and corrected. But we can rest assured that there will be a final decision as to what is right and what is wrong. This decision will not depend on the belief, race or origin of the scientists, but it will be taken by a higher power and will then apply to all men for all time. While we cannot avoid in political life a constant change of values, a struggle of one set of illusions and misleading ideas against another set of illusions and equally misleading ideas, there will always be a "right or wrong" in science. There is a higher power, not influenced by our wishes, which finally decides and judges. The core of science is formed, to my mind, by the pure sciences, which are not concerned with practical applications. They are the branches in which pure thought attempts to discover the hidden harmonies of nature. Mankind today may find this innermost circle in which science and art can hardly be separated, in which the personification of pure truth is no longer disguised by human ideologies and desires.

You may, of course, object that the great mass of people has no access to this truth and that it can therefore exert little influence on the attitude of people. But at no time did the great mass of people have direct access to the center and it may be that people today will be satisfied to know that though the gate is not open to everyone there *can* be no deceit beyond the gate. We have no power there—the decisions are taken by a higher power. People have used different words at different times for this "center." They called it "spirit" or "God," or they spoke in similes, or in terms of sound or picture. There are many ways to this center, even today, and science is only one of them. Perhaps we have no longer a generally recognized language in which we can make ourselves intelligible. That may be the reason why so many people cannot see it, but it is there today as it has always been, and any world order must be based on it. Such a world order must be guided by men who have not lost sight of it.

Science can contribute to the understanding between peoples. It can do so not because it can render succor to the sick, nor because of the terror which some political power may wield with its aid, but only by turning our attention to that "center" which can establish order in the world at large, perhaps simply to the fact that the world is beautiful. It may appear presumptuous to attribute such importance to science, but may I remind you that though we have cause to envy previous epochs in many aspects of life, our age is second to none in scientific achievement, in the pure cognition of nature.

Whatever may happen, interest in knowledge itself will remain a potent force in mankind for the next few decades. Even though this interest may for some time be overshadowed by the practical consequences of science and by the struggle for power it must eventually triumph and link together people of all nations and races. In all parts of the world people will be happy when they have gained new knowledge and they will be grateful to the man who first discovered it.

You are gathered here to contribute in your circle to an understanding between the peoples. There can be no better way of doing this than by getting to know, with the freedom and spontaneity of youth, people of other nations, their ways of thought and their feelings. Take from your scientific work a serious and incorruptible method of thought, help to spread it, because no understanding is possible without it. Revere those things beyond science which really matter and about which it is so difficult to speak.

XIII / PHILOSOPHY OF A MAN CONDEMNED TO BE FREE

BEING AND NOTHINGNESS, AN ESSAY ON PHENOMENOLOGICAL ONTOLOGY, BY Jean-Paul Sartre, made its first appearance in English in 1956. The translation of the 632-page book involved its translator, Hazel E. Barnes of the University of Colorado, for two years, and was the first opportunity readers not familiar with French were given to appraise the chief opus of the now fifty-one-year-old Frenchman whose name in literary circles, if not in purely philosophical ones, had become almost synonymous with modern disillusion, despair and an over-all meaningless in life.

The appearance of the book in English, as its appearance in French more than a dozen years before in Paris, found reviewers and readers concurring that here was no dilettante in philosophy but one who had formulated his thought into a framework of structure and style, and that the point of view that "existence is prior to essence" and that man is alone responsible, through his own choice, for his own destiny, was more than the thematic utterance of a playwright or novelist out to shock the bourgeoisie.

(Between the French publication of the book and its American publication, Sartre defined, for his critics, in *"L'Existentialism est un humanism* (1946), his "new humanism" as "without illusions (that is to say, divorced from religious experience), but full of confidence in the grandeur of humanity; hard, but without useless violence; passionate yet restrained; striving to paint the metaphysical condition of man while fully participating in the movements of society.")

Sartre was born in Paris, June 21, 1905, and at the École Normale Supérieure in 1925 he majored in philosophy. He completed his studies with high academic honors and became a teacher in the secondary schools. In 1933 and 1934 he studied in Germany under two of the most influential German philosophers, Edmund Husserl and Martin Heidegger, and continued his studies of Sören Kierkegaard, the nineteenth-century Danish philosopher and forerunner of the contemporary existentialist movement; he then began work on his own philosophy.

From 1935 until September, 1939, when he entered the French Army as a private, Sartre was the center of a section of Parisian intellectual life on the Left Bank, known as the author of essays on contemporary literature, advocate of certain American authors just being translated into French, and author of a novel, *Nausea,* and a collection of short stories. Captured by the Germans upon the fall of France, Sartre spent nine months in a prison camp, where he wrote and directed plays for his fellow prisoners. On his release he was active in the French Resistance movement and concluded his philosophical treatise. In 1946 he founded the review *Les Temps Modernes,* which he has edited since. He has taken part in several international congresses, Communist inspired or directed, and Communist leanings have been evident in his magazine writings.

Pleading pressure on his time, Sartre suggested that someone else select something from the over-all expression of his philosophy and this task was performed for this book, accordingly, by his American publisher, Dr. Dagobert Runes, president of The Philosophical Library.

Out of *Being and Nothingness*

BY JEAN-PAUL SARTRE

I. FREEDOM AND RESPONSIBILITY

Man, being condemned to be free, carries the weight of the whole world on his shoulders; he is responsible for the world and for himself as a way of being. We are taking the word "responsibility" in its ordinary sense as "consciousness (of) being the incontestable author of an event or of an object." In this sense the responsibility of the "for-itself"[1] is overwhelming since he[2] is the one by whom it happens that

[1] See Definitions.

[2] I am shifting to the personal pronoun here since Sartre is describing the for-itself in concrete personal terms rather than as a metaphysical entity. Strictly speaking, of course, this is his position throughout, and the French "*il*" is indifferently "he" or "it."— Translator.

there is a world; since he is also the one who makes himself be, then whatever may be the situation in which he finds himself, the for-itself must wholly assume this situation with its peculiar coefficient of adversity, even though it be insupportable. He must assume the situation with the proud consciousness of being the author of it, for the very worst disadvantages or the worst threats which can endanger my person have meaning only in and through my project; and it is on the ground of the engagement which I am that they appear. It is therefore senseless to think of complaining since nothing foreign has decided what we feel, what we live, or what we are.

Furthermore this absolute responsibility is not resignation; it is simply the logical requirement of the consequences of our freedom. What happens to me happens through me, and I can neither affect myself with it nor revolt against it nor resign myself to it. Moreover everything which happens to me is mine. By this we must understand first of all that I am always equal to what happens to me *qua* man, for what happens to a man through other men and through himself can be only human. The most terrible situations of war, the worst tortures do not create a nonhuman state of things; there is no nonhuman situation. It is only through fear, flight, and recourse to magical types of conduct that I shall decide on the nonhuman, but this decision is human, and I shall carry the entire responsibility for it. But in addition the situation is mine because it is the image of my free choice of myself, and everything which it presents to me is *mine* in that this represents me and symbolizes me. Is it not I who decides the coefficient of adversity in things and even their unpredictability by deciding myself?

Thus there are no *accidents* in a life; a community event which suddenly bursts forth and involves me in it does not come from the outside. If I am mobilized in a war, this war is *my* war; it is in my image and I deserve it. I deserve it first because I could always get out of it by suicide or by desertion; these ultimate possibles are those which must always be present for us when there is a question of envisaging a situation. For lack of getting out of it, I have *chosen* it. This can be due to inertia, to cowardice in the face of public opinion, or because I prefer certain other values to the value of the refusal to join in the war (the good opinion of my relatives, the honor of my family, etc.). Anyway you look at it, it is a matter of a choice. This choice will be repeated later on again and again without a break until the end of the war. Therefore we must agee with the statement by Jules Romains, "In war there are no innocent vic-

213

tims."[3] If therefore I have preferred war to death or to dishonor, everything takes place as if I bore the entire responsibility for this war. Of course others have declared it, and one might be tempted perhaps to consider me as a simple accomplice. But this notion of complicity has only a juridical sense, and it does not hold here. For it depended on me that for me and by me this war should not exist, and I have decided that it does exist. There was no compulsion here, for the compulsion could have got no hold on a freedom. I did not have any excuse; for as we have said repeatedly, the peculiar character of human-reality is that it is without excuse. Therefore it remains for me only to lay claim to this war.

But in addition the war is mine because by the sole fact that it arises in a situation which I cause to be and that I can discover it there only by engaging myself for or against it, I can no longer distinguish at present the choice which I make of myself from the choice which I make of the war. To live this war is to choose myself through it and to choose it through my choice of myself. There can be no question of considering it as "four years of vacation" or as a "reprieve," as a "recess," the essential part of my responsibilities being elsewhere in my married, family, or professional life. In this war which I have chosen I choose myself from day to day, and I make it mine by making myself. If it is going to be four empty years, then it is I who bear the responsibility for this.

Finally, as we pointed out earlier, each person is an absolute choice of self from the standpoint of a world of knowledges and of techniques which this choice both assumes and illumines; each person is an absolute upsurge at an absolute date and is perfectly unthinkable at another date. It is therefore a waste of time to ask what I should have been if this war had not broken out, for I have chosen myself as one of the possible meanings of the epoch which imperceptibly led to war. I am not distinct from this same epoch; I could not be transported to another epoch without contradiction. Thus *I am* this war which restricts and limits and makes comprehensible the period which preceded it. In this sense we may define more precisely the responsibility of the for-itself if to the earlier quoted statement, "There are no innocent victims," we add the words, "We have the war we deserve." Thus, totally free, undistinguishable from the period for which I have chosen to be the meaning, as profoundly responsible for the war as if I had myself declared it, unable to live without integrating it in my situation, engaging myself

[3] Jules Romains: *Les hommes de bonne volonté, "Prélude à Verdun."*

214

in it wholly and stamping it with my seal, I must be without remorse or regrets as I am without excuse; for from the instant of my upsurge into being, I carry the weight of the world by myself alone without anything or any person being able to lighten it.

Yet this responsibility is of a very particular type. Someone will say, "I did not ask to be born." This is a naïve way of throwing greater emphasis on our facticity. I am responsible for everything, in fact, except for my very responsibility, for I am not the foundation of my being. Therefore everything takes place as if I were compelled to be responsible. I am *abandoned* in the world, not in the sense that I might remain abandoned and passive in a hostile universe like a board floating on the water, but rather in the sense that I find myself suddenly alone and without help, engaged in a world for which I bear the whole responsibility without being able, whatever I do, to tear myself away from this responsibility for an instant. For I am responsible for my very desire of fleeing responsibilities. To make myself passive in the world, to refuse to act upon things and upon Others is still to choose myself, and suicide is one mode among others of being-in-the-world. Yet I find an absolute responsibility for the fact that my facticity (here the fact of my birth) is directly inapprehensible and even inconceivable, for this fact of my birth never appears as a brute fact but always across a projective reconstruction of my for-itself. I am ashamed of being born or I am astonished at it or I rejoice over it, or in attempting to get rid of my life I affirm that I live and I assume this life as bad. Thus in a certain sense I *choose* being born. This choice itself is integrally affected with facticity since I am not able not to choose, but this facticity in turn will appear only insofar as I surpass it toward my ends. Thus facticity is everywhere but inapprehensible; I never encounter anything except my responsibility. That is why I cannot ask, "Why was I born?" or curse the day of my birth or declare that I did not ask to be born, for these various attitudes toward my birth—i.e., toward the fact that I realize a presence in the world—are absolutely nothing else but ways of assuming this birth in full responsibility and of making it *mine*. Here again I encounter only myself and my projects so that finally my abandonment—i.e., my facticity—consists simply in the fact that I am condemned to be wholly responsible for myself. I am the being which *is* in such a way that in its being its being is in question. And this "is" of my being is as present and inapprehensible.

Under these conditions since every event in the world can be revealed to me only as an *opportunity* (an opportunity made use of, lacked, neglected, etc., or better yet since everything which happens to us can be considered as a *chance* i.e., can appear to us only as a way of realizing this being which is in question in our being) and since others as transcendences-transcended are themselves only *opportunities* and *chances,* the responsibility of the for-itself extends to the entire world as a peopled-world. It is precisely thus that the for-itself apprehends itself in anguish; that is, as a being which is neither the foundation of its own being nor of the Other's being nor of the in-itselfs which form the world, but a being which is compelled to decide the meaning of being—within it and everywhere outside of it. The one who realizes in anguish his condition as *being* thrown into a responsibility which extends to his very abandonment has no longer either remorse or regret or excuse; he is no longer anything but a freedom which perfectly reveals itself and whose being resides in this very revelation. But as we pointed out at the beginning of this work,[4] most of the time we flee anguish in bad faith.

II. THE DESIRE TO BE GOD

The most discerning ethicists have shown how a desire reaches beyond itself. Pascal believed that he could discover in hunting, for example, or tennis, or in a hundred other occupations, the need of being diverted. He revealed that in an activity which would be absurd if reduced to itself, there was a meaning which transcended it; that is, an indication which referred to the reality of man in general and to his condition. Similarly Stendhal in spite of his attachment to ideologists, and Proust in spite of his intellectualistic and analytical tendencies, have shown that love and jealousy cannot be reduced to the strict desire of possessing a *particular* woman, but that these emotions aim at laying hold of the world in its entirety through the woman. This is the meaning of Stendhal's crystallization, and it is precisely for this reason that love as Stendhal describes it appears as a mode of being in the world. Love is a fundamental relation of the for-itself to the world and to itself (selfness) through a particular woman; the woman represents only a conducting body which is placed in the circuit. These analyses may be inexact or only partially true; nevertheless they make us suspect a method other than pure analytical description. In the same way Catholic novelists immediately see in carnal love its surpassing toward God—in Don Juan, "the eternally unsatisfied," in sin, "the place empty

[4] *Being and Nothingness*, Philosophical Library, 1956.

216

of God." There is no question here of finding again an abstract behind the concrete; the impulse toward God is no *less concrete* than the impulse toward a particular woman. On the contrary, it is a matter of rediscovering under the partial and incomplete aspects his impulse toward being, his original relation to himself, to the world, and to the Other, in the unity of internal relations and of a fundamental project....

... The best way to conceive of the fundamental project of human reality is to say that man is the being whose project is to be God. Whatever may be the myths and rites of the religion considered, God is first "sensible to the heart" of man as the one who identified and defines him in his ultimate and fundamental project. If man possesses a preontological comprehension of the being of God, it is not the great wonders of nature nor the power of society which have conferred it upon him. God, value and supreme end of transcendence, represents the permanent limit in terms of which man makes known to himself what he is. To be man means to reach toward being God. Or if you prefer, man fundamentally is the desire to be God.

It may be asked, if man on coming into the world is borne toward God as toward his limit, if he can choose only to be God, what becomes of freedom? For freedom is nothing other than a choice which creates for itself its own possibilities, but it appears here that the initial project of being God, which "defines" man, comes close to being the same as a human "nature" or an "essence." The answer is that while the *meaning* of the desire is ultimately the project of being God, the desire is never *constituted* by this meaning; on the contrary, it always represents a particular discovery of its ends. These ends in fact are pursued in terms of a particular empirical situation, and it is this very pursuit which constitutes the surroundings *as a situation*. The desire of being is always realized as the desire of a mode of being. And this desire of a mode of being expresses itself in turn as the meaning of the myriads of concrete desires which constitute the web of our conscious life. Thus we find ourselves before very complex symbolic structures which have *at least* three stories. In empirical desire I can discern a symbolization of a fundamental concrete desire which is the person himself and which represents the mode in which he has decided that being would be in question in his being. This fundamental desire in turn expresses concretely in the world within the particular situation enveloping the individual, an abstract meaningful structure which is the desire of being in general; it must be considered as human reality in the person, and it brings about his community with others, thus making it possible to state that there is a truth concerning man and not only concerning individuals who cannot be compared. Absolute concreteness, completion, existence as a totality belong then to the free and fundamental desire which is the unique person. Empirical desire is only a symbolization of this; it refers to this and derives its meaning from it while remaining partial and reducible, for the empirical desire cannot be conceived in isolation. On the other hand, the desire of being in its abstract purity is the *truth* of the concrete fundamental desire, but it does not exist by virtue of its reality. Thus the fundamental project, the person, the free realization of human truth is everywhere in all desires. . . . It is never apprehended except through desires—as we can apprehend space only through bodies which shape it for us, though space is a specific reality and not a concept. Or, if you like, it is like the *object* of Husserl, which reveals itself only by *Abschattungen,* and which nevertheless does not allow itself to be absorbed by any one *Abschattung.* We can understand after these remarks that the abstract ontological "desire to be" is unable to represent the fundamental, *human* structure of the individual, it cannot be an obstacle to his freedom. Freedom is strictly identified with nihilation. The only being which can be called free is the being which nihilates its being. Moreover we know that nihilation is *lack of being* and cannot be otherwise. Freedom is precisely the being which makes itself a lack of being. But since desire, as we have established, is identical with lack of being, freedom can arise only as being which makes itself a desire of being, that is, as the project for itself of being in-itself-for-itself. Here we have arrived at an abstract structure which can by no means be considered as the nature or essence of freedom. Freedom is existence, and in it existence precedes essence. The upsurge of freedom is immediate and concrete and is not to be distinguished from its choice; that is, from the person himself. But the structure under consideration can be called the *truth* of freedom; that is, it is the human meaning of freedom.

III. EXISTENTIAL PSYCHOANALYSIS

It should be possible to establish the human truth of the person, as we have attempted to do by an ontological phenomenology. The catalogue of empirical desires ought to be made the object of appropriate psychological investigations, observation and induction and, as needed, experience can serve to draw up this list. They will indicate to the philosopher the comprehensible relations which can unite to each other various desires and various patterns of behaviors, and will bring to light certain concrete connections between the subject of experience and "situations" experientially defined (which at bottom originate only from limitations applied in the name of positivity to the fundamental situation of the subject in the world). But in establishing and classifying fundamental desires of *individual persons* neither of these methods is appropriate. Actually there can be no question of determining *a priori* and ontologically what appears in all the unpredictability of a free act. This is why we shall limit ourselves here to indicating very summarily the possibilities of such a quest and its perspectives. The very fact that we can subject any man whatsoever to such an investigation—that is what belongs to human reality in general. Or, if you prefer, this is what can be established by an ontology. But the inquiry itself and its results are on principle wholly outside the possibilities of an ontology.

On the other hand, pure, simple empirical description can only give us catalogues and put us in the presence of pseudo-irreducibles (the desire to write, to swim, a taste for adventure, jealousy, etc.). It is not enough in fact to draw up a list of behavior patterns, of drives and inclinations, it is necessary also to *decipher* them; that is, it is necessary to know how to *question* them. This research can be conducted only according to the rules of a specific method. It is this method which we call existential psychoanalysis.

The principle of this psychoanalysis is that man is a totality and not a collection. Consequently he expresses himself as a whole in even his most insignificant and his most superficial behavior. In other words there is not a taste, a mannerism, or an human act which is not *revealing*.

The *goal* of psychoanalysis is to decipher the empirical behavior patterns of man; that is, to bring out in the open the revelations which each one of them contains and to fix them conceptually.

Its point of departure is experience; its pillar of support is the fundamental, preontological comprehension which man has of the human person. Although the majority of people can well ignore the indications contained in a gesture, a word, a sign and can look with scorn on the revelation which they carry, each human individual nevertheless possesses *a priori* the *meaning* of the revelatory value of these manifestations and is capable of deciphering them, at least if he is aided and guided by a helping hand. Here as elsewhere, truth is not encountered by chance; it does not belong to a domain where one must seek it without ever having any presentiment of its location, as one can go to look for the source of the Nile or of the Niger. It belongs *a priori* to human comprehension and the essential task is an hermeneutic; that is, a deciphering, a determination, and a conceptualization.

Its *method* is comparative. Since each example of human conduct symbolizes in its own manner the fundamental choice which must be brought to light, and since at the same time each one disguises this choice under its occasional character and its historical opportunity, only the comparison of these acts of conduct can effect the emergence of the unique revelation which they all express in a different way. The first outline of this method has been furnished for us by the psychoanalysis of Freud and his disciples. For this reason it will be profitable here to indicate more specifically the points where existential psychoanalysis will be inspired by psychoanalysis proper and those where it will radically differ from it.

Both kinds of psychoanalysis consider all objectively discernible manifestations of "psychic life" as symbols maintaining symbolic relations to the fundamental, total structures which constitute the individual person. Both consider that there are no primary givens such as hereditary dispositions, character, etc. Existential psychoanalysis recognizes nothing *before* the original upsurge of human freedom; empirical psychoanalysis holds that the original affectivity of the individual is virgin wax *before* its history. The libido is nothing besides its concrete fixations, save for a permanent possibility of fixing anything whatsoever upon anything whatsoever. Both consider the human being as a perpetual, searching historization. Rather than uncovering static, constant givens they discover the meaning, orientation, and adventures of this history. Due to this fact both consider man in the world and do not imagine that one can question the being of a man without taking into account all his *situation*. Psychological investigations aim at reconstituting the life of the subject from birth to the moment of the cure; they utilize all the objective documentation which they can find; letters, witnesses, intimate diaries, "social" information of every kind. What they aim at restoring is less a pure psychic event than a twofold structure: the crucial event of infancy and the psychic crystallization around this event. Here, again we have to do with a *situation*. Each "historical" fact from this point of view will be considered at once as a *factor* of the psychic evolution and as a *symbol* of that evolution. For it is nothing in itself. It operates only according to the way in which it is taken and this very manner of taking it expresses symbolically the internal disposition of the individual.

Empirical psychoanalysis and existential psychoanalysis both search within an existing situation for a fundamental attitude which cannot be expressed by simple, logical definitions because it is prior to all logic. and which requires reconstruction according to the laws of specific syntheses. Empirical psychoanalysis seeks to determine the *complex,* the very name of which indicates the polyvalence of all the meanings which are referred back to it. Existential psychoanalysis seeks to determine the *original choice.* This original choice operating in the face of the world and being a choice of position in the world is total like the complex; it is prior to logic like the complex. It is this which decides the attitude of the person when confronted with logic and principles; therefore there can be no possibility of questioning it in conformance to logic. It brings together in a prelogical synthesis the totality of the existent, and as such it is the center of reference for an infinity of polyvalent meanings.

Both our psychoanalyses refuse to admit that the subject is in a privileged position to proceed in these inquiries concerning himself. They equally insist on a strictly objective method, using as documentary evidence the data of reflection as well as the testimony of others. Of course the subject can undertake a psychoanalytic investigation of himself. But in this case he must renounce at the outset all benefit stemming from his peculiar position and must question himself exactly as if he were someone else. Empirical psychoanalysis in fact is based on the hypothesis of the existence of an unconscious psyche, which on principle escapes the intuition of the subject. Existential psychoanalysis rejects the hypothesis of the unconscious; it makes the psychic act coextensive with consciousness. But if the fundamental project is fully experienced by the subject and hence wholly conscious, that certainly does not mean that it must by the same token be *known* by him; quite the contrary. . . . We distinguish between consciousness and knowledge. To be sure, as we have seen earlier, reflection can be considered as a quasi-knowledge. But what it grasps at each moment is not the pure project of the for-itself as it is symbolically expressed—often in several ways at once—by the concrete behavior which it apprehends. It grasps the concrete behavior itself; that is, the specific dated desire in all its characteristic network. It grasps at once symbol and symbolization. This apprehension, to be sure, is entirely constituted by a preontological comprehension of the fundamental project; better yet, insofar as reflection is almost a nonthetic consciousness of itself as reflection, it is this same project, as well as the nonreflective consciousness. But it does not follow that it commands the instruments and techniques necessary to isolate the choice symbolized, to fix it by concepts, and to bring it forth into the full light of day. It is penetrated by a great light without being able to express what this light is illuminating. We are not dealing with an unsolved riddle as the Freudians believe; all is there, luminous; reflection is in full possession of it, apprehends all. But this "mystery in broad daylight" is due to the fact that this possession is deprived of the means which would ordinarily permit *analysis* and *conceptualization*. It grasps everything, all at once, without shading, without relief, without connections of grandeur—not that these shades, these values, these reliefs exist somewhere and are hidden from it, but rather because they must be established by another human attitude and because they can exist only by *means of* and *for* knowledge. Reflection, unable to serve as the basis for existential psychoanalysis, will then simply furnish us with the brute materials toward which the psychoanalyst must take an objective attitude. Thus only will he be able to know what he *already understands*. The result is that complexes uprooted from the depths of the unconscious, like projects revealed by existential psychoanalysis, will be apprehended *from the point of view of the Other*. Consequently the *object* thus brought into the light will be articulated according to the structures of the transcended-transcendence; that is, its being will be the being-for-others even if the psychoanalyst and the subject of the psychoanalysis are actually the same person. Thus the project which is brought to light by either kind of psychoanalysis can be only the totality of the individual human being, the irreducible element of the transcendence with the structure of *being-for-others*. What always escapes these methods of investigation is the project as it is for itself, the complex in its own being. This project-for-itself can be experienced only as a living possession; there is an incompatibility between existence for-itself and objective existence. But the object of the two psychoanalyses has in it nonetheless the *reality of a being*; the subject's knowledge of it can in addition contribute to *clarify* reflection, and that reflection can then become a possession which will be a quasi-knowing.

At this point the similarity between the two kinds of psychoanalysis ceases. They differ fundamentally in that empirical psychoanalysis has decided upon its own irreducible instead of allowing this to make itself known in a self-evident intuition. The libido or the will to power in actuality constitutes a psychobiological residue which is not clear in itself and which does not appear to us as *being beforehand* the irreducible limit of the investigation. Finally it is experience which establishes that the foundation of complexes is this libido or this will to power; and these results of empirical inquiry are perfectly contingent, they are not convincing. Nothing prevents our conceiving *a priori* of a "human reality" which would not be expressed by the will to power, for which the libido would not constitute the original, undifferentiated project.

On the other hand, the choice to which existential psychoanalysis will lead us, precisely because it is a choice, accounts for its original contingency, for the contingency of the choice is the reverse side of its freedom. Furthermore, inasmuch as it is established on the *lack of being,* conceived as a fundamental characteristic of being, it receives its legitimacy as a *choice,* and we know that we do not have to push further. Each result then will be at once fully contingent and legitimately irreducible. Moreover it will always remain *particular*; that is, we will not achieve as the ultimate goal of our investigation and the foundation of all behavior an abstract, general term, libido for example, which would be differentiated and made concrete first in complexes and then in detailed acts of conduct, due to the action of external facts and the history of the subject. On the contrary, it will be a choice which remains unique and which is from the start absolute concreteness. Details of behavior can express or *particularize* this choice, but they cannot make it more concrete than it already is. That is because the choice is nothing other than the being of each human reality; this amounts to saying that a particular partial behavior *is* or expresses the original choice of this human reality since for human reality there is no difference between existing and choosing for itself. From this fact we understand that existential psychoanalysis does not have to proceed from the fundamental "complex," which is exactly the choice of being, to an abstraction like the libido which would explain it. The complex is the ultimate choice, it is the choice of being and makes *itself such*. Bringing it into the light will reveal it each time as evidently irreducible. It follows necessarily that the libido and the will to power will appear to existential psychoanalysis neither as general characteristics common to all mankind nor as irreducibles. At most it will be possible after the investigation to establish that they express by virtue of particular ensembles in certain subjects a fundamental choice which cannot be reduced to either one of them. We have seen in fact that desire and sexuality in general express an original effort of the for-itself to recover its being which has become estranged through contact with the Other. The will to power also originally supposes being-for-others, the comprehension of the Other, and the choice of winning its own salvation by means of the Other. The foundation of this attitude must be an original choice which would make us understand the radical identification of being-in-itself-for-itself with being-for-others.

The fact that the ultimate term of this existential inquiry must be a *choice*, distinguishes even better the psychoanalysis for which we have outlined the method and principal features. It thereby abandons the supposition that the environment acts mechanically on the subject under consideration. The environment can act on the subject only to the exact extent that he comprehends it; that is, transforms it into a situation. Hence no objective description of this environment could be of any use to us. From the start the environment conceived as a situation refers to the for-itself which is choosing, just as the for-itself refers to the environment by the very fact that the for-itself is in the world. By renouncing all mechanical causation, we renounce at the same time all *general* interpretation of the symbolization confronted. Our goal could not be to establish empirical laws of succession, nor could we constitute a universal symbolism. Rather the psychoanalyst will have to rediscover at each step a symbol functioning in the particular case which he is considering. If each being is a totality, it is not conceivable that there can exist elementary symbolic relationships (e.g.; the faeces = gold, or a pincushion = the breast) which preserve a constant meaning in all cases; that is, which remain unaltered when they pass from one meaningful ensemble to another ensemble. Furthermore the psychoanalyst will never lose sight of the fact that the choice is living and consequently can be *revoked* by the subject who is being studied. We have shown . . . the importance of the *instant,* which represents abrupt changes in orientation and the assuming of a new position in the face of an unalterable past. From this moment on, we must always be ready to consider that symbols change meaning and to abandon the symbol used hitherto. Thus existential psychoanalysis will have to be completely flexible and adapt itself to the slightest observable changes in the subject. Our concern here is to understand what is *individual* and often even instantaneous. The method which has served for one subject will not necessarily be suitable to use for another subject or for the same subject at a later period.

Precisely because the goal of the inquiry must be to discover a *choice* and not a *state,* the investigator must recall on every occasion that his object is not a datum buried in the darkness of the unconscious but a free, conscious determination—which is not even resident in consciousness, but which is one with this consciousness itself. Empirical psychoanalysis, to the extent that its method is better than its principles, is often in sight of an existential discovery, but it always stops part way. When it thus approaches the fundamental choice, the resistance of the subject collapses suddenly and he *recognizes* the image of himself which is presented to him as if he were seeing himself in a mirror. This involuntary testimony of the subject is precious for the psychoanalyst; he sees there the sign that he has reached his goal; he can pass on from the investigation proper to the cure. But nothing in his principles or in his initial postulates permits him to understand or to utilize this testimony. Where could he get any such right? If the complex is really unconscious—that is, if there is a barrier separating the sign from the thing signified—how could the subject *recognize* it? Does the unconscious complex recognize itself? But haven't we been told that it lacks *understanding?* And if of necessity we granted to it the faculty of understanding the signs, would this not be to make of it by the same token a conscious unconscious? What is understanding if not to be conscious of what is understood? Shall we say on the other hand that it is the subject as conscious who recognizes the image presented? But how could he compare it with his true state since that is out of reach and since he has never had any knowledge of it? At most he will be able to judge that the psychoanalytic explanation of his case is a *probable* hypothesis, which derives its probability from the number of behavior patterns which it explains. His relation to this interpretation is that of a third party, that of the psychoanalyst himself; he has no privileged position. And if he *believes* in the probability of the psychoanalytic hypothesis, is this simple belief, which lives in the limits of his consciousness, able to effect the breakdown of the barriers which dam up the unconscious tendencies? The psychoanalyst doubtless has some obscure picture of an abrupt coincidence of conscious and unconscious. But he has removed all methods of conceiving of this coincidence in any positive sense.

Still, the enlightenment of the subject is a fact. There is an intuition here which is accompanied by evidence. The subject guided by the psychoanalyst does more and better than to give his agreement to an hypothesis; he touches it, he sees what it is. This is truly understandable only if the subject has never ceased being conscious of his deep tendencies; better yet, only if these drives are not distinguished from his conscious self. In this case as we have seen, the traditional psychoanalytic interpretation does not cause him to attain *consciousness* of what he is; it causes him to attain *knowledge* of what he is. It is existential psychoanalysis then which claims the final intuition of the subject as decisive.

This comparison allows us to understand better what an existential psychoanalysis must be if it is entitled to exist. It is a method destined to bring to light, in a strictly objective form, the subjective choice by which each living person makes himself a person; that is, makes known to himself what he is. Since what the method seeks is a *choice of being* at the same time as a *being*, it must reduce particular behavior patterns to fundamental relations—not of sexuality or of the will to power, but *of being*—which are expressed in this behavior. It is then guided from the start toward a comprehension of being and must not assign itself any other goal than to discover being and the mode of being of the being confronting this being. It is forbidden to stop before attaining this goal. It will utilize the comprehension of being which characterizes the investigator inasmuch as he is himself a human reality; and as it seeks to detach being from its symbolic expressions, it will have to rediscover each time on the basis of a comparative study of acts and attitudes, a symbol destined to decipher them. Its criterion of success will be the number of facts which its hypothesis permits it to explain and to unify as well as the self-evident intuition of the irreducibility of the end attained. To this criterion will be added in all cases where it is possible, the decisive testimony of the subject. The results thus achieved —that is, the ultimate ends of the individual—can then become the object of a classification, and it is by the comparison of these results that we will be able to establish general considerations about human reality as an empirical choice of its own ends. The behavior studied by this psychoanalysis will include not only dreams, failures, obsessions, and neuroses, but also and especially the thoughts of waking life, successfully adjusted acts, style, etc. This psychoanalysis has not yet found its Freud. At most we can find the foreshadowing of it in certain particularly successful biographies . . . [as in] Flaubert and Dostoevsky. But it matters little to us whether it now exists; the important thing is that it is possible.

IV. THE HOLE

Here at its origin we grasp one of the most fundamental tendencies of human reality—the tendency to fill. We shall meet with this tendency again in the adolescent and in the adult. A good part of our life is passed in plugging up holes, in filling empty places, in realizing and symbolically establishing a plenitude. The child recognizes as the results of his first experiences that he himself has holes. When he puts his fingers in his mouth, he tries to wall up the holes in his face; he expects that his finger will merge with his lips and the roof of his mouth and block up the buccal orifice as one fills the crack in a wall with cement; he seeks again the density, the uniform and spherical plenitude of Parmenidean being; if he sucks his thumb, it is precisely in order to dissolve it, to transform it into a sticky paste which will seal the hole of his mouth. This tendency is certainly one of the most fundamental among those which serve as the basis for the act of eating; nourishment is the "cement" which will seal the mouth; to eat is among other things to be filled up.

It is only from this standpoint that we can pass on to sexuality. The obscenity of the feminine sex is that of everything which "gapes open." It is an appeal to being as all holes are. In herself woman appeals to a strange flesh which is to transform her into a fullness of being by penetration and dissolution. Conversely woman senses her condition as an appeal precisely because she is "in the form of a hole." This is the true origin of Adler's complex. Beyond any doubt her sex is a mouth and a voracious mouth which devours the penis—a fact which can easily lead to the idea of castration. The amorous act is the castration of the man; but this is above all because sex is a hole. We have to do here with a presexual contribution which will become one of the components of sexuality as an empirical, complex, human attitude but which far from deriving its origin from the sexed being has nothing in common with basic sexuality.... Nevertheless the experience with the hole, when the infant sees the reality, includes the ontological presentiment of sexual experience in general; it is with his flesh that the child stops up the hole and the hole, before all sexual specification, is an obscene expectation, an appeal to the flesh.

We can see the importance which the elucidation of these immediate and concrete existential categories will assume for existential psychoanalysis. In this way we can apprehend the very general projects of human reality. But what chiefly interests the psychoanalyst is to determine the free project of the unique person in terms of the individual relation which unites him to these various symbols of being. I can love slimy contacts, have a horror of holes, etc. That does not mean that for me the slimy, the greasy, a hole, etc. have lost their general ontological meaning, but on the contrary that because of this meaning, I determine myself in this or that manner in relation to them. If the slimy is indeed the symbol of a being in which the for-itself is swallowed up by the in-itself, what kind of a person am I if in encountering others, I love the slimy? To what fundamental project of myself am I referred if I want to explain this love of an ambiguous, sucking in-itself? In this way tastes do not remain irreducible givens; if one knows how to question them, they reveal to us the fundamental projects of the person. Down to even our alimentary preferences they all have a meaning. We can account for this fact if we will reflect that each taste is presented, not as an absurd datum which we must excuse but as an evident value. If I like the taste of garlic, it seems irrational to me that other people cannot like it.

To eat is to appropriate by destruction; it is at the same time to be filled up with a certain being. And this being is given as a synthesis of temperature, density, and flavor proper. In a word this synthesis signifies a certain being; and when we eat, we do not limit ourselves to knowing certain qualities of this being through taste; by tasting them we appropriate them. Taste is assimilation; by the very act of biting the tooth reveals the density of a body which it is transforming into gastric contents. Thus the synthetic intuition of food is in itself an assimilative destruction. It reveals to me the being which I am going to make my flesh. Henceforth, what I accept or what I reject with disgust is the very being of that existent, or if you prefer, the totality of the food proposes to me a certain mode of being of the being which I accept or refuse. . . .

Generally speaking there is no irreducible taste or inclination. They all represent a certain appropriative choice of being. It is up to existential psychoanalysis to compare and classify them. Ontology abandons us here; it has merely enabled us to determine the ultimate ends of human reality, its fundamental possibilities, and the value which haunts it. Each human reality is at the same time a direct project to metamorphose its own For-itself into an In-itself-For-itself and a project of the appropriation of the world as a totality of being-in-itself, in the form of a fundamental quality. Every human reality is a passion in that it projects losing itself so as to found being and by the same stroke to constitute the In-itself which escapes contingency by being its own foundation, the *Ens causa sui,* which religions call God. Thus the passion of man is the reverse of that of Christ, for man loses himself as man in order that God may be born. But the idea of God is contradictory and we lose ourselves in vain. Man is a useless passion.

V. ETHICAL IMPLICATIONS

Ontology itself cannot formulate ethical precepts. It is concerned solely with what is, and we cannot possibly derive imperatives from ontology's indicatives. It does, however, allow us to catch a glimpse of what sort of ethics will assume its responsibilities when confronted with a *human reality in situation.* Ontology has revealed to us, in fact, the origin and the nature of *value*; we have seen that value is the *lack* in relation to which the for-itself determines its being as a *lack.* By the very fact that the for-itself *exists,* as we have seen, value arises to haunt its being-for-itself. It follows that the various tasks of the for-itself can be made the object of an existential psychoanalysis, for they all aim at producing the missing synthesis of consciousness and being in the form of value or self-cause. Thus existential psychoanalysis is *moral description,* for it releases to us the ethical meaning of various human projects. It indicates to us the necessity of abandoning the psychology of interest along with any utilitarian interpretation of human conduct— by revealing to us the *ideal* meaning of all human attitudes. These meanings are beyond egoism and altruism, beyond also any behavior which is called *disinterested.* Man makes himself man in order to be God, and selfness considered from this point of view can appear to be an egoism; but precisely because there is no common measure between human reality and the self-cause which it wants to be, one could just as well say that man loses himself in order that the self-cause may exist. We will consider then that all human existence is a passion, the famous *self-interest* being only one way freely chosen among others to realize this passion.

But the principal result of existential psychoanalysis must be to make us repudiate the *spirit of seriousness.* The spirit of seriousness has two characteristics: it considers values as transcendent givens independent of human subjectivity, and it transfers the quality of "desirable" from the ontological structure of things to their simple material constitution. For the spirit of seriousness, for example, *bread* is desirable because it is *necessary* to live (a value written in an intelligible heaven) and because bread *is* nourishing. The result of the serious attitude, which as we know rules the world, is to cause the symbolic values of things to be drunk in by their empirical idiosyncrasy as ink by a blotter; it puts forward the opacity of the desired object and posits it in itself as a desirable irreducible. Thus we are already on the moral plane but concurrently on that of bad faith, for it is an ethics which is ashamed of itself and does not dare speak its name. It has obscured all its goals in order to free itself from anguish. Man pursues being blindly by hiding from himself the free project which is this pursuit. He makes himself such that he is *waited* for by all the tasks placed along his way. Objects are mute demands, and he is nothing in himself but the passive obedience to these demands.

Existential psychoanalysis is going to reveal to man the real goal of his pursuit, which is being as a synthetic fusion of the in-itself with the for-itself; existential psychoanalysis is going to acquaint man with his passion. In truth there are many men who have practiced this psycho-analysis on themselves and who have not waited to learn its principles in order to make use of them as a means of deliverance and salvation. Many men, in fact, know that the goal of their pursuit is being; and to the extent that they possess this knowledge, they refrain from appropriating things for their own sake and try to realize the symbolic appropriation of their being-in-itself. But to the extent that this attempt still shares in the spirit of seriousness and that these men can still believe that their mission of effecting the existence of the in-itself-for-itself is written in things, they are condemned to despair; for they discover at the same time that all human activities are equivalent (for they all tend to sacrifice man in order that the self-cause may arise) and that all are on principle doomed to failure. Thus it amounts to the same thing whether one gets drunk alone or is a leader of nations. If one of these activities takes precedence over the other, this will not be because of its real goal but because of the degree of consciousness which it possesses of its ideal goal; and in this case it will be the quietism of the solitary drunkard which will take precedence over the vain agitation of the leader of nations.

But onotology and existential psychoanalysis (or the spontaneous and empirical application which men have always made of these disciplines) must reveal to the moral agent that he is *the being by whom values exist.* It is then that his freedom will become conscious of itself and will reveal itself in anguish as the unique source of value and the nothingness by which the *world* exists. As soon as freedom discovers the quest for being the appropriation of the in-itself as *its own possibles,* it will apprehend by and in anguish that they are possibles only on the ground of the possibility of other possibles. But hitherto although possibles could be chosen and rejected *ad libitum,* the theme which made the unity of all choices of possibles was the value or the ideal presence of the *ens causa sui.* What will become of freedom if it turns its back upon this value? Will freedom carry this value along with it whatever it does and even in its very turning back upon the in-itself-for-itself? Will freedom be reapprehended from behind by the value which it wishes to contemplate? Or will freedom by the very fact that it apprehends itself as a freedom in relation to itself, be able to put an end to the reign of this value? In particular is it possible for freedom to take itself for a value as the source of all value, or must it necessarily be defined in relation to a transcendent value which haunts it? And in case it could will itself as its own possible and its determining value, what would this mean? A freedom which wills itself freedom is in fact a being-which-is-not-what-it-is and which-is-what-it-is-not, and which chooses as the ideal of being, being-what-it-is-not and not-being-what-it-is.

This freedom chooses then not to *recover* itself but to flee itself, not to coincide with itself but to be always at a distance *from* itself. What are we to understand by this being which wills to hold itself in awe, to be at a distance from itself? Is it a question of bad faith or of another fundamental attitude? And can one *live* this new aspect of being? In particular will freedom by taking itself for an end escape all *situation?* Or on the contrary, will it remain situated? Or will it situate itself so much the more precisely and the more individually as it projects itself further in anguish as a conditioned freedom and accepts more fully its responsibility as an existent by whom the world comes into being. All these questions, which refer us to a pure and not an accessory reflection, can find their reply only on the ethical plane. We shall devote to them a future work.

—Translation by Hazel E. Barnes

DEFINITIONS[5]

1. BEING (*être*). "Being is. Being is in-itself. Being is what it is." Being includes both Being-in-itself and Being-for-itself, but the latter is the

[5] Technical terms coined by Sartre and familiar words to which he gives special meanings, direct quotations being from *Being and Nothingness.*—Translator.

nihilation of the former. As contrasted with Existence, Being is all-embracing and objective rather than individual and subjective.

2. BEING-IN-ITSELF (*être-en-soi*). Nonconscious Being. It is the Being of the phenomenon and overflows the knowledge which we have of it. It is a plenitude, and strictly speaking we can say of it only that it is.

3. BEING-FOR-ITSELF (*être-pour-soi*). The nihilation of Being-in-itself; consciousness conceived as a lack of Being, a desire for Being, a relation to Being. By bringing Nothingness into the world the For-itself can stand out from Being and judge other beings by knowing what it is not. Each For-itself is the nihilation of a particular being.

4. COGITO. Sartre claims that the prereflective *cogito* (see "consciousness") is the precognitive basis for the Cartesian *cogito*. There is also, he says, a sort of *cogito* concerning the existence of Others. While we cannot abstractly prove the Other's existence, this *cogito* will disclose to me his "concrete, indubitable presence," just as my own "contingent but necessary existence" has been revealed to me.

5. CONSCIOUSNESS. The transcending For-itself. "Consciousness is a being such that in its being, its being is in question insofar as this being implies a being other than itself." Like Husserl Sartre insists that consciousness is always consciousness of something. He sometimes distinguishes types of consciousness according to psychic objects; e.g., pain-consciousness, shame-consciousness. Two more basic distinctions are made:

> 1. Unreflective consciousness (also called nonthetic consciousness or nonpositional self-consciousness). This is the prereflective *cogito*. Here there is no knowledge but an implicit consciousness of being conscious of an object.

> 2. Reflective consciousness (also called thetic consciousness or positional self-consciousness).

6. EKSTASIS. Used in the original Greek sense of "standing out from." The For-itself is separated from its Self in three successive ekstases:

> 1. Temporality. The For-itself nihilates the In-itself (to which in one sense it still belongs) in the three dimensions of past, present, and future (the three temporal ekstases).

> 2. Reflection. The For-itself tries to adopt an external point of view on itself.

> 3. Being-for-others. The For-itself discovers that it has a Self for-the-Other, a Self which it is without ever being able to know or get hold of it.

7. ENGAGE. (*engager*). Includes both the idea of involvement and the idea of deliberate commitment. Thus the human being is inescapably engaged in the world, and freedom is meaningful only as engaged by its free choice of ends.

8. ESSENCE. For Sartre as for Hegel, essence is what has been. Sartre calls

it man's past. Since there is no pre-established pattern for human nature, each man makes his essence as he lives.

9. EXISTENCE. Concrete, individual being here and now. Sartre says that for all existentialists existence precedes essence. Existence has for them also always a subjective quality when applied to human reality.

10. FACTICITY (*facticité*). The For-itself's necessary connection with the In-itself, hence with the world and its own past. It is what allows us to say that the For-itself *is* or *exists*. The facticity of freedom is not able not to be free.

11. PROJECT. Both verb and noun. It refers to the For-itself's choice of its way of being and is expressed by action in the light of a future end.

12. REFLECTION (*réflexion*). The attempt on the part of consciousness to become its own object. "Reflection is a type of being in which the For-itself is in order to be to itself what it is."

13. ONTOLOGY. The study "of the structures of being of the existent taken as a totality." Ontology describes Being itself, the condition by which "there is" a world, human reality, etc.

14. NIHILATE. (*néantir*) A word coined by Sartre. Consciousness exists as consciousness by making a nothingness (q.v.) arise between it and the object of which it is consciousness. Thus nihilation is that by which consciousness exists. To nihilate is to encase with a shell of nonbeing. The English "nihilate" was first used by Helmut Kuhn in his *Encounter with Nothingness*.

15. NOTHINGNESS (*néant*). Nothingness does not itself have Being, yet it is supported by Being. It comes into the world by the For-itself and is the recoil from fullness of self-contained Being which allows consciousness to exist as such.

16. HUMAN-REALITY. Sartre's term for the human being or For-itself. Used both generally like "mankind" and for the individual man.

17. BAD FAITH. A lie to oneself within the unity of a single consciousness. Through bad faith a person seeks to escape the responsible freedom of Being-for-itself. Bad faith rests on a vacillation between transcendence and facticity which refuses to recognize either one for what it really is or to synthesize them.

18. WORLD. The whole of nonconscious Being as it appears to the For-itself and is organized by the For-itself in "instrumental complexes." Because of its facticity the For-itself is inescapably engaged in the world. Yet strictly speaking, without the For-itself, there would be not a world but only an undifferentiated plenitude of Being.

19. ABSCHATTUNGEN. Used by Sartre in the usual phenomenological sense to refer to the successive appearances of the object "in profile."

XIV / A PHILOSOPHER AMONG THE NIHILISTS

IGNAZIO SILONE, WHO WAS BORN ON MAY DAY AS THE NEW CENTURY came to birth, May 1, 1900, in a village in Italy, where his father was a small landowner and his mother a hand weaver, entered into the labor problems of the century at the age of seventeen, when he was made secretary of the land workers in his mountain district of the Apennines. His first act was organization of a demonstration against the war for which he was hailed into court. In 1921 he helped found the Italian Communist party, opposed the growth of Fascism, was imprisoned, expelled and finally in 1930 settled in Switzerland and left the Communist party. In 1940 he took over the direction of the foreign center of the Italian Socialist party. He is the author of several novels, including the world-famous fictional portrayals of his hill country compatriots, *Fontamara* and *Bread and Wine*. He is married and lives now in Rome. "The Choice of Comrades" was written recently and has appeared in the London magazine *Encounter* and in New York in *Dissent,* from whose pages it is taken at Mr. Silone's suggestion.

The Choice of Comrades

BY IGNAZIO SILONE

The last forty years have witnessed the collapse of most of the great politico-social myths bequeathed to us by the nineteenth century. As a result, certain kinds of people who had relied on these myths as a compass find themselves in a state of spiritual vagueness and ambiguity

234

that is still far from being clarified. This situation is one aspect of the general crisis of capitalism and anticapitalism. We are confronted with the need for reassessment, not only of the problems of human behavior but also of the greater question of the meaning of our existence. It is not a matter, be it said, even in its subsidiary aspects, of literary diversion. There will always be a number of perfectly respectable people who interpret in their own fashion, by their haircut or the way they knot their ties, the spirit of the age in which they live. For others less fortunate, however, times of crisis may bring graver consequences. My concern in these pages is with them.

Suicide among writers in various countries during the past thirty years has reached an unparalled figure. It seems to me that however much they may differ outwardly, the majority of these episodes have a common source: what Nietzsche called the nihilism of modern times. The lives of writers are, I think, not less significant than the books they write. Whenever I happen to consider the sense of bewilderment, tedium, and disgust characteristic of our age, my mind turns not to the books of Heidegger, Jaspers, and Sartre but to the suicides of Essenin, Mayakovsky, Ernst Toller, Kurt Tucholsky, Stefan Zweig, Klaus Mann, Drieu La Rochelle, F. O. Mathiessen, Cesare Pavese, and other lesser-known figures. What a flock of terrifying ghosts they seem, when one names them all together! Persecution, exile, isolation, poverty, illness, abnormality—one or the other of these external reasons has been suggested in each case to explain how a man of talent could have sought such a desperate end. But the last writings of these men before death, or their last confidences to their friends, are invariably a confession of anguish or despair at the effort and the futility of living.

These suicides are not to be easily explained away. To pin responsibility for them on any one political regime would clearly be a misrepresentation, since we know that they occurred under widely differing regimes, in Russia, America, and Western Europe. Still less can we blame the pernicious influence of some pessimistic doctrine; Mayakovsky was the poet of a victorious revolution, and the others, from Zweig to Pavese, were deeply rooted in the humanist or religious traditions of the society from which they came. (Indeed, one might well reverse the explanation and say it was precisely because they were not pessimistic enough, because they had banished *Angst* from their doctrine and their art, that some of them were to end by succumbing to it so miserably. Inhibition is more deadly than sincerity.

The decadence of our age, however, had already begun prior to

235

these tragic episodes. It has not merely engulfed a number of cultivated and hypersensitive individuals; it has invaded entire classes and institutions, not even sparing the people. Nietzsche was the first to define this decadence, calling it nihilism, as I said, and giving the word a new meaning that it has retained, a meaning different from that found in Turgenev's famous novel. Since then, wars and revolutions in constant succession have borne out Nietzsche's prophecy, making evident what in his day was still perhaps obscure.

Nihilism, as Nietzsche conceived it, is the identification of goodness, justice, and truth with self-interest. Nihilism is the conviction that beliefs and ideas are, ultimately, a mere facade with nothing real behind them, and that consequently only one thing really matters, really counts: success. It is nihilistic to sacrifice oneself for a cause in which one does not believe, while pretending to believe in it. It is nihilistic to exalt courage and heroism independently of the cause they serve, thus equating the martyr with the hired assassin. And so on.

How did we come to this pass? The First World War is generally blamed as the cause and origin of the disaster; but would that war ever have broken out in the first place had the civilized world not already been in a state of crisis? The war merely demonstrated how fragile were the myths of progress on which capitalist civilization was based. Even in the victorious countries, venerable institutions were subjected to such terrible ordeals that they began to totter like rotten scaffolding. And from them, skepticism and corruption spread and seeped downward to the very foundation of society. Traditional moral and religious values, rashly invoked to prop up the vested interests which were being threatened, were thereby compromised.

The authoritarian restoration which followed the war—first in Italy and the Balkans, later in Germany and elsewhere—was a remedy worse than the disease. How could conservatives ever have deluded themselves into thinking that political tyranny of any kind would eliminate nihilism? On the contrary Fascism in all its forms meant that nihilism was installed in power. The dictatorships strengthened the old instruments of coercion and created new ones, but they did not create a new moral order; indeed, with their atmosphere of fear and servility, they aggravated and exacerbated the general decadence. With the collapse of these regimes, the basic nihilsm remained, buried deep in peoples' consciences.

And so in many ways we are back where we were, except that we

236

are once again free to discus the moral situation of man without having to make concessions to a false optimism, dissimulation not being a civic virtue in a democracy.

Political regimes may come and go, bad habits remain. The big difficulty is this: nihilism is not an ideology, it cannot be legislated about, it is not a subject for school curricula; it is a disease of the spirit which can be diagnosed only by those who are immune from it or have been cured of it, but to which most people are quite oblivious, since they think it corresponds to a perfectly natural mode of being. "That's how it has always been; that's how it will always be."

We are all familiar with the picture which post-Nietzschean and existentialist literature has drawn of the predicament of present-day man. It can be summarized as follows: all links between the existence and the being of man are broken; existence has no meaning beyond itself; what is human is reduced to mere vitality. Before commenting on what I consider the provisional and transient nature of this representation, I feel bound to state that in some respects I find it praiseworthy. I think sincerity is always to be admired, especially if it requires a certain amount of courage, for without sincerity neither morality nor art can exist. And moreover, at the stage to which things are now reduced, I as a writer see no other way, outside the freedom of art, of placing before the minds of men the problems which elude them, and of presenting them with a truer image of themselves than that which they see daily in the mirror. However, literature cannot take up a permanent abode in a nihilist situation, and the only way out for it, I think, is to explore courageously the entire surface of this situation. Anyone undertaking to do so with absolute intellectual honesty and an uncorrupted heart should sooner or later be able to reach its farthest limit. At that point, one of two things will happen to him: either he will find the abyss of suicide yawning at his feet, or else he will rediscover some valid meaning in human existence. This is no abstract hypothesis, but the plain truth of what has happened to quite a number of people.

The examples are far from insignificant. Here I shall only mention two: the literary path of Ernst Jünger and that of Albert Camus. The German writer reached the farthest limit of nihilism in his famous message *Der Arbeiter*. In this description of a new type of proletarian, depersonalized and standardized, without heart, soul, or brain—a living robot—he depicted the protagonist of the transformation which is taking place in modern society. The greatest freedom of this human robot would consist in being mechanically employed in the series of civil and imperialist wars on which we have already embarked and which will dominate the coming centuries. "To sacrifice oneself for a faith," wrote Ernst Jünger, "means to reach one's maximum, irrespective of whether that faith is true or false. The mere fact that men throw themselves into the fray, even though they are knotted up with a fear that no discipline and no love of country can dispel, makes them, like martyrs, bear witness to an ultra-human reality that is beyond and within them." The heroism of Jünger's proletarian robots would therefore be all the more sublime the remoter it was from the traditional human sphere and the more closely it resembled that of highly perfected machines. This was a final point beyond which it was impossible to advance. Ernst Jünger retreated from it in time, while Hitler was still in power. In his subsequent works, among which may be mentioned the pages on pain, the novel *Auf den Marmorklippen,* and the diary he kept during the invasion of France in the second World War, his condemnation of nihilism is increasingly explicit and increasingly based on human motives.

The experience of Albert Camus is different but analogous. No reader of his books can fail to discern the sharp contrast dividing *Le Mythe de Sisyphe* and *L'Étranger* on the one hand, from *La Peste* and the book of essays entitled *L'Homme Révolté* on the other. Camus opens *Le Mythe de Sisyphe* with the concept of suicide, in order to distill from it an explanation of the meaning of life. He bluntly defines as absurd the reasons for living. "To die voluntarily," he writes, "implies that one has recognized, at least instinctively, the absurd nature of this habit, the absence of any serious reason for living, the senselessness of this daily agitation and the futility of suffering." To kill oneself means "simply to recognize that life is not worth the trouble." In compassion Camus finds the cure for this desolate sense of the absurd. "The world in which I live repels me," he wrote later, in *L'Homme Révolté,* "but I feel with its suffering inhabitants." In his novel *La Peste* the existence of the characters is presented, not as the impassive unfolding of arbitrary and meaningless facts, but as the compassionate encounter of human beings suffering and struggling against a common destiny.

At a certain point in *La Peste* one of the characters—Rieux, a doctor —meets a municipal clerk named Grand whose wife has just left him, with no ill-will on either side.

238

From a distance he looked at Grand, who was standing almost glued to a shop window full of roughly carved wooden toys. Tears were streaming down the cheeks of the old clerk. And those tears shook Rieux, because he understood them and could feel them in the dryness of his own throat. He could even remember the day when the poor fellow had got engaged to be married; he had seen him standing in front of a shop decked out for Christmas, with Jeanne bending toward him, telling him she was happy. No doubt but that Jeanne's fresh voice was echoing now to Grand across the distant years. Rieux knew what the old, weeping man was thinking of at that moment, and he too thought that without love this world of ours is a dead world, and that there always comes a time when, weary of the prisons of work and courage, one wants the face of another human being and a heart filled with the wonder of tenderness. . . . He felt Grand's unhappiness as his own, and something gnawed at his heart at that moment—the fierce anger that comes over one at the suffering which human beings have to endure.

Even the revolt born of pity alone can restore meaning to life.

André Malraux presents a more remarkable case because this French descendant of Nietzsche, through his progress from Communism back to nationalism, gives the impression of having remained a Nietzschean at heart all the time. The stormy curve of his life's journey does indeed seem the adventure of a "superman" seeking tests and opportunities for his own dreams of glorification. Nevertheless it would be unjust to consider it as a superficial movie-hero affair. Between *La Tentation de l'Occident* and *La Psychologie de l'Art* there is more than a change of scene. In 1926 Malraux was announcing the historical downfall of Europe, "this century where only dead conquerors sleep." The Communist revolt of the colored peoples seemed to offer him hope; but how ambiguous was his adherence to it. The virile sense of a new brotherhood of man alternated, in the pages of *La Condition Humaine,* with the intoxication of action for its own sake. In *Le Temps du Mépris,* brotherhood was invoked more wholeheartedly, as the last resort against nihilist desperation. It was an active sympathy, consecrated by the sacrifices which culminated in the act of an unknown comrade who saved Kassner, the Communist leader, from Nazi torture. But did this member act on his own initiative or by order of the party machine? And can brotherhood be founded on anything but freedom and personal responsibility? "Economic servitude is hard," old Alvear was to say in *L'Espoir,* "but if in order to destroy it we are obliged to strengthen political or military or religious or police servi-

239

tude, then what does it matter to me in comparison?" Revolutions, like trees, are to be judged by their fruits, and not by the effort they cost.

I know that these are isolated examples, and that one or even two swallows do not make a summer. Still they do point to a path of salvation, a true way out of nihilism, which springs from a sure and indestructible element deep-rooted in man.

But to return to my point. The particular spiritual condition I wish to discuss has affinities with the instances I have just mentioned. However, it follows a different path and has a significance of its own. For example, it never starts from philosophical or scientific conviction, but almost always from simple instinctive revolt against family or social surroundings. One fine Sunday some of us stopped going to Mass, not because Catholic dogma seemed to us, all of a sudden, false, but because the people who went began to bore us and we were drawn to the company of those who stayed away. A young man's revolt against tradition is a frequent occurrence in every age and every country, and his reasons are not always clear to the onlooker. According to circumstances, it can lead to the Foreign Legion, to common crime, to a film career, to a monastery, or to political extremism. What characterized our revolt was the choice of comrades. Outside our village church stood the landless peasants. It was not their psychology that we were drawn to: it was their plight. A choice once made, the rest, as experience shows, follows automatically. Without the slightest attempt at resistance, indeed with the well-known fervor of neophytes, one accepts the language, symbols, organization, discipline, tactics, program and doctrine of the party to which one's new comrades belong. It is hardly surprising that rarely should anything learned in the catechism and schoolbooks hinder one's docile acceptance of the new orthodoxy. Indeed, one does not even feel the need of refuting them, because all of that has become part of the world one has left behind. They are neither true nor false: they are "bourgeois," dead leaves. The choice is emotional, beyond logic. And the claim of the new orthodoxy, which one has accepted so completely, to be scientific and objective—that is not the least of the inconsistencies which you will vainly seek to force on the attention of the convert.

This is the rule. I have read a certain number of biographies of Anarchists, Socialists, Communists and Facists, and I am more or less familiar with the circumstances that led some of my acquaintances into political activity; so far I have found no exceptions to the pattern I

240

have just described, and if any do exist, I think they are rare. We proclaim ourselves revolutionaries or conservatives for motives, often ill defined, that are deep within us, and before choosing we are, unknown to ourselves, chosen. As for the new ideology, we learn that, usually, at the schools of the party to which we have already pledged allegiance by an act of faith. Altogether similar—and just as it should be—is the opposite process of abjurement. Ideology is now given the same rough treatment once meted out to the catechism and to patriotic stories. To speak in old-fashioned terms, the head, even in the process of relearning, is towed along by the heart—or, according to the health of the person in question, by the stomach.

There is one Duty, however, that we cannot evade: to be aware of what is happening. What could the landless peasants of his Southern Italian village have meant to a young student, in the years immediately preceding the First World War, that he should embrace their cause? He was certainly not thinking of politics as a career. Besides, he as yet knew nothing of the proud Marxist prophecy acclaiming the proletariat as the legitimate heir of modern philosophy. Neither did he know that, after the Milanese revolution of 1848, Carlo Cattaneo had declared the cause of the proletariat to be indissolubly linked thenceforth with that of freedom, one destined to travel through the coming ages with the other, like horseman and rider. He had as yet heard nothing of Rosa Luxemburg's theory of the natural impulse to revolution of the working class, or of Lenin's theory of the forces which propel modern society on the path of progress. Nor did he know of Sorel or other prophets of the new Messiah. But if the new revolutionary theories of the historical mission of the proletariat had not yet reached that remote district of Southern Italy, emigrants returned from America were already prompting the landless peasants to form their first resistance leagues. It is not to be wondered at that a young man already secretly disgusted with his surroundings, witnessing this unaccustomed ferment, should undergo a profound change of heart and become convinced that in an old, tired decrepit, blasé society such as the one in which he lived, the poor represented the final refuge of life—something real, to which it would be wholesome to attach oneself.

Those were the declining years of an epoch in which a number of events had seemed to prove the myth about the liberating mission of the proletariat. The fascination of that myth spread far beyond the narrow limits of party politics. It was the great popular alternative to the nihilist decadence of Nietzsche's prophecy—the promise of a new earth and a new heaven. Morals, art, philosophy were all directly influenced by it. And events seemed to indicate that Rosa Luxemburg was right. In those years one did not yet risk contradiction if one claimed that wherever a workers' organization was active, under whatever regime, in whatever climate or social conditions, despite its shortcomings it would move "naturally" toward freedom and renewal. Indeed, a certain episode occurred around 1905 in Moscow which has remained a classic in the history of the workers' movement and seemed to have been created for the express purpose of proving even to skeptics how well founded was the theory of Rosa Luxemburg about the liberating impulse of the working class. The Tsarist secret police, the Okhrana, decided to encourage the formation of a labor union in the hope of drawing underground agitators into it and arresting them. These, however, scented a trap and kept clear of it; but the labor union, despite its police origin, became of its own accord a revolutionary organization, so that the Okhrana was soon obliged to disband it.

Since then, as we all know, the myth of the liberating power of the proletariat has dissolved along with that other myth of the inevitability of progress. The recent examples of the Nazi labor unions, those of Salazar and Peron and, in a broader sense, all reformist and co-operative unions have at last convinced of this even those who were reluctant to admit it on the sole grounds of the totalitarian degeneration of Communism. Now, however, the decline of that myth must be obvious to anyone who takes the trouble to inform himself of the conditions prevailing in the world beyond his own backyard. It is no longer merely a question of a few privileged workers (the so-called "proletarian aristocracy" of the imperialist countries, made possible by the exploitation of colonial peoples); nor of the inferior groups on the margin of the productive process (the so-called *Lumpenproletariat*); but of the normal working classes. Today an experiment such as the Okhrana made in 1905 would not necessarily be doomed to failure. For Marxists the moral to be drawn is clear: a similar way of living no longer determines an identical or analogous way of thinking. Class consciousness is no longer a natural product of class. Ever since this situation arose, ever since there ceased to exist a world-wide trend of the working classes toward freedom, human life has acquired a new aspect, spiritually as well as politically. The workers' world is spiritually broken up. It is multiform. The horse of Carlo Cattaneo has thrown its rider and gone wild again. The worker, as we have seen and as we continue to see, can work for the most conflicting causes; he can be blackshirt or partisan, executioner or victim, or simply, in rich and peaceful countries, a lazy philistine with no ideals, insured against unemployment, old age, illness, and also against the risk that the insurance company might go bankrupt. But generally, in poor countries, because of his relative political simplicity, he can still be the prey of extremists. He can still be Christ, taking on himself the sins of others; and he can also be Barabbas, an ignoble totalitarian Barabbas, trampling on all that is most human in man. Either way, he is a protagonist on the world stage. He is the *deus ex machina* of modern politics. It is futile to think that this fact can be abolished, or that any democracy can maintain itself for very long, propped by police tribunals in the face of working-class opposition. The vital role of the workers in production, their numbers, their greater social compactness and homogeneity—the sum of these factors in every country gives them the decisive voice in politics. No other single element is so powerful. On it depends the freedom of mankind, and much else. But since it is no longer class that decides, but conscience, we are back where we started.

One need only look around one to see the state to which consciences have been reduced. Nihilism has spread from the upper classes over the entire surface of the social fabric: the epidemic has not spared the working-class districts. Today the nihilist cult of force and success is universal. And the widespread virtue that identifies History with the winning side, the ignoble cowardice that leads so many intellectuals to Communism or to McCarthy—that too is nihilism. Are the dead, are the weak always in the wrong? Was Mazzini wrong? Was Trotsky wrong only because he was defeated? Were Gobetti and Matteotti wrong? And did Gramsci begin to be right only after April, 1945? Will he cease to be right if the strength of his party declines? And is fear of the hydrogen bomb the fear of a stronger right, a right therefore more convincing than the others?

To the general feeling of personal insecurity which in our age has been engendered by the economic crisis and the intrusion of the state and politics into every field of human activity, there corresponds the anxious search by individuals for some kind of security and protection in one or other of the political mass parties. This by no means excludes, incidentally, a double game with the opposing party, which might be the winner tomorrow. If ideological criticisms and moral

243

campaigns cannot shake the compactness of the mass parties, if they leave the majority of their members indifferent, it is precisely for the reason already mentioned: those joining the mass parties out of inner ideological conviction are very few. And to the opportunism of individuals obsessed with their own security and that of their families, there is added the usurping tendency of collective organizations. Frankly, I cannot think of a single collective organization today which could be said to be untainted by the leprosy of nihilism. Group living, it would almost seem, creates the most favorable temperature for the incubation of its germs. Human stupidity is so monotonous. The deathly mechanism is always the same: every group or institution arises in defense of an ideal, with which it rapidly comes to identify itself and for which it finally substitutes itself altogether, proclaiming its own interests as the supreme value. "Whoever injures the Party is against History." The members of the group in question are unruffled by this procedure; in fact, they find it serves their purposes. The advantages are by no means negligible, because they are completely absolved from all personal responsibility. In the deplorable event of someone having a scruple, all he need do is bring his problem to the propaganda office. If the matter is delicate, the answer will be delivered to him at home. Few people realize that the tyranny of means over ends is the death of even the noblest ends. And it is a mere mystification to claim that the reduction of human beings to the status of instruments and raw materials can ever ensure human happiness.

There is no more melancholy image than that of the persecuted who in their turn become persecutors. Here I should like to recall the terrible letter which Simone Weil wrote to Georges Bernanos in the spring of 1938 about the Spanish Civil War. The Catholic-Royalist writer's vehement indictment of the excesses of the Franco repression in Majorca is countered by the anguished confession of the young revolutionary intellectual, then a volunteer on the Republican side. The letter has been published only recently. It expresses a sensitive woman's horror at the useless massacres which accompanied these events. But she had witnessed something else that had made an even more painful impression on her than brute violence. A purer-hearted witness or a more exemplary circumstances would be hard to find.

I have never seen, [she writes] either among the Spaniards or among the French who have come here to fight or to amuse themselves (the latter often being gloomy, harmless intellectuals) anyone who expressed, even in private conversation, repugnance or disgust for, or even only disapproval of, unnecessary bloodshed. You talk of fear. Yes, fear has played a part in these killings; but where I was I did not find that it played as large a part as you ascribe to it. Men to all appearances courageous, when dining with friends, would relate with a warm, comradely smile how they had killed priests or "Fascists" —a word of elastic meaning. I felt that whenever a certain group of human beings is relegated, by some temporal or spiritual authority, beyond the pale of those whose life has a price, then one finds it perfectly natural to kill such people. When one knows one can kill without risk or punishment or blame, one kills; or at least one smiles encouragingly at those who kill. If at first one happens to feel some revulsion, one hides it, stifles it, fearing to seem lacking in virility. There seems to be in this some impulse or intoxication which it is impossible to resist without a strength of mind which I am obliged to consider exceptional, since I have not found it in anyone. On the contrary, I have seen sober Frenchmen whom I had not previously despised—men who of their own accord would never have thought of killing anyone—plunging with obvious relish into that blood-soaked atmosphere. The very aim of the struggle is blotted out by an atmosphere of this kind. Because the aim can be formulated only in terms of the public good, the good of human beings; and human beings have no value.

And the letter ends: "One sets out as a volunteer, with ideas of sacrifice, only to find oneself in a war of mercenaries, with a great deal of unnecessary cruelty thrown in."

Of course there will be people foolish enough to dismiss Simone Weil's letter as defeatist; but the defeat had preceded it, as an illness precedes its diagnosis. In this world-wide moral shipwreck, what scrap of driftwood can one clutch in order not to drown? Among the reflections of Simone Weil collected under the title *La Pesanteur et la Grâce,* we find this indirect answer, the validity of which goes far beyond politics: one must, she says, "always be ready to change sides with justice, that fugitive from the winning camp."

We have come a long way now from the very simple situation in which some of us revolted against our family surroundings and went over to the side of the proletariat. The proletariat of this world are no longer in agreement among themselves; they are no longer the incarnation of a myth, and if one were to follow them blindly and unconditionally one might find oneself where least one wants to be. The initial choice must now be followed by another. To judge men, it is no longer enough to see if they have callused hands: one must look into their eyes. There is no mistaking the look of Cain. Do we side with the inmates of the slave-labor camps or with their jailers? This dilemma we can no longer evade, because the executioners themselves are forcing it on us. Threateningly they demand: "Are you with us or against us?" We must call a spade a spade. We are certainly not going to sacrifice the poor to the cause of freedom, nor freedom to the poor, or rather to the usurping bureaucrats who have climbed on the shoulders of the poor. It is a matter of personal honor to keep faith with those who are being persecuted for their love of freedom and justice. This keeping faith is a better rule than any abstract program or formula. In this age of ours, it is the real touchstone.

It should be apparent from the foregoing why humanism in general, literary or philosophical, means very little to us. Perhaps the time for it will come again, but at present we feel very remote from the serenity and harmony it represents. To us it seems that the self-complacency of man implicit in humanism has scant foundation nowadays. Mankind today is in poor shape. Any portrait of modern man, if at all faithful to the original, cannot but be deformed, split, fragmentary— in a word tragic.

This confession of humility does not cost us an effort, since we have no answers to the supreme questions about man's origin and his destiny. Frankly, these traditional problems do not even trouble us. We have stopped pondering the riddle of egg-or-chicken priority, for what is perhaps a very banal reason: we are not responsible for it, and whichever way things may originally have happened, it was not our fault. That is not the sort of problem that can give us sleepless nights. The problems that beset us are those of our present existence, of our responsibility as men of today. Only within these limits can we reach a true definition of ourselves.

This amounts to saying that we are not believers, we are not atheists, and still less are we skeptics. These labels, with their conventional implications, do not concern us. Anyone who tries to attach them to us will merely increase terminological confusion. A distaste for verbalism and facile consolations holds us back from more general statements. A proper awe of the transcendental prevents us from taking its name in vain and using it as a narcotic. And if we are not too proud to confess that there have been moments of anguish and solitude when our thoughts returned with piercing nostalgia to the tradition-bound order, the peace and security, of the home we knew in childhood, we are nevertheless obliged to add that love of truth has always ended by prevailing over considerations of personal convenience.

In a situation where the premises of metaphysics and even of history are uncertain and open to question, the moral sense is forced to extend its scope, taking on the additional function of guide to knowledge. The pitfall of abstract and superficial moralism can be a real one, but only if the moral sense is operating on a *tabula rasa*. In reality, even beyond one's frontiers of awareness, one remains a creature of flesh and blood, a man of a certain region, a certain class, and a certain time. For our part, the vital resource which saves us from the extremist situation of nihilism can be easily identified: the same emotional charge which impelled us to our initial choice has not been exhausted by disillusionment. This is not an individual case. I am not using the pronoun "we" as a puffed-up form of the first person singular. Our number is an ever-swelling legion: the legion of refugees from the International. There are really a great many, belonging to no church or political party, who now bear in secret these same burning stigmata.

Does anything at all remain to us? Yes, there are some unshakable certainties. To my way of feeling, they are Christian certainties. They appear to me so deeply immured in human existence as to be identified with it. Man disintegrates when they are denied.

This is too little to constitute a profession of faith, but it is enough for a declaration of trust. The trust is founded on something more stable and more universal than the mere compassion of Albert Camus. It is founded, in the last analysis, on the certainty that we human beings are free and responsible; that we feel the need of reaching out to touch the inmost reality of our fellow men; and that spiritual communion is possible. The fact that spiritual communion is possible—surely this is the irrefutable proof of human brotherhood? Furthermore, it contains a rule of life. Love of the oppressed is born from it as a corollary that the disillusionments of history—the love being of a disinterested nature—can never place in doubt. To be valid, it does not need success. With these certainties as a basis for existence, how can we resign ourselves to seeing man's noblest faculties stifled in so many human creatures born to poverty and wretchedness? How can we conceive of a moral life from which this fundamental concern is absent?

Need I add that this is not to be interpreted in political terms of power or tyranny? To use the oppressed as a steppingstone to power and then betray them is undoubtedly the most wicked of all sacrileges, because of all human beings they are the most defenseless. Frankly we must confess that we have no panacea. There is no panacea for social evils. All we have—and it is a great deal—is this trust that makes it possible for us to go on living. We are forced to pick our steps beneath a sky that is, ideologically speaking, dark. The clear, ancient Mediterranean sky, once filled with shining constellations, is overcast; but this small circle of light that remains to us enables us at least to see where to place our feet for the next step.

This amounts to saying that the spiritual situation I have just described admits neither of defense nor of arrogance. Frankly, it is merely an expedient. It resembles a refugee encampment in no man's land, an exposed makeshift encampment. What do you think refugees do from morning to night? They spend most of their time telling one another the story of their lives. The stories are anything but amusing, but they tell them to one another, really, in an effort to make themselves understood.

As long as there remains a determination to understand and to share one's understanding with others, perhaps we need not altogether despair.

—Translation by Darina Silone

XV / A PHILOSOPHER AFTER
ST. THOMAS AQUINAS

JACQUES MARITAIN, BORN IN PARIS IN 1882, NOW THE WORLD'S LEADING advocate of the thinking of St. Thomas of Aquinas as applicable to the problems of today, has lived for some years in America, at times as visiting professor at Columbia, as professor at the Institute of Medieval Studies at Toronto, and until 1953 as professor emeritus at Princeton University. He is the author of many books on art, scholasticism, freedom, humanism, logic, philosophy, politics and education. It has been said of him, in connection with his influence in the revival of religious and philosophical thinking in America, that Professor Maritain believes "philosophy is not removed from the human life of man and that the most profound philosophical questions are those which the common sense of mankind seeks for an answer." The "Confession of Faith," which first appeared in English in *I Believe,* edited by Clifton Fadiman and published by Simon and Schuster, Inc., appears here as Professor Maritain's selection. An essay published in France as *"Confession de Foi,"* the translation is a new one made at his request from his own revised text, by Dr. Joseph W. Evans and the Reverend Father Leo R. Ward of Notre Dame University. It is included in *The Social and Political Philosophy of Jacques Maritain,* published by Charles Scribner's Sons, New York, 1955.

Confession of Faith

BY JACQUES MARITAIN

As a child I was brought up in "Liberal Protestantism." Later on I became acquainted with the different phases of secularistic thought. The scientist and phenomenist philosophy of my teachers at the Sorbonne at last made me despair of reason. At one time I thought I might be able to find complete certitude in the sciences, and Félix Le Dantec thought that my fiancée and I would become followers of his biological materialism. The best thing I owe to my studies at that time is that they let me meet, in the School of Sciences, the woman who since then has always, happily for me, been at my side in a perfect and blessed communion. Bergson was the first to answer our deep desire for metaphysical truth —he liberated in us the sense of the absolute.

Before being captured by St. Thomas Aquinas, I underwent some great influences, those of Charles Peguy, Bergson, and Léon Bloy. A year after we met Bloy, my wife and I were baptized Catholics, and we chose him as our godfather.

It was after my conversion to Catholicism that I came to know St. Thomas. I had voyaged passionately among all the doctrines of modern philosophers and had found in them nothing but deception and grandiose uncertainty. What I now experienced was like an illumination of reason. My vocation as philosopher became perfectly clear to me. "Woe to me if I do not Thomisticize," I wrote in one of my first books. And through thirty years of work and battles I have kept to this same path, with the feeling of sympathizing all the more profoundly with the researches, the discoveries and the agonies of modern thought, the more I tried to penetrate them with the light which comes to us from a wisdom worked out through the centuries, a wisdom resistant to the fluctuations of time.

In order to advance in this path we are obliged constantly to bring together singularly distant extremes, for no solution of our problems is found ready-made in the heritage of the ancients. We are also obliged to make a difficult sifting of the pure substance of truths which many a modern rejects in his loathing of the trashy opinions of the past, from all the dross, the prejudices, the out-of-date images and arbitrary constructions which many a traditionalist confuses with what is really worthy of being venerated by intelligence.

I have spoken of the different experiences through which I passed, because they gave me the occasion to try personally the state of mind of the idealist free-thinker, of the inexperienced convert, and of the Christian who becomes aware, in proportion as his faith takes root, of the purifications to which that faith must be subjected. I was also able to obtain some experimental idea of what the antireligious camp and the straddlers' camp are worth. Neither of them is worth very much. And the worst disgrace of the second camp is that it runs the risk of

250

compromising along with itself the innocent and persecuted Church, the Mystical Body of Christ, whose essential life, *sine macula sine ruga*, is in the Truth and in the saints, and which travels toward its fullness through the weaknesses of its own and the ferocity of the world. In my view, God educates us through our deceptions and mistakes, in order to make us understand at last that we ought to believe only in Him and not in men—which readily brings one to marvel at all the good which is in men despite everything and at all the good they do in spite of themselves.

I have decidedly come to the conclusion that in practice there are only two ways to know the depths of things, or, if one wishes, two "wisdoms," each of them a kind of folly, though in opposite manners. One is the way of sinners, who in order to drain things to the dregs embrace the nothingness of which all things are made and thereby have a full experience of this world, in the evil of the world more than in its good. The other way is the way of the saints, who adhere to subsisting Goodness, maker of all things, and receive in love a full experience of God and of creation, and who stand surety for all the world by their suffering and compassion. Well, it is normal to hope that the disciples of vain wisdom, if they are not hardened by pride and if they are loyal to their own experience, will finally be saved "through fire" by the lovers of true wisdom. And if they should live to be converted, they will perhaps be harsher than others in censuring any of their brothers still in darkness, so that, after having long tasted the delights of the world, they will taste for a moment the delights of their virtues and will continue vain till the last day, till they enter eternity.

This is not the place to give an exposition of theses in speculative philosophy. I will only say that I consider Thomistic philosophy to be a living and present philosophy, with all the greater power to make conquests in new fields of discovery just because its principles are so firm and so organically bound together. Confronted with the succession of scientific hypotheses, some minds are surprised that anyone could find inspiration today in metaphysical principles acknowledged by Aristotle and Thomas Aquinas and rooted in the oldest intellectual heritage of the race. My reply is that the telephone and the radio do not prevent man from still having two arms, two legs and two lungs, or from falling in love and seeking happiness as did his faraway ancestors. Besides, truth recognizes no chronological criteria, and the art of the philosopher is not to be confused with the art of the great dressmakers.

On a deeper level, we must explain that progress in the sciences of phenomena, where the "problem" aspect is so characteristic, takes place chiefly by *substitution* of one theory for another which saved less well the known facts and phenomena; but in metaphysics and philosophy, where the "mystery" aspect is predominant, progress takes place chiefly by *deeper penetration*. Besides, the different philosophical systems, however ill-founded they may be, constitute in some way, in their totality, a virtual and fluent philosophy, overlapping contrary formulations and unfiendly doctrines and carried along by the elements of truth they all contain. If, therefore, there exists among men a doctrinal organism entirely supported by true principles, it will incorporate—more or less tardily, due to the laziness of its defenders—it will progressively realize within itself this virtual philosophy, and this will thereby, and in a proportionate degree, take on form and organic arrangement. Such is my idea of progress in philosophy.

If I say next that the metaphysics which I hold to be founded on truth may be described as a critical realism and as a philsophy of intelligence and of being, or still more precisely as a philosophy of the *act of existing* regarded as the act and perfection of all perfections, these formulas, of course, will be of interest only to specialists. A brief reflection on the historical significance of modern philosophy will no doubt be more appropriate.

In the Middle Ages, philosophy was in fact ordinarily treated as an instrument in the service of theology. Culturally, it was not in the state required by its nature. The coming of a philosophical or lay wisdom which had completed its own formation for itself and according to its own finalities was therefore a response to an historical necessity. But unfortunately this work was brought about under the aegis of division and of a sectarian rationalism; Descartes *separated* philosophy from any higher wisdom, from anything in man which comes from above man. I am convinced that what the world and civilization have lacked in the intellectual order for three centuries has been a philosophy which would develop its autonomous exigencies in a Christian climate, a wisdom of reason not closed but open to the wisdom of grace. Today reason must battle an irrational deification of elemental and instinctive forces that threatens to ruin all civilization. In this struggle, reason's task is one of integration; understanding that intelligence is not the enemy of mystery, but lives on it, reason must come to terms with the irrational world of affectivity and instinct, as well as with the world of the will, of freedom and of love, and the suprarational world of grace and of divine life.

The dynamic harmony of the degrees of knowledge will at the same time become manifest. From this point of view, the problem proper to the age we are entering will be, it seems, to reconcile *science* and *wisdom*. The sciences themselves seem to invite intelligence to this work. We see them stripping themselves of the remains of materialistic and mechanistic metaphysics which for a time hid their true features. They call for a philosophy of nature, and the wonderful progress in contemporary physics restores to the scientist the sense of the mystery stammered by the atom and by the universe. A critique of knowledge formed in a genuinely realist and metaphysical spirit has a chance henceforth to be heard when it affirms the existence of structures of knowledge specifically and hierarchically distinct—distinct, but not separated—and shows that they correspond to original types of explanation which cannot be substituted one for another.

The Greeks recognized the great truth that contemplation is in itself superior to action. But they at once transformed this truth into a great error: they believed that the human race exists for a few intellectuals. As they saw it, there was a category of specialists, the philosophers, who lived a superhuman life, and the properly human life, namely, civil or political life, existed to serve them. To serve civil or political life, in turn, there was the subhuman life of labor, which in final analysis was the life of the slave. The lofty truth of the superiority of the contemplative life was thus bound to a contempt for labor and to the evil of slavery.

Christianity transfigured all this. It taught men that love is of more value than intelligence. It transformed the notion of contemplation, which henceforth does not stop in the intellect, but only in the love of God, the contemplated object. It restored to action its human significance as a service to our neighbor, and rehabilitated work by disclosing in it a value of natural redemption, as it were, and even a natural prefiguration of the communications of charity. It called to the contemplation of the saints and to perfection, not a few specialists or privileged persons, but all men, who are all bound proportionately by the law of work. Man is at once *"homo faber"* and *"homo sapiens"* and he is *"homo faber"* before truly and actually being *"homo sapiens"* and in order to become the latter. In this way Christianity saved, by transforming and delivering from the error which tainted it, the Greek idea of the superiority of the contemplative life.

The saints' contemplation completes and consummates a natural aspiration to contemplation consubstantial to man, of which the sages of India and Greece especially give testimony. It is through love that the knowledge of divine things becomes experimental and fruitful. And precisely because this knowledge is the work of love in act, it also passes into action by virtue of the very generosity and abundance of love, which is gift of self. Then action proceeds from the superabundance of contemplation, and that is why, far from suppressing action or being opposed to it, contemplation vivifies it. It is in this sense, which relates to the essential generosity of the contemplation of love, that we must recognize with Bergson, in the superabundance and excess of the giving of self shown by the Christian mystics, the sign of their success in reaching the heroic summit of human life.

The pursuit of the highest contemplation and the pursuit of the highest freedom are two aspects of the same pursuit. In the order of spiritual life, man aspires to a perfect and absolute freedom, and therefore to a superhuman condition; sages of all times give evidence of this. The function of law is a function of protection and education of freedom, the function of a pedagogue. At the conclusion of this tutelage the perfect spiritual man is freed from every servitude, even, St. Paul says, from the servitude of the law, because he does spontaneously what is of the law and is simply one spirit and one love with the Creator.

To my way of thinking, the pursuit of freedom is also at the base of the social and political problem. But in the order of temporal life, it is not a divine freedom which is the object of our desires, but rather a freedom proportionate to the human condition and to the natural possibilities of our earthly existence. It is important not to deceive ourselves on the nature of the good thus pursued. It is not simply the preservation of each one's *freedom of choice,* nor the social community's *freedom of power.* The good in question is the *freedom of expansion* of human persons making up a people and participating in its good. Political society has as an end to develop conditions of life in common which, while assuring first of all the good and peace of the whole, will positively aid each person in the progressive conquest of this freedom of expansion, a freedom which consists above all in the flowering of moral and rational life.

Thus justice and friendship are the very foundations of society's life; and it is to truly human goods that society ought to subordinate all material goods, technical progress and the implements of power which also make up part of society's common good.

I believe that historical conditions and the yet backward state of human development make it difficult for social life fully to reach its end, and that in regard to the possibilities and demands which the Gospel brings to us in the sociotemporal order, we are still in a pre-historic age. As we see in the psychoses of the masses which adored Stalin or Hitler, or dream of exterminating certain groups that they judge to be diabolical, in particular the Jews, doubtless because they are the people of God, human collectivities bear such a burden of will-ingly diseased animality that it will still require many centuries for the life of personality to be able truly to take on among the masses the fullness to which it aspires. But it still remains that the end toward which social life of itself tends is to procure the common good of the multitude in such a way that the concrete person, not merely in a privileged class but in the entire mass, may truly reach that measure of independence which belongs to civilized life and which is assured alike by the economic guarantees of work and property, by political rights, civic virtues and the cultivation of the mind.

These ideas are tied up with wider views which seem to me most properly designated by the expression *integral humanism,* and which involve a whole philosophy of modern history. Such a humanism, con-sidering man in the integral wholeness of his natural and supernatural being and setting no a priori limits to the descent of the divine into man, may also be called a humanism of the Incarnation.

In the sociotemporal order it does not ask men to sacrifice themselves to the imperialism of race, of class or of nation. It asks them to sacrifice themselves to a better life for their brothers and to the concrete good of the community of human persons. That is why it cannot be less than a heroic humanism.

It has often been remarked that "bourgeois" liberalism, which tries to base everything on the individual taken as a little god and on his good pleasure, on an absolute freedom of ownership, of business and the pleasures of life, ends up fatally in statism. The rule of numbers produces the omnipotence of the State, of a ruminant or plutocratic State. Communism may be regarded as a reaction against this individ-ualism. It claims to be orientated toward the absolute emancipation of man, who would thus become the god of history, but in reality this emancipation, supposing it were accomplished, would then be that of collective man, not that of the human person. Society as economic community would enslave the whole life of the person, because the essential work of civil society would be made to consist in economic functions, instead of subordinating this work to the freedom of expansion of persons: what the Communists propose as the emancipation of collective man would be the enslavement of human persons.

What of the anti-Communist and anti-individualistic reactions of a totalitarian or dictatorial type? It is not in the name of the social community and the freedom of collective man, it is in the name of the sovereign dignity of the State, a state of the carnivorous type, or in the name of the spirit of a people, in the name of race or of blood, that they would annex man in his entirety to a social whole where the person of the ruler is the only one, properly speaking, to enjoy the privileges of personality. This is why totalitarian states, needing for themselves the total devotion of the person and having no sense of or respect for the person, inevitably seek a principle of human exaltation in myths of external grandeur and in the never-ending struggle for power and prestige. By its nature this tends to war and the self-destruction of the civilized community. If there are people in the Church—and they are fewer and fewer—who count on dictatorships of this kind to promote the religion of Christ and Christian civilization, they forget that the totalitarian phenomenon is an aberrant religious phenomenon in which an earthly mysticism devours every other mysticism whatever it may be, and will tolerate none besides itself.

Confronted with "bourgeois" liberalism, Communism and totalitarian statism, what we need, I do not cease to say, is a new solution, one that is at the same time personalist and communal, one that sees human society as an organization of freedoms. We are thus brought to a conception of democracy, the community of free men, very different from that of Jean-Jacques Rousseau. We may call it *pluralist,* because it requires that the body politic guarantee the organic freedoms of the different spiritual families and different social bodies assembled within it, beginning with the basic natural community, the society of the family. The drama of modern democracies is that, under the appearance of an error—the deification of a fictitious individual entirely closed up in himself—they have without knowing it pursued a good thing: the expansion of the real person open to higher realities and to the common service of justice and friendship.

Personalist democracy holds that each is called, by virtue of the common dignity of human nature, to participate actively in political life, and that those who hold authority—which is a vital function in society and a real right to direct people—should be freely designated by the people. This is why personalist democracy sees in universal suffrage the first practical token by which a democratic society becomes aware of itself and which it may not in any case renounce. It has no better or more meaningful motto than the republican motto, understood as indicating, not an established condition in which man has only to be installed, but an end to be reached, a difficult and lofty goal to which man must tend by force of courage, justice and virtue. For freedom must be conquered, by the progressive elimination of the several forms of servitude, and it is not enough to proclaim equality of the fundamental rights of human persons, whatever one's race, one's religion, one's condition. This equality ought to pass in a real way into custom and into social structures and ought to yield fruit in a larger and larger participation by all in the common good of civilization. Finally, fraternity in the body politic requires that the loftiest and most generous of virtues, the love to which the Gospel has called our ungrateful species, pass into the very order of political life. A personalist democracy is not really conceivable without the superelevations which nature and temporal civilizations receive, each in its own order, from the energies of the Christian leaven.

I am convinced that the coming of such a democracy, which presupposes that class antagonism has been overcome, demands that, by a genuine renewal of life and of justice, we truly go beyond "capitalism" and beyond socialism, each of which is vitiated by a materialistic conception of life. Nothing is more opposed to personalist democracy than Fascist totalitarianism—whether social-nationalist or national-socialist; for it goes beyond "capitalism" only through the paroxysm of the evils it begets.

Let me remark that Christians are confronted today, in the socio-temporal order, with problems quite similar to those their sixteenth- and seventeenth-century ancestors encountered in the area of the philosophy of nature. At that time modern physics and astronomy, then in their beginnings, were simply one with philosophies set against tradition. The defenders of tradition did not know how to make the necessary distinctions. They took sides against what was to become modern science, at the same time that they took sides against the philosophical errors which at the start were parasitic on science. It took three centuries

257

to get rid of this misunderstanding, if indeed the world is yet rid of it. It would be a sad story if we should be guilty today, in the field of practical and social philosophy, of like errors.

In the words of Pope Pius XI, the great scandal of the nineteenth century was the divorce of the working classes from the Church of Christ. In the temporal order, the moral secession of the working masses from the political community was a comparable tragedy. The awakening in the working masses of what the socialist vocabulary calls "class consciousness" appears to us as a great gain, so far as we see in it man's becoming aware of an offended and humiliated human dignity and of a vocation. But it has been chained to an historic calamity, because this awakening has been spoiled by the gospel of despair and of social warfare which is at the bottom of the Marxist idea of class struggle and the dictatorship of the proletariat. And it was precisely into this *secessionist* conception, whose protagnist was Marx and whose demand is that proletarians of all countries should recognize no other common good than that of their class, that the blindness of the possessing classes in the nineteenth century precipitated the working masses.

Whoever has pondered on these fundamental facts and on the history of the labor movement understands that the central problem of our times is the temporal and spiritual problem of the *reintegration of the masses*. In my view, it is only an artificial and illusory solution of this problem when the attempt is made, as in the case of German National Socialism, to manufacture happy slaves through violence linked up with material ameliorations good in themselves but achieved in a spirit of domination, and with a psychotechnic solicitude vowed to satisfy and to benumb appetites. The fact is that one manufactures only unhappy slaves, robots of nonbeing.

However difficult, slow and painful it may be, the reintegration of the proletariat within the national community, not to exercise a class dictatorship in it, but to collaborate body and soul in the work of the community, will take place really, which means humanly, only by a recasting of social structures worked out in the spirit of justice. I am not naïve enough to believe that this reintegration can be accomplished without knocks and sacrifices, on the one hand as regards the well-being of the privilegd sons of fortune and on the other as regards the theories and the destructive instincts of fanatical revolutionaries. But I am persuaded that it requires above all else the free co-operation of the workers' leaders (elites) and of the masses who follow them, and this co-operation must go along with a better general understanding of historical realities and with an awareness, not wiped out but heightened, of the human being's dignity as worker and citizen. In like manner the return of the masses to Christianity will be brought about only through love, I mean love stronger than death, the fire of the Gospel.

We shall never give up hope of a new Christendom, a new temporal order of Christian inspiration. Now the means should correspond to the end, and already are the end itself as in the state of movement and preparation. If this is so, it is clear that in order to prepare a Christian social order we must use Christian means, that is to say true means, and these are means animated, even when they are of necessity harsh, by a genuine spirit of love. In two books published in 1930 and 1933[1] I have insisted at length on these axiomatic truths. Nothing is more serious or scandalous than to see, as we have for some years seen in certain countries, iniquitous and barbarous means used by men in the name of Christian order and Christian civilization. It is a truth embedded in the very nature of things that Christendom will be renewed through Christian means or it will be completely eclipsed.

The present state of nations obliges us to declare that never has the spirit been so profoundly humiliated in the world. And yet pessimism in the end always dupes itself. It disregards the great law which may be called the law of the double movement involving the energy of history. While the wear and tear of time naturally dissipates and degrades the things of this world and the "energy of history," and this means the mass of human activity on which the movement of history depends, the creative forces which are characteristic of spirit and freedom and are a witness to them, forces which ordinarily find their point of application in the effort of the few—who are thereby bound to sacrifice—improve more and more the quality of this energy. This is exactly the work of the sons of God in history, it is the work of Christians if they do not belie their name.

People do not understand this work at all if they imagine that it aims at installing the world in a state from which all evil and all injustice would have disappeared. If this were the aim, it would be quite easy, considering the results, stupidly to condemn the Christian as utopian. The work the Christian has to do is to keep up and to increase in the world the internal tension and movement of slow and painful deliverance, a tension and movement due to the invisible powers of truth and

---

[1] *Religion et culture, Du régime temporel et de la liberté.* English translation, *Religion and Culture, Freedom in the Modern World.*

justice, of goodness and love, acting on the mass which is opposed to them. This work cannot be in vain, it assuredly bears its fruit.

Woe to the world should Christians turn their back on it, should they fail to do their work, which is to heighten here on earth the charge and tension of the spiritual; should they listen to blind leaders of the blind who seek the means to order and to good in things which of themselves lead to dissolution and death. We have no illusions about the misery of human nature and the malice of this world. But neither have we any illusions about the blindness and malfeasance of pseudo realists who cultivate and exalt evil in order to fight evil, and who take the Gospel as a decorative myth which cannot be regarded seriously without wrecking the machinery of the world. They themselves, meantime, take it upon themselves to ruin, to distract, and to torment this unhappy world.

The ferment of the Pharisees, against which Christ put us on our guard, is a permanent temptation for the religious conscience. Undoubtedly, this ferment will not be altogether driven out of the world till the end of history. Meantime, in the social as well as in the spiritual order, we must never let up the fight against it. However great may be the mass of evil which a mass of Pharisaism means to oppose, the latter is always as great an evil, because the good it sets against that evil is a good which does not give life but kills, as does the letter without the spirit: it is a good which leaves God without resources in man.

One of the gravest lessons afforded us by the experience of life is that, in fact, in the practical conduct of most people, all those things which in themselves are good and very good—science, technical progress, culture, etc., and even the knowledge of moral laws, and religious faith itself, faith in the living God (which of itself demands the love of charity)—all these things, *without love and good will,* serve to make men all the more evil and the more unhappy. So far as religious faith is concerned, this was demonstrated in the Spanish Civil War by the inhuman feelings that surged up in the "crusaders" as well as in the "Reds," but were confirmed in the former in the sanctuary of the soul. What happens is that, without love and charity, man turns the best in him into an evil that is yet greater.

When one has understood this, he no longer puts his hope on earth in anything less than that good will of which the Gospel speaks—it speaks of good will, not of good velleity; he puts his hope in those obscure energies of a little real goodness which persist in making life germinate and regerminate in the secret depths of things. There is

260

nothing more destitute, nothing more hidden, nothing nearer to the weakness of the infant. And there is no wisdom more fundamental or more effective than that simple and tenacious confidence, not in the means of violence, deceit and malice, which certainly are capable of crushing men and of triumphing, but which a grain of sand is nevertheless enough to cause to be smashed one against the other—but simple and tenacious confidence in the resources of personal courage to give oneself, and of good will set to do as one ought the tasks of every day. Through this disinterested spirit flows the power of nature and the Author of nature.

—Revised translation of *Confession de foi,*
by Joseph W. Evans and Leo R. Ward, 1955

A PHILOSOPHER

IN A BROADWAY

SEMINARY

DR. REINHOLD NIEBUHR, WHO HAS BEEN TEACHING CHRISTIAN ETHICS AND philosophy of religion at Union Theological Seminary on upper Broadway in New York since 1928, has devoted most of his adult life to the relation of religion to social and political problems. In 1915 he accepted his first call, taking over a "struggling little church" in Detroit, where his influence grew with the town (and the automobile era), the city swelling from half a million to a million and a half in thirteen years.

Dr. Niebuhr's spiritual influence has widened with the years and with his writings and later his editing of the quarterly *Christianity and Society* and still later the biweekly *Christianity and Crisis*. His Gifford Lectures at the University of Edinburgh now compose one of his most important books, *The Nature and Destiny of Man*.

Dr. Niebuhr is married and has a son and a daughter. He is a former member of the Socialist party and while he describes himself as still "a liberal in economics," since 1940 or so his religious thinking has been characterized generally as orthodox. He was born in Wright City, Missouri, June 21, 1892, the son of the pastor of an Evangelical church.

"I think," the author wrote the editor, "our age is one of great anxiety about the future."

On Freedom, Virtue and Faith

BY REINHOLD NIEBUHR

There is a grim irony in the fact that mankind is at the moment in the toils of the terrible fate of a division between two great centers of power, one of which is informed by the Communist and the other by the bourgeois liberal creed of world redemption. Both creeds imagine that man can become the master of historical destiny. The Communists assume that the rationalization of particular interest will disappear with a revolutionary destruction of a society which maintains special interests. The very fury of Communist self-righteousness, particularly the identification of ideal ends with the tortuous policies of a particular nation and its despotic oligarchy, is rooted in its naïve assumption that the rationalization of partial and particular interests is merely the product of a particular form of social organization and would be overcome by its destruction.

Meanwhile the liberal world dreams of the mastery of historical destiny by the gradual extension of the "scientific method" without recognizing that the objectivity and disinterestedness which it seeks by such simple terms represents the ultimate problem and despair of human existence. The two creeds are locked in seemingly irreconcilable conflict. Whether the conflict eventuates in overt hostilities or not, it has already produced an historical situation which cannot be encompassed in the philosophy of history of either creed. An adequate frame of meaning to encompass it would have to contain the motif of the Tower of Babel myth of the Bible. In that myth God reduced the pride of men who wanted to build a tower into the heavens by confounding their languages, thereby reminding them that they were particular, finite, and conditioned men, who do not find it an easy matter to become simply "man."

Is it not significant that a culture which expects "man" to become master of his historical fate, and "man" to decide what direction his historical development should take, arrives at this tragic end? And that the difficulty is created by the fact that the natural scientist, who is the only scientist faintly approximating the universal *mind* which is to become master of historical destiny, discovers atomic power; and that, confronted with the necessity of bringing this new power of creativity and destructiveness under social and moral control, our generation should find *mind* dissolved into various national minds, whose social objectives are as varied as their language? And that they should find the greater difficulty in achieving a tolerable community, across this chasm of mutual fear, because each is armed with a social philosophy which obscures the partial and particular character of its objective?

When all the elements which enter our present world situation are explicated, it becomes apparent that history's pattern of meaning is more complex than either the Communist or the liberal conception of historical progress. Men do not, whether by evolutionary or revolutionary means, exchange their position of creatures of historical process to that of history's masters. They remain rather in the continuous ambiguity both of being mastered and mastering the course of history. Whatever mastery they may achieve over historical processes must still operate in a wide realm of meaning in which both natural and historical factors beyond the control of any particular human will frustrate, deflect and negate, as well as fulfill, human desires and ambitions.

The modern version of an historical redemption from the human predicament of finiteness and freedom is, in short, a particularly flagrant expression of the *Hybris* which tempts man to overestimate the degree of his freedom and which Christian thought recognizes as the root of sin.

The general belief in modern thought, that religion is an expression of impotence, must be understood in the light of this exaggerated conception of the limitless power of man. If it should be true that history radically changes the human situation and that man's mastery over, rather than subordination to, the natural and historical process is the primary proof and fruit of that change, it would follow that religious conceptions of a providential purpose and pattern would become irrelevant through historial development. The warning of Christ, "Which of you by taking thought can add one cubit unto his stature?" (Matthew 6:27) seems from the viewpoint of modern pride a typical religious expression of impotence, which ceases to have meaning in a day in which technics have extended the power of the human foot in transportation, of the human hand in manufacture, and of the ear and eye in fabulous forms of communication.

Engel's indictment of religion as an expression of weakness states the mood of typical moderns in classical form: "All religion," he declares

is nothing but the fantastic reflection in men's minds of those external forces which control their daily life. . . . Although bourgeois political economy has given a certain insight into the causal basis of this domination by extraneous forces, this makes no essential difference. Bourgeois economics can neither prevent general crises nor protect the individual capitalist from losses. . . . It is still true that man proposes and God (that is, the extraneous forces of the capitalist mode of production) disposes. Mere knowledge . . . is not enough. What is above all necessary is a social act. When this act has been accomplished . . . and society has freed itself and all its members

264

from the bondage in which they are now held . . . when therefore man not only proposes but also disposes, only then will the last extraneous force which is still reflected in religion vanish and with it will also vanish the religious reflection itself.[1]

Marxism gives the thesis, that religion is the expression of impotence, a particular color because it accuses the bourgeois world of having emancipated man only from bondage to nature and not from the inevitabilities of historic catastrophe. But the essential idea was borrowed by Marxism from the liberal culture of the eighteenth and nineteenth centuries. It was generally believed that "the illusion of power over the external world, promised by religion, has been achieved by science, which accounts for the decline of the religious mentality."[2]

Mr. Calverton's observation proves that religion is subject to contrasting indictments. It is accused of seeking to give man control over the natural world but also of expressing an attitude of impotence and defeatism toward "extraneous forces." Actually the primitive magic which sought to bend nature to human ends by magical formulae and incantations was a kind of prescientific science, which must be distinguished from the more typical religious attitude of reverence and awe before the power or powers of the world of nature and history which determine human destiny beyond man's contriving. While this primitive magic insinuates itself into even advanced religions of later ages; and while men do seek to use religion as a tool for a fancied manipulation of natural forces, the sense of submission toward omnipotent power is certainly more characteristically religious. It cannot be denied that this religious sense of human limitations has frequently been misapplied in the realm of man's growing power and has prompted a defeatist attitude toward scientific efforts to ameliorate natural evils or toward social efforts to overcome historical evils.[3] While these errors of the religious mind prove that orthodox religions have had difficulty in appreciating the meaning of man's growing power over nature, they do not validate the curious belief of modern culture that religion is merely an expression of impotence, which man's growing power will overcome. This belief is succinctly expressed in the observation of Bertrand Russell that fishermen with sailboats incline to be religious while those who

[1] Engels, *Anti-Dühring*, Part III, v.

[2] V. F. Calverton, *The Passing of the Gods*, p. 320.

[3] Andrew White's *History of the Warfare between Science and Religion* is a fruitful source-book of specific instances of such religious defeatism. Gandhi's opposition to surgery and projects for the arrest of the disease of leprosy is one example of a non-Christian religious opposition to the elimination of natural evil.

boast the possession of motorboats divest themselves of religion. "Modern technics," declares Mr. Russell, "is giving man a sense of power which is changing his whole mentality. Until recently the physical environment was something that had to be accepted. But to the modern man physical environment is merely the raw material for manipulation and opportunity. It may be that God made the world. but there is no reason why we should not make it over."[4] The modern man's sense of power does not stop with a sense of mastery over the immediate natural conditions of his life. "A cosmic process has come to consciousness," boasts Eustace Hayden, "and to the capacity for purposive self-control on the social level. . . . The task is to impose human purposes upon the cosmic process, to shape the course of the flowing stream of life."[5]

The illusion of budding omnipotence, which inspires the charge that a religious sense of Providence is the expression of a primitive impotence, could not be stated more clearly.

The extravagant estimate of the degree of freedom and power which may accrue to man through historical development is hardly as grievous an error as the estimate of the virtue of that freedom, implied in most modern interpretations of the human situation.

Since modern rationalism inherited the belief from classical rationalism that the evil in human nature is the consequence of natural finiteness and physical impulses, it naturally inclined to the conclusion that the development of rational capacities was, in itself, a process of gradual emancipation from evil. Race prejudice is generally regarded as a vestigial remnant of barbarism. Manifestations of national pride or other parochial bigotries are, in a similar fashion, thought of as forms of inertia which the ever more inclusive purposes and visions of reason will overcome. Individual and collective egotism is believed to be the consequence of a primitive ignorance which must ultimately either yield to more enlightened and therefore more inclusive forms of self-interest, or which will be brought under the dominion of the moral force implicit in man's rational faculties.

In more recent scientific forms of this identification of virtue and reason, the hope is to bring the irrational stuff of human nature under control by more adequate psychiatric technics or by establishing rational political checks upon the irrational impulses of men.

In any event evil is always a force of the past, which must be over-

---

[4] *Scientific Outlook*. p. 151. London. George Allen and Unwin Ltd.
[5] *Quest of the Ages*. pp. 207-9.

come by present and future possibilities. The triumph of virtue is more or less guaranteed because historical development assures both the increasing purity of reason and the efficacy of its scientific technics. This error of identifying increasing freedom with increasing virtue is primarily responsible for the false estimates of history by contemporary culture. The increasing evils which arose with increasing power could be neither anticipated nor comprehended within terms of these presuppositions.

In its most naïve form modern rationalism identifies technical competence with rational profundity and sees in the conquest of nature a proof of man's capacity to bring the irrational stuff of human nature under control. All that is necessary is to apply the "methods of science" as rigorously to the world of human affairs as to the realm of nature.[6] In forms less crude there is some recognition of the wide gulf which separates the world of history from the world of nature; but confidence in the final dominion of reason over this more complex world is no less sanguine.

One reason why it never occurs to the typical modern that evil in human nature may be due to a corruption of human freedom, rather than to some inertia of nature or history, is because the human self in its integrity and unity has been lost.

Despite all modern protest against dualism and idealism, the real self in its unity is dissolved into an intelligible and a sensible self. But the intelligible self is not really a self. It is pure mind. And the sensible self is not really a self. It is a congeries of physical impulses. It conforms fairly well to Freud's "id" which is defined as a "caldron of seething excitement." When the modern man speaks of mastering human nature, or ordering society, or manipulating historical destiny, he dismisses the real self with its anxieties and fears, its hopes and ambitions both from the concept of the man who is to become master of historical destiny, and from the picture of the stuff of history which is to be mastered. This

[6] Occasionally the suggestion is made that since human nature is slightly more complex than nature, a mastery of more varied technics is required. Thus Alexis Carrel in *Man the Unknown* comes to the conclusion that the management of human affairs requires a thorough knowledge of "anatomy and physics, physiology and metaphysics, pathology, chemistry, psychology, medicine, and also a thorough knowledge of genetics, nutrition, pedagogy, aesthetics, ethics, religion, sociology, and economics." He estimates that about twenty-five years would be required to master all these disciplines so "that at the age of 50 those who have submitted themselves to these disciplines could effectively direct the *reconstruction of human beings*" (p. 285).

This vision of world salvation through the ministrations of an elite of encyclopedists is a nice symbol of the inanity to which the modern interpretation of life may sink.

real self as a force to be mastered has unique powers of recalcitrance not known in nature; and as the instrument of mastery it is betrayed by confusions not known in pure mind.

This dismissal of the real self in the unity of its finiteness and freedom is responsible for the note of unreality in the more theoretic disciplines of our culture, as compared either with the common sense which informs the practical life of men or the profounder insights of poets and artists, seeking to portray life in its wholeness and complexity. The common sense of ordinary men is seldom under the illusion that the jealousies and envies which infect even the most intimate human relations are merely the defects of an undisciplined mind. They are known to be temptations for saint as well as sinner; for the wise man and fool. Practical statesmen do not regard the will-to-power of a strong man as the vestigial remnant of barbarism. All common-sense political wisdom seeks to harness and to restrain, to make use of, and to guard against, the power impulse. A common-sense regulation of economic life does not treat the economic motive as a force which is about to be eliminated from human society. It knows that motive to be one facet of the power of self-interest, which must be harnessed, deflected, beguiled and transmuted in the interest of the commonweal but which can never be completely suppressed.

The common-sense wisdom of mankind is even more aware of the recalcitrant power of egoistic interest in collective action. Nations and groups do not possess an integral consciousness as does the individual. But they do have an inchoate will; and that will is capable of only vagrant affirmations of ideals and values beyond its own interest. No one is particularly shocked by George Washington's dictum that a nation is not to be trusted beyond its own interest. That bit of cynicism is common currency in the affairs of mankind; and statesmen would be impeached if their policies ventured too far beyond its warning.

Some poets and artists, novelists and historians have been so much influenced by the modern temper as to have become incapable either of picturing human character in the complexity of its motives or of describing human relations in the bewildering confusion of interactions in which human lives impinge upon one another. Recently a few novelists have sought to do justice to the complex unity of human life by inserting psychiatric techniques into their stories, as if this little bit of science could compensate for the lack of a poetic grasp of human nature in both its grandeur and its misery. But no matter how much our imaginative literature has suffered from the illusions of our age, no respectable novel has ever quite pictured human life as vapidly as some of our more theoretic social and historical sciences. When either common sense or poetry are not completely robbed of their art of observation they are not wholly obtuse to the reality of the human self (including an inchoate collective self) whose "ideals" are interlaced with anxieties and fears not known in the kingdom of pure reason; and whose hopes and ambitions betray a guile of spirit not known in the realm of nature.

Even the social, psychological and historical scientists are, despite their theories, unable to deny the real self, in the unity of its finiteness and freedom, completely. Thus a modern psychologist who seeks to equate the complex causation of human motives with the type of causality known in nature admits by inadvertence that a transcendent self interferes with the natural process. In L. J. Shaffer's *Psychology of Adjustment* the self is reduced to the level of nature in this fashion: "In sharp contrast to the moralistic viewpoint the objective psychological attitude places no blame or judgment upon the individual. Human behavior is the result of causes just as physical phenomena arise from certain sufficient antecedents. Not many centuries ago material events were blamed upon the wrath of deity or the perversity of nature. Conduct problems have only recently emerged in the realm of natural occurrences to be treated impartially as physical events."[7] The self, thus dismissed from responsibility for its actions, is, however, so full of guile that the same psychologist warns against placing the tools of self-knowledge too much at its disposal; for it will use them to its own advantage: "Thus one student complains of his inability to achieve because of his inferiority complex," he declares. "Another points to the fact that he is the product of his heredity and environment. Such statements must be recognized as products of rationalization rather than of reasoning."[8]

Another psychologist is rather disconcerted by the intrusion of "naïve egotism" into the nicely laid plans for a rational world. William McDougall uses the lives of Woodrow Wilson and of Lord Curzon as illustrations of the "disastrous effects" of this naïve egotism which makes even a great man "unwilling to dim the glory of his achievement by sharing it with others." He thinks something "drastic" must be done to break the power of this residual evil in an otherwise rational world.

[7] P. 8.
[8] *Ibid.*, p. 543.

He suggests that nothing less than "inducing all our young people to make some study of psychology" will be adequate for the solution of this problem.[9]

Thus rationalism, defined as primarily confidence in the virtue and omnipotence of reason, can sink to a low level of unreason, if discernment of the facts of life is a mark of reason's competence.

The division of the self into a rational and natural, or an intelligible and a sensible, self leads to a false estimate of human virtue. The real self, in its transcendent unity and integrity, is involved in the evils, particularly the evils of self-seeking, which it commits. This self is always sufficiently emancipated of natural necessity, not to be compelled to follow the course dictated by self-interest. If it does so nevertheless, it is held culpable both in the court of public opinion and in the secret of its own heart. The self finds itself free; but, as Augustine suggested, not free to do good. The self seeks its own despite its freedom to envisage a wider good than its own interest. Furthermore it uses its freedom to extend the domain of its own interests. It is this use of freedom which makes the moral effect of the extension of human power so ambiguous. New technical skills become the servants of particular interest in the first instance; and come under the control of a wider community or value only by tortuous process. The ability of the self to envisage a wider world than its immediate environment is the occasion for the rise of imperialism long before it leads to the establishment of any universal concord between particular interests. It is always through some particular center of power that the human community is organized; or from some particular viewpoint that meaning is given to the course of history.

Thus the increasing freedom of the self over natural limitations aggravates and enlarges the conflicts of life with life as nature knows them. Yet the self can never use its wider freedom for itself with complete complacency. It has some knowledge of a responsibility toward life beyond itself and a vagrant inclination to be loyal to it. But there is a "law in its members" which wars against the "law that is in its mind," a powerful inclination to bend every new power to its own purposes and to interpret every situation from the standpoint of its own pride and prestige.

The selfishness of men and of nations is a fixed datum of historical science. Election results can be confidently predicted if the economic

[9] *The Energies of Men*, p. 382.

interests of the voters can be carefully enough analyzed. Yet this human egotism does not belong to nature. The eighteenth-century rationalists were wrong in asserting that men sought their own, just as every animal seeks to preserve its existence. The human self is different from other creatures in two respects: (1) It is able by its freedom to transmute nature's survival impulse into more potent and more destructive, more subtle and more comprehensive forms of self-seeking than the one-dimensional survival impulse of nature. (2) It is able to envisage a larger good than its own preservation, to make some fitful responses to this more inclusive obligation and to feel itself guilty for its failure to make a more consistent response.

Every animal will run as fast as it can from a superior foe, a strategy which subjects human beings to the charge of cowardice. Naturalists may argue that human actions have been reduced to the level of "physical events" to which no praise or blame can be attached because they always have "sufficient antecedents." But the common sense of mankind has never accepted this ridiculous denial of a unique freedom in human life and of a consequent responsibility and guilt in human action. The life and literature of the ages is replete with condemnation of cowardice and self-seeking and of praise for acts of bravery and lives of selfless devotion. Even the deterministic Marxists, who assume that moral ideals are inevitably pretentious rationalizations of self-interest, are unable to carry their determinism to its logical conclusion; for their political propaganda abounds in invectives against the dishonesty of their foes. This invective could have meaning only upon the assumption that men might be honest, rather than dishonest, and might actually seek, rather than merely pretend to seek, the good of the commonwealth rather than their own advantage.

In a smilar fashion a liberal idealist who ostensibly believes that the progress of mankind depends upon the extension of the scientific method, periodically censures his fellow men for their laziness and dishonesty, and for their inclination to make compromises with outmoded authoritarianism. "All I know about the future of progress," declares John Dewey, "is that it depends upon man to say whether he wants it or not."[10] Thus the responsible self (and the guilty self insofar as it always falls short of its highest responsibilities) peeps through even the most intricate and elaborate façades of modern thought.

The real situation is that the human self is strongly inclined to seek its own but that it has a sufficient dimension of transcendence over self

[10] Joseph Ratner, *The Philosophy of John Dewey*. p. 461.   London. George Allen and Unwin Ltd.

to be unable to ascribe this inclination merely to natural necessity. On the other hand, when it strives for a wider good it surreptitiously introduces its own interests into this more inclusive value. This fault may be provisionally regarded as the inevitable consequence of a finite viewpoint. The self sees the larger structure of value from its own standpoint. Yet this provisional disavowal of moral culpability is never finally convincing. The self's ignorance is never invincible ignorance. It sees beyond itself sufficiently to know that its own interests are not identical with the wider good. If it claims such identity nevertheless, there is an element of moral perversity, and not mere ignorance in the claim. Thus the cynical attitude of all common-sense judgments toward the pretensions of nations and individuals is justified by the facts. Common sense at least touches the periphera of the mystery of original sin which uncommon sense so easily dismisses.

The common sense of mankind, embodied in the judgments which men and nations make of each other, recognizes that there is indeed an internal debate in the life of individuals and groups between the claims of the self and the claims of some wider system of value, but that this debate is within the self and not between mind and body, or between reason and impulse. The self is indeed divided. It would do the good but does not do it; it would avoid evil but finds an inclination more powerful than its will toward the evil which it would avoid.[11] The power of this inclination to self-seeking is more potent and more mysterious than the natural impulses. The self in its totality is in the force of the inclination. Yet in moments of high reflection the self feels the inclination to be a power not its own "but sin that dwelleth in me."[12]

The will of nations is not as clearly integrated as the "will" which symbolizes the individual self. Yet it is possible to observe this debate in the "spiritual life" of nations as well as in individuals; and to recog-

[11] Cf. Romans 7.

[12] We have previously observed how much closer to the ultimate mysteries of good and evil the poets and artists are than the psychologists and social scientists of our day. André Gide refers again and again in his journal to the mystery of evil inclinations within himself, which are his own and not yet his own. He objectifies this inclination in "the devil" though he declares, "I am utterly indifferent as to whether this name of the demon is the right name for what I mean and I grant that I give it this name out of convenience. . . . When I say: the Evil One I know what this expression designates just as clearly as I know what is designated by the word God. . . . Since he is more intelligent than I, everything he thought up to hurl me toward evil was infinitely more precious, more specious, more convincing, more clever than any argument I could have brought up to persevere in honor." *The Journals of André Gide,* Vol. II, p. 189.

nize that something more than a struggle between reason and ignorance is involved.

Thus American isolationism can be explained by reference to the geographic fact of the nation's seeming continental security. But though one may call attention to geographic conditions, which influence political judgments, one instinctively adds moral censure to such an analysis. If a nation ignorantly believes itself secure when it is not, it has failed to exercise its intelligence. The ignorance and finiteness of the human mind is never at a fixed limit. "We are living in a day," declared a political scientist recently, "in which knowledge of world-wide political conditions has become a possibility and a necessity. The refusal of men and nations to cultivate such knowledge has therefore become a crime." Here again the will of the self, capable of extending or restricting the knowledge required for adequate mutual relations, is revealed as a factor in a human situation, despite every effort to dismiss so incalculable an element from the rational analysis.

Though, on the whole, nations are not expected to conform to a moral standard higher than that of a prudent self-interest, yet common-sense moral judgments do cast blame upon nations for a too consistent devotion to their own interests, involving indifference to a wider good. This moral blame is justified; for though no nation will venture beyond its own interest into a system of mutual security, yet the power of even enlightened self-interest is not sufficient alone to prompt such a venture. It must be supported by a concern for a wider good, beyond its own interests. Nations are thus subject, as are individuals, to an internal tension between the claims of the self and a larger claim. Whether the second claim is tolerably met represents a spiritual issue beyond the mere calculations of prudence. Here is the responsible self in the collective life of mankind. Insofar as nations, even more than individuals, never adequately meet the wider claim the responsible self is also the guilty self.

The simple facts which we have enumerated are so obvious, supported by so much evidence and sustained by so many judgments of common sense in contravention to the prevailing theories of our age, that one is forced to the conclusion that something more than an honest error has entered into modern miscalculations of human behavior and historical destiny. An honest error has indeed contributed to the confusion of our culture. It did discover the fact of historical growth and it did see that specific evils, due to specific forms of human impotence, may be overcome by the growth of human power; and that particular evils due to human ignorance may be overcome by the growth of man's intelligence; and it may well have been led astray by this evidence to the false conclusion that all human problems were being solved by historical development.

But meanwhile there was also mounting evidence that the growth of human freedom and power enlarges the scope of human problems. The problems in their larger scope are not insoluble. Proximate solutions, at least, may be found for them in time. But there is no evidence that the proximate solutions of man's perennial problems become by degrees absolute solutions. There is no evidence that highly intelligent individuals find it easier than simple folk to come to terms with their fellow men, though intelligence may produce a social system of wider scope and greater complexity than the primitive community. There is no proof that a universal community will ever annul the partial and particular loyalties of smaller groups, rooted in nature and elaborated by history. Every wide community represents, not some simple triumph of universal over particular interest but an artful equilibration, suppression, extension, and deflection of particular interest for the sake of the wider community. Nor is there proof that history represents a gradual spiritualization or rationalization of human nature so that in some absolute sense "methods of mind" supplant methods of force. On the contrary there is mounting evidence that men act in the unity of their physical and spiritual capacities and use all resources at their command to effect what they most deeply desire or to prevent what they most profoundly abhor. In this connection the development from partial to total wars, while a culture dreamed of the gradual abolition of war, is instructive. The engagement of the total capacities of a nation for its military ventures proved to be a late achievement of culture. Precisely those technical and rational developments, which were supposed to lead to a detachment of the spiritual from the physical vitalities of men, proved to be the prerequisites for the total harnessing of all resources for the attainment of whatever end the pride or the fear, the ambition or idealism of a nation prompted.

Since there is so much proof that the development of man's power and freedom is not redemptive, the question is justified whether the modern faith in historical redemption could have been due merely to an "honest" error. The question is justified particularly because of the persistence with which modern men cling to this error in defiance of its cumulative refutation by historical experience.

These facts prompt the supposition that a more "existential" element is involved in these miscalculations. The modern interpretation of human life and history was a highly plausible evasion of some very inconvenient and embarrassing facts about human nature. It was an evasion both of the dimension of responsibility in human nature and of the fact of guilt. It made man the judge of his world and of himself and seemed to free him from the scrutiny of a higher judgment. Above all it annulled and erased the indictment of guilt contained in that higher judgment. It refuted the embarrassing suspicion that man himself is the author of the historical evils which beset him. The whole structure of the modern interpretation of life and history was, in short, a very clever contrivance of human pride to obscure the weakness and the insecurity of man; of the human conscience to hide the sin into which men fall through their efforts to override their weakness and insecurity; and of human sloth to evade responsibility.

The monotonous reiteration of the eighteenth century and of the belated children of the eighteenth century in our own age that their primary concern is to establish and to guard the "dignity of man" has the quality of a peculiar irony, when these evasions are considered.

The more consistent naturalistic versions of our culture are involved in the absurdity of ostensibly guarding the dignity of man while they actually deny the reality of a responsible self, by reducing human behavior to the dimension of "facts of nature" about which no moral judgments can be made since every human act is the consequence of some "sufficient cause." The less consistent naturalist and the idealist do indeed exalt the dignity of the human mind; but they do not understand its involvement in finite conditions. Thus they promise a mastery of historical destiny which contradicts the permanent ambiguity of the human situation. And they construct confident "philosophies of history" as if man completely surveyed the stuff of history in his mind even as he mastered the forces of history by his power. Meanwhile man's involvement in the forces which he ostensibly masters periodically produces a shock of disillusionment in modern complacency. The vaunted master of historical destiny is subject to fits of despair when he finds himself tossed about among historical forces beyond the power of his will; and the proud interpretator of the meaning of history is periodically reduced to despair, wondering whether any truth can be known, since every truth known is known only from a special and peculiar historical locus.

Though sometimes the dignity of man is denied because the responsible self is annulled, and sometimes the dignity is exaggerated because the weakness of man is forgotten, an even more grievous error dogs all these modern calculations. The misery of man, the fact of his guilt is evaded. The fact that human power and freedom contain destructive, as well as creative, possibilities is not recognized. The responsibility of the self in the center and quintessence of its will and personality for the destructive side of human freedom is denied with particular vehemence. Even if the self is regarded as a responsible self, the idea that guilt accompanies responsibility is denied as a monstrous form of religious morbidity.

These evasions are much more serious than any of the modern rational miscalculations. They suggest that the human situation cannot be understood in some simple system of rational intelligibility. Man in his strength and in his weakness is too ambiguous to understand himself, unless his rational analyses are rooted in a faith that he is comprehended from beyond the ambiguities of his own understanding. The patterns of meaning in his history culminate in a realm of meaning and mystery which, if too easily dissolved into rational intelligibility, lead to nonsense, particularly to the nonsense of contradiction. But above all there is the mystery of man's responsibility and of his guilt in failing to fulfill it. That the recalcitrance of the human heart should not be simply the lag of nature but a corruption of freedom and should not be overcome by increasing freedom: this is the mystery of original sin.

Thus an analysis of the modern conception of rationally intelligible history proves that such a conception gives history a too simple moral meaning. A profound consideration of the antinomies and mysteries which modern rationalism has been unable to digest suggests that man's life and history can be made intelligible only within the framework of a larger realm of mystery and meaning discerned by faith. In proceeding to an exposition of the Christian interpretation of life and history, in comparison with the modern one, it is necessary to disavow the purpose of proving the Christian interpretation rationally compelling, in the sense that such a comparison could rationally force modern man to accept the Christian faith. The Christian interpretation of life and history is rooted in a faith prompted by repentance. It will not be convincing except to the soul which has found the profoundest enigma of existence not in the evil surrounding it but in itself. There is therefore no simple Christian "philosophy of history" which could be set against a modern or a classical one in such a way as to prove its superior profundity through rational comparison. Yet it may be possible to prove its relevance rationally, even as it has been possible to make a rational analysis of the limits of a theory of history's rational intelligibility.

We have previously noted that the primary root of modern complacency is to be found in the belief that historical development insures man's triumph over whatever is fragmentary, tragic, and contradictory in human experience. A Christian (Quaker) version of this faith states the modern creed exactly: "Quietly underneath the iceberg of corruption, which causes false pessimism, the warm waves of Christian progress are doing their work; and soon it will topple over. . . . Our scepticism results from the fact that we expect immediate results and are not willing to abide the process of nature."[13]

Though the complacency is drawn primarily from the idea of progress, it has been enchanced by the characteristic circumstances of a bourgeois civilization. This civilization, in the period of its expansion, was able to obscure the conflict of interest and passion which expresses itself in even the most ordered community and in even the most delicate equilibrium of power between the nations. The predominance of economic power, which operates covertly rather than overtly, gave rise to the illusion that human relations are, or will soon become, a meeting of mind with mind, in which no appeal to force will be necessary. The fragmentary and contradictory aspects of human culture and civilization were partly veiled; and insofar as they were apparent, historic development was expected to overcome them. Modern complacency was supported, in short, not only by a creed of progress, but by momentary historic circumstances which gave the creed a special plausibility.

That is why the more tragic contemporary historical facts are beginning to undermine this complacency. The hidden despair, which is never absent from complacency, is beginning to reveal itself. One development in modern culture adds a special depth of pathos to our situation; for the most obvious challenge to the complacency of our culture, Marxism, has become the source of a new and more fanatic complacency. The Marxist dialectic challenged the confidence of Hegelian rationalism in the power of reason. It saw that reason may be an instrument of interest and passion. But unfortunately it transmuted this discovery into a mere weapon of social and political conflict by attributing an ideological taint to the moral and social ideals of every group except

---

[13] Isaac Sharpless, *Quakerism in Politics*, p. 97. The identification of "Christian progress" with "process of nature" is an illuminating confession of the capitulation of Christian thought to the modern creed.

the proletariat. The pretension that one group in human society is free of sin, naturally became the source of new and terrible fanaticisms. Marxism also challenged the bourgeois confidence in the virtue and stability of a democratic society. It discerned the social conflicts of society where bourgeois idealists saw nothing but a harmony of social interests. It predicted the doom of a civilization, when liberal society hoped to achieve ever wider and more perfect forms of social justice. Marxism became a new religion, to which not only industrial workers but a vast section of the intellectual classes repaired when the pretensions of a bourgeois culture were shaken by the realities of history. However, Marxism did not challenge the moral complacency of modern culture, essentially. It only substituted new illusions for discredited ones. It has therefore been more fruitful of a demonic idolatry than the liberal culture. It sacrificed one great source of virtue, possessed by the liberal culture: the latter's provisional recognition of the contingent and conditioned character of all forms of historic virtue. This relativism of the liberal culture is the source of the democratic virtue of tolerance. It may be superior not only to Marxism but to forms of the Christian faith which encourage a too simple identification of the goodness of Christ with whatever social value to which an ecclesiastical institution or a devout believer may be committed.

The Marxist misapplication of the discovery of the sinful taint in human knowledge and virtue leaves this problem still unsolved. The liberal culture tries to avoid disillusionment by regarding the ideological taint in human knowledge and virtue as the consequence of finite perspectives which may be progressively eliminated by a more and more astute sociology of knowledge.[14] The theory unfortunately leaves one important aspect of the process of rationalization out of account. Men are inclined to make the worse appear the better reason, not only unwittingly but wittingly. Ideology is a compound of ignorance and dishonesty. The dishonest element in it, the tendency of men to justify self-interest by making it appear identical with the common good, is an expression of the person, and not of the mind. It betrays a corrupted will, which is a mystery with which rationalism does not deal. Insofar as Freud does deal with the problem, at

---

[14] As, for instance, in Karl Mannheim's effort to overcome ideology by ferreting out the various bases of ideology. He hopes to lay the foundation for a rational politics by a rational purge of the irrational elements in moral and political ideals. See *inter alia* his *Ideology and Utopia* and *Man and Society.*

least in individual life, he arrives at morally cynical conclusions, thus moving toward the abyss of despair.[15]

The complacency of the liberal culture is most unshaken in America, where the social and political situation, which supported it, still bears some semblance to the stability of previous centuries. The opulence of American life and the dominant position of American power in the world create the illusion of a social stability which the total world situation belies. The absence of overt social conflict permits sentimental versions of social harmony and stability to arise, which are overtly refuted only by the fears and hatreds of racial antagonisms. The fragmentary and contradictory character of human virtues and ideals is recognized; but the abyss of meaninglessness is avoided by the confidence that a critical analysis of all historic political and moral positions will gradually establish the universal truth.

In Europe the movement from complacency to despair may be seen much more clearly than in America. The rise of Nazism in the past decade was, in one of its aspects, the growth of a demonic religion out of the soil of despair. Politically men were willing to entertain the perils of tyranny in order to avoid the dangers of anarchy; and spiritually they were ready to worship race, nation or power as god in order to avoid the abyss of meaninglessness.

The military defeat of this political religion has not altered the spiritual situation of modern culture essentially. The rise of French existentialism is another manifestation of the same despair. There are fortunately no immediate political perils in this expression of despair; for it contains no effort to escape from the continguent character of the human situation by the worship of false gods. It is, in fact, a remarkably consistent effort to remain within the abyss of despair and to abjure the obvious idolatries which seem to offer an escape. Existentialism recognizes that life and history are not as coherent rationally as the liberal culture assumed. It also knows that moral ideals are contingent and fragmentary. Lacking a faith which sees a higher coherence beyond the immediate incoherences, it seeks nevertheless to assert the meaning of the present moment and the present experience in defiance of the chaos of existence. Its islands of meaning in the sea of meaninglessness are, however, tiny and periodically inundated. Existentialism is a desparate affirmation of meaning within the framework of despair. It is a very accurate index of

[15] Cf. Sigmund Freud, *Civilization and Its Discontents.*

the spiritual crisis in contemporary culture.

Perhaps a more perfect example of the movement from complacency to despair in modern culture can be found in the thought of a typical liberal optimist. H. G. Wells was, in some respects, the most representative evolutionary idealist of the past generation. After the first world war his *Outline of History* expressed the characteristic hope of our culture. The forces and processes of history were, according to his conviction, moving toward a universal community, democratically organized. By 1933 when his *Shape of Things to Come* was published, a note of desperation became apparent in his optimism. He saw no possibility of overcoming the fragmentary, parochial, and contingent elements in the various human cultures except by a desperate expedient. Modern technicians, symbolized by a group of conspirational aviators, would establish a world authority, sufficiently powerful to dictate the standards of universal truth which would inform an educational program for the whole of mankind. This educational program would ultimately create the universal mind and the comprehensive culture, essential for the stability of the universal community. The movement of his thought from democracy to tyranny is evidence of his desperation.

Shortly before his death Mr. Wells' desperate optimism had finally degenerated to complete despair. He wrote: "A frightful queerness has come into life. Hitherto events have been held together by a certain logical consistency as the heavenly bodies have been held together by the golden cord of gravitation. Now it is as if the cord had vanished and everything is driven anyhow, anywhere at a steadily increasing velocity. . . . The writer is convinced that there is no way out, or around, or through the impasse. It is the end."[16]

The despair which follows upon complacency could not be more consistently or tragically expressed. The spiritual pilgrimage of Mr. Wells is an almost perfect record in miniature of the spiritual pilgrimage of our age, though in its totality it will not reveal so neat a pattern. Yet the general movement in our day is from complacency to despair. The Christian faith which "is perplexed, but not in despair" (II Corinthians 4:8) seemed completely irrelevant to a culture which had no perplexities. It has become relevant, though not necessarily acceptable, to a generation which has moved from faith without perplexity to despair. It is, in any event, the apprehension

[16] H. G. Wells, *The Mind at the End of Its Tether*, pp. 4-5.

of a wisdom which makes sense out of life on a different level than the worldly wisdom which either makes sense out of life too simply or which can find no sense in life at all.

The wisdom which leads to complacency seeks both to overcome the ambiguity of human existence by the power of reason and to deny the sinful and dishonest pretension in this enterprise. The wisdom which leads to despair understands the limits of reason. It also sees something of the dishonesty by which a more idealistic culture seeks to hide the contingent character of human knowledge and virtue, and the fanaticisms and power lusts which are the fruit of this pretension. The moral cynicism which results from this discovery is delicately balanced between complacency and despair. Insofar as it recognizes the power lusts and pretensions of other men and nations but not its own, it leads to a new and more terrible complacency. Insofar as it recognizes the sinfulness of all men, including the self, but knows of no forgiving love which can overcome this evil, moral cynicism is despair.

The Christian Gospel is negatively validated by the evidence that both forms of worldly wisdom, leading to optimism and to pessimism, give an inadequate view of the total human situation. This evidence is partly derived from the testimony which the optimists and the pessimists bear against each other. The optimists rightly insist that the pessimists do not fully appreciate the dignity of man, the integrity of human reason, and the tentative coherences of life and history which establish provisional realms of meaning. The pessimists rightly declare that the optimists do not understand the misery of man in the ambiguity of his subordination to and transcendence over nature; that they hide or willfully deny the elements of dishonesty and pretension in human culture which are the consequence of man's effort to obscure his true situation; and that they give a false estimate of the stability of cultures and civilization because they do not understand the destructive character of human pretensions.

The Christian Gospel is thus distinguished from both forms of worldly wisdom; but its truth lies closer to the testimony of the pessimists than the optimists because it is a truth which cannot be apprehended at all from the standpoint of intellectual, moral or social complacency. That is why Jeremiah condemns those prophets as false who make the "word of the Lord" to conform to the world's complacency by assuring those "who walketh after the imagination of their own heart, No evil shall come upon you" (Jeremiah 23:17). This also is the reason for Christ's preference of the moral derelicts over the righteous of his day; for the former have some contrite recognition of the real situation and the latter have not.

Yet the truth of the Christian Gospel is not logically established from the standpoint of the position of the pessimist, the moral cynic and the social catastrophist. There is no knowledge of the true God in it, and therefore neither hope of redemption through genuine repentance, nor confidence that a power, not our own, can complete what is fragmentary and purge what is evil in human life. Since this knowledge cannot be supplied by a further rational analysis of the human situation or the course of history, there is no force of reason which moves from despair to hope or transmutes remorse into repentance. Ultimately the acceptance of the truth of the Gospel is a gift of grace which stands beyond both forms of worldly wisdom and cannot be achieved by the testimony of either one against the other.

While the negative proof of the Christian truth cannot be transmuted into a positive one, which would compel conviction on purely rational grounds, there is nevertheless a positive apologetic task. It consists in correlating the truth, apprehended by faith and repentance, to truths about life and history, gained generally in experience. Such a correlation validates the truth of faith insofar as it proves it to be a source and center of an interpretation of life, more adequate than alternative interpretations, because it comprehends all of life's antinomies and contradictions into a system of meaning and is conducive to a renewal of life.

In pursuing the task of correlating the truth of the Gospel as apprehended by faith to truth otherwise known, Christian theology is subject to three temptations to error. Each error tends to destroy the redemptive power of the truth of faith. The first error is to regard the tuth of faith as capable of simple correlation with any system of rational coherence and as validated by such a correlation. Thus many modern versions of Christian theism are embarrassed by the traditional Christian trinitarian definitions of God and seek to construct a theistic metaphysical system without reference to it. Trinitarian definitions are indeed embarrassing rationally; but they are necessary to embody what is known about the character of God, as apprehended in faith's recognition of the revelation of divine mercy, to what is otherwise known about God. At worst such theistic interpretations may hardly be distinguished from pantheistic systems. At best they acknowledge God as creator, thus drawing upon what may be known about God in terms of "general revelation." Thereby they acknowledge that the world we know points beyond itself to a creative ground which we do not immediately know but yet apprehend by faith. But this worship of God the Creator may still be devoid of all the deeper problems of human existence for which the "mercy" of God is the answer.

Naturally the ascription of divinity to Christ is equally embarrassing in such systems of thought. This embarrassment is overcome by fitting Christ into some general scheme of the history of culture. He becomes the great teacher or exemplar of the moral ideal or either the anticipator or the culmination of the law of moral progress. His perfect love is regarded as a simple possibility for all men, if only they are able to recover knowledge of the "historic Jesus'" persuasiveness as a teacher of the law of love or his rigor as its lawgiver. The moral complacency of modern culture is supported, rather than challenged, by a faith which thus brings Christ into a system of simple historical possibilities.

The second error arises when the effort is made to guard the uniqueness of the truth of faith and to prevent its absorption into a general system of knowledge by insisting that Christian truth is miraculously validated and has no relation to any truth otherwise known. This is the error to which Protestant literalism is particularly prone. Its consequence is cultural obscurantism. The truth of faith, thus jealously guarded, degenerates into a miraculous historical fact. Miracles may be believed without the repentance which is the prerequisite of the renewal of life. The tendency to transmute a truth of faith, which can be known only by a person in the totality and wholeness of his life, into a miraculous fact, which the credulous but not the sophisticated may easily believe, accounts for the frequent spiritual aridity of Protestant orthodoxy. The whole Biblical story of redemption is not inwardly known in such orthodoxy. There is therefore no power of a new life in its wisdom and no grace in its truth. The knowledge of a series of miraculous events may be perfectly compatible with a graceless legalism or with racial and religious hatreds of every kind.

Failure to relate the truth of faith to other knowledge and experience furthermore leads to a cultural obscurantism which denies the obvious truths about life and history, discovered by modern scientific disciplines. The cultural obscurantism of this kind of literalism not only brings Christian truth in contradiction with the facts, known

L

by natural science and indisputable on their own level. It also makes that truth completely irrelevant to the truths discovered by the social, political, psychological, and historical sciences.

Ideally there should be a constant commerce between the specific truths, revealed by the various historical disciplines and the final truth about man and history as known from the standpoint of the Christian faith. In such a commerce the Christian truth is enriched by the specific insights which are contributed by every discipline of culture. But it also enriches the total culture and saves it from idolatrous aberrations. Thus every discipline of psychology and every technique of psychiatry may be appreciated as contributing to the cure of souls provided the self in its final integrity is not obscured by detailed analyses of the intricacies of personality, and provided techniques are not falsely raised into schemes of redemption. In the same manner the social and historical sciences may give constantly more accurate accounts of cause and effect in the wide field of human relations. But without relation to the Christian truth they finally generate structures of meaning which obscure the profounder perplexities of life, offer some plan of social enlightenment as a way of redemption from evil, and lose the individual in the integrity of his spirit to the patterns of cause and effect which they are able to trace.

The third error, to which Catholic rationalism is particularly prone, is to validate the truth of faith but to explicate it rationally in such a way that mystery is too simply resolved into ostensible rational intelligibility. The rational exposition of Christian trinitarianism illustrates this difficulty from the Christological controversies of the early church to this day. It is not possible to state the truth about God, as known from the standpoint of Christian faith, except in trinitarian terms. God was revealed in Christ in actual history. The Second Person of the Trinity thus defines that aspect of the divine power which is engaged in history, and which is known primarily by faith. The relation of the Son to the Father is most simply stated in the Scriptural word: "God so loved the world, that he gave his only begotten Son, that whosoever believeth in him should not perish, but have eternal life" (John 3:16). The relation of the Son to the Father, in which the Father's love is on the one hand the force of redemption and the Son's suffering is on the other hand the revelation of redemptive love in contrast to the "wrath" or the justice of the Father, reveals to us a partly understandable mystery, without the understanding of which either the Christian doctrine of redemption degenerates into

284

sentimentality or the Christian conception of law and justice degenerates into legalism. This is a mystery rich in meaning. If we seek to reduce it to simple intelligibility by pretending to know too much about the relation of Son to Father and to Holy Spirit, we fall either into an impossible tritheism or a too simple monism. In the same manner the doctrine of the Holy Spirit, as the third person of the Trinity is important, if we would understand that all forms of holiness and all signs of redemption in actual history are not merely extensions of human wisdom or human virtue but are the consequence of a radical break-through of the divine spirit through human self-sufficiency. Without relating these manifestations to God's nature, Christian faith degenerates into a shallow spiritualism. Yet this fact hardly justifies the long *"filioque"* controversy in Christian history in which theologians sought abortively either to prove or disprove that the Holy Spirit proceeded from only the Father or from both the Father and the Son.

The effort to validate the divine nature of Christ by attributing divine omniscience to the human person is an equally abortive attempt to explicate a truth about Christ, as known to faith, in rational terms, with the consequence of reducing it to rational nonsense.

Thus a modern Anglo-Catholic theologian engages in the tortuous effort to prove that Christ both was, and was not, omniscient. He does this by supposing that there was a "stratification of knowledge in such a way that quite apart from the experimental knowledge which he acquired by the normal human use of the intellect, the Christ includes in himself, by the infusion of omniscience which the divine person possesses through its real identity with the divine nature, the possession in principle of everything that is knowable by man." But he does not always use this possession because "the exercise of his knowledge is adjusted with the most precise and exquisite accuracy to the precise needs of every situation with which he is confronted." This picture of an omniscient person who usually hides his omniscience comes into conflict with the plain Scriptural confession that Jesus did not know the "day and hour" of the final judgment. Jesus' admission of ignorance, we are told, "is neither on the one hand a mere affectation which would be difficult to reconcile with truthfulness, nor yet on the other hand the sign of the absence of knowledge in the mind considered in its totality."[17]

It is difficult to understand what could possibly be gained by such implausible efforts. The meaning of Christ's revelatory power, as ap-

[17] E. L. Mascall, *Christ, the Christian and the Church*, p. 59.

prehended by faith, is imperiled and a logical absurdity takes its place.

It is interesting that Christian piety and art are usually closer to the truth than various theologies in seeking to symbolize the true nature of Christ in both the historical dimension and in the revelatory depth or height which reveals Jesus to be the Christ. Christian art wisely centers upon the Cross in seeking to portray this deeper significance of the person of Christ and of the whole drama of his life. Other portrayals easily degenerate into sentimentality. Christian piety follows the same course, though it is not insensible to the fact that the teachings of Christ have a rigor which point beyond simple historical possibilities and that the life of Christ is filled with signs of that suffering *Agape* of which the Cross is the supreme symbol. The Cross is the symbolic point where this story most obviously ceases to be merely a story in history and becomes revelatory of a very unique divine "glory," namely the glory and majesty of a suffering God, whose love and forgiveness is the final triumph over the recalcitrance of human sin and the confusion of human history.

That history is fulfilled and ended in this *Agape* of God, as revealed in Christ, is the basic affirmation of the Christian faith. Such a love both completes and contradicts every form of historic virtue. It cannot be comprehended as the completion of life, by faith, if that which stands in contradiction to it in historic forms of virtue and wisdom is not contritely acknowledged. If this truth of faith ceases to be a truth requiring such repentance, it ceases to be a truth which contains "grace," which is to say it loses its power to complete what is fragmentary and to overcome what is wrongly completed in human existence.

If the truth of faith merely becomes a "fact" of history, attested by a miracle, or validated by ecclesiastical authority, it no longer touches the soul profoundly. If it is made into a truth of reason which is validated by its coherence with a total system of rational coherence, it also loses its redemptive power. The truth of the Christion Gospel is apprehended at the very limit of all systems of meaning. It is only from that position that it has the power to challenge the complacency of those who have completed life too simply, and the despair of those who can find no meaning in life.

XVII / A PHILOSOPHER
OF A SINGLE
CIVILIZATION

"IN THE RIPENESS OF YEARS I AM INCLINED TO A MOMENT OF PROPHECY," writes William Ernest Hocking in the opening of his latest book, *The Coming World Civilization* (Harper & Brothers, 1957). Professor Hocking is eighty-four, and while not all the scope of his prophecy is given in his selection for *This Is My Philosophy* enough is here to show that Professor Hocking believes there is some hope for man. "I wish," he says, "to discern what character our civilizations, now unsteadily merging into a single world civilization, are destined to take in the foreseeable future, assuming that we have a foreseeable future."

About his own personal philosophy of life, Professor Hocking, who has varied his activities over the fields of education, religion and philosophy, as well as active participation in the responsibilities of peace and war, says: "I could sum up my life in four words—I have enjoyed living. I have found it a wonderful and holy thing. And . . . in the several lives lived abreast, or rather braided . . . I surely ought to put in somewhere the strand of fighting; for what is life without its inner angers, wills-to-eliminate this and that blemish from a fair world? And what is love without the hatred of all that destroys or degrades it? There is a lot to hate, *ergo* a lot to fight."[1]

He was born August 10, 1873, into a Cleveland home in which science and religion were joined, son of a Canadian-born doctor and a mother of old New England stock. Professor Hocking says his religion was "undermined" early, in his first readings in philosophy, mathematics and science. "Dr. Hocking, my father, was very keen for the scientific phase of medicine, as well as for its philosophy. As a good Methodist he had a shelf of books for 'Sunday reading.' One of these books was Drummond (Scottish biologist), *Natural Law in the Spiritual World*. I got hold of that book as a kid of thirteen; noted

[1] *Twentieth Century Authors*, H. W. Wilson Co., 1955.

his frequent references to a stranger called Herbert Spencer; made up my mind that Spencer would bear being looked into; got his *First Principles* out of the public library and read it with increasing fascination until one day, Father, looking over my shoulder indicated that this book was unfit to be read by one of my years—would I kindly take it back to the library. As a dutiful son I obeyed. Next day I took it out again, read it by stealth in the haymow over the horses' stalls— I being in charge of the stable. Father's fears were correct: Spencer finished me off!"

At twenty-one Professor Hocking first read William James and set himself to four years of teaching in the public schools of Iowa to earn his way to study under the Harvard master. "One begins by being educated, and goes on to educate others while continuing being educated," he wrote in a recent autobiographical note. His own philosophical system, influenced by both William James and Josiah Royce, as well as by early initiation into science and engineering, took its independent development in the early part of the century. His thinking he has described as composed, philosophically, of "realism . . . mysticism . . . idealism also, its identity not broken."

After receiving his Ph.D. from Harvard in 1904, he taught at Andover Theological Seminary from 1904 to 1906, at the University of California from 1906 to 1908, when he joined the philosophy department at Yale. In 1914, he left to become professor of philosophy at Harvard, remaining until his retirement in 1943. He is now emeritus professor and lives in Madison, New Hampshire. He married Agnes Boyle O'Reilly, now deceased, and has a son and two daughters. His wife, of a completely different background, was the daughter of the poet and editor of the Boston *Pilot*, herself a lover of poetry and people, "instinctively a teacher and of an astounding courage. . . . We had fifty years from 1905 to 1955 together. Our experience in education was joint experience," Professor Hocking writes. "What I have done in this field is hers-and-mine."

His interests in education, philosophy, political and legal theory, and religion have taken him into many countries and posts. His studies after graduation from Harvard were continued at the universities of Göttingen, Berlin and Heidelberg; he has been Gifford Lecturer at Glasgow University, Hibbert Lecturer at Oxford and Cambridge, lecturer on the Juridical Faculty at Leyden, and he was a trustee of Lingnan University, Canton, China. He was instructor of military engineering at Harvard in the First World War, later an observer at the American and British fronts, and in 1948 a lecturer at Munich and Erlangen under the Office of Military Government.

Professor Hocking's first book, in 1912, expressed a theory of the human self which he later described as a "break-through" from the prevailing modern theories stemming from Descartes—theories which made the self a solitary monad—into a recognition of "intersubjectivity." The book was entitled *The Meaning of God in Human Experience*. Its originality was not that it denounced "solipsism"[2]—many denounced it, and more ignored the problem—but that by careful analysis it showed the root of the Cartesian error, and justified common sense in its assumption of an experience of community with other minds, or, as Whitehead later put it, *"Here we are*; we don't go behind that, we begin with it."* With this analysis first propounded by Hocking in his thesis of 1904, the normal intersubjectivity of human experience, he believes, ceases to conflict with the scientific outlook, and the "modernity" of the Cartesian era, characterized by a split between subjective and objective analysis, is overcome. Though the new analysis "has taken until now to become generally accepted," the world of thought has now fairly passed beyond the Cartesian phase, he thinks, or "beyond modernity."

His latest book treats the significance of the "secularization of modern life, the extrusion of religion, not wholly, but from omnicompetence, in science, law and politics, business, education and the fine arts." He regards the secularization "as an advance, having a certain necessity and therefore a degree of permanence . . . and destined to work not only to the net advantage of the West, but also to that of a reconceived Christianity." He believes it has helped to cure Christianity of a "hampering Westernism, revealing to each (the secular movements and Christianity) its latent universality, and stripping both for the severe labors of world functions lying before whatever is universal in art or science or law or religion, and whatever can become universal."

Even the "despair" of the existentialists Professor Hocking does not see as unrelieved and hopeless gloom, as he indicates in a "Note on Despair" he has appended, for this book, from a paper in *Philosophy and Phenomenological Research*. Commenting on the French philosopher Gabriel Marcel, a Christian existentialist, Professor Hocking hints at the possibility of a dialectic in man's despair which may

[2] That the self is the only existent thing.

289

"enable him to pass out of modernity with its split-mentality into what lies 'beyond modernity,' the era here heralded in whose dawn we now live."

Tentative Outlook for the State and Church

BY WILLIAM ERNEST HOCKING

Our concern is with the shape of the civilization to come. As guiding lines we consider especially the place in that civilization of the state and the religious community, since each of these undertakes in its own way to reflect and satisfy the whole of human nature.

We have first examined the state. For if, as intelligent humanists, we can get on without religion, the state becomes our trust. However great our faith in the human individual, we have never thought him self-sufficient. Man is a creator; but he is a creator who must first be created. If it were only on the basis of everyday wants, he must live in society; and while the economic necessity is instructive as to his shaping and being shaped, we are today less than ever persuaded by the Marx-Engels following—illuminating for its time—that the logic of his economic needs can explain man's social history or his cultural prowess, still less outline his destiny. As modern men, we still see with Aristotle the political community as the specific instrument of "the good life" in its human amplitude; and modern man still nearer approaches Aristotle's persuasion that in this respect the state is "nearly if not quite self-sufficient." We recall that Greece had almost nothing corresponding to a church. As for economy, we see that it is the political community that shapes the economy, not the economy that makes the nation. It is the state which holds within the grasp of a unified will-to-power both the economic and the social needs of man.

This does not mean that we have ever mistaken the state for the cosmos, or imagined that for practical purposes the state is equivalent to "the whole." We simply see in it the one representative of the totality of being *with which we can converse*: it is for us the responsible, and in general the responsive, image of the whole of things. We may in a sense pray to it, and sometimes be heard: of what other symbol of totality can this be said? The state, like all things human, is finite: and the gap between the finite and the infinite remains—infinite. If, as some say, and I am with them, it is with the infinite that we have always to do, the state must be infinitely short of complete competence. Agreed. But the gap that is logically infinite may be psychologically negligible. If, as seems evident, everything tangible is finite, and the state's purview reaches to all the relevant tangibles, trust in the state, slowly perfectible through infinite time, seems the path of available wisdom. Secular modernity has, in effect, committed itself to this experiment. We have followed some of its findings.

At this its strongest point, we have found modernity vulnerable, and with modernity, the state. Its Achilles' heel, if we are right, is not itself a tangible and overt weakness—say the rationalizing or technicalizing of society, or the functional character that thus descends on the individual's self-definition, or the simple existence of the "mass man" with his diminished and derivative mentality. These are indeed disturbing traits of the life of modern man, proud in his newly won dignity, freedom, and scientific power, and those who, like Ortega y Gasset, dwell on them are on the right scent. But as evils-flowing-from-goods they are, I believe, symptoms of a malady simpler and deeper rooted, an inner surrender, the gradual abandonment of the individual's native rapport with a genuine—not representative—total-and-real, an immediate Thou-art, which is at the same time his avenue of rapport with his fellow men.

With this surrender has come the tacit relinquishment of his certitude of the universality of his private experience and therefore of his confidence. For man in the same moment, and by the same fact, that makes him solidary-at-root with his tribe and with humanity, is individualized and set beyond crowd pressures. It is his private tryst with the Absolute, whereby his certitude is at once every man's certitude so that he can think and speak for man-in-general, that normally enables him to hold his own in presence of whatever strains arise from social organization. Losing that rapport, he loses what makes him a state-sustaining being. The state by itself cannot insure its own perpetuity.

This diagnosis, which I have offered as an experimental and also as a dialectical outcome of modernity, exemplifies an ancient paradox, the paradox of power. The secular state has become not only the greatest of tangible powers, but in concrete terms, the sole power—the trusted repository of all the physical forces of the community. And Leviathan at the peak of his all-might is lamed. By what? By deficiency in the field of motivation, a lack of control in the region of "mere feeling." It is the nonassertive Tao of Lao-tse that still bends the strongest to its demand.

But while a diagnosis may and should point to a remedy, it is not itself a prescription. The integrating of human motives is the business of religion; but religion is not a commodity that can be prescribed, nor is it a staple. It exists for itself alone, and while always the same, as the bond between the soul of man and the Real, it varies internally with its specific tasks. For what that bond requires depends on the depth and character of the separation between the soul and its object due to varying experience and thought. The Real is by definition eternal; but the religious questioning of modern man is not necessarily met by the expositions of religion for premodern man. That issue lies before us.

Meanwhile, if we may tentatively assume that there exists a mode of religion prepared or preparable to mend the lost rapport between the modern soul and the Absolute, our analysis provides certain indications of the role of its community in any future civilization.

Because religion can never serve as a "means only"—a means for curing the ills of the state—the dependence between church and state is not mutual. *The state is dependent for its vital motivation upon an independent religious community.* It must therefore allow the free exercise of religion so far as religion is honest—i.e., so far as it serves its function of integrating the human will in view of the whole—simply because nothing that is not free and universal can be religion.

This duty of the state does not infringe the state's conceptual sovereignty, nor is it in general onerous. It leaves sovereignty intact, because the duty in question is not a legal duty: it is a duty arising simply from the logic of the state's self-preservation.

It is not, in general, onerous, because the civilized state takes it for granted that its citizens are full-grown men, having their own hold on principle; it knows that it can be served only by individuals who are first of all servants of truth and honor. To this extent, the modern state is entirely at home with the principle that the primary loyalty of its subjects is and ought to be beyond itself. At the same time, the possibility of clash between state and church is written into the situation.

For example, the religious community is by definition universal in extent as well as in norms of will: it speaks not primarily to the man-within-the-nation but to the man-within-the-world. It spins the web of a potential world society. Reaching across all boundaries it fosters a moral unity among men without which international order lacks a necessary precondition—that of psychological fraternity. For peace and order must be built on mutuality of feeling before they can be built on laws and powers. This preliminary work toward world community can never be of indifference to the state. On the whole it tends to be in accord with national purposes; but it can bring a radical criticism to bear on national egoism, the more effective as its own fellowship becomes actually as well as intentionally world-wide.

And the state has no choice but to accept this possibility of clash, whether in foreign policy or in domestic affairs, a possibility which—in spite of all efforts to make a firm line between the standards of politics and morals—effectively limits its freedom of action to courses that do not massively violate the consciences of its people. The state has no choice, because the subjects for their part—unable to escape their knowledge of the state's finitude—have themselves no choice but to find their primary loyalties in whatever glint they may discover through inward clues of an absolute good.

It can never be the state's duty—as premodernity sometimes assumed possible—to deduce positive law and policy from the premises of religion and ethics, for which these premises are incompetent, as Aquinas clearly saw. But it will always be the duty of the state, unless by persuasion it can transvalue the values of its people, to create policies that do not contradict these premises. This is a principle of politics as old as Confucius, in which Machiavelli shrewdly concurs, a principle which will remain valid as long as the state must live in the freely accorded respect and consent of its members.

But if the state has a duty, so has the church. For the continuing historical community of religion, undertaking to offer an unshakable world affirmation in which primary loyalties may be anchored, must probe the depth of the soul's lostness in the given era of man's thought, even while distraction and despair may be far off. Religion has frequently to disturb the undisturbed, to create anew a sense of that moral aloneness-with-the-Absolute which is the sole security against the anaesthesia of crowd insouciance. For the individual, circumstance and the current temper may benumb his "cosmic anxiety"; yet that anxiety remains a measure of his realism, not of his folly, it must be the groundwork of all his building. Religion must always spur the soul not to evade experience nor new-opening truth but to descend into the caverns, psychological and other, that science or public crisis may open for exploration. Religion must *descend with the soul,* while keeping intact the thread of recovery of a true universality. "Saving the soul" in this sense must be the ever-renewed and ever-changing duty of religion.

It becomes here especially apparent that in this duty the state has no competence; and yet depends for its vitality on that well-grounded firmness of character which it cannot of itself supply. With this understanding, the relation of church and state cannot be either now or in the future one of rivalry, nor of duplication in the task of interpreting human nature. It is a natural symbiosis, on the ground of the priority and autonomy of the religious consciousness.

But what can we discern of the shape of the civilization that is to succeed what we call modernity? What guidance can history give us as to the passage toward recovery? Is humanity perhaps following a rhythm, now passing from its upward to its downward phase, so that we must anticipate a period of confusion, if not of *Untergang?*

History has indeed its repetitions of rhythmic tracery, lending force to the judgment that civilizations, too, are mortal. But as a whole, history never repeats; partly because civilizations have seldom perished —perhaps never *in toto.* Commonly in their phase of ebb they have injected something of their essence into a rising movement elsewhere, ruder and fuller of will-to-live—within chaos, continuity. By whatever it thus inherits, that rising movement starts from an altered level, excluding the concept of recurrence. Is this inherited element ephemeral and accidental, or may some of it keep its place?

There is in history a certain tough cumulativeness at two levels— levels at which mankind cannot forget—the level of technic and the level of insight. At these levels there is set into human nature *a mental ratchet* which prevents total slipping back, a selective holding function which can easily escape notice amid apparently unlimited change. Arts have been lost, but not all arts—the art of fire-making, the taming of animals, the conquest of the sea, the art of printing. . . . Sciences have been lost, even astronomies and geometries, but not the multiplication table, nor once devised in India the arithmetical zero, nor once mastered in Greece the science of proof. . . . Poetry is born profuse as the flowers of the field, and vanishes as they do; and there is poetry the race cannot forget. . . . Religions likewise. In religion, the unforgettable may be more evident than the rationally final, and perhaps ought to be.

I point out simply that there are odd durabilities that cut through the vast rhythm of rising and falling civilizations, checking each fall at a higher point, and that may in due time put an end to the ending. History, for good reasons, finds it hard to identify the cumulative characters. Yet unless they are recognized the total structure of history threatens to be that of a record—on the one hand of perpetual passing, *das Einmalige,* or on the other, of the recurrent and sterile, losing sight of its most significant ingredient, *the unlosable.*

If through the role of the unlosable—without appeal to any "law of progress"—we can eliminate to some extent the rule of rhythm, and so of periodic downfall in the broad swing of human affairs, as well as of the "eternal occurrence," might we not with the same stroke *eliminate the element of plurality* in our picture of civilization? In my judgment, this is now taking place.

Today, we seem to stand on the threshold of a new thing, civilization in the singular. We still have civilizations: the distinction between The East and The West still has validity. And what Toynbee calls the aggression of the West upon the East has had an indubitable basis in fact. But whether it has been the whole fact, I doubt; and certainly, it has long ceased to be the main part of the fact. Much of what was once transmitted from West to East by the methods of imperialism has become self-propagating—first imposed, then sought, then demanded as of right. A siphon flow has usually to be forced to begin with. No one who has seen a Western technical school in the Orient, or an agricultural station, or a hospital, can entertain the picture of "aggression" as the dominant fact in these fields, though aggression has frequently been the frame in which these transactions have occurred.

In any case, our present period is one of general and reciprocal osmosis of thought, technique, art and, law. The assimilation proceeds from both sides; though the West is only beginning to realize its potential property in the unlosables of the East. These processes can neither be stopped nor undone; the lines that have "gone forth into all the world" cannot return to their origin. The making of a single civilization is contained in the two concepts, the universal and the unlosable, plus the simple existence of the arts of unlimited human communication.

Hence we may say that for the first time our entire world space is permeated with ideas which, as Locke said about truth and the keeping of faith, "belong to man as man and not as a member of society." Here and there in the Orient there is still revulsion from clinging localisms of Western thought and practice, but none toward what we may call the Clean Universals, the sciences, the mathematics, the technics—these it claims *not as borrowings from the West, but as its own.* In giving birth to the universal, the West has begotten something that can never again be private property.

For the first time, too, among these ideas are certain discoveries of the inner dynamics of material particles which deliver into our hands the power to destroy massively whatever man has built—including conceivably, though not probably, the recondite trails leading to those very discoveries. The era of "the civilizations" being past, what we now enter is either the era of civilization or the era of universal desolation. I shall write as though only the former alternative were before us; but I shall be writing of the conditions under which alone that alternative can be realized.

What is the extent, at present, of this common property?

As I have suggested, not all parts of a civilization spread with equal pace. Custom, happily, remains local; together with folklore and folk arts, and therewith the *Volksgeist* itself, in which Savigny rightly saw the genius of positive law. These all have universal ingredients, but also ingredients incurably local; they are not "clean universals." It is the abstract universal that most swiftly makes its way, the logic and mathematic, the commercial habits which in the nature of the case have to cross boundaries, so that commercial and maritime law are the earliest ingredients of a working *jus gentium.* Among technical devices, arts of agriculture spread more slowly than arts of metallurgy and mining. Political forms, having to link together past, present, and future of a persistent national group, cannot spread as easily as a turn of industrial artifice.

Nevertheless, there are no important political or legal ideas that are not today shelled out from their local wrappings and everywhere discussed as universal. Libraries of Buddhist monasteries, and even of the department stores of Tokyo prior to the war, commonly contained political classics in European languages, not omitting the works of Marx and Engels. The budding Civil Code of prewar China, as the codes of Japan and Siam at that time relatively new, was fully cognizant of earlier European and American codes. The Chinese code was especially alive to the universal aspect of a workable civil law; the preface to the first volume, *General Principles* (in English translation, Shanghai, 1930), refers to the elements of "juridical science which are now becoming world-wide," while indicating that the principles of the law of real property and of the family must retain Chinese localisms.

Partly because of the more rapid spread of the abstract universal, and partly because of the instinct of modernity for separation of distinguishable functions, the modern state everywhere tends to be the secular state, in Asia as well as in the West. And so far as this is the case, the new states of Asia inherit the problems which tend to enfeeble the secular state—as I pointed out earlier.

With this illustration in mind, I hazard the generalization that it is precisely because of the superior speed and penetrating power of the abstract universals that the coming civilization is threatened by an unbalance which may imperil its advent.

The claim of the East upon the universals of the West is invulnerable. It is supported by contributions from the Orient to fields of theory formerly considered the peculiar provinces of Western minds. Fields which are essentially abstract, as mathematics and logic, raise no question of balance. Fields in which the universal is extracted from its setting, as in law or cosmology, may raise such question. Let me illustrate:

The theory of "rights" as a basis of law is one of the abstractions whose potential menace to the societies of its origin we have already noticed. It has nevertheless a universal trait which the nineteenth century has been unable, with the united denunciation of its leading schools of jurisprudence, wholly to repress. The new nation-states of our era, eastern as well as western, totalitarian as well as liberal, have been unable to escape at least lip service to the rights of the natural man. The elaborate Declaration made by United Nations was not addressed to democracies alone; and the Soviet Constitution of 1936 has a place for the idea.[3] It has been the pride of the modern state of the

[8] When the subcommission engaged in formulating this Declaration came to consider the "right to work," the Soviet delegate favored an unrestricted assertion of that right, whereas Mrs. Eleanor Roosevelt, in the chair of the subcommittee, demurred as representing the American view that economic conditions may not always allow everyone to be employed. The Soviet delegate urged that the Declaration must present not the actual but the right! The Soviet view prevailed. Today (1955) in the U.S.A. it is labor—i.e., organized labor—that contests the universality of the "right to work."

West that it can concede to its individual members the maximum of liberty and right without losing its coherence (a point which drew the admiring comment of Hegel, presumably with England in mind). But just on this account, the maximum in question confesses having given the highest possible gage to the uncontrollable factor of individual morale. And the contemporary Western individual is no longer the custom-and-conscience-borne person of John Locke, nor yet of Blackstone of Jefferson. He presents, as we have noted, a far wider political incalculability. And if this is true in lands still aware of traditional premodern intangibles of social control, what of lands whose intangibles are far different?

And in both hemispheres today, this incalculability is increased by the swift persuasive force of an abstract universal in the field of cosmology, on which I have barely touched.

It belongs to the empirical conscience of modern science to relieve nature, not alone of all purpose in the shape of "final causes," but as well of all quality and value. If "nature" is synonymous with the cosmos, we men inhabit a universe purposeless and meaningless, a realm of fact and event ideally mathematical in process, ideally empty of choice. If this is indeed "the Real" with which we have to do, our human purposes find there no objective support. But Descartes, who on one side of his dualism has given us this purpose-purged world picture, is the same as he who on the other side has given us the sole certitude of the subjective I-think. May we then take refuge in our subjective being, claiming not only the "secondary qualities," but the entire realm of value as our own? Since values have no other source, they are "our kingdom"; they impose no obligation—we are free to make them as we will. Indeed, since there is nothing in the nature of things to steady our aim, we are foredoomed to this freedom; and if, as M. Sartre sees it, our value-setting decision tends—in strangely Kantian fashion—to universalize its maxim, it can be attended with the unique anguish of unguided responsibility.

But this same empirical conscience that provides the purposeless universe allows us no rest in value-setting subjectivity. For eventually it turns its searching light upon man himself as an object within nature: it creates a science of man, a psychology, a sociology, an anthropology. And since the human phenomenon cannot disavow the character of the whole, it, together with its value-setting activities, must share the resulting desiccation: value-setting is itself a product of valueless necessity.

Our modern self-awareness is thus torn between two opposing pictures of its own nature, each claiming a certain necessity—not pacing along in parallel time orders as Spinoza would have them do—but each professing to swallow the other, and neither of them offering a foothold for the notion of a right common to all men.

We cannot abandon our empirical conscience, and its consequences. The methods of a value-free science are genuine universals, however abstract. And this theory of human rights, renascent in the present century, becoming part of a world-wide political pattern, without the conceptions of human nature that once made democracy inwardly strong, can only contribute to its disintegration, and tend to dissolve the coming civilization even while we build it.

But we must look again at this scientific world picture which is at the heart of at least part of the political embarrassment of our time, and which, like our individualism, cannot be simply rejected. For this world picture has also become an integral part of the entire contemporary civilization. The present moment is indeed one of widespread revolt against what Fechner called the "night view" of nature—that purposeless and qualityless cause-tight universe which a perfected science, including the sciences of man, would insist upon. His classic statement deserves rereading, for its prophecy is fulfilled in our day. Its opening represents an experience of perhaps 1840, when he was recovering from an eye malady which had compelled him to give up his university post. I translate some of the opening paragraphs:

One morning I sat on a bench in the Leipzig Rosenthal in the neighborhood of the little Swiss chalet, and looked through an opening among the bushes over the wide and lovely meadow there spread out, in order to refresh my ailing eyes on its expanse of green. The sun was bright and warm . . . There were flowers . . . butterflies . . . birds . . .; and notes from a morning concert reached my ear. But for one accustomed to thinking, gradually upon this enjoyment of the senses a play of thought began to spin itself out. . . .

Strange illusion, said I to myself. In reality is everything before me and around me Night and Silence; the sun that seems to me so blazing-bright that I refrain from turning my eyes to it, is in truth only a dark hall seeking its way in perfect gloom. The flowers, butterflies, deceive with their colors, the violins and flutes with their tones. In this universal darkness, desolation, silence engulfing heaven and earth, there are scattered beings, as it were (conscious) points, inwardly illumined, colored, sounding; they emerge from the night and sink back into it, without leaving anything behind of light and sound. . . . So today, and so from the beginning, and so will it be forever. . . .

How could I come on such absurd thoughts? . . . They are the thoughts of the entire thinking world around me. However else they differ, in this, philosophers and physicists, Darwinians and Anti-Darwinians, orthodox and rationalists, reach each other the hand. This is not a building stone, it is *the foundation stone* of the contemporary world view.

This is the night view! And, as Fechner continues, "if the world had ever presented to itself the complete improbability, the entire weakness of the ground of this view as they came to me in that hour, it could never have become a world view."

And with this illumination—for it was such—Fechner finds complete confidence that as day succeeds night, so the day view will eventually succeed the night view.[4] Certainly the purposeless universe is the negation in advance of all religion in the sense of a cosmic call to right living, or a rootage in the Real of man's subjective valuations.

Nevertheless, that night view is itself an achievement of the first magnitude. It is a conception made possible by the mathematical genius of modernity, and by the empirical honor of a host of scientific observers. The building of that corporate body of truth called science is a monumental accomplishment of thought disciplined by a relentless moral ideal. A godless world picture? Yes; unless, as Gandhi seemed to think, truth is itself a god; for truth as an abiding and growing totality is certainly not a material structure. As a product of honor-governed thought the edifice of science can never be abandoned, even though the world it displays, devoid of inherent purpose, is inanimate, and in this sense a dead world.

Both in its value-purged structure and in its extent, it is a world in which man is lost. Hegel remarks of the Roman world that there for the first time the soul of man could be thoroughly lost. In our present immeasurably vaster world room of uncountable galaxies and unsayable time ranges—all indifferent to human fate—the lostness of

[4] Gustav Theodor Fechner (1801-87), professor of physics in Leipzig, and the chief initiator of experimental and metrical psychology, was a thinker whose genius broke through the crust of then prevalent conceptions of nature founded on a Cartesian-Newtonian physics. In 1879 he published a small book called *The Day View over against the Night View (Die Tagesansicht gegenueber der Nachtansicht)*.

the human soul attains a depth incomparably greater.

And note that this is an exigency no prior civilization has faced. Neither India nor Egypt nor China nor Greece had any conception of the dead world of astrophysics implied in the clear vision of Descartes. Karma has indeed an inexorable legality; but it is a legality sensitive to moral qualities, hence not possibly inanimate. In none of these earlier civilizations had the physical and the mental been sundered, still less the sense qualities of nature from the equationable qualities. For instance, a Chinese philosopher mentioned to me as a point of superiority the fact that China "had *no Descartes*." Prior to our seventeenth century there had never been anywhere a "bifurcation of nature" such as Whitehead has well named and denounced, together with Goethe and Fechner. And this bifurcation is without doubt an unnatural malady. But unless this malady is experienced, the actual implications of scientific method have not been fully encountered. It is necessary to the soul's maturity that the thought of man should descend into this pit of the meaningless universe. If he is to be saved from that pit, his metaphysical insight, his religion, must descend with him.

And in point of fact, this his religion has already by anticipation done.

For if we rightly read the story of the genesis of modern science, and answer the question why its relentless logic appeared only in Europe, we shall see that it is the religion of Europe which begot the empirical conscience, and thus indirectly all its fruits. It is not an accident that Bacon in formulating the principle of empirical observation fell into a form of words recalling the fundamental paradox of Christian morals, "He that loseth his life for my sake shall find it." Bacon's words are, "We cannot command nature except by obeying her"—clearly the mental phase of that same paradox. It is the willful curbing of self-will which had been the discipline of Christian morals for a millennium and a half.[5] It was the purposeful exclusion of purpose from the field of theoretical physics that swung the door open to a universal science and technology.

Once we have traced this concept of the meaningless universe to its moral origins, we can begin to interpret its apparent threat. The original moral purpose is a purpose to "objectify." But it cannot objectify itself—it may *per contra* even forget itself; yet it cannot expunge itself from the world picture. The cause-tight character of that

[5] I have commented on this parental relationship in *What Man Can Make of Man*, 26 f.

universe is a property, not of the whole but solely of what can be objectified and set into calculable group relations: the night view, then, valid for its own data, is an abstraction: it omits *quality*—yet quality is part of the fact; *consciousness*—yet consciousness is the condition of any value or "importance" whatever; *volition*—the response to meaning and truth—yet volition is *there*!

The night view, I say, is an abstraction; but it is a *necessary abstraction*. Necessary not alone for the community of scientific labor, but also because it is only the nonpurposive that purpose can be wholly free to utilize. It is only an inanimate world segment that can be exploited for human end without consideration or compunction. If all actual being were conscious and purposive, plowing a field would be inflicting microscopic tragedies on an immense scale! Hence those who like Fechner and Whitehead seek to remedy the appalling vacuousness of nature's intricate fabric by a universal reanimation are, I fear, surrendering a genuine and world-changing human advance.

When it is once seen that the purpose of science cannot extrude purpose and value from an empirical account of the real, the essential step is taken; and the succeeding steps must preserve an equally rigorous economy of hypothesis. The purpose which has revealed the purposeless process *within nature* has for its goal, what? The goal of the explorer, who must climb Annapurna "because it is there"? Yes. The mapping of our finite situation within the endless wonder of fact? Yes. A fading hope of practical adjustments of human living to infinite contingency? Perhaps. But at least this: a recovery of proportion, of fearlessness toward the limitless inanimate, through some glimpse of the ulterior purpose of the simple existence of any island of purpose whatever. The progress of physical science has its own intrinsic joy of mastery—it needs no ulterior aim; but with the mastery implied in its powerful (and beautiful) equations, there is joined the anticipation of a further mastery of "understanding." And it is in this sense that "to master nature" we first yield to her our unreserved empirical "obedience."

For this reason, I can only with qualification follow Toynbee in his judgment that the modern period has rejected the guidance of religion in accepting the guidance of man-made science. Unless I am mistaken, the characteristic development of science in modern Europe is not only a corollary of the religion of Europe but in a significant sense part of that religion. Scientific empiricism is simply the constant and unreserved will to truth in yielding one's preconceptions and wishes to the evidence of fact and of the universal lawfulness embodied in event.

The vast defection of modernity is not that it has been scientific but that its science has been at critical points untruthful and therefore unscientific. Through excess of zeal and through forgetting the auspices of its own search for truth it has made or implied metaphysical assertions to which it has no right, such as that mathematical nature is the whole of reality, and that what empirical science can show of man is the whole of human nature. A scrupulous empiricism of the positivist type would refrain from any such implication. A wider empiricism shows both of these judgments false.

A truthful science will admit that in the strict sense of the term there is no science of man; there is science only of the manikin, the robot. Man embodies the duality of the world, the events which are his life flow both from reasons (including ends) and from causes; but they flow from causes only by the consent of his reasons. If he fails to eat he will die; but his instinctive eating is none the less an act of rational will. The life process of man is end-seeking, involving an organism of causes; it is definitely not one of causes excluding ends. And the end-seeking is a function of his interpretation of reality. In a living universe it may become a phase of love; and that love a participation in a purpose which is the final cause of the whole. On the validity of this interpretation, a truthful science passes no judgment.

But the untruthful science has permeated our incipient world civilization, and is especially deadly where the course of science has entered new ground. The vices of the West become the poison of the East, which has no acquired immunity. In the transmissions of culture, a new civilization frequently tends to borrow the perversities of the old; and in this present matter, the englobement of all world process and of human nature in the nexus of physical law, with the resulting secularization of all life, has a peculiar plausibility and sanction. The character of the ensuing stage of history will depend much on whether with this perversity there can go also the specific remedy already potentially present in the West.

The immediate practical suggestion would appear to be that with the science should go the religion from which its method sprang, both in the West and in the East. This suggestion is significant, but only on two conditions: One, that Christianity in the West should recover its vitality, and reconceive its message, to the extent of meeting in its own house the malaise of its own offspring. Two, that Christianity can show itself universal and not "western," and therefore as belonging—with as good a claim as that of science—to all men, not as something borrowed or imported or imposed from outside, but as their own birthright.

These are questions to be pursued further.

A NOTE ON DESPAIR

The "tragic sense of life" of which Unamuno[6] speaks, and to which existential philosophy bears witness, is not to be set over against a fundamental joy in living as an alternative view: both views are veracious. The tragic aspect of our being is a necessary preparation for emotional security and freedom. It is essential to the task of philosophy in our time to take this tragedy upon itself in full measure; otherwise it can have nothing to say to mankind. It must follow the path of doubt. And it must do so with a similar faith—or at least a similar hope—that the path of doubt in its own completion will light upon the dialectical revelation of certitude. The existential movement in its broader character may prove to be a *Cartesian dialectic of the passions.* How this may take place I can here but sketchily suggest. . . . In the same sense in which *summa jus* can become *summa injuria,* the height of civilization is precisely the condition in which the frustration of high hopes means the deepest perdition. The moment of the achieved mastery of nature, the possession of ultimate secrets and ultimate powers, the full wonder of science and the machine-that-seems-to-think—this is the moment of the most appalling emptiness of spirit, the most unbelievable treasons to human sensitivity: *summa ratio summa corruptio.*

The lostness of contemporary man is not the lostness that weighed on Kierkegaard: it is not the terror toward an undying Hell that besets us. The source of despair today has an opposite theme: not the malign possibilities of another world but the visible danger that what we see of this world may be all there is to see! What we see is the moment-to-moment boundary of our being, the nothingness that completes itself in death, our own and that of the race: in such a world, riddled the while with horror-filled actualities, how can a being aspiring and infinite be other than condemned to frustration? And

[6] Miguel de Unamuno, the Spanish philosopher (1864–1936).

in just this world we are nevertheless condemned to engage and to act as men: is it possible?

It is always in order to inquire whether and how this dark world-picture can sustain any passion for justice, such as alone can redeem the world of technology—whether it is to be supplemented by an order of mystery, in Marcel's terms, lying nearer the real than the order of nature: this, the true metaphysical inquiry should have precedence of all else. But we may also follow the Cartesian clue in asking whether at the heart of world-despair there may be a glint of affirmation.

World-despair begins in world-condemnation on the score of the incidence of pain and suffering, indiscriminate, meaningless, devoid of justice, rendering the notion of a world-justice repellent. Schopenhauer was concerned only with the pain itself, not with any question of its justice; and finding pain inseparable from the life of will, he condemned the world as a product of will. His cure was simple: reverse the will to live, and thus uncreate the world! Existentialism rejects the pain-calculus as decisive, and still more the cure by de-creation, or by any form of escape by world-flight. Sartre finds a palliative—hardly a remedy—in the euphoria of a self-building freedom, overcoming the palsy of a cause-and-effect naturalism whereby, via the science of man, we must see ourselves as products of nature: man is product of nothing anterior—of no nature, no society, no God—man makes himself and chooses his own values. This repudiation of nature-determined man is timely and nearly valid: human freedom includes this history-changing, destiny-molding capacity. But Titanism as perpetual effort-strain is no genuine relief, and no universal resource: nor is it meeting the issue of world-despair. The clue lies in a closer examination of the nature of pain.

Were there no endless seeking and striving, pain could be vastly diminished. If human striving is eternal, it must be that the pain incident to striving is an integral part of the joy of living. The pain of the artist, of all creative workers, exists solely because of the perfection one contemplates and suffers through incapacity to achieve: it can be canceled at once by rejecting the vision. But the vision, wholly without biological necessity, is a gift of the gods: to cancel it would be to cancel what life has now come to mean. We freely prefer to pay its price, which is the acceptance of pain.

In other words, the human mode of existing has as one ingredient a pain-absorbing, more than this a pain-requiring aspect. Every wakening of the mind to love, as every opening of the eyes to beauty, carries this—I will not say paradox, I will say with Marcel this mystery; for the gift of love exercises a command over the receiver of the gift, he seeks an opportunity to serve what he cannot deserve. It follows that the "best of all possible worlds" could not consist of an aggregate of "goods": purely for the love of love the endurable world must allow occasion for suffering. And further, these perceptions of love and beauty with their hunger for pain are at the same time perceptions of the nature of "the real": they are the empirical glints of entrance to the secret of "the ontological mystery." For whatever else we know of the world, we know it as a world in which loving and being loved are possible.

And this perception is contained in the experience of despair. To despair confesses at least an earlier hope; but since it refuses to take the world "realistically" as dead fact, it retains the wraith of that hope: "*désespoir*" contains "*espoir*." And if one hopes, it is because of a value in what is hoped for; one could not hope unless he also loved. Thus, in despair itself there lies a confession of love, which the nature of existence-as-being-lived sustains. "I doubt, therefore I think, therefore I exist"; let us now say, "I despair, therefore I hope, therefore I exist as loving." And therefore, whether in this sphere of things or in a sphere transcending that of nature, I am justified in denying tragedy the last word: I may retain the *will to suffer in creating* that which I love.

XVIII / NEO-SOCRATIC QUESTIONINGS OUT OF FRANCE

GABRIEL MARCEL, WHO WAS BORN IN 1887, IS LIKE HIS FELLOW PARISIAN, Jean-Paul Sartre, a critic and playwright as well as a philosopher. Unlike Sartre, however, neither his philosophy nor dramaturgy is based on atheism and despair, but both are investigations into the values of faith, the impulse to believe and man's necessity for love.

A member of the Institute of France, and a winner of the Grand Prix de Littérature of the Académie Française, Dr. Marcel is the author of several volumes, just recently being translated into English, including the Gifford Lectures, The Mystery of Being, Metaphysical Journal, Being and Having, and Man Against Mass Society. He lives in Paris.

The Universal Against the Masses

BY GABRIEL MARCEL

I. PREFACE

The dynamic element in my philosophy, taken as a whole, can be seen as an obstinate and untiring battle against the spirit of abstraction. Since the years 1911 and 1912, the time of my first researches and my still unpublished earliest philosophical writings, I have played the part of a prosecuting counsel against every philosophy that seemed to me to remain the prisoner of abstractions. Was this attitude, in these early days, a result of Bergson's influence? I should not like to swear to it, one way or the other, but it may well have been so.

But this distrust of abstractions explains, for instance, the fascination which the Hegelian system exercised on me for such a long time. For, in spite of appearances to the contrary, Hegel did make a very splendid effort to preserve the primacy of the concrete; and no philosopher has protested more strongly against the confusion of the concrete with the immediately given. My severe and hostile criticism, on the other hand, of a pseudo philosophy like that of Julien Benda is to be explained by the fundamentally abstract trend of Benda's thinking; he has never even suspected the existence of the true philosopher's urgent inner need to grasp reality in it concreteness.

On the other hand, this hostility of mine toward the spirit of abstraction is quite certainly *also* at the roots of the feeling of distrust aroused in me, not exactly by democracy itself, but by the sort of ideology which claims to justify democracy on philosophical grounds. At no time in my life, for instance, has the French Revolution inspired in me anything at all akin to admiration or even attachment; one reason may be that, when I was still very young, I became aware of the ravages in French social life that are due to a sort of egalitarian bigotry. But another feeling had its effect. It was also when I was still very young that my parents—for what reason, I am still not too clear—compelled me to read Mignet's very dry history of that great event; and the other feeling, which that reading aroused, was my innate horror of violence, disorder, cruelty. At that time, the glaring abuses in French social and political life which had dragged on *until* 1789 struck less feelingly home to me than the crimes of the Terror. Naturally, as time went on, I arrived at a more just or at least more balanced estimate of the French Revolution. But the feelings of indignation which the September Massacres and the other mass crimes of the Revolutionary period aroused in me in adolescence, were not, in the end, *essentially* very different from those much more recently aroused by the horrors of Stalinism or Nazism, or even by the shameful aspects of a purge nearer home.

Can there be any doubt, then, that a bent of mind so deeply rooted is the point of departure of my whole philosophical development? But my readers, very naturally, will want to ask me if there is any connection *that can be grasped* between my horror of abstraction and my horror of mass violence. My answer is that such a connection does certainly exist. Even for myself, however, it existed for a long time below the level of conscious understanding. It is, certainly, only at a fairly recent date that it has become explicit for me: since . . . the spirit of abstraction is essentially of the order of the passions, and since conversely, on the other hand, it is passion, not intelligence, which forges the most dangerous abstractions. Now, I can say without hesitation that my own thought has always been directed by a passionate love (but passionate at another level) for music, harmony, peace. And when I was still very young I grasped the truth that it is impossible to build true peace on abstractions; though I grasped it, of course, in a form that had not yet reached the stage of conceptual elaboration. (In passing, the fact that it is impossible to build true peace on abstractions is the deepest reason for the failure of the League of Nations, and of other pretentious organizations which resemble it). Perhaps also the sort of prejudice which I have always had in favor of Christianity, even during the very long period in which I could not envisage the possibility of becoming a practicing and confessing Christian, may be explained by the unconquerable conviction I had that, so long as Christianity remained true to itself, Christianity could be the only authentic peacemaker.

A reader may ask, "But so far as that goes, Christians of the Left think as you do; and is it not perfectly permissible to suppose that a Christianity of the Right will always remain conformist in spirit, that its essence is to try to appease and to manage by tact those who hold power in the world, or even to lean on them for support?" To that my answer would be that in fact I have always been extremely suspicious of a Christianity of the Right—I have always thought that such a Christianity runs the risk of distorting in the most sinister fashion the true message of Christ. (I have even been tempted to adopt as my own certain phrases of Pascal Laumière's, from the final act of my play, *Rome n'est plus dans Rome*). Only, I should like to add immediately that the men of the Right are very far from having a monopoly of the spirit of conformity and appeasement: there is a conformism of the Left, there are men of the Left who hold power in the world, there are "right-thinking people" (in the conformist sense of the phrase) on the Left as well as the Right; I remember one day before the war saying something of this sort at the Ambassadeurs, thus greatly shocking Jacques and Raïssa Maritain.

One must add that conformism of the Left, not only because it has, if I may put it so, the wind behind its sails these days, but because it is in such glaring contradiction with the principles that the Left claims to be defending, must be denounced just as ruthlessly as conformism of the Right. Not, of course—this hardly needs saying—

that there is any excuse for allowing conformism of the Right, with all it too often implies of blindness and unconscious cruelty, to cash in on that weight of reprobation with which, on this count, one must load the shoulders of the Left. One must recognize the fact that, in certain countries of Europe and the Americas, the spirit of clericalism, with the hateful political connivances that it implies, is tending to take on a character that, for a truly Christian conscience, becomes more and more offensive. The note of a truly honest mode of thinking in these matters, as in bookkeeping, is to have a system of double entry, and to prohibit oneself from marking down—by an intellectually fraudulent operation—to the credit of the Right what one has to mark down to the debit of the Left. I am thinking now of people who, because of their horror of the Soviet world, are today tending to regard Nazism with a certain retrospective tolerance. That is an aberration—and a criminal aberration. In any case, who could fail to see at once the simple mechanism of the mental conjuring trick by which we belittle a danger that is past, simply because it *is* past, or because we believe it past? It is really past? Or may it not in fact appear again, and in a form not radically altered? In this realm of discourse, we must learn once more to express ourselves categorically and to denounce the errors of a moral relativism which is, as may be easily shown, radically self-centered. Human nature being what it is, the movement which I condemn morally is too often the movement which hurts me personally; and I am likely to go on condemning it for so long as (and just for so long as) it is really able to hurt me.

But having said this, I should add immediately that there is an historical dogmatism no less disastrous in its consequences than this self-centered moral relativism. Simone de Beauvoir wrote a few years ago that crimes against the common law—crimes, that is, against person and property—ought not to be judged with too much severity; but that political crimes, on the other hand, are inexpiable. Such an assertion, as soon as one reflects on it a little, opens out gulfs beneath one's feet; it can be properly understood only if one lays bare the dogmatic philosophy of history which it presupposes. If political crime is a mortal sin, the reason must be that it goes against the meaning of history and that the latter, of course, is supposed to be generally known. To the already rather odd maxim, "Nobody is assumed to be ignorant of the law," we must now add another even odder: "Nobody is assumed to be ignorant of the meaning of history." From the point of view of somebody like Simone de Beauvoir, an ordinary crime against person or property has no interest for history, it exists on the margin of history, and counts, so to say, as a merely venial sin. To be sure, we are all perfectly well aware that to a certain type of philosophic man of letters today those whom we call criminals often appear as extremely attractive: the novels and characters of Jean Genêt are a striking case in point. From such a novelist's point of view, a middle-class hero practicing the dreary virtues of his retrograde social group is a much less brilliant character than a thief and pervert who has the courage to put into action those desires which, for the plodding bourgeois, never get beyond the stage of unadmitted daydreams. I am thinking for instance of a play I propose to write in which we see a young married woman, all keyed up, confronting her husband, who is just about to play the host, with all the respect due to such a personage, to a rival and imitator of M. Jean Genêt, with this question: "Tell me, Jo: can you swear to me that in the presence of Jacques Framboise, who has just come out of prison, you experience nothing that at all resembles a feeling of superiority?" Jo, confused and quite taken aback, remains silent. The lady presses her point: "Answer me, Jo: the whole future of our relations depends on your answer." In her discreet way, she then adds that Jo ought to feel a little ashamed, if anything, of wearing the white flower of a, legally at least, blameless life. . . . If I have allowed myself a somewhat farcial digression here, it is to throw a clearer light on those generally inverted values which a contemporary literary elite—an international elite, too—is rapidly today tending to adopt for its own. And here, also, we find conformism and "right-thinking persons." One would be judged a "wrong-thinking person" in such circles if one persisted in pointing out that theft, in itself, is a reprehensible act. And in art generally, in all the arts, we find the same sort of unarguable preconceived false opinion, the same sort of aberration. Our period is offering us the spectacle of a coherence in moral absurdity. But just because of this very coherence, we are forced to assert without a shadow of hesitation that this cult of the morally absurd is very rapidly becoming a cult of the positively evil.

On the nature of evil . . . there is a sort of meditation of mine; a meditation which has so far arrived only at very general results, and with which I am very far from being satisfied myself. Evil is a mystery; it is not something which can be assimilated to the notion of something lacking, even to the sort of lack which is a deformity.

On this point I should be tempted to say, very broadly, that the gnostics, from Jacob Boehme to Schelling and Berdyaev, are right: here again the rationalizing philosophers have been led away by the spirit of abstraction.

But this word "mystery" is not a simple signboard placed at the entrance to a straight path. The reflections which follow all imply, I think, that mystery is coextensive with what I should like to call (on the analogy of the metaphysical) the *metatechnical*: by which term I merely intend to mark off roughly that infrangible sphere of being to which techniques are never able to gain access. In Great Britain, neopositivistic philosophies have been making alarming inroads lately, and it was partly for that reason that I found myself making to a student audience there observations to the following effect: "Calculating machines rightly astonish us, and for my own part I am quite incapable of saying to what degree of perfection they may be brought. But what we can quite certainly affirm is that it will never be possible to construct a machine capable of *interrogating itself* on the conditions that make it possible and on the limits of its own range of operations. . . . "These remarks were an illustration of that notion of an intimate link between reflection and mystery which lies at the foundation of all my work. Yet we are forced to admit that the more techniques advance, the more reflection is thrust into the background —and I believe that this cannot be a matter of mere chance. Not, for that matter, that I should like to assert that there is anything necessarily fated, or fatal, about the connection; but what does seem certain is that the progress and above all the extreme diffusion of techniques tends to create a spiritual and intellectual atmosphere (or more precisely, an antispiritual and anti-intellectual atmosphere) as unfavorable as possible to the exercise of reflection; and this observation may prepare us to understand why today the idea of the universal can be affirmed only outside the mass world and against that world.

The universal against the masses: no doubt that should really be the title of this book.[1] But what *is* the universal? What are we to understand by it? Not, of course, it goes without saying, a wretched abstract truth reducible to formulas that could be handed down and learned by rote. The universal is spirit or mind—and spirit or mind is love. On this point, as on so many others, we have to go back to Plato. Not, of course, to the mere letter of a philosophy of which, for that matter, hardly more than the letter, than the outward, un-

[1] *Man against Mass Society,* Henry Regnery, 1952.

312

secret aspect, has come down to us—but to the essential message which that philosophy still has for us today. Between love and intelligence, there can be no real divorce. Such a divorce is apparently consummated only when intelligence is degraded or, if I may be allowed the expression, becomes merely cerebral; and, of course, when love reduces itself to mere carnal appetite. But this we must assert, and as forcibly as possible: where love on one side, where intelligence on the other, reach their highest expression, they cannot fail to meet: do not let us speak of their becoming identical, for there can be no mutual identity except between abstractions; intelligence and love are the most concrete things in the world, and at a certain level every great thinker has recognized this or had a presentiment of it.

But in point of fact the masses exist and develop (following laws which are fundamentally purely mechanical) only at a level far below that at which intelligence and love are possible. Why should this be so? Because the masses partake of the human only in a degraded state, they are themselves a degraded state of the human. Do not let us seek to persuade ourselves that an education of the masses is possible: that is a contradiction in terms. What is educable is only an individual, or more exactly a person. Everywhere else, there is no scope for anything but a *training*. Let us say rather that what we have to do is to introduce a social and political order which will withdraw the greatest number of beings possible from this mass state of abasement or alienation. One mark of that state is that the masses are of their very essence—I repeat, *of their very essence*—the stuff of which fanaticism is made: propaganda has on them the convulsive effect of an electrical shock. It arouses them not to life, but to that appearance of life which particularly manifests itself in riots and revolutions. Also, of course, it is usual—and I do not know that the essential principle of this necessity has ever been grasped—on such occasions for the very dregs of the population to rise to the surface and take command of events. It is at the lowest level that the crystallization of mass impulses to violences takes place. Yet this is not to say that, if revolutions are bad in themselves, they are without some element of counterbalancing good; they might be compared to certain crises in the development of a living organism, which are pathological in themselves, but which seem to be needed to secure, in a very risky fashion, the future growth of that organism by snatching it from torpor and death.

At the end of this book, it will be my duty to indicate some of the more positive conclusions to which such reflections on the antagonism between the universal and the masses ought to lead us.

II. CONCLUSION

What sort of general conclusion can the arguments of a book like this imply? There can be no question, certainly, of anything resembling a prophecy. From man's point of view—and that expression is pleonastic, since there is no point of view that is not man's, that does not start with man—it must be said as firmly as possible that everything is not finished, that we have not "had our chance," that fatalism is a sin and a source of sin. The philosopher is not a prophet, he is no prophet in any sense, and that means above all that it is not for him to put himself in the place of God. To do so, at his own level of thought, would not only be an absurdity but an act of sacrilege. Yet it is important to remember, here, that the prophet himself, the true prophet, never puts himself in the place of God, but effaces himself so that God may speak, which is something very different. However, that sublime vocation is not that of the philosopher. Today, the first and perhaps the only duty of the philosopher is to defend man against himself: to defend man against that extraordinary temptation toward inhumanity to which—almost always without being aware of it—so many human beings today have yielded.

But a tragic difficulty arises here: for a century past, and perhaps for longer, man has been led to call his own nature into question, and this has been necessarily so from the moment in which he no longer acknowledged himself to be a creature made in the image of God. That, no doubt, is the fundamental reason why what Nietzsche called the "Death of God" could only be followed, and almost immediately followed, by the death-throes of man. Let us make our meaning clear: something which, for the thinker, is *brought into question* is, for the nonthinker, almost bound to become pure negation. Self-questioning and suspended judgment seem almost incompatible with the demands of action: think of Shakespeare's Prince Hamlet. Thus the man who is nonreligious—which is to say, the man who has broken his bonds— becomes the man who rejects, who refuses. But we have to go further into this dialectical process, which, for that matter, is suffered rather than thought. The man who rejects, if he is perfectly consistent with himself, will be the integral nihilist. But for reasons which have to do with the very conditions and, as it were, the structure of existence, the integral nihilist can only be an extreme case, an exception which fundamentally is not a practicable one. Let us beware, in any case, of attempted discourse about an ideal single being, the man who rejects: such singleness only exists subjectively. It is what speaks, not what can be objectively spoken of. What can be objectively spoken of is *men,* the objective is plural. It is only *between* men who reject that there can come into being what I should like to call unnatural bonds—I am contrasting them with the natural bonds that link together members of the same family or citizens of the same city, when family or city is in a healthy state.

It is starting from such observations that we ought to reread Dostoevsky's *The Possessed,* one of the most profound novels—and one of the most essentially prophetic novels—that has ever been written. What I really mean is this: in the world that we know—I make this qualification, for there would be no point in referring to other types of civilization, to which we have not the key—human beings can be linked to each other by a real bond only because, in another dimension, they are linked to something which transcends them and comprehends them in itself. Now, the men who reject have broken with that superior principle, and it is in vain that they attempt to replace it by a fiction wholly lacking in ontological attributes and in any case projected into the future. In spite of all the phrases we make use of in our attempt to confer an appearance of reality on such fictions, all that actually happens is that a reality is displaced and a fiction replaces it.

But what happens at this point is something extremely serious. We know very well that abstractions cannot remain at the stage of mere abstraction. It is just as if they took on concrete life; though an abnormal and unhealthy life, which we could properly compare to that of a cancer-tissue. It is experience alone that can throw light on when, where, and how such life is able to take shape. We should have to look, in the first place, into just how the mass condition is able to come into being, particularly in great urban and industrial agglomerations; and secondly into how these masses—to whom we must refuse all ontological dignity, that is, we must not consider them as having substantial being—can be galvanized and magnetized, invariably, as it would seem, by fanatical groups growing up round a nucleus of dictatorship. I am myself neither a sociologist nor an historian, and so must be broad and sketchy here. However, it would be necessary to transcend such data as history and sociology might provide us with in order to isolate, if not exactly the laws, at least the more or less constant conditions, of a social dynamism which imitates life but reaches its climax only in what we ought rather to call death: that is, in servitude and terror. And no doubt it is from that night of servitude and terror that we ought then to seek once more to rise, like a diver coming up to the surface, if we wished to rediscover the human in its dignity and plenitude.

But there is another aspect of this topic on which it is important now to insist. Techniques, as I have repeatedly said, cannot be considered as evil in themselves, quite the opposite. Nevertheless, we ought to recognize that unless we make a truly ascetic effort to master techniques and put them in their proper subordinate place, they tend to assemble themselves, to organize themselves, around the man who rejects. It is a mysterious and significant fact about our contemporary world that nihilism is tending to take on a technocratic character, while technocracy is inevitably nihilist. I say, *technocracy* is: there is an absolute distinction in theory between *technocracy* and *the proper sphere of techniques,* even though in practice the distinction may appear today to have reached vanishing point. However, it is no less obvious that this connection, between nihilism and technocracy, is not a patent one, and no doubt it is of its essence not to be so. Nothingness or mere negation is, as it were, the secret which technocracy jealously hides in its heart, and this under whatever aspect technocracy presents itself to us. In the end—but only in the end—it is permissible to pass the same verdict of condemnation on American technocracy as on that at which the Soviet world is aiming. But I should add that such a condemnation based, in this case, on a possible extreme development of existing American tendencies must arouse suspicion, just because it is too easy. It is a sort of condemnation at which intellectuals excel, just because they are frivolous and usually without concrete and circumstantial knowledge of what they are talking about.

From this certainly rather confused bundle of observations it is, I think, possible to pick out a number of more precise warnings that each of us could take to heart.

The most urgent and imperative of all these warnings might be put in the following way. As soon as I start thinking,—and by thinking I mean reflecting, here—I am forced not only to take notice of the extreme danger in which the world today stands but also to become aware of the responsibilities which fall upon myself in such a situation. This should be strongly emphasized: for the very act of thinking, as the whole history of philosophy shows us, brings with it a temptation, that of detachment, that of *self-insulation*. But this temptation only persists where reflection has not yet deployed itself in every possible dimension. I discover that it is a temptation, and by the same act I surmount it, as soon as I have understood that what I call the self is not a source but an obstacle; it is not from the self, it is *never* from the self that the light pours forth, even though, through an illusion which is hard to dissipate, it is of the very nature of our ego to take itself as a projector when it is only a screen. The ego is essentially pretentious, it is its nature to be a pretender in every sense of the word.

But when we have recognized this fundamental responsibility, what sort of effort should we make to face it? In other words, what is the first ethical commandment to which I ought, as a philosopher, to conform? Without any possible doubt it is that I ought not to sin against the light. But what exact meaning are we to give to this term "light"? I do not say to this metaphor of light; for in fact we are not in possession of any word in relation to which the term can be judged metaphorical. The expression at the beginning of the Gospel according to St. John, "That was the true Light, which lighteth every man that cometh into the world," defines in the most rigorous fashion and in terms of unsurpassable adequacy what is in fact the most universal characteristic of human existence; one can see that clearly if one adds by way of corollary that man is not man except insofar as that light lights him. And if nevertheless, yielding to an almost uncontrollable inner necessity, we do after all attempt to elucidate the meaning of the word "light," we shall have to say that it denotes what we can only define as the identity at their upper limit of Love and Truth: we should have to add that a truth which lies below that limit is a pseudo truth and conversely that a love without truth is in some respects a mere delirium.

We must now ask ourselves what are the still singular and in many ways mysterious conditions under which we can have access to this light? Leaving on one side Revelation properly so called, which has always remained in relation to any thoughts put forward in this work at, as it were, the horizon, I would say that we all have to radiate this light for the benefit of each other, while remembering that our role consists above all and perhaps exclusively in not presenting any obstacle to its passage *through us*. This, in spite of all appearances to the contrary, is an active role: it is an active role just because the self is a pretender, and a pretender whose duty it is to transcend or to destroy its own false claims. This can only be achieved through freedom and in a sense this *is* freedom.

But on our way to these conclusions we have been able to isolate other temptations which we ought to resist. One of the most dangerous and diffused of these is linked to the prestige of numbers (and of statistics). It is at this level of thought that the most sinister collusion takes place between a degraded philosophy and a simple-minded dogmatism deriving from the natural sciences; it seems as if the mind becomes corrupt as soon as it accustoms itself to juggling with numbers that correspond to nothing in the imagination—this is true both of the infinitely great and the infinitely little. To be sure, it would be mere madness to refuse to recognize the necessity, for the astronomer and the physicist in their specialized domains, of such dangerous manipulations. But the danger begins when such methods, which in themselves must always remain open to suspicion, are transferred from such domains to another domain: I mean from a specialized field of thought, which has to make use of special methods, to the field of concrete general activity which is that of man *qua* man. Here we ought to restore in their plenitude the meaning, and the implicit affirmation, of the word "neighbor"; and at no point does the essential agreement between the Gospels and the results of philosophical reflection more fully reveal its fertility. It is impossible not to allude here to the kind of aberration of which a famous French paleontologist once gave an example. He is a man who sincerely believes that he is a Christian, but who has succumbed more thoroughly than anyone else to the intoxication of great numbers. On one occasion, when he was dilating on his confidence in world progress, and somebody was trying to call to his attention the case of the millions of wretches who are slowly dying in Soviet labor camps, he exclaimed, so it seems: "What are a few million men in relation to the immensity of human history?" A blasphemy! Thinking in terms of millions and multiples of millions, he could no longer conceive, except in terms of "cases," of abstractions, of the unspeakable and intolerable reality of the suffering of the single person—a suffering literally masked from him by the mirage of numbers.

In the foreword to my *Mystery of Being,* I proposed that my thought should henceforth be designated under the name of neo-Socratism. In this context, that description takes on its full meaning. The return to one's neighbor appears to be the real condition of a neo-Socratic approach to being; and I would add that the more we estrange ourselves from our neighbor, the more we are lost in a night in which we can no longer even distinguish being from nonbeing. But can one fail to see that technocracy consists precisely of making an abstraction of one's neighbor and, in the long run, denying him? I shall remember a remark made to me by a man who has remarkable intellect but one too much contaminated, alas, by the errors of our time! As I was speaking to him of my admiration for so many young French Christians, almost all of middle-class background, who are today courageously and under very great difficulties bringing up large families, "On the contrary," he said vigorously, "there is nothing to admire. When one is aware of the conclusions recently arrived at by the board set up in the United States to make an estimate of world stocks of primary commodities, this fecundity for which you feel such wondering admiration seems mere madness." The dramatist in me—and I might add, the comic dramatist—immediately imagined a young couple who, before deciding to start a baby on the way, hurried away to some set of technical experts to discover the state of the harvests in South America or Central Africa. My friend was forgetting that, in France itself, as a result of the accumulated errors of the governmental system, whole fertile regions are being allowed to lie fallow. A family does not have to think on the world scale, it does not have to make its horizon an unlimited one. To think the contrary is to be a technocrat.

I should, of course, be guilty of bad faith if I refused to agree that there is, in fact, a real and terrible problem of possible overpopulation in the world; but is man as he is made today capable of facing this problem or even of stating it in acceptable terms? It is, in reality, a problem for a demiurge; but the idea of a human demiurge is self-contradictory, and we are paying a high price for not having recognized that earlier: the price of the low spiritual level at which we find ourselves today. For my own part, here I think that the role of the philosopher consists above all in putting men of science and action on their guard against such *hubris:* against, that is, such unmeasured arrogance.

It is our duty not only to make the imprescriptible rights of the universal currently recognized, but also to plot out with the greatest care the terrain on which these rights can be effectively defended. In my introduction, I said that the word "universal" seems fated to give rise to misunderstandings of the very sort most likely to darken and confuse its real meaning. We are almost irresistibly inclined to understand "the universal" as that which presents a maximum of generality. But that is an interpretation against which one cannot too strongly react. The best course here is for the mind to seek its support among the highest expressions of human genius—I mean among those works of art which have a character of supreme greatness. Being a musician myself, for instance, I am thinking of the last works of Beethoven. How can anybody fail to see that any sort of notion of generality is quite inapplicable here? On the contrary, if a sonata like Opus 111 or a quartet like Opus 127 introduces us to what is most intimate and I would even say most sacred in our human condition, at the level where that condition transcends itself in a significance which is at once self-evident and beyond any possible formulation, at the same time it addresses itself only to a very restricted number of people, without for that reason at all losing its universal value. We must understand that universality has its place in the dimension of depth and not that of breadth. Shall we say that the universal is accessible only to the individual? There again is a notion about which we must be terribly cautious. We have to reject the atomic just as much as the collective conception of society. Both, as Gustave Thibon has so pregnantly remarked, are complementary aspects of the same process of decomposition—I would say of local mortification.

There can be no authentic depth except where there can be real communion; but there will never be any real communion between individuals centered on themselves, and in consequence morbidly hardened, nor in the heart of the mass, within the mass-state. The very notion of intersubjectivity on which all my own most recent work has been based presupposes a reciprocal openness between individuals without which no kind of spirituality is conceivable.

But this fact has a particular importance from the point of view of action, and it opens up new horizons to us. It is only within groups that are fairly restricted in size and animated by a spirit of love that the universal can really embody itself. From this point of view, it is very important to rehabilitate that aristocratic idea, which has been today discredited, for the worst possible reasons, in the name of an egalitarianism that cannot stand up for a moment to critical thought. Only, of course, the content of this idea of aristocracy must be renewed. We ought to think, particularly, of what an aristocracy of craftsmanship might have been; I say "might have been," for the almost systematic destruction of the craftsman in France to which an idiotic legislation has contributed obliges us, here, to project our conjectures into the past. But it is absolutely necessary that aristocracies should be recreated, for we must face the terrible fact that every leveling process must proceed downward, to the base of the hierarchy: there is not, and cannot be, such a thing as "leveling up." There can be no more serious problem than that of investigating around what centers, what focal points, these new aristocracies can constitute themselves. It is probable that this very worrying problem does not imply an abstract and general solution; there are and only can be the particular cases, groups managing to form themselves according to the circumstances around an institution, a personality, a living idea, and so on.

But there is a complementary remark to be made. In every case such a group runs the risk of shutting itself up in itself and becoming a sect or a "little clan," and as soon as it does so it betrays the universal value which it is supposed to be embodying. It is therefore the duty of each group to remain in a sort of state of active expectation or availability in relation to other groups moved by a different inspiration, with whom it ought to have fertilizing exchanges of view; and it is on this condition alone that each group can remain a living group and avoid the morbid hardening that results from its becoming the seat of a sort of self-idolatry. This life of the group, moreover, can only develop in time; it has its bearings set toward an achievement outside of time, which it would be futile to seek to anticipate in imagination, but whose joyous presentiment is, as it were, the mainspring of all activity worthy of the name, of all true creation. Such a life is by its very nature one of adventure; it does not exclude risks, it rather presupposes them; and on the other hand the principles of such a life cannot be generalized and put forward as a kind of system. I would say, rather, that what can be reduced to a system is incompatible with the profoundest inner need that animates such a life, and that this need itself implies the mysterious encounter of the mind and heart.

It should be added that it is up to each of us to make what we call a reality of, that is, to incarnate, such guiding ideas as this; for these guiding ideas will be lies if they are not given definite practical shape. It is true to say that there is nobody at all—and I am thinking here at least as much of the most humble lives as of those that attract our attention —who does not find himself placed in a concrete setting in which such incarnation of these guiding ideas is possible and even requisite: there is nobody at all who is not in a position to encourage, within himself and beyond himself, the spirit of truth and love. But one should immediately add the converse proposition: there is nobody at all who is not in a position, through the powers of rejection which he possesses, to put obstacles in the way of such encouragement and thus to maintain in the world a state of blindness, of mutual mistrust, of internal division, that are paving the way for the world's destruction and his own. What is asked of all of us, such as we are—and here truly is what one might call our existential secret—is that we should discover what that sphere is, however restricted it may be, in which our own activity can be vitally connected with that universal purpose, which is the purpose of love and truth in the world. Our error or our fault invariably consists in our wanting to persuade ourselves that no such sphere exists and that our contribution to the task that has to be accomplished in the world cannot amount to anything. An even more serious error consists in denying the existence or the imperativeness of this task and shutting ourselves up in the awareness of a sterile liberty.

I am very far of course from disguising from myself the objections to which this attempt of mine once more to make the outcome of philosophical reflection a kind of practical wisdom may give rise. The most serious of these objections might be stated as follows: "Is not this attempt to recall us to the feeling for our neighbor and the consciousness of our immediate surroundings essentially reactionary? Doesn't it come down, in the end, to making a clean sweep of everything that has been laboriously achieved in the last few centuries? Are you not instituting a ruinous divorce, not only between science and philosophy, but between the infinitely enlarged world of modern science and technical activity, on the one hand, and on the other hand the narrow field in which it seems, according to you, that philosophical reflection, guided by a sense of intimacy, ought to exercise itself? For you, the sense of intimacy claims to ally itself with the sense of Being, evoked and invoked by you in its plenitude. Whether or not you acknowledge this explicitly, are you not inciting anyone who shows himself docile to the instructions, or rather to the appeal, of the philosopher, to remain on one side of the world of techniques and to use the resources which it offers him only with a distrustful parsimony? But unless the sage is willing in some sense to take charge of the world of modern techniques, is he not condemning it, is he not devoting it to destruction?"

It is, in fact, very doubtful whether the problem can really be stated in such general terms as this, terms which presuppose that the critic is taking the extreme case. I have denounced already the disquieting ease with which arguments based on an imagined extreme case can be built up. My first point, however, is this: it is not the business of the philosopher or the sage to take charge of a technocratic world; he could only do so by making himself its slave. The ideal of the philosopher as king which seduced Comte and Renan, or at least Renan in certain moods, is chimerical, and it is also to be numbered among our temptations. But here, as everywhere else, we must also denounce the error which consists in thinking *grosso modo,* of constituting in the imagination unities or totalities which do not exist in fact. "The world of techniques" is such an imaginary unity and "philosophy" is another. We have every reason for believing that the unification of the world, from the moment at which it could be effected at the level and from the point of view of power, would coincide with the world's destruction. If one does not allow oneself to be snared by mere words, one sees very clearly that such a material unification has no relationship at all to the only kind of unity which has spiritual importance, that of hearts and minds. As for Philosophy with a capital letter, that is an idol; what is real is a kind of life of reflective thought that can and ought to be pursued at every level of human activity; I am thinking as much of the administrator as of the doctor and the magistrate. However, when one talks today of the philosopher, it is in fact almost always of the university teacher of philosophy that one thinks. But, alas, as we have already seen in developing our argument, the professor of philosophy is himself today exposed to the worst possible temptations. I am thinking, for instance, of what a young philosopher of remarkable intellect recently said to me at Basel. Criticizing, with much courtesy and discretion, the ideas which I had just been publicly expounding about the duties of the philosopher in the world today, he said that possibly the philosopher as such ought never to pose the question of whether some course of action is opportune. He did not see that a philosopher who made a claim of this sort to speak only in terms of the absolute would at the same time totally disqualify himself from having a relevant contribution to make to any concrete problem. And, very generally, we *can* say that nothing is more characteristic than the incredible blindness of professors of philosophy when they decide to take a stand on political questions. One recognizes in them a spirit of rashness which can be explained, as Alain, I think, very clearly saw, by the simple fact that, unlike doctors, architects, or engineers, they are in contact chiefly with words and ideas and hardly ever with things. The illusion that one is flying is a melancholy one in the case of man who does not even know how to walk and, for that matter, rather despises walking. And our world is made in such a way that a man can believe he is flying, today, when he has not left his armchair; there is a condition of waking dream which, by its very nature, cannot become conscious of itself, and it exists at the level of thinking in pure abstractions.

During a recent trip to Morocco, I was able to observe with trepidation the incredible misdeeds of which devotees of ideologies can become guilty when, rejecting reality, they claim to judge by their chosen categories even men and events to which these categories are strictly inapplicable. What is tragic . . . is that such abstractions are far from

M *

being without practical impact: latent in them are almost infinite possibilies of disorder. Thus I end as I began: the philosopher can help to save man from himself only by a pitiless and unwearying denunciation of the spirit of abstraction. No doubt he will be denounced as a conservative, a reactionary, possibly even a Fascist—though he knows that it is his duty to denounce Fascism as one of the cancers of democracy—but what does that matter? It is the masses who hurl these accusations at him or, at the most, the man who is only an echo of the masses. But the philosopher knows that the mass itself is a lie and it is *against the mass* and *for the universal* that he must bear witness.

—Translated from the French by G. S. Fraser

XIX / PHILOSOPHY OF A LIBERAL

Salvador de Madariaga, Spanish author and diplomat, was born in 1886 and trained as an engineer. In 1916 in London he became a journalist and in 1921 entered the Secretariat of the League of Nations and served the following year as head of the disarmament section. Between 1928 and 1931 he was professor of Spanish literature at Oxford, Ambassador to the United States and Delegate of Spain on the Council of the League of Nations. He has also served as Ambassador to France. He writes in English, French and Spanish; has devoted himself to the analysis of the different national types in Europe and been a strong advocate of internationalism. The following excerpt is the first English translation from his most recent book, *From Anguish to Liberty,* which appeared in 1954 in French in Paris. Dr. Madariaga lives in Oxford, England.

From Anguish to Liberty: Faith of a Liberal Revolutionary

BY SALVADOR DE MADARIAGA

I. INTRODUCTION

"In our days," says the professor, "the average man dreams less about his liberty than about his ham and eggs." He says that in a tone which leaves little doubt of *his* attitude. He is in perfect accord with his "average man." And I reply to him: "To cure this state of the spirit, there is nothing like ten years of prison with ham and eggs every day for breakfast." I certainly had reason for correcting his error of judgment; but he certainly had reason for thinking that such is the general attitude today with the average man.

The average man. Yes. But where is he? We all know, for they have told it to us enough times at school, that the abundance of a thing brings down its value. It is then quite possible that, in free countries, liberty abounds to such a degree that one ends by undervaluing it. What is more precious than air or water? And we attach little value to them because they are everywhere. Nevertheless, so far as liberty is concerned, one is tempted to put forth another explanation: evolution toward a hedonism purely materialistic is leading humanity to the pleasures of the body in preference to the joys of the spirit—the first of which is liberty.

In any event, let us assert that some cases are known of men in great need not of ham and eggs but of plain dry bread who have preferred liberty. In the course of one of the general elections under the Second Spanish Republic, between 1931 and 1936, a farm worker carrying all the stigmata of chronic hunger was standing in a line before an election booth at Granada. An agent of the conservatives, in the service then of the landowners who held him and his family in a starveling state, flashed a piece of silver in the hollow of his hand. No reaction from the workman. The agent showed him a bank note five times the value of the coin. The workman gazed impassively at the paper, a symbol of wages for a week when anyone hired him. Piqued with the indifference, the agent brought out a bill four times higher, a real fortune for the living skeleton he wished to buy. This time the impassivity gave way to contempt, and the workman let drop a phrase the native force of which requires the Spanish: *En qui hambre mando yo* (I'm the one who is the master of my hunger).

This jeweled phrase might be worthy of being the motto and symbol of liberty. It would widen the sense of the word hunger to include in it all the vital needs of man. For the instinct of liberty is no other at base than a vast hunger of being, an unlimited hunger, the hunger for that which is not yet. And this hunger for that which is not yet is imposed on man by that which already is, because the one is already in the other in germ, as the whole of the parabola is already in its first three points. So the instinct of liberty finally is fidelity to oneself. Whatever might be the intimacy of the ties which unite us with other human beings, each of us has the sense of his own destiny, unique and alone. If life throws out a challenge to our destiny, we sense that, whatever may be the value of the moral support or the advice of others, whatever may be the consequences our decision entails for others, we must retain the sovereign power of deciding: we must remain masters of our own hunger.

He is free then who knows how to keep in his own hands the power to decide, at each step, the course of his life, and who lives in a society which does not block the exercise of that power. Positive liberty results then from two systems of forces: the attitude of the individual toward his own liberty, and the attitude of society toward that of each of its members. Our modern world distinguishes today two types of societies: those modeled on Moscow, and those which have conserved their traditional autonomous evolutions, and which, in a first approximation at least, one might consider as free. The first type has almost entirely destroyed the margin of choice of its citizens. Individual liberty in this society moves in an extremely narrow path. There is scarcely a vital decision for the individual which the state does not take over for him.

The attempt is often made to say that in these societies, the loss of political liberty is compensated for by a gain in economic liberty. This is not true. Certainly one admits the transfer, after all purely theoretical, of the ownership of the means of production from the "capitalists" to the "workers." But because of the fact that, in reality, the new owner is the State, the workers under Soviet Communism enjoy an economic liberty much less wide than under capitalism even if only due to the fact that they have to work for only one boss. But even so, supposing that this loss of economic liberty should become a gain, what would it serve? What good is economic liberty without the political liberty which guarantees it? States modeled on Moscow may well offer to the workers all the economic liberty they want: without a public opinion, without liberty of press, political organization, the rights of assembly, who will impede the bureaucrats, who are in fact the bosses and the government, from mocking economic liberty and sending into Siberia with all their economic liberties on their backs the workers who might protest?

Such subtleties on the subject of liberty (economic liberty? political liberty?) are no more than scholastic *distinguos* invented by the Stalinists, the most medieval spirits the modern world ever dreamed of seeing in our days, invented for the purpose of sidetracking the public attention to the adjective from the noun—liberty—which they are maltreating. If, in the course of a discussion on liberty, your opponent starts to split hairs in four parts with questions like: "Of what liberty are you speaking exactly?" you may deduce that liberty does not interest him at all. Liberty, like justice, truth, love, is one of the pure essences which reject adjectives. Imagine a mathematician engaged with a calculus problem asking if the solution of his equations should be political or economic; a judge anxious to know if his sentence ought to be dictated by economic or political considerations; Romeo saying to Juliet: "I love you with a love economic. That will compensate for my lack of political love." No. We say no to all this gibberish, and we declare that liberty is one and indivisible and if you tread on her big toe you tread on all of her.

But the abominable torture to which liberty is subjected in the Communist countries should not make us forget that she is also in danger in the countries called free. It is not a matter of temporary restrictions imposed on liberty exclusively by the Soviet menace. A besieged city is certainly forced to restrain the liberty of its citizens as long as the threat lasts. But, regardless of these provisional restrictions, liberty is menaced in a fashion entirely inexcusable in the so-called free West. Two dangers line up against her: the State tends to extend increasingly its sphere of action; and the individual seems more and more inclined to prefer his ham and eggs to his liberty.

The tendency to acquire more and more power is natural to man. If, in fact, the State is incarnate in M. Durand or Mr. Smith or Herr Schultz, these human beings, already powerful behind their big desks, want to become more so. The subjective factor finds itself reinforced by another factor, the objective. For example: the government decides that the price of milk will be reduced to X. The inevitable consequence is that the producers which have not happened to peg their accounts at that price withdraw from the market. Scarcity of milk. The Durand-Smith-Schultzes, who in this affair *are* the State, should do something. What? Procure more milk? Not at all. Procure for themselves more power. They demand and obtain the power of subvention, of being underwritten as marginal producers which the arbitrary price had driven out of the market. At the smell of subsidies, other producers become "marginal." Whereupon—controllers, accountants. . . . The State grows bigger.

This voracity of the State for power coincides with the secret desire of too many citizens to give up their power to it. Dostoyevsky said it in an unforgettable fashion in his narrative of the Grand Inquisitor: "They will marvel at us and look on us as gods, because we are ready to endure the freedom which they have found so dreadful and to rule over them—so awful it will seem to them to be free." "No science will give them bread so long as they remain free. In the end they will lay their freedom at our feet, and say to us, 'Make us your slaves, but feed us.'"

By these words the great Russian writer has clearly predicted the deplorable shift of orientation of modern man from liberty toward security, which results in augmenting day by day the power of the State and which leads fatally to a society the ideal of which will be a model stable. Each day, men and women, obsessed by security, place at the feet of the State new areas of their liberty. Fear ousts hunger from its role as the moving power of human actions. Human life migrates from the masculine hemisphere of its spirit to the feminine.

Who will dare to predict the consequences of this evolution? After this hunger for new life has been repressed for a generation at the placid breast of a feminine society, must one be astonished if all this peace and placidity flies to bits under the effect of an explosion of masculine hunger?

And even if this disaster does not take place, what a loss for humanity in this constant diminution of the areas of human liberty! History, which might have been able to evolve in many directions, diverse and various, shrinks into a level canal flat and gray, and the most marvelous of the faculties of man, the power to fashion his own life, sees itself bereft of its vigor.

Born liberal (for one is born liberal as one is born blond or brunette), I did not become officially so until the centenary of the Belgian Liberal Party, in 1947. The liberals of Belgium invited to their centenary liberal parties from many countries. They did me the honor of inviting me personally. The liberal parties, thus reunited, laid out the basis for a permanent association which has become the Union Liberale Internationale. I was president of this until 1952 and I have remained attached to it ever since.

In the course of the studies made at Brussels first, at Oxford later by the liberals associated in their international constitution, considerable differences in points of view came to light. They were not only differences on the ways of applying the principles of liberalism, but they were differences over the principles themselves. Thus, the Belgian liberals, radical French, Italian liberals, and Spanish and even, in some cases, German liberals, considered anti-clericalism as an integral part of their liberalism; and many pushed their anticlericalism to a fierce opposition to the Church of Rome, all churches, all religion, even to God himself. On the other hand, British liberals see in their religion the very foundation of their liberalism; and it is the same, although perhaps to a lesser degree, with the liberals among the peoples of the North and of the countries of the British Commonwealth in general.

These differences explain themselves perhaps by the fact that liberalism is an attitude and a temperament rather than a doctrine or a philosophy. This attitude presents at once a positive or active aspect and a negative or passive aspect. The born liberal above all holds on to liberty. And liberty is one of those words which run the risk of sinking under the weight of the commentaries made upon them ... for this word, liberty, lends itself very well to different points of view, since it designates a human experience which one may live through at every stage of existence, from the darkest caverns of the subconscious to the most luminous belvederes of thought.

The born liberal senses liberty rumbling in him like a powerful spring of vital sap, and has no need at all of the analyses of the philosopher to render an account of his essential character. Liberty is experienced before being thought out or compromised. A workman who never has consecrated a minute of his life to abstraction *knows* that liberty is necessary to him and that it is necessary to the men around him without ever having analyzed the idea of liberty, or of *necessity* or of *man,* nor even ever having glimpsed the existence of such ideas.

The tendency to liberty is, then, innate with the man born a liberal. (It is only obscurely there with all men.) Like all natural tendency it can be defined by its *stretch,* that is to say its capacity to push in its own direction as far as it can, against the outside resistances of natural and social surroundings, and also against the internal resistances of the human being himself upon whom liberty acts. This tendency to liberty is then a force of nature, whose role would seem to be of assuring to every man a radius of effective action equal to that with which he has been endowed by nature.

This positive or active aspect of the liberal attitude and of the liberal temperament is duplicated by a negative aspect. The born liberal has not only, regarding the liberty of others, a respect, almost a deference; he manifests also a certain impatience at seeing himself charged with responsibilities which are not his own. Instinctively, he apportions to each the burden of his own life; or, as the Spanish proverb has it, he wants each mast to carry its own sail. This instinct, so liberal, which wishes each to be the master of his own destiny, is thus two sides of the medal, respect for man on one side, and on the reverse, independence of him. That each man know himself free from all hindrance emanating from me; but that no one look to me to load myself down with his affairs for him—these are the active and the passive aspects of liberalism.

—Of liberalism, of course, in the beginning stage. At this deep but formless level, the conservatives will explain themselves as a heterogeneous group composed of an elite gifted with a very strong tendency to liberty—going so far as the control of the liberty of others—and herds of others not having more than an attenuated instinct for liberty. With the socialists, the situation will be found more complex. In the main, it wil be found identical with that of the conservatives, except that the leaders will strive to hide in the crowd of their co-religionists the true countenance of their ambitions; for a good part too, the elite themselves will be animated by equalitarian tendencies and the mass strongly oriented toward security, and will sense in only a moderate degree the instinct of liberty.

If we return now to the liberals, we will find that the negative aspect of their attitude, that respect plus indifference to the welfare of others, may well extend to translating itself into a certain neutrality in regard to the opinions of others. The liberal will thus have a tendency to react by a "Maybe you're right" at the assertion of the most monstrous heresies. We are, once more, before an attitude of two aspects: the one positive, creative tolerance; the other negative, indifference in the face of error. "For myself, I get along very well, because I never argue. If somebody puts up an argument with me, I give up," someone said. And the other put in: "But certainly you must have to argue sometimes." "Yes, of course, sometimes." The anecdote is typical of a certain kind of liberalism, the easygoing good fellow. But is this really what one should mean by liberalism?

It is this intellectual hospitality to all comers which tends to make of liberalism an open house where the most badly assorted travelers may run into each other as in a huge caravansery. As a result of flinging open all doors to their widest, liberalism ends by having no more walls, by losing, in short, the very boundaries which should define it. It is not by disappearing in the thin air of the indefinite that liberalism may hope to rejuvenate the world. It must commence by

331

defining the liberal doctrine and then fixing precisely what the true liberal means by tolerance. For it would be absurd to see in liberalism a school ready to accept everything, even that which is plainly contrary to its very essence and its reason for existence. We have seen in our time the most rabid enemies of liberalism, the Communists and the Fascists, calling on the name of liberalism the better to kill it; and some so-called liberals defending the right of the Communists to kill liberty.

It is time to draw this all out into the open. The liberal is ready to listen to all doctrines; but he does not admit that they may all be compatible with the liberal doctrine. He is still ready to listen to all they say in public, but he will not have to admit that all he hears said there is true, just or reasonable. Once defined, the liberal doctrine should be defended by its adherents with the intransigence it needs: for intransigence is nothing but the shadow thrown by the light of our faith.

These pages[1] are an offering to liberty made at the moment when she has most need of it. From all sides, in world public opinion, a clamor is arising which demands intellectual aid and guidance. This clamor only liberalism can satisfy. A debate of universal scope must be opened on this question. I am not forgetting that works on the collective civilized life of the highest interest have already poured out; and that some of these works have presented with force and clarity a liberal point of view. If, nevertheless, I dare to put forward other views it is because I think the ideas invoked up to now by liberals suffer from a timid traditionalism and an attachment to political prejudices which the experience of nearly two centuries has rejected.

The liberal will not be able to save liberty, in danger of death, unless he has the courage to speak in public against these prejudices. He, the sole revolutionary of our days, ought to have the courage to pass for a reactionary in the eyes of the capitalist-conservative reactionaries and those of the Marxist-Communists. But this courage one must not yet demand from the political man. Indeed, politicians don't lack courage, but theirs is of an entierly different kind; and if a man engaged in active politics risks an exploration of ideas implicit in the liberal faith without regard for the positive consequences of his eventual conclusion, he would be giving a proof not of courage but of temerity.

The political man is a man of action. He owes himself to the useful. The writer is a man of thought. He owes himself to truth. Thus

[1] The book, *De L'Angoisse à la Liberté*.

it is the liberal writer upon whom devolves the task of exploring the ideas implicit in the liberal faith in order to renew it, and in so doing of defining liberalism and giving it its vigor; and it is only when the debate so begun has gushed forth new ideas and purified the old ones that a rejuvenated liberal opinion will permit the political men of tomorrow to direct positive politics into new channels.

Beset with the daily tasks of the political battle, the political man is not one to be too embarrassed with general ideas and principles. His job consists in gaining tactical positions; and it is human that from time to time he will let himself be disoriented in his strategy. So it is even more important that those who are able to indulge in the luxury of braving the public opinion of today in order to better prepare for tomorrow remind him at times of the study of those general ideas and those principles which are the *raison d'être* of his battle. "One may do everything with bayonettes, except sit down on them," said Napoleon. It should not be possible for the cynic to say: "One may do everything with principles, everything without exception."

But liberalism, hail-fellow-well-met, admits under its hospitable roof too many positive fellows and so-called realists, who see nothing more in the principles than means of making money. Let us speak out plainly: There are liberals who defend the liberty of man; and some liberals who defend the liberty of dividends. The true liberal sees no objection to the quest for dividends. To make money is neither "good" nor "evil." Money is a neutral medium, like water, air or paper. One may scatter in the water, or in the air, life-giving elements or poisons; one may write on paper sublime thoughts or vanities. One may, with money, do big things, little things, nice things or villainies. The true liberal is not against money—the prejudice which afflicts so many of the needy and incapable. But he would like money to stay in its place, and be an instrument and not an end.

The true liberal understands the close ties which unite economic liberalism to spiritual liberalism, but knows how to submit the first, a simple instrument, to the second, the true end of his doctrine. In this he is ready to temper the extremist individualism of the liberals of former times, adapting it as the experience of two centuries has proved necessary.

It is thus that liberalism, born from an irrational instinct, matured by reason and experience, flowers into wisdom. This liberalism, composed of equilibrium, of experience, of understanding of men and of

333

things, is then the natural conclusion of the long lives of men of good will.

Pressed by time, I have very often had to resign myself, when being published in Paris, to having my books translated into French from their original whether written in English or Spanish. This work, however, I have written directly in French. It seems to me, indeed, that the deviation imposed on liberalism by the Revolution of '93 and by Anglo-Saxon ideas has carried over to the political life of the Latin countries the most formidable effects. Neither France, nor Italy, nor Spain (nor the twenty Spains across the Atlantic) is able to felicitate itself on how the liberal democratic system functions among them. France and Italy are reduced to two-thirds of their liberal ranks by a Communist occupation of the other third which makes precarious the life of their public institutions. The liberal "space" of Spain is entirely occupied by military Fascism.

I offer this book in French, not, certainly, as a panacea to cure the three Latin sisters, but as a call to debate which should be instigated to discuss in all frankness and loyalty the very basis of our beliefs and institutions. I know very well that in doing this I am going to run counter to those ideas considered until now as inherent in liberalism. I deny that they are so, and I fight them precisely because I consider them contrary to the true liberal spirit. But if I have tried formulating my opinions, even the most "heretical," with all the precision of which I am capable, I must repeat here what is said in the text of the work, that I recognize the extreme difficulty which the spirit encounters in the application of the clearest principles; and that I do not present concrete examples of proposed political reforms at the end of the work other than as a guaranty of the importance which I attach to the principles these examples apply to—always ready to recognize the errors which I may have committed because of the complexity of the problem.

With these reservations, I hope that this essay may not be too unworthy of the end which I have assigned myself: to stimulate a debate which might one day end in the establishment of a liberal doctrine and of a concrete liberal movement. Too often the liberals are considered (even by themselves) as socialists of the second class. What is this if not socialist etiquette adhering to an important sector of the radical party? No: the liberal should not cut a figure as a moderate socialist or as a conservative open to the fads of the times. He has his own word to say. He even has the most important word to say. Liberalism alone marks and defines the line which human progress must take. It is not without meaning that one speaks of the ship of state. Well, with a ship, the part which is the furthest ahead is neither the left nor the right but the prow, which, being in the fore, cuts through the waters of history with a sharp clean edge.

II. UNIVERSAL FEDERATION: THE CO-WORLD

It is by virtue of nothing but a relatively recent deformation of thought and emotion that national frontiers have acquired the exceptional importance with which we see them invested today. Men of the elite have always declared themselves citizens of the world; and one might gather from their works a superb anthology of universalism whose motto might well be the phrase of Dante: *Nos autem cui mundus est patria, velut piscibus aequor. . . .*

If we try to reduce the national frontiers to their natural importance, we would be forced to admit that they really only express the extension of the same social condition we see established in the interior of each country: the tendency to create in each indentation of the physical landscape a social landscape in strict conformity with it. . . . And we will conclude that the liberal and reasonable solution of the problem of peace ought to be sought for in a federation of nations.

But precisely because we are liberals, we have, from the start, taken pains in constructing our states, not beginning from on high and from the center, but beginning from the base and ranging to the periphery. And, beginning with the family and with the parish, we have been anxious to affirm the right of each local ensemble to all its natural sovereignty in all the fields of activity it possesses. Thus we have extolled the constitution of communes, countries and regions each endowed with a maximum of political power and with autonomous decision. And we have favored also considering each community as a federation of the communities immediately inferior in size and, consequently, constituting each assembly by delegates elected by the assemblies of the constituent communities. It is only in this fashion of doing things that we seem organic and to conform to social nature.

When, passing beyond the boundaries of the nation, we envisage a federation of nations, we will remain faithful to those practical rules which social nature has dictated to us. We will not then be at all

335

disposed to imagine an abstract universal federation, which takes no account whatever of the forms of the planet and its inhabitants. And we lament above all the absurd plans put forth by some unrealistic people who think themselves idealists, and want to elect a president of the Republic of the World by a world assembly elected by universal suffrage.

Happily, nature is there to stop us from falling into ridicule and chaos. There are the seas which outline the continents where our countries are rooted. Let us proceed by steps to federalization. Here is Europe. When the nightmare in which our co-Europeans of the East live is brought to an end, Europe must federate. Meantime, free Europe must federate. But, once more, there will be no assembly elected by universal suffrage—and for many reasons which we have stated again and again in presenting liberal ideas in conformance with social nature as against "statistical" ideas and inorganic ideas in favor today. Since we have been led to reserve for the communities closest to the people—the commune, the country, the region—the greatest political liberty possible, we would not be disposed to sacrifice lightly on the altar of the Super-State the political liberties of the nations. Federalists we are, since we see all collective life as a pyramid of federations; but we ask ourselves with trepidation if many of the militants who believe sincerely that they are federalists might not be rather centralists desirous of overcentralizing power in a European Super-State. Let us say then: *Federation must be, but only of that which it is indispensable to federate and nothing more.* For it is always wise to disperse power. Certainly, it is too much dispersed today on the international plane, and not only dispersed but divergent to the point of incoherence. It is this incoherence which must be corrected by the co-ordination and the sense of unity which will emanate from federal institutions; but it is not necessary to go as far as concentration. That fashion of looking at things suffices to condemn the assembly elected by direct universal suffrage.

But there are other reasons which support the same opinion. Universal suffrage elections in Europe would resolve themselves into an abominable cacaphony of incoherent tendencies disguised as ideas. The people of Europe have a solidarity of destiny, but in it they remain no less marvelously diverse in natural gifts according to the stages of their evolution. The languages in which they express themselves are different; the idioms in which they think and feel are still more different. From European elections there would come nothing more than an artificial sum of quantities which are incoherent and could not be compared, something as bizarre as the petition which an old soldier presented one day at a review to Napoleon: "Joseph Durand. Age: 53; years of service: 26; campaigns: 14; wounds: 5; children: 8; total 106. Asks the Legion of Honor."

This is nothing but the persistence of statistics and arithmetic against life and integration. For—and this is again a reason for rejecting election by universal direct suffrage in what concerns the European Assembly—Europe is not and never will be a nation. Europe is a cluster of nations. Never, no matter what one does, can there be success in creating a European electoral body. The European federalists should undertake original work and imitate neither a European country already formed, like France, nor a federation already achieved, like Switzerland or the United States. Europe is *sui generis*. She resembles nothing. She should be given original institutions.

It is without doubt that the very base of these institutions should be an assembly. But for the true liberal, this assembly ought to be elected by the senates of the national federations. The assembly, in its turn, furnished with powers analogous to those of the national senates in respect to the common interests of the continent, will elect the government. One must have no illusions as to the power which the nations will be ready to accord to this European government. Conscious solidarity will make but very slow progress for a long time and neither the European assembly nor the European government will enjoy for a long time an authority comparable to that of the national states. It is even probable that at the beginning the European laws voted by the assembly will not attain their full strength until after ratification by the national senates.

Whatever it may be, the European political body should possess an authority sufficient to vote its own budget and apportion the expenses to the component nations, to organize its courts and its police and to co-ordinate the armed forces of the component nations either by merging into one European force or by linking them. Its economic services will tend also toward continental integration, which will take care of national interests.

It is not at all necessary to anticipate organizations absolutely parallel for the other continents. Historic, political and human facts may well be able to supersede in all or in part the physical facts. The British Commonwealth, the Spanish-American bloc, Islam, so many factors of nature complicate the design. But, with this reservation,

337

the principle remains the same. For us, liberals of the twentieth century, it is not a question of federating in one act all the nations of the world by leaping over the continental balustrade. Some federal organisms ought to be foreseen for the British Commonwealth, Iberic-America, Africa, Asia, perhaps Islam. These great human groups, in their turn, would constitute a Council of no more than twenty representatives which would govern the Co-World. The United Nations would then be able to stop encumbering universal affairs and this would be a fine economy of money, time and paper.

III. CONCLUSION

If now we look backward for a glance at the road covered, and how this road is situated in the landscape of modern thought, we might be tempted to ask if our manner of seeing doesn't permit the evolution of ideas since the eighteenth century to receive light from a new day. It was, indeed, in the eighteenth century that the critical, ironic, corrosive attitude toward the official religion took form and became general and that attitude has from then till now manifested itself at all times in the margin, so to say, *extra muros* of European culture. The great spirits of that century are all in revolt against dogmatic religion, but they are not against God nor against the existence of God; or, to return to our nomenclature, they are all searchers but not all atheists. D'Alembert, for example, is atheist, but Voltaire is not.

Unwittingly, these men of the eighteenth century initiated an era of purification and simplification of the idea of God; the net gain of their efforts has been to permit men of all countries and all cultures to "live" God in a fashion if not unique, or, so to speak, identical for all, at least no longer disparate and incoherent to the point of incompatibility. Gradually, the intellectual ambiance changes, in such a way that the enlightened opinion of the world, including the opinion of enlightened men in dogmatic religions, takes note of the absurdity that is implied in the "wars of religion." Isn't even the expression absurd? Is it possible that men have been able to tear one another to pieces over the differences in the fashion of comprehending that which surpasses them and of defining that which floods over them? The movement launched by the encyclopedists, preceded by names as glorious as those of Cervantes and Montaigne, had as historic function the shaking of the great religions, the tumbling down of the dead leaves and rotten branches, the parasitic ivy and even some bats and owls, in order to prepare, certainly not for a unique religion, which is a snare, but for a possible *entente* with God, without which the *entente* between men is inconceivable.

But this movement had also profound roots in the Reformation as much as among the Jews. Man being what he is, a kind of river of life, sometimes a mirror clear and transparent from the light of heaven, sometimes a torrent bursting and shaken by terrestrial forces, these movements of ideas which he creates and maintains through history scarcely resemble beautiful regular crystals, but rather mixtures to such an incoherent degree that one has trouble sometimes believing that they could possibly emanate from one and the same brain.

The leaders of the Reformation were all afflicted with a certain incoherence, Luther above all. It is perfectly possible to represent them as theologians tainted with dogma of the same style as Rome if not more so. Calvin putting to death Servetus yielded nothing to Torquemada unless it was in quantity. So far as they simplfied dogma and cult, and so far as they broke the monopoly of Rome, the men of the Reformation prepared the movement of the encyclopedists and in some way were a part of it, at least in the aspect in which it is considered here.

It is the same with the Jews and particularly with the converted Jews. The study of the influence of the *conversos* on the Spanish church shows that the tendency of these theologians, enlightened, erudite, but strictly orthodox, which Jewry gave to the Church, was all oriented toward simplification, toward elimination of the secondary aspects of the cult in order to retain nothing but the essential. What must be seen here perhaps is a "transfer," to the religion of Christ, of the abstract attitude which characterized the religion of Jehovah. But the dominant trait which unites the three branches of the movement, the Protestant, the Israelite and the encyclopedist, is intellectualism. The simplification and the purification of the idea of God are the work of the intellectuals.

Therein lies the force of the movement, for it is by intellectual criticism that the idea of God is able to attain universality among men. But there also is its weakness, and for two reasons. The first is that the average man holds less with God than with his own ideas of

339

God. Indeed, the Universal God finds himself always in opposition with the local god, and the critical work of purification and of simplification of the local gods in order to transmute them into Universal God is constantly started anew. This tension, nevertheless, is fertile, and the intellectual movement finds itself invigorated by it.

The other cause of weakness of the movement of intellectual criticism is more serious. It involves an excess of corrosive action of the intellectual acid which, after having scoured off all impurities which tarnished the metal of religion, attacks the metal itself. We have seen d'Alembert differing with Voltaire in that one is atheist and the other deist. From these two men, considered as symbols, emerge two currents of opinion which diverge—one going toward Jacobinism, the other toward liberalism.

What does nature say to us? Nature tells us that ever since life appeared on the planet the universal law of the physical world has found itself in a struggle with a law clearly contrary. Even when the physical world tends toward the common, the equal, quantity without quality, the surface without heights or depths, immobility and death, the organic world tends always toward the singular, the hierarchy, the unique quality, heights and depths, movement and life. The opposition is plain. It is irreducible.

We are able then to give to the advent of life on the planet the value of an incarnation of the Spirit. At the moment when this event takes place a battle begins between the Spirit and the Earth whose anguish is visible in the eyes of dogs before it bursts out in the Ninth Symphony, *King Lear* or *The Brothers Karamazov*. Human history is the history of that struggle. Humanity, facing the adversary, does not form a single front. It divides, rather it is naturally divided, into human groups—races, tribes, nations, empires, religions, philosophies—which lend their form and color to the natural social landscape which they inhabit. To describe them would be to write the universal history. Let us limit ourselves here to passing in review the fashions in which the different groups of the modern intellectual movement react before this conflict.

Atheist Jacobinism leads to denying the advent of the spirit. It does not recognize the contradiction between the laws of biology and the laws of physics; it hopes always to find a best way to fit vital phenomena together, like flagstones, under the principles of Clausius-

340

Carnot-Boltzmann,[2] meantime seeing in life nothing but complexes of physical phenomena.

The collective life which the Jacobin understands obeys the principle of Clausius-Carnot. It is doubtful that a single active politician preoccupied himself with it. But one finds that the political schools which spring from atheist Jacobinism work precisely in the sense of the second principle of thermodynamics. They are, in effect, favorable to leveling, opposed to hierarchy, always ready to bow before quantity and wrinkle their brows before quality. Cooped up in the steel cage of determinism, they are incapable, no matter what they say, of believing in liberty or even of comprehending it. The perfect conclusion of this mode of thinking is Communism; its intermediary step, socialism. This road leads to the mineralization of men, the grinding up of their institutions, classes and social strata in order to reduce their society to a heap of gravel. Triumph of earthly forces.

At the other end, the movement makes a pact with the national gods. It accepts the hierarchy, quality, but only under the supremacy of the nation and its nationals. The Spirit, here, not finding itself forsworn, denied, disowned, as in the materialistic atheistic and determinist schools, will still seem bent and even turned back on itself by its shock with the earthly forces. We are in the world of the demoniacal man who shows himself among the wild beasts and the ferocious fish like a shark. This is the world which Darwin tried to explain if not excuse with his thesis of the survival of the fittest: the world of the forest, the seas and the birds of prey.

The political schools which take their inspiration from this wing, the black wing of the intellectualist movement, are distinguished from those of the red wing in that the red wing does not recognize God, while the black wing recognizes him, but only in the form of a national animal—eagle, lion, cock, leopard, bear. We are now in a cannibal world which, if it does not eat individual men, makes whole peoples fodder for cannons. This demoniacal spirit does not operate as a pure state except in totalitarian doctrines. But the national and imperialist faith, diluted in doses more or less concentrated in the liberal solvent, is met with again in the majority of the political non-Marxist schools of the Western world, above all among the great

[2] The German, French and Austrian nineteenth-century founders of modern thermodynamics, relating to the conversion of mechanical energy and heat.

powers where power is in itself a temptation to which few of their citizens are in a condition to resist.

Human evolution, it must be admitted, is dominated by these two wings of the intellectualist movement stemming from the Reformation of the eighteenth century. Neither one nor the other is in harmony with social nature. Each denies liberty. One, the red wing, does not deny human unity; on the contrary, it affirms it. But, incapable of conceiving the free and creative essence of liberty, it is not able to guide men toward anything but the unity of death, the desert of sand. The other generally denies human unity and even when it affirms it, it is only as a tactic the better to fight in the "struggle for existence," in the war to the death waged by the national gods in the prehistoric jungle.

True liberalism alone opens the road lying between the red desert and the black jungle and leading toward the future. It understands, respects and tries to incarnate the Spirit. It takes into account the opposition between the physical law—the leveling, equalitarian and the quantitative—and the vital law—hierarchical, differentiated, qualitative. It proclaims above all the absolutely essential nature of liberty. In this regard, liberalism is the sole principle conforming to social nature and its evolution. For it knows that the opposition between physical nature and social nature is irreducible and that the line of human evolution should seek not at all to approximate physical nature, as the red wing wishes it, nor animal nature, as the black wing wishes it, but to withdraw from these two forms of nature in order to conform to social nature, and thus raise man toward the Spirit.

—Translated from the French by Whit Burnett

XX / A PHILOSOPHER OF
THE EAST AND WEST

SARVEPALLI RADHAKRISHNAN, GENERALLY CONSIDERED THE ABLEST EXPONENT of the rich philosophical traditions of the Far East and the leading advocate of a coming together of the Orient and the Occident in a reconciliation of spiritual values, is a native of a small town in South India, but his adult years saw him a citizen of the world, both European and Asiatic.

His first studies were in a Christian missionary institution of the Lutherans at Tirupati. He started his professional life as a teacher of philosophy in the Madras Presidency College in 1909 where, for the next seven years, he studied and taught the classics of Hinduism, as well as the scholastic works of Buddhism and Jainism.

"Although I admire the great masters of thought, ancient and modern, Eastern and Western, I cannot say that I am a follower of any, accepting his teaching in its entirety. I do not suggest that I refused to learn from others or that I was not influenced by them. While I was greatly stimulated by the minds of all those whom I have studied, my thought does not comply with any fixed traditional pattern. For my thinking had another source and proceeded from my own experience, which is not quite the same as what is acquired by mere study and reading. It is born of spiritual experience rather than deduced from logically ascertained premises. Philosophy is produced more by our encounter with reality than by the historical study of such encounters. In my writings I have tried to communicate my insight into the meanings of life. I am not sure, however, that I have succeeded in conveying my inmost ideas. I tried to show that my general position provides a valid interpretation of the world, which seems to me to be consistent with itself, to accord with the facts as we know them, and to foster the life or spirit.

". . . I think today Indian wisdom is essential not only for the revival of the Indian nation but also for the re-education of the human race."

Sir Sarvepalli Radhakrishnan, who is Fellow of All Souls College,

Oxford, honorary Fellow of the Royal Asiatic Society of Bengal, Spalding Professor of Eastern religions and ethics at Oxford, and holder of honorary degrees from universities in many parts of the world, was chosen Vice President of India in May, 1952, a post he still holds. Prior to that he was Indian Ambassador to the U.S.S.R., and before that was a member of the Indian Constituent Assembly, member of the executive board of Unesco, and President of the executive board of Unesco, in Paris. Sir Sarvepalli was president of the Silver Jubilee Session of the Indian Philosophical Congress in Calcutta in 1950 and twenty years before was president of the All-Asia Education Conference at Benares.

"Never in the history of philosophy," writes Professor George P. Conger, in "Radhakrishnan's World," the first of twenty-three articles by world-famous authorities on the philosophy of the Eastern thinker in *The Library of Living Philosophers,* "has there been quite such a world-figure. With his unique dual appointment at Benares and Oxford, like a weaver's shuttle he has gone to and fro between East and West, carrying a thread of understanding, weaving it into the fabric of civilization. We hear him and hear of him in China and South Africa, in Chicago and Mexico City. . . . Except for an occasional Marcus Aurelius, philosophers never will be king, but sometimes a philosopher wields among his contemporaries an influence which any king might envy."

The Religion of the Spirit and the World's Need

BY SARVEPALLI RADHAKRISHNAN

THE RELIGION OF THE SPIRIT

When rational thought is applied to the empirical data of the world and of the human self, the conclusion of a Supreme who is Pure Being and Free Activity is reached; but it may be argued that it is only a necessity of thought, a hypothesis, however valid it may be. There

344

is also an ancient and widespread tradition that we can apprehend the Eternal Being with directness and immediacy. When the Upanishads speak of *jñāna* or gnosis, when the Buddha speaks of *bodhi* or enlightenment, when Jesus speaks of the truth that will make us free, they refer to the mode of direct spiritual apprehension of the Supreme, in which the gap between truth and Being is closed. Their religion rests on the testimony of the Holy Spirit, on personal experience, on mysticism as defined by St. Thomas Aquinas, *cognitio dei experimentalis.* From the affirmations of spiritual experience, we find that it is possible to reconcile the conclusions of logical understanding with the apprehensions of integral insight.

There are different types of knowledge: perceptual, conceptual, and intuitive and they are suited to different kinds of objects. Plotinus tells us that sense perceptions are below us, logical reasonings are with us, and spiritual apprehensions are above us.

The last type of knowledge may be called integral insight, for it brings into activity not merely a portion of our conscious being, sense of reason, but the whole. It also reveals to us not abstractions but the reality in its integrity. Existentialists dispute the priority of essence to existence. Whereas the possible is prior to the actual insofar as the genesis of the universe is concerned, in the world itself thought works on and in existence and abstracts from it. Thought reaches its end of knowledge insofar as it returns to being. Thought is essentially self-transcendent. It deals with another than thought and so is only symbolic of it. Thinking deals with essences, and existences are unattainable to it. Existence is one way of being, though it is not the only way. Knowledge is reflection on the experience of existence. It is within being. The inadequacy of knowledge to being is stressed by Bradley in his distinction between *what* and *that,* between a logical category and actual being. In integral insight we have knowledge by identity. Although logical knowledge is mediate and symbolic, it is not false. Its construction is not an imaginative synthesis. It falls short of complete knowledge, because it gives the structure of being, not being itself. In integral insight we are put in touch with actual being. This highest knowledge transcends the distinction of subject and object. Even logical knowledge is possible because this highest knowledge is ever present. It can only be accepted as foundational. Being is Truth. *Sat* is *cit.*

We use the direct mode of apprehension, which is deeper than logical understanding, when we contemplate a work of art, when we enjoy

345

great music, when we acquire an understanding of another human being in the supreme achievement of love. In this kind of knowledge the subject is not opposed to the object but is intimately united with it. By calling this kind of knowledge integral insight, we bring out that it does not contradict logical reason, though the insight exceeds the reason. Intellect cannot repudiate instinct any more than intuition can deny logical reason. Intellectual preparation is an instrument for attaining to the truth of the spirit, but the inward realization of the truth of spirit transcends all intellectual verification, since it exists in an immediacy beyond all conceivable mediation.

The Supreme is not an object but the absolute subject, and we cannot apprehend it by either sense-perception or logical inference. Kant was right in denying that being was a predicate. We are immersed in being. When the Upanishads ask us to grow from intellectual to spiritual consciousness, they ask us to effect an enlargement of our awareness by which the difficulties of insecurity, isolation, and death are overcome. We are called upon to grow from division and conflict into freedom and love, from ignorance to wisdom. Such wisdom cannot come except to those who are pure not only in heart but also in the intellect, which has to rid itself of all preconceptions. Unmediated apprehension of the primordial Spirit is the knowledge of God. It is achieved by a change of consciousness, the experience of a new birth. It means an illumined mind, a changed heart, and a transformed will. Wisdom composes the various elements of our mental life, modifies our being, restores our community with nature and society, and makes living significant. Wisdom is freedom from fear, for fear is the result of a lack of correspondence between the nature of the individual and his environment, the clash of the ego and the nonego which is alien and indifferent to it. The struggle against the alien is the source of suffering. Man is a being who is straining toward infinity, in quest of eternity; but the condition of his existence, finite and limited, temporal and mortal, causes the suffering. When he attains "integrality," there is harmony in his life and its expression is joy.

Through wisdom we grow into likeness with the Spirit. St. Thomas Aquinas observes: "By this light the blessed are made deiform, that is like God, according to the scriptural saying 'When he shall appear, we shall be like him and we shall see him as he is.' "[1]

There is a tradition of direct apprehension of the Supreme in all

[1] I. John 3:2, quoted in *Summa Theologica* 1, q, 12, a, 5, C.

lands, in all ages and in all creeds.[2] The seers describe their experiences with an impressive unanimity. They are "near to one another on mountains farthest apart." They certify, in words which ring both true and clear, of a world of spirit alive and waiting for us to penetrate. Indian religions take their stand on spiritual experience, on divine-human encounter, *kṛṣṇārjunasaṁvāda,* and so do the prophets and saints of other religions. Augustine writes: "I entered and beheld with the eye of my soul above the same eye of my soul, above my mind, the Light unchangeable."[3] St. Bernard wrote that happy and blessed was he "who once or twice—or even once only—in this mortal life for the space of a moment has lost himself in God." St. John of the Cross speaks of that steady and established certitude of essential creative union which alone he considers worthy to be called the "spiritual marriage" of the soul.

What God communicates to the soul in this intimate union is utterly ineffable, beyond the reach of all possible words . . . in this state God and the soul are united as the window is with the light or the coal with the fire . . . this communication of God diffuses itself substantially in the whole soul or rather the soul is transformed in God. In this transformation the soul drinks of God in its very substance and its spiritual powers.

Spiritual experience, as distinct from religious feeling of dependence or worship or awe, engages our whole person. It is a state of ecstasy or complete absorption of our being. When the flash of absolute reality breaks through the normal barriers of the conscious mind it leaves a trail of illumination in its wake. The excitement of illumination is distinct from the serene radiance of enlightenment. The experience is not of a subjective psychic condition. The contemplative insight into the source of all life is not an escape into the subjective. The human individual can strip himself one after the other of the outer sheaths of consciousness, penetrate to the nerve and quick of his life

---

[2] "The close agreement which we find in these records (of mystic life), written in different countries, in different ages, and even by adherents of different creeds (for Asia has here its own important contribution to make) can only be accounted for, if we hold that the mystical experience is a genuine part of human nature, which may be developed, like the arts, by concentrated attention and assiduous labour, and which assumes the same general forms whenever and wherever it is earnestly sought." W. R. Inge: *The Philosophy of Plotinus* (1918), Vol. I, p. 2. Rudolf Otto, in the Introduction to his book on *Mysticism: East and West,* observes: "We maintain that, in mysticism, there are wide and strong primal impulses working in the human soul which as such are completely unaffected by differences of climate, of geographical position or of race. These show, in their similarity, an inner relationship of types of human experience and spiritual life which is truly astonishing." (English translation, 1932), XVI.

[3] *Confessions* VII, 16.

until all else fades away into illimitable darkness, until he is alone in the white radiance of a central and unique ecstasy. This is the fulfillment of man. This is to be with God. This is to be of God. During our hurried passage through life there may come to us a few moments of transcendent joy, when we seem to stand literally outside our narrow selves and attain a higher state of being and understanding. All religions call upon us to renew those great moments and make the experience of spirit the center of our lives.

When the vision fades, the habitual awareness of this world returns. The so-called proofs of the existence of God are the results of critical reflection on the spiritual intuitions of the ultimate Fact of Spirit. These intuitions inspire the acts of reflection, which only confirm what has been apprehended in another way. The reflections are pure and true to the extent that they refer to the intuited facts. There is a perpetual disquiet because ultimate Being is not an object. Reflective accounts are thus only approximations.

Being as such is uncharacterizable and our descriptions and translations are in forms of objects which are less than Being and consequently are inadequate. Abstract ideals and intellectualizations do not deal justly with Being which is given to us as Absolute Presence in adoration and worship. It is through religious contemplation that we realize the Holy. It is not simple apprehension. It is the surrender of the self, its opening to the Supreme.

The experience of a pure and unitary consciousness in a world divided gives rise to the twofold conception of the Absolute as Pure Transcendent Being lifted above all relativities, and the Free Active God functioning in the world. Some emphasize the transcendent aspect, the fullness of being, the sublime presence, the sovereignly subsistent "other," above all names and thought; others the immanent aspect, the fullness of life, the living personal God of love who made the world, gave us freedom, and wishes us to participate in the riches of life. St. John of the Cross says:

Beyond all sensual images, and all conceptual determination, God offers Himself as the absolute act of being in its pure actuality. Our concept of God, a mere feeble analogue of a reality which overflows it in every direction, can be made explicit only in the judgment: Being is Being, an absolute positing of that which, lying beyond every object, contains in itself the sufficient reason of objects. And that is why we can rightly say that the very excess of positivity which hides the divine being from our eyes is nevertheless the light which lights up all the rest: *ipsa caligo summa est mentis illuminatio.*

We have here the two aspects of supracosmic transcendence and cosmic universality, the divine mystery which is inexpressible, Eckhart's Godhead, and the mystery which is directed toward the world, Eckhart's God. The God who reveals Himself to the world and to man is not the Absolute which is inexpressible, relationless mystery.

Attempts to rationalize the mystery, to translate into the language of concepts that which is inexpressible in concepts, have resulted in different versions. We may use the trinitarian conception to unfold the nature of the Supreme Being; the Brahman, the Absolute, is the first person, the second is Iśvara, and the third is the World-Spirit. The three persons are different sides of the one Supreme. They are not three different persons but are the one God who hides himself[4] and reveals himself in various degrees. In communicating their experiences the seers use words and symbols current in their world.

The liberated souls have overcome the power of time, the force of Karma. There is something in common between the wisdom of the sage and the simplicity of the child, serene trust and innocent delight in existence. The happy state of childhood is almost the lost paradise of the human mind. The free spirits are the rays of light that shine from the future, attracting us all who still dwell in darkness. They do not separate themselves from the world but accept the responsibility for perfecting all life. There is no such thing as individual salvation, for it presupposes the salvation of others, universal salvation, the transfiguration of the world. No man, however enlightened and holy he may be, can ever really be saved until all the others are saved. Those individuals who have realized their true being are the integrated ones who have attained personal integrity. Their reason is turned into light, their heart into love, and their will into service. Their demeanor is disciplined and their singleness of spirit is established. Selfish action is not possible for them. Ignorance and craving have lost their hold. They are dead to pride, envy, and uncharitableness. The world in which they live is no more alien to them. It is hospitable, not harsh. It becomes alive, quakes, and sends forth its greetings. Human society becomes charged with the grace and grandeur of the eternal. These free spirits reach out their hands toward the warmth in all things. They have that rarest quality in the world, simple goodness, beside

[4] "Verily Thou art a God that hidest Thyself." Psalm 103.

which all the intellectual gifts seem a little trivial. They are meek, patient, long-suffering. They do not judge others because they do not pretend to understand them. Because of their eager selfless love they have the power to soothe the troubled heart. To those in pain their presence is like the cool soft hand of someone they love, when their head is hot with fever. The released individuals are artists in creative living. With an awareness of the Eternal, they participate in the work of the world. Even as the Supreme has two sides of pure being and free activity, these liberated souls, who are the vehicles of divine life,[5] have also two sides: the contemplative and the active.

Their life is socially minded. We are members of a whole, parts of *brahmāṇḍa* (the cosmic egg), which is one, which is perpetually in transition until its final purpose is achieved. "No man liveth unto himself and no man dieth unto himself" (St. Paul). Their attitude is not one of lofty condescension or patronizing pity to lift a debased creature out of mire. But it is a conviction of the solidarity of the world *loka-saṁgraha* and a recognition that the low and the high are bound together in one spirit. Vicarious suffering, not vicarious punishment, is a law of spiritual life. The free spirits bend to the very level of the enslaved to emancipate their minds and hearts. They inspire, revive and strengthen the life of their generation.

From the time I was a student, I have heard criticisms made against Indian religions that they are world-negating and that the attitude of our religious men is one of withdrawal from the world. Though the supreme quest is for the freedom of the spirit, for the vision of God, there is also the realization of the ever-present need of the world for the light and guidance of free spirits. A life of service and sacrifice is the natural and inevitable expression and the proof of the validity of spiritual experience. After years of solitary contemplation the Buddha attained enlightenment. The rest of his life was devoted to intense social and cultural work. According to Mahāyāna Buddhism, the released spirits retain their compassion for suffering humanity. Even those whose activities are limited to the instruction of their disciples participate in social leadership insofar as they aim at refashioning human society. Gandhi, well known as a religious man, did not strive to escape from the human scene to forge a solitary destiny. He said: "I am striving for the kingdom of salvation which is spiritual deliverance. For me the road to salvation is through incessant toil in the

[5] "Grace makes us participants of the divine nature." II Peter 1:4.

service of my country and of humanity. I want to identify myself with everything that lives. I want to live at peace with both friend and foe." He reckoned social reform and political action among his religious duties. He founded not a monastic order but a revolutionary party. Gandhi brought home to us the lessons of the saints of old, that no one who believes in spiritual values can abandon to their fate the millions of people whom misery and impossible conditions of life have condemned to a hell on earth. Active service is a part of spiritual life.

Although the unitive knowledge of God here and now is the final end of man, it remains true that some forms of social and cultural life put more obstacles in the way of individual development than others. It is our duty to create and maintain forms of social organization which offer the fewest possible impediments to the development of the truly human life. By improving the conditions of social life we remove powerful temptations to ignorance and irresponsibility and encourage individual enlightenment. Every man, whatever may be his racial or social origin, is potentially a son of God, made in his image. Human personality is sacred. The human person has a claim to be treated as an end in himself and is therefore entitled to the rights to life, freedom, and security. Freedom to be himself is the right of personality. These rights involve duties. Our legal and political systems must help the realization of our rights and the acceptance of our obligations. Our civilization has failed to the extent to which these ideals are denied or betrayed. We must work for the achievement of these ideals in accordance with the principles of freedom, truth, and justice. This is not to reduce religion to a sublimated social engineering.

There is a tendency in all religions, Eastern or Western, to neglect the practical side. Anyone who approaches the New Testament will find that the emphasis is on other-worldliness. Jesus' teaching about the Kingdom of God and its righteousness, of its coming and of the conditions of our partaking in it, does not betray any interest in the structures of our temporal life. The letters of the Apostles are concerned with the preaching of salvation, the proclamation of Resurrection, of the divine judgment, of the restoration and perfection of all things beyond their historical existence. The few brief comments on the state, on marriage and family life, on the relations between masters and slaves, do not take away the essentially other-worldly character of the teaching of Jesus and his disciples. In the last century his teaching has been interpreted in a manner that shows its kinship with our social and cultural problems.[6]

Religion is not a particular way of life but is the way of all life. Jesus said: "I am the Way, the Truth and the Life." Religious life is neither ascetic nor legalistic. It condemns mere externalism and does not insist on obedience to laws and ordinances. "Where the spirit of the Lord is there is liberty." Liberty is freedom from all taboos and restrictions. We are not called upon to hate the world because it is the creation of a hostile demiurge. To look upon the world as undivine is a speculative aberration. God is not jealous of his own works. The world is an abyss of nothingness, if we take away its roots in the Divine. What the Indian thinkers aim at is action without attachment. It is action of an individual who is no more a victim of selfishness, who has identified himself with the divine center which is in him and in all things. Since he is not emotionally involved in the "fruits of action," he is able to act effectively. True religion has elements in it of withdrawal from the world and of return to it. Its aim is the control of life by the power of spirit.

Our social conscience has been anesthetized by a formal religion and it has now to be roused. In recent times, it is the atheists and not the saints that have taken the lead in the work of social enlightenment and justice. In the history of religions, however, the role of the religious leader has been important. Though dedicated to a life of contemplation he is led to act like a ferment of renewal in the structure of society. That great tradition of which Gandhi is the latest example, requires to be renewed.[7]

The integrated individuals are the rare privileged beings who are in advance of their time. They are the forerunners of the future race,[8] who set to us the path we have to take, to rise from fallen to transfigured nature. They are not, however, to be regarded as unique

[6] "All New Testament scholars nowadays would admit that this nineteenth century interpretation, whether we like it or not, was a falsification of the historical facts. Whether you understand the Kingdom of God more as a present reality or as something to come, in either case it is a reality which entirely transcends the sphere of civilisation." Emil Brunner, *Christianity and Civilisation*, First Part (1948), p. 7.

[7] God inquires of Israel: "Is this such a fast that I have chosen? a day for a man to afflict his soul? is it to bow down his head as a bullrush, and to spread sackcloth and ashes under him? Wilt thou call this a fast, and an acceptable day to the Lord? Is not this the fast that I have chosen; to loose the bonds of wickedness, to undo the heavy burdens, and to let the oppressed go free, and that ye break every yoke?" Isaiah 58:5, 6.

[8] Christ, said St. Paul, was to be the first born of a great brotherhood. Romans 8:29.

and absolute manifestations of the Absolute. There cannot be a complete manifestation of the Absolute in the world of relativity. Each limited manifestation may be perfect in its own way, but is not the Absolute which is within all and above all. The life of a Buddha or a Jesus tells us how we can achieve the same unity with the Absolute to which they had attained and how we can live at peace in the world of manifested being. The light that lighteth everyone that cometh into the world shone in those liberated spirits with great radiance and intensity. The Kingdom of God is the Kingdom of persons who are spiritually free, who have overcome fear and loneliness. Everyone has in him the possibility of this spiritual freedom, the essence of enlightenment, is a *bodhisattva*. The divine sonship of Christ is at the same time the divine sonship of every man. The end of the cosmic process is the achievement of universal resurrection, redemption of all persons who continue to live as individuals till the end of history.

The function of the discipline of religion is to further the evolution of man into his divine stature, develop increased awareness and intensity of understanding. It is to bring about a better, deeper and more enduring adjustment in life. All belief and practice, song and prayer, meditation and contemplation, are means to this development of direct experience, an inner frame of mind, a sense of freedom and fearlessness, strength and security. Religion is the way in which the individual organizes his inward being and responds to what is envisaged by him as the ultimate Reality. It is essentially intensification of experience, the displacement of triviality by intensity.

Each individual is a member of a community where he shares work with others; but he is also an individual with his senses and emotions, desires and affections, interests and ideals. There is a solitary side to his being as distinct from the social, where he cherishes thoughts unspoken, dreams unshared, reticences unbroken. It is there that he shelters the questionings of fate, the yearning for peace, the voice of hope and the cry of anguish. When the Indian thinkers ask us to possess our souls, to be *ātmavantam,* not to get lost in the collective currents, not to get merged in the crowd of those who have emptied and crucified their souls, *ātmahano janāh,* who have got their souls bleached in the terrible unmercy of things, they are asking us to open out our inward being to the call of the transcendent. Religion is not a movement stretching out to grasp something, external, tangible and good, and to possess it. It is a form of being, not having, a mode of life. Spiritual life

353

is not a problem to be solved but a reality to be experienced. It is new birth into enlightenment.

The Upanishads speak to us of three stages of religious life, *śravaṇa,* hearing, *manana,* reflection, *nididhyāsana* or disciplined meditation. We rise from one stage to another. Joachim of Floris in the twelfth century sees the story of man in three stages. The first is of the "Father" of the Letter, of the Law, where we have to listen and obey. The second is of the "Son"; here we have argument and criticism. Tradition is explained, authority is explicated. The third stage is of the Spirit, where we have "prayer and song," meditation and inspiration.[9] Through these, the tradition becomes a vital and transforming experience. The life of Jesus, the witness of St. Paul, of the three apostles on the Mount of Transfiguration, of Ezekiel, and of scores of others are an impressive testimony to the fact of religion as experience. Mohammed is said to have received his messages in ecstatic states. St. Thomas, in the beginning of the fourth book of his *Summa Contra Gentiles,* speaks of three kinds of human knowledge of divine things. "The first of these is the knowledge that comes by the natural light of reason," when the reason ascends by means of creatures to God. The second "descends to us by way of revelation." The third is possible only to the human mind "elevated to the perfect intuition of the things that are revealed." Dante symbolized the first by Virgil, the second by Beatrice, the third by St. Bernard.

Though God is everywhere, he is found more easily in the soul. The inward light is never darkened and it enlightens with understanding the minds of those who turn to it. Our self is a holy temple of the Spirit into which we may not enter without a sense of awe and reverence.

Behold Thou wert within and I abroad, and there I searched for Thee. Thou wert with me but I was not with Thee. Thou calledst and shoutedst, burstedst my deafness. Thou flashedst, shonedst, and scatteredst my blindness. Thou breathedst odours, and I drew in breath, and pant for Thee. I tasted and hunger and thirst. Thou touchedst me, and I was on fire for Thy peace.[10]

"Thou wert more inward to me than my most inward part, and higher than my highest."[11] Bishop Ullathorne says:

[9] See Gerald Heard: *The Eternal Gospel* (1948), p. 6.
[10] St. Augustine, *Confessions* X, 38.
[11] *Confessions* III, 11.

Let it be plainly understood that we cannot return to God unless we enter first into ourselves. God is everywhere, but not everywhere to us. There is but one point in the universe where God communicates with us, and that is the center of our own soul. There He waits for us; there He meets us; there He speaks to us. To seek Him, therefore, we must enter into our own interior.[12]

When Kierkegaard tells us that truth is identical with subjectivity, he means that if it is objectified, it becomes relative. He does not mean that the truth is peculiar to and private to the individual. He makes out that we must go deep down into the subject to attain the experience of Universal Spirit. Professor A. N. Whitehead says that "religion is what the individual does with his solitariness."[13] Each individual must unfold his own awareness of life, witness his own relation to the source or sources of his being and, in the light of his experience, resolve the tragedies and contradictions of his inward life. "If you are never solitary, then you are never religious." It is in solitude that we prepare the human candle for the divine flame. This does not mean a facile commensurability between God and man. It means that man can transcend himself, can exceed his limits. To get at the transcendent within oneself, one must break through one's normal self. The revelation of the divine in man is of the character of an interruption of our routine self. We must impose silence on our familiar self, if the spirit of God is to become manifest in us. The divine is more deeply in us than we are ourselves. We attain to spirit by passing beyond the frontiers of the familiar self. If we do not mechanize the doctrine of Incarnation, of "God manifest in the flesh," we make out that man has access to the inmost being of the divine, in these moments of highest spiritual insight. The highest human life is life in God. In the words of Eckhart, "God in the fullness of his Godhead dwells eternally in His Image, the soul."

Religions prescribe certain conditions to which we have to submit if we are to gain religious illumination. Discipline of the intellect, emotions and will is a prerequisite for spiritual perception. Religious spirits use the catastrophes of the world as opportunities for creative work. The world is the field for moral striving. The purpose of life is not the enjoyment of the world but the education of the soul.

In the middle of January, 1946, was published the Report of the

[12] *Groundwork of Christian Virtues*, p. 74.
[13] *Religion in the Making* (1926), p. 16.

N *

355

Commission appointed by the Archbishop of Canterbury "to survey the whole problem of modern evangelism with special reference to the spiritual needs and the prevailing intellectual outlook of the non-worshipping members of the community and to report on the organisation and methods by which the needs can most effectively be met." This Report, entitled *The Conversion of England,* points out that religion has become a waning influence in the national life of the country and calls for a strengthening and quickening of spiritual life. Religion, it urges, is a conversion, a mental and spiritual revolution, a change from a self-centered to a God-centered life. It is a call to a new vision and understanding of life. The Report asks for the assertion of the primacy of spirit over the long dominant external forms of religion, submission to authority, subscription to a formula. The discipline of religion consists in turning inward, deepening our awareness and developing a more meaningful attitude to life which frees us from bondage and hardening of the spirit. "Except ye be converted and become as little children, ye shall not enter into the kingdom of heaven."

There are different ways which are prescribed by religions to achieve this inward change. *Yoga* is used in Indian religions for the methods of drawing near to the Supreme. *Yoga* is a path, a praxis, and training by which the individual man, bleeding from the split caused by intelligence, becomes whole. Intellectual concentration, *jñāna,* emotional detachment, *bhakti,* ethical dedication, *karma,* are all types of *Yoga.* In Patañjali's *Yoga Sūtra,* we have a development of what Plato calls recollection, the way by which we steadily withdraw from externality, from our functions which are at the mercy of life and enter into our essential being, which is not the individual ego but the Universal Spirit. It is the act of recollection by which the recollecting self distinguishes its primal being from all that is confused with it, its material, vital, psychological and logical expressions. By recollection the self is assured of its participation in ultimate being, the principle of all positivity, the ontological mystery. We have power over the outer expressions. We may submit ourselves to despair, deny physical being by resorting to suicide, surpass all expressions and discover that deep down there is something other than these empirical manifestations. Even the thinking subject is only in relation to an object, but the spirit in us is not the subject of epistemology. It is primordial being.

When we are anchored in the mystery which is the foundation of our very being, our activities express "Thy will and not mine." When we are in Being we are beyond the moral world of freedom.

Our deeds flow out of the heart of reality and our desires are swallowed up in love. Spiritual freedom is different from moral autonomy. The inward hold we get makes us the masters of life. Religion then is experience turning inward toward the realization of itself.

RELIGION AND RELIGIONS

The Report on the *Conversion of England* deplores the unhappy divisions, the lack of charity among particular congregations, which obscure the fellowship of the Christian Church and calls upon the different Christian sects to continue and co-operate in the task of the conversion of England. It asks us to adopt the principle of unity in variety, which is not only a profound spiritual truth but the most obvious common sense.

If we accept this principle seriously we cannot stop at the frontiers of Christianity. We must move along a path which shall pass beyond all the differences of the historical past and eventually be shared in common by all mankind. Belief in exclusive claims and monopolies of religious truth has been a frequent source of pride, fanaticism and strife. The vehemence with which religions were preached and the savagery with which they were enforced are some of the disgraces of human history. Secularism and paganism point to the rivalries of religions for a proof of the futility of religion. A little less missionary ardor, a little more enlightened skepticism will do good to us all. Our attitude to other religions should be defined in the spirit of that great saying in a play of Sophocles, where Antigone says, "I was not born to share men's hatred, but their love." We must learn the basic principles of the great world religions as the essential means of promoting international understanding.

Besides, Whitehead observes that "the decay of Christianity and Buddhism as determinative influences in modern thought is partly due to the fact that each religion has unduly sheltered itself from the other. They have remained self-satisfied and unfertilized."[14] A study of other living religions helps and enhances the appreciation of our own faith. If we adopt a wider historical view we obtain a more comprehensive vision and understanding of spiritual truth. Christian thinkers like St. Thomas Aquinas were willing to find confirmation of the truths of Christianity in the works of pagan philosophers. We live in a world which is neither Eastern nor Western, where every one of us is the heir

[14] Quoted in Inge: *Mysticism and Religion* (1947), p. 40.

to all civilization. The past of China, Japan, and India is as much our past as is that of Israel, Greece, and Rome. It is our duty and privilege to enlarge our faculties of curiosity, of understanding, and realize the spaciousness of our common ground. No way of life is uninteresting so long as it is natural and satisfying to those who live it. We may measure true spiritual culture by the comprehension and veneration we are able to give to all forms of thought and feeling which have influenced masses of mankind. We must understand the experience of people whose thought eludes our categories. We must widen our religious perspective and obtain a world wisdom worthy of our time and place.

Religious provincialism stands in the way of a unitary world culture which is the only enduring basis for a world community. "Shall two walk together except they have agreed?" To neglect the spiritual unity of the world and underline the religious diversity would be philosophically unjustifiable, morally indefensible, and socially dangerous.

The arrogant dislike of other religions has today given place to respectful incomprehension. It is time that we accustom ourselves to fresh ways of thinking and feeling. The interpenetration of obstinate cultural traditions is taking place before our eyes. If we have a sense of history we will find that human societies are by nature unstable. They are ever on the move giving place to new ones. Mankind is still in the making. The new world society requires a new world outlook based on respect for and understanding of other cultural traditions.

The procedure suggested here provides us with a basis for interreligious understanding and co-operation. It involves an abandonment of missionary enterprises such as they are now. The "compassing of sea and land to make one proselyte"[15] is not possible when our ignorance of other peoples' faiths is removed. The main purpose of religious education is not to train others in our way of thinking and living, not to substitute one form of belief for another, but to find out what others have been doing and help them to do it better. We are all alike in need of humility and charity, of repentance and conversion, of a change of mind, of a turning round. The missionary motives are derived from the conviction of the absolute superiority of our own religion and of supreme contempt for other religions. They are akin to the political motives of imperialist countries to impose their culture and civilization

[15] Matthew 23:15. Cf. C. S. Lewis: "Democrats by birth and education, we should prefer to think that all nations and individuals start level in the search for God, or even that all religions are equally true. It must be admitted at once that Christianity makes no concessions to this point of view"! *Miracles* (1947), p. 140.

on the rest of the world. If missionary activities such as they are now are persisted in, they will become a prime factor in the spiritual impoverishment of the world. They are treason against Him who "never left himself without a witness." St. Justin said: "God is the word of whom the whole human race are partakers, and those who lived according to Reason are Christians even though accounted atheists . . . Socrates and Heracleitus, and of the barbarians, Abraham and many others." St. Ambrose's well-known gloss on I Corinthians 12:3, "All that is true, by whomsoever it has been said, is from the Holy Ghost," is in conformity with the ancient tradition of India on this matter. "As men approach me, so I do accept them, men on all sides follow my path" says the *Bhagavadgītā.* "If the follower of any particular religion understood the saying of Junayd, 'The color of the water is the color of the vessel containing it,' he would not interfere with the beliefs of others, but would perceive God in every form and in every belief," says ibn-ul-'Arabi.[16] Our aim should be not to make converts, Christians into Buddhists or Buddhists into Christians, but enable both Buddhists and Christians to rediscover the basic principles of their own religions and live up to them.

Every religion is attempting to reformulate its faith in accordance with modern thought and criticism. Stagnant and stereotyped religions are at variance with the psychology of modern life. If, in the name of religion, we insist on teaching much that modern knowledge has proved to be untrue, large numbers will refuse to accept devitalized doctrines. Aware of this danger, religions are emphasizing the essential principles and ideals rather than the dogmatic schemes. For example, the moral and spiritual truths of Christianity, faith in the Divine Being, in the manifestation of the spiritual and moral nature of the Divine in the personality of Jesus, one of the eldest of many brothers, faith that we can receive strength and guidance by communion with the Divine, are regarded as more important than beliefs in the miraculous birth, resurrection, ascension and the return of Jesus as the judge of mankind at the end of human history. The *Report of the Commission on Christian Doctrine*[17] appointed by the Archbishops of Canterbury and York, made it permissible for the English

---

[16] R. A. Nicholson: *Studies in Islamic Mysticism* (1921), p. 159. Cf.: Faridu'd Din Attar in *Manṭiqu't Tayr:* "Since then there are different ways of making the journey, no two (soul) birds will fly alike. Each finds a way of his own, on this road of mystic knowledge, one by means of the Mihrab and another through the Idol." See Ananda K. Coomaraswamy, *The Bugbear of Literacy* (1947), Ch. III.

[17] 1938, Society for Promoting Christian Knowledge.

Churchmen to hold and to teach the Christian faith in accordance with the verified results of modern scientific, historical, and literary criticism. Other religions are also attempting to cast off the unessentials and return to the basic truths. Whereas the principles of religions are eternal, their expressions require continual development. The living faiths of mankind carry not only the inspiration of centuries but also the encrustations of error. Religion is a "treasure in earthen vessels" (St. Paul). These vessels are capable of infinite refashioning and the treasure itself of renewed application in each succeeding age of human history. The profound intuitions of religions require to be presented in fresh terms more relevant to our own experience, to our own predicament. If religion is to recover its power, if we are to help those who are feeling their way and are longing to believe, a restatement is essential. It is a necessity of the time. "I have many things to say unto you, but ye cannot bear them now; when he, the Spirit of Truth, is come, he will guide you into all the truth."[18] Every religion is growing under the inspiration of the Divine Spirit of Truth in order to meet the moral and spiritual ordeal of the modern mind. This process of growth is securing for our civilization a synthesis on the highest level of the forces of religion and culture and enabling their followers to co-operate as members of one great fellowship.

The world is seeking not so much a fusion of religions as a fellowship of religions, based on the realization of the foundational character of man's religious experience. William Blake says: "As all men are alike (though infinitely various), so all Religions, as all similars, have one source." The different religions may retain their individualities, their distinctive doctrines and characteristic pieties, so long as they do not impair the sense of spiritual fellowship. The light of eternity would blind us if it came full in the face. It is broken into colors so that our eyes can make something of it. The different religious traditions clothe the one Reality in various images and their visions could embrace and fertilize each other so as to give mankind a many-sided perfection, the spiritual radiance of Hinduism, the faithful obedience of Judaism, the life of beauty of Greek Paganism, the noble compassion of Buddhism, the vision of divine love of Christianity, and the spirit of resignation to the sovereign lord of Islam. All these represent different aspects of the inward spiritual life, projections on the intellectual plane of the ineffable experiences of the human spirit.

If religion is the awareness of our real nature in God, it makes

[18] John 16:12ff.

360

for a union of all mankind based on communion with the Eternal. It sees in all the same vast universal need it has felt in itself. The different religions take their source in the aspiration of man toward an unseen world, though the forms in which this aspiration is couched are determined by the environment and climate of thought.[19] The unity of religions is to be found in that which is divine or universal in them and not in what is temporary and local. Where there is the spirit of truth there is unity. As in other matters, so in the sphere of religion there is room for diversity and no need for discord. To claim that any one religious tradition bears unique witness to the truth and reveals the presence of the true God is inconsistent with belief in a living God who has spoken to men "by diverse portions and in diverse manners."[20] God is essentially self-communicative[21] and is of ungrudging goodness, as Plato taught.[22] There is no such thing as a faith once for all delivered to the saints. Revelation is divine-human. As God does not reveal His Being to a stone or a tree, but only to men, His revelation is attuned to the state of the human mind. The Creative Spirit is ever ready to reveal Himself to the seeking soul provided the search is genuine and the effort intense. The authority for revelation is not an Infallible Book or an Infallible Church but the witness of the inner light. What is needed is not submission to an external authority but inward illumination which, of course, is tested by tradition and logic. If we reflect on the matter deeply we will perceive the unity of spiritual aspiration and endeavor underlying the varied upward paths indicated in the different world faiths. The diversity in the traditional formulations tends to diminish as we climb up the scale of spiritual perfection. All the paths of ascent lead to the mountaintop. This convergent tendency and the remarkable degree of agreement in the witness of those who reach the mountaintop are the strongest proof of the truth of religion.

Religious life belongs to the realm of inward spiritual revelation; when exteriorized it loses its authentic character. It is misleading to

---

[19] Plutarch observes: "Nor do we speak of the 'different Gods' of different peoples, or of the Gods as 'Barbarian' and 'Greek,' but as common to all, though differently named by different peoples, so that for the One Reason (Logos) that orders all these things, and the One Providence that oversees them, and for the minor powers (i.e. gods, angels) that are appointed to care for all things, there have arisen among different peoples different epithets and services, according to their different manners and customs." *Isis and Osiris*, p. 67.

[20] Epistle to the Hebrews I:I.

[21] *Bhagavadgītā*, IV, 3.

[22] *Timaeus*, 29B.

speak of different religions. We have different religious traditions which can be used for correction and enrichment. The traditions do not create the truth but clothe it in language and symbol for the help of those who do not see it themselves. They symbolize the mystery of the spirit and urge us to move from external significations, which reflect the imperfect state of our consciousness and social environment, to the thing signified. The symbolic character of tradition is not to be mistaken for reality. These are secondhand notions which fortify and console us so long as we do not have direct experience. Our different traditions are versions in a series, part of the historical and relative world in which we live and move. It we cling to these historically conditioned forms as absolute they will not rescue us from slavery to the momentary and the contingent. They leave us completely immersed in the relative. It does not mean that there is nothing central or absolute in religion. The unchanging substance of religion is the evolution of man's consciousness. The traditions help to take us to the truth above all traditions and of which the traditions are imperfect, halting expressions. If we love truth as such and not our opinions, if we desire nothing except what is true and acceptable to God, the present religious snobbery and unfriendliness will disappear. If we open ourselves up unreservedly to the inspirations of our age, we will get to the experience of the one Spirit which takes us beyond the historical formulations. Averroes, the Arab philosopher, distinguished between philosophic truth (*secundum rationem*)[23] and religious views (*secundum fidem*).[24]

No single religion possesses truth compared with philosophic knowledge, though each religious view may claim to possess a fragment of the truth. "Yet every priest values his own creed as the fool his cap and bells." Our quarrels will cease if we know that the one truth is darkened and diversified in the different religions. If we are to remove the present disordered, divided state of the world, we have to adopt what William Law called

a catholic spirit, a communion of saints in the love of God and all goodness, which no one can learn from that which is called orthodoxy in particular churches, but is only to be had by a total dying to all worldly views, by a pure love of God and by such an unction from above as delivers the mind from all selfishness and makes it love truth and goodness with an equality of affection in every man, whether he is Christian, Jew or Gentile.

William Law says also:

23 Tattvam.
24 Matam.

The chief hurt of a sect is this, that it takes itself to be necessary to the truth, whereas the truth is only then found when it is known to be of no sect but as free and universal as the goodness of God and as common to all names and nations as the air and light of this world.

Maitrī Upanishad says:

Some contemplate one name and some another. Which of these is the best? All are eminent clues to the transcendent, immortal, unembodied Brahman; these names are to be contemplated, lauded and at last denied. For by them one rises higher and higher in these worlds; but where all comes to its end, there he attains to the unity of the Person.

In the midst of the travail in which we are living we discern the emergence of the religion of the Spirit, which will be the crown of the different religions, devoted to the perfecting of humanity in the life of the spirit, that is, in the life of God in the soul. When God is our teacher, we come to think alike.

The thought of the Upanishads, the humanism of Confucius, the teaching of the Buddha are marked by the comparative absence of dogma, and their followers are, therefore, relatively free from the evils of obscurantism and casuistry. This is due to the fact that there is greater emphasis in them on the experience of Spirit. Those whose experience is deepest do not speak of it because they feel that it is inexpressible. They feel that they are breaking, dividing, and betraying the experience by giving utterance to it. By their attitude of silence they affirm the primacy of Being over knowledge with the latter's distinction of subject and object. In the deepest spiritual experience we are not self-conscious. When we describe it, it is by way of second reflection, in which we turn the inward presence into an object of thought. We take care to observe that the truth goes beyond the traditional forms. Ruysbroeck says about the reality known by the seer: "We can speak no more of Father, Son and Holy Spirit, nor of any creature, but only of one Being, which is the very substance of the Divine Persons. There were we all one before our creation, for this is our super-essence. There the Godhead is in simple essence without activity." A devout Catholic of the Counter-Reformation period, J. J. Olier, observes: "The holy light of faith is so pure, that compared with it, particular lights are but impurities: and even ideas of the saints, of the Blessed Virgin and the sight of Jesus Christ in his humanity are impediments in the way of the sight of God in His purity." When the seers try to communicate their vision in greater detail they use the tools put into their hands by their cultural milieu. Jesus interprets his experience in terms of notions current in contemporary Jewish thought. We perhaps owe the doctrine of the world's imminent dissolution to the Jewish circle of ideas. So long as we are on earth we cannot shake off the historical altogether.

Sometimes we exteriorize the mystery of spiritual life. Religions which believe in the reality of spiritual life interpret the dogmas with reference to it. Religious views are not so much attempts to solve the riddle of the universe as efforts to describe the experience of sages. The concepts are verbalizations of intense emotional experience. They are lifted out of their true empiricism and made historical rather than experimental, objective instead of profound inward realization. Christ is born in the depths of spirit. We say that He passes through life, dies on the Cross and rises again. These are not so much historical events which occurred once upon a time as universal processes of spiritual life, which are being continually accomplished in the souls of men. Those who are familiar with the way in which the Kṛṣṇa story is interpreted will feel inclined to regard Christhood as an attainment of the soul; a state of inward glorious illumination in which the divine wisdom has become the heritage of the soul. The annunciation is a beautiful experience of the soul. It relates to the birth of Christhood in the soul, "the holy thing begotten within." The human soul from the Holy Breath, *Devakī* or *daivī prakṛti,* divine nature is said to be the mother of Kṛṣṇa. Mary, the mother of the Christ child, is the soul in her innermost divine nature. Whatever is conceived in the womb of the human soul is always of the Holy Spirit.

The mandate of religion is that man must make the change in his own nature in order to let the divine in him manifest itself. It speaks of the death of man as we know him with all his worldly desires and the emergence of the new man. This is the teaching not only of the Upanishads and Buddhism but also of the Greek mysteries and Platonism, of the Gospels and the schools of Gnosticism. This is the wisdom to which Plotinus refers, when he says, "This doctrine is not new; it was professed from the most ancient times though without being developed explicitly; we wish only to be interpreters of the ancient sages, and to show by the evidence of Plato himself that they had the same opinions as ourselves."[25] This is the religion which Augustine mentions in his well-known statement: "That which is called the Christian Religion existed among the Ancients, and never did not

[25] *Enneads* V, 1.8.

exist, from the beginning of the human race until Christ came in the flesh, at which time the true religion, which already existed, began to be called Christianity."[26] This truth speaks to us in varying dialects across far continents and over centuries of history. Those who overlook this perennial wisdom, the eternal religion behind all religions, this *sanātana dharma,* this timeless tradition, "wisdom uncreate, the same now that it ever was, and the same to be forevermore,"[27] and cling to the outward forms and quarrel among themselves, are responsible for the civilized chaos in which we live. It is our duty to get back to this central core of religion, this fundamental wisdom which has been obscured and distorted in the course of history by dogmatic and sectarian developments.

At the level of body and mind, physique and temperament, talents and tastes, we are profoundly unlike one another; but at the deepest level of all, that of the spirit which is the true ground of our being, we are like one another. If religion is to become an effective force in human affairs, if it is to serve as the basis for the new world order, it must become more inward and more universal, a flame which cleanses our inward being and so cleanses the world. For such a religion the historical expressions of spiritual truth and the psychological idioms employed by religions to convey the universal truth cease to be rocks of offense. The barriers dividing men will break down and the reunion and integration of all, what the Russians call *sobornost,* an altogetherness in which we walk together creatively and to which we all contribute, a universal church will be established. Then will the cry of St. Joan in Bernard Shaw's epilogue to that play be fulfilled: "O God that madest this beautiful earth, when will it be ready to receive thy saints?" Then will come a time when the world will be inhabited by a race of men, with no flaw of flesh or error of mind, freed from the yoke not only of disease and privation but of lying words and of love turned into hate. When human beings grow into completeness, into that invisible world which is the kingdom of heaven, then will they manifest in the outer world the Kingdom which is within them. That day we shall cease to set forth God dogmatically or dispute about his nature but leave each man to worship God in the sanctuary of his heart, to feel after him and to possess him.

While I never felt attracted to traveling for its own sake, I have traveled a great deal and lived in places far from home, in England

[26] *Librum de vera religione:* Ch. 10.
[27] *St. Augustine.*

and France, America and Russia. For some years, I have spent long periods in England and the qualities of the English people, such as their love of justice, their hatred of doctrinairism, their sympathy for the underdog, made an impression on me. All Souls College, which has provided a second home for me all these years, has given me an insight into English intellectual life with its caution and stability, confidence and adventure. Whatever one may feel about the character of the Russian government, the people there are kindly and human and their lives are filled as anywhere else with jokes and jealousies, loves and hates. Though I have not been able to take root in any of these foreign countries, I have met many, high and low, and learned to feel the human in them. There are no fundamental differences among the peoples of the world. They have all the deep human feelings, the craving for justice above all class interests, horror of bloodshed and violence. They are working for a religion which teaches the possibility and the necessity of man's union with himself, with nature, with his fellow men, and with the Eternal Spirit of which the visible universe is but a manifestation and upholds the emergence of a complete consciousness as the destiny of man. Our historical religions will have to transform themselves into the universal faith or they will fade away. This prospect may appear strange and unwelcome to some, but it has a truth and beauty of its own. It is working in the minds of men and will soon be a realized fact. Human unity depends not on past origins but on future goal and direction, on what we are becoming and whither we are tending. Compared with the civilization that is now spreading over the earth's surface, thanks to science and technology, the previous civilizations were restricted in scope and resources. Scientist claim that organic life originated on this planet some 1200 million years ago, but man has come into existence on earth during the last half-million years. His civilization has been here only for the last ten thousand years. Man is yet in his infancy and has a long period ahead of him on this planet. He will work out a higher intergration and produce world-minded men and women.

The eternal religion, outlined in these pages, is not irrational or unscientific, is not escapist or asocial. Its acceptance will solve many of our desperate problems and will bring peace to men of good will.

This is the personal philosophy which by different paths I have attained, a philosophy which has served me in the severest tests, in sickness and in health, in triumph and in defeat. It may not be given to us to see that the faith prevails; but it is given to us to strive that it should.

INDEX

INDEX

INDEX

Happiness, defined, 5
    possibility of, 5
Harold of England, 101
Hartmann, Eduard von, 121, 130 n.
Harvard Research Center in Creative
    Altruism, 179, 187
Hastings, Battle of, 101
Hayden, Eustace, 266
Hedonism, 9
Hegel, Georg Willhelm Friedrich, 96, 123,
    308
Hegelian philosophy, psychic background
    of, 124
Heidegger, Martin, 211-212
Heisenberg, Werner, 200-210
Hemophilia, 45
Herbart, J. F., 118-119
Herman Melville, 8
Herzen, Alexander, 11
Historical destiny, vs. despair, 275
Historical events, mixture of good and evil
    in, 100 ff.
Historical progress, Communist vs. liberal
    view of, 263-264
Historical redemption, modern version of,
    264
History, alleged repetition of, 97
    Christian interpretation of, 276
    modern interpretation of, 275
    pattern of meaning in, 276
    philosophy of, 96
    place of crime in, 311
    poetic value of, 95
    rhythmic pattern of, 294
    social, 97
History of England, 94
History of Western Philosophy, 1-2
Hitler, Adolf, 4, 35, 37, 45, 80
Hocking, William Ernest, 287-306
Holes, "plugging up" of, in existentialist
    philosophy, 227-229
Holmes, Oliver Wendell, 18
Homeopathic medicine, 10
Homo faber, and *homo sapiens,* 253
Homosexual vs. heterosexual love, 16
Hormones, and gland functions, 131
House, "grammar" of, 177
Human ancestry, history of, 44
Human being, animal ancestry of, 36, 44
    full, defined, 15
Human biology, and human evolution,
    35-50
Human body, concealment of, 15
Human diversity, political implications of,
    41-43
Human evolution, domination of by intel-
    lectualist movement, 342
Human history, earliest date in, 38

Humanism, diminished meaning of, 246
    integral, 255
*Human Knowledge: Its Scope and Its
    Limits,* 1-2
Human maturation, 39
Human nature, evil in, 266
Human personality, sacredness of, 351
Human race, double crisis of, 73-93
Human-reality, concept of, in existentialist
    philosophy, 229, 233
Human Society in Ethics and Politics, 2
Human stupidity, 244
Hunger, international project for relief of,
    92
    vs. liberty, 326
Husserl, Edmund, 211, 218
Huxley, Aldous, 71-93
Huxley, Julian, 71
Huxley, Leonard, 71
Huxley, Thomas Henry, 71
Hydrogen bomb, fear of, 243

"id," concept of, 267
Idealism, German, 123
"Idealistic" culture, 186
Ideological universe, 183
Ideology, likened to catechism and patriotic
    stories, 241
Ignatius Loyola, 144
Illumination, 347
Inborn ideas, rejection of, 119-120
Indirect lighting, 169
Individuality, consciousness of, 116
Individuals, as sociocultural persons, 183
Individuation process, 146
    consciousness and, 167
Industrial Revolution, 98
Inge, W. R., 347
Insanity, increase in incidence of, 88
Inside Africa, 52
Insight, contemplative, 347
Instant, importance of, in existentialist
    philosophy, 224
Instinct, and will, 130-135
Instincts, meaning and purpose of, 133
    vs. reason, 252
    and situational patterns, 145
    theory of, 131
Institute for Analytical Psychology, 114
Institutions, historic, modification of, 10-11
Integralism, defined, 180-189
Integration, dynamic, 25
Integrity, psychology of, 229
Intelligence, active, task of, 197
Interest, psychology of, 229
Interhuman and intergroup conflicts, 185
International trade, as curse or blessing, 90
Introduction to Mathematical Philosophy, 2

INDEX

INDEX

DATE DUE